Buddha Shakyamuni.

Guru Rinpoche.

A Guide to
THE WORDS *of* MY PERFECT TEACHER

A Guide to
THE WORDS *of*
MY PERFECT TEACHER

KHENPO NGAWANG PELZANG

Translated under the auspices of
DIPAMKARA
in collaboration with
THE PADMAKARA TRANSLATION GROUP

SHAMBHALA
Boston & London
2004

SHAMBHALA PUBLICATIONS, INC.
HORTICULTURAL HALL
300 MASSACHUSETTS AVENUE
BOSTON, MASSACHUSETTS 02115
www.shambhala.com

© 2004 by Padmakara Translation Group

All rights reserved. No part of this book may be
reproduced in any form or by any means, electronic
or mechanical, including photocopying, recording,
or by any information storage and retrieval system,
without permission in writing from the publisher.

9 8 7 6 5 4

Printed in the United States of America

♾ This edition is printed on acid-free paper that meets
the American National Standards Institute z39.48 Standard.
Distributed in the United States by Random House, Inc.,
and in Canada by Random House of Canada Ltd

Library of Congress Cataloging-in-Publication Data
Nag-dban-dpal-bzan, Mkhan-po, 1879–1941
A guide to the words of my perfect teacher/Khenpo
Ngawang Pelzang; translated by the Dipamkara Translation
Group in collaboration with the the Padmakara Translation
Group.—1st ed.
p. cm.
Includes bibliographical references and index.
ISBN 978-1-59030-073-2 (alk. paper)
1. Rdzogs-chen (Rnin-ma-pa) 2. Spiritual life—Buddhism.
3. Buddhism—China—Tibet—Doctrines. I. Kun bzan bla
ma'i zal lun. II. O-rgyan-'jigs-med-chos-kyi-dban-po, Dpal-
sprul, b. 1808. Kun bxan bla ma'i zal lun. III. Title.
BQ7662.4 .N3315 2004
294.3'923—dc22
2003016978

༄༅། །རྫོགས་པ་ཆེན་པོ་ཀློང་ཆེན་སྙིང་ཐིག་གི་སྔོན་འགྲོའི་
ཁྲིད་ཡིག་ཀུན་བཟང་བླ་མའི་ཞལ་ལུང་གི་
ཟིན་བྲིས་ཞུགས་སོ།།

དེ་པོ་ཀ་རའི་སྐྱ་བསྒྱུར་མཐུན་ཚོགས་ནས་
སྐྱ་བསྒྱུར་ཞུས།།

Contents

List of Illustrations	xvii
Foreword by Alak Zenkar Rinpoche	xix
Translators' Introduction	xxi

A Guide to *The Words of My Perfect Teacher*
Introduction ... 3

PART ONE
THE ORDINARY OR OUTER PRELIMINARIES ... 13

Chapter One
The Difficulty of Finding the Freedoms and Advantages ... 17
    I. THE PROPER WAY TO LISTEN TO SPIRITUAL TEACHING ... 18
        1. Attitude ... 18
        2. Conduct ... 35
    II. THE TEACHING ITSELF ... 39
        1. Reflecting on the Nature of Freedom ... 44
        2. Reflecting on the Ten Particular Advantages
           Related to Dharma ... 47
        3. Reflecting on Images That Show How Difficult It Is
           to Find the Freedoms and Advantages ... 50

Chapter Two
The Impermanence of Life ... 55
    I. THE IMPERMANENCE OF THE OUTER UNIVERSE IN WHICH
       BEINGS LIVE ... 55
    II. THE IMPERMANENCE OF BEINGS LIVING IN THE UNIVERSE ... 57

VI. The Uncertainty of the Circumstances of Death	58
VII. Intense Awareness of Impermanence	61

Chapter Three
The Defects of Samsara — 62
    I. The Defects of Samsara in General — 64
    II. The Particular Sufferings Experienced by the Beings of Each of the Six Realms — 64

Chapter Four
Actions: The Principle of Cause and Effect — 67
    I. Negative Actions to be Abandoned — 74
        1. Explanation of the Negative Actions to be Abandoned — 74
        2. Explanation of Their Effects — 74
    II. Positive Actions to be Adopted — 75
    III. The All-determining Quality of Actions — 75

Chapter Five
The Benefits of Liberation — 83

Chapter Six
How to Follow a Spiritual Friend — 87
    I. Examining the Teacher — 87
    II. Following the Teacher — 89
    III. Emulating the Teacher's Realization and Actions — 89

Part Two
THE EXTRAORDINARY OR INNER PRELIMINARIES — 91

Chapter One
Taking Refuge, the Foundation Stone of All Paths — 93
    I. Approaches to Taking Refuge — 95
    II. How to Take Refuge — 99

III.	Precepts and Benefits of Taking Refuge	128
	1. The Precepts of Taking Refuge	128
	2. The Benefits of Taking Refuge	130

Chapter Two
Arousing Bodhichitta, the Root of the Great Vehicle — 133

I.	Training the Mind in the Four Boundless Qualities	134
	1. Impartiality	137
	2. Love	145
	3. Compassion	148
	4. Sympathetic Joy	150
II.	Arousing Bodhichitta, the Mind of Supreme Enlightenment	151
III.	Training in the Bodhichitta Precepts	162
	1. Training in the Precepts of the Bodhichitta of Aspiration	162
	2. Training in the Precepts of the Bodhichitta of Application	181

Chapter Three
Meditating on the Teacher as Vajrasattva and Reciting His Mantra so as to Cleanse All Adverse Circumstances, Negative Actions, and Obscurations — 221

I.	How Negative Actions Can Be Purified through Confession	221
II.	How to Confess Negative Actions	226
III.	The Actual Meditation and Recitation on Vajrasattva	227

Chapter Four
Offering the Mandala to Accumulate Merit and Wisdom — 233
   I. THE NEED FOR THE TWO ACCUMULATIONS — 233
   II. THE ACCOMPLISHMENT MANDALA — 239
   III. THE OFFERING MANDALA — 240

Chapter Five
The Kusali's Accumulation: Destroying the Four Demons at a Single Stroke — 244
   GIVING ONE'S BODY — 245
   THE MEANING OF CHÖ — 246
   THE ACTUAL PRACTICE OF OFFERING THE BODY — 249

Chapter Six
The Profound Guru Yoga, the Ultimate Method for Arousing the Wisdom of Realization in One's Mind — 253
   I. THE REASON FOR GURU YOGA: A COMPARISON OF THE ROLE OF THE TEACHER IN THE NINE YANAS — 253
   II. HOW TO PRACTICE GURU YOGA — 265
      1. Visualizing the Field of Merit — 266
      2. Offering the Seven Branches — 267
      3. Praying with Resolute Trust — 274
      4. Taking the Four Empowerments — 277

PART THREE
THE SWIFT PATH OF TRANSFERENCE — 281
   I. THE FIVE KINDS OF TRANSFERENCE — 282
      1. Superior Transference to the Dharmakaya through the Seal of the View — 282
      2. Middling Transference to the Sambhogakaya through the Union of the Generation and Perfection Phases — 283

	3. Lower Transference to the Nirmanakaya through	
	Immeasurable Compassion	283
	4. Ordinary Transference Using Three Images	283
	5. Transference Performed for the Dead	284
II.	THE PRACTICE OF TRANSFERENCE USING THREE IMAGES	284
	1. Training for Transference	284
	2. Actual Transference	284

Concluding Instructions	287
Prayers	289
Notes	295
Glossary	319
The Three Worlds	327
The Five Bodhisattva Paths and the Thirty-seven Elements	
* Leading to Enlightenment*	329
Comparative Glossary	331
Bibliography	341
Index	347

List of Illustrations

All drawings are by Olivier Philippot unless otherwise stated.

Buddha Shakyamuni (woodblock from Derge)	*i*
Guru Rinpoche (painting by Orgyen Lhundrup)	*iii*
Vimalamitra	*xviii*
Kunkhyen Longchen Rabjam	2
Rigdzin Jigme Lingpa	16
Jigme Gyalwai Nyugu	92
Patrul Rinpoche	132
Nyoshul Lungtok Tenpai Nyima	220
Khenpo Ngawang Pelzang (photo © The Terton Sogyal Trust, reproduced by kind permission)	252
Gönpo Lekden (woodblock by Gomchen Ulekshé)	358
Gönpo Maning Nagpo (drawing by Konchok Lhadrepa)	358
Ekajati (drawing by Konchok Lhadrepa)	359
Khyabjuk Rahula (woodblock by Gomchen Ulekshé)	359
Damchen Dorje Lekpa (woodblock by Gomchen Ulekshé)	360
Tseringma (from the Chöling collection)	360

Vimalamitra.

Foreword

KHENCHEN NGAGI WANGPO was Kunkhyen Longchen Rabjam reborn in the Khromtha region of Kham (eastern Tibet) as the protector of the doctrine and beings. He received *The Words of My Perfect Teacher*, a guide to the preliminaries for the *Heart Essence of the Vast Expanse* from the Great Perfection, on several occasions from the great Khenpo Lungtok, who was the heart son of Dzogchen Palge Tulku, and at different times he made notes on the oral instructions handed down from Patrul Rinpoche and the experiential instructions he received from his root teacher. All these his disciples put together unedited and included in Khenpo Ngaga's collected works.

Now Choktrul Pema Wangyal Rinpoche, director of Padmakara, and translators Anne Benson, Christian Bruyat, John Canti, and Stephen Gethin, together with Ani Jinba, Patrick Gaffney, and Peter Roberts, have painstakingly translated these notes into English with meticulous reference to editions from both India and Tibet and are having them published. To all of them, and to Mr. Patrick Godwin Naylor, president of Dipamkara, Padmakara's sister organization, whose financial support made this project possible, and Jenny Kane, Dipamkara's manager, who nurtured the project and acted as editor, I would like to express my immense heartfelt gratitude.

It is my sincere wish that this book may serve to sow the seed of liberation in the minds of numerous readers, help them engender the shoot of bodhichitta, and finally benefit both themselves and others.

Alak Zenkar Thubten Nyima Rinpoche

Translators' Introduction

Ever since its publication in the middle of the nineteenth century, Patrul Rinpoche's *Kunzang Lama'i Shelung*, known to many Western readers as *The Words of My Perfect Teacher*, has been acknowledged as an indispensable guide to the preliminary practices, not only for followers of the Longchen Nyingtik tradition in the Nyingma school of Tibetan Buddhism, for whom it was originally written, but also for anyone with a sincere desire to put the Buddhist teachings into practice. Patrul Rinpoche's work has a special place within the Tibetan commentatorial tradition with its direct, often humorous style and wealth of anecdotes. It makes the teachings immediately accessible to complete beginners while providing frequent reminders of the obstacles on the path that can all too easily prove the undoing of seasoned practitioners.

In the *Kunzang Lama'i Shelung* Patrul Rinpoche put down in writing for the first time teachings that had hitherto been passed from master to disciple only in the form of oral advice and instruction. This tradition of oral transmission did not stop with the publication of his book, however. Even for the fortunate students who now had access to these teachings in printed form, it was no less important to receive transmission and instruction directly from their teacher. In the first place, the Buddhist tradition of oral transmission (*lung*) is considered an essential step in studying the scriptures and their commentaries and in practicing ritual instructions. Through the transmission from mouth to ear starting from the original teacher (in this case, Rigdzin Jigme Lingpa) and continuing down the lineage, the disciple's chance of fully understanding and realizing the words thus transmitted is immeasurably enhanced and thence his or her ability to transmit the same understanding and realization to the next generation of disciples. It is as if the disciple were receiving the teaching directly from its original author. Furthermore, so vast is the scope of the Buddhist teachings that no text, however voluminous or apparently complete, could ever be exhaustive. Every disciple studying a particular text needs to receive a greater or lesser amount of commentary in order to understand it fully, and the *Kunzang Lama'i Shelung* is no exception in this respect.

It is in order to give the oral transmission and expand on the original text that all the masters in the lineage, beginning with Patrul Rinpoche himself, have explained the *Kunzang Lama'i Shelung* to their disciples on numerous occasions down to the present day. And it is just such a teaching, given by Patrul Rinpoche's disciple Lungtok Tenpai Nyima, that Khenpo Ngawang Pelzang received as a young man and recorded as his notes, the *Kunzang Lama'i Shelung Zintri*.

KATHOG KHENPO NGAWANG PELZANG (1879–1941)[1]

Khenpo Ngawang Pelzang, also known as Osel Rinchen Nyingpo Pema Lendrel Tsel and popularly called Khenpo Ngakchung or Ngaga, is a remarkable example of a particular kind of lineage holder among the broad variety of personalities of those who held and transmitted the different traditions of Buddhism in Tibet, for if they were all similar in their wisdom and compassion, they differed widely in the particular guises each took in order to pass the teachings on to others most effectively. Some lamas were recognized *tulku*s, enthroned as the heads of great monasteries, with considerable spiritual influence over the large communities of monks under their care and over the local lay populations. Others, like Patrul Rinpoche and Milarepa, were respected on account of their total disregard for wealth, fame, and position, inspiring and teaching through the example of their humility and simple lifestyle. Yet others chose to undertake many years of intensive academic training, mastering the texts of sutra and tantra and their commentaries in order to qualify as *khenpo*s. The khenpos were learned professors responsible for the education of the tulkus and monks in the monasteries and at the same time faultless upholders of the Vinaya who continued its transmission in ordaining thousands of monks and supervising their training. It should not be imagined, however, that they confined themselves to their duties in the monasteries, for many of them also spent years meditating in retreat and transforming the texts they taught into inner spiritual realization. And if they did not occupy the thrones of recognized incarnations, this did not necessarily mean that they had not been "someone" in their previous births.

In Khenpo Ngakchung's case that "someone" was a whole series of accomplished beings in India and Tibet—scholars, yogis, translators, Dharma kings, treasure discoverers—summarized in one biography as twenty-five great incarnations. Foremost among these was Vimalamitra, the great Indian master who was responsible, with Guru Padmasambhava, for introducing the Nyingtik teachings to Tibet and who promised on his departure from Tibet to send an emanation every hundred years. Khenpo Ngakchung had also been, in a previous life, the Indian master Sthiramati, Vasubandhu's foremost Abhidharma student, and this was to hold him in good stead when he came to study this difficult subject.

His teacher Nyoshul Lungtok Tenpai Nyima (1829–1901/2*), himself an incarnation of the great abbot Shantarakshita, spent twenty-eight years constantly in the company of Patrul Rinpoche, receiving from him all the Nyingtik teachings, practicing them under his guidance, and attaining full realization of the Great Perfection. When at the end of this time Patrul Rinpoche told him to return home, he could not bear to leave, but Patrul Rinpoche comforted him by telling him that in due course he would meet Kunkhyen Longchenpa. The truth of this prediction duly became clear when, following a series of significative dreams, a small boy, the future Khenpo Ngakchung, was presented to him.

Khenpo Ngakchung was indeed a most unusual child. Even as a baby he displayed miraculous powers and had visions of deities. From his early teens he accompanied Lungtok Tenpai Nyima constantly, serving him, listening to his teachings, and, in his spare time, practicing. Even before completing the preliminary practice he had meditative experiences usually associated with the main practice of the Great Perfection. While doing the mandala practice he had a vision of Longchenpa, in which he was introduced to the nature of mind. Lungtok Tenpai Nyima downplayed these experiences, insisting that Ngawang Pelzang go through the whole path in the proper order so that he could achieve stable realization and truly benefit beings. In this way, he completed all the stages of the practice—the preliminaries, *sadhana* recitations, yogas, and the two aspects of the Great Perfection, *trekchö* and *thögal*—by the time he was twenty-one, when his teacher recognized him as his Dharma heir and sent him to Dzogchen Monastery to study under the learned khenpos at the monastery's Shri Singha *shedra* (college). While there he met Mipham Rinpoche, who entrusted him with the *Introduction to Scholarship*

---

*The exact date of Nyoshul Lungtok Tenpai Nyima's death appears uncertain.

(*mkhas 'jug*) which he had just finished writing. Two years later, after Lungtok Tenpai Nyima had passed away, he performed several retreats, all marked by extraordinary signs of accomplishment. He continued to study and practice, and to receive further teachings and empowerments from other great teachers, in particular the second Kathog Situ, Chokyi Gyatso (1880–1925). He also began giving teachings himself. His calling as a khenpo was no doubt encouraged by a vision he had of Patrul Rinpoche in which the latter stressed the importance of education and monastic observance. At the age of thirty he was appointed to teach at Kathog Monastery's newly opened shedra, at first as assistant to Khenpo Kunpel (author of an important commentary that synthesizes Patrul Rinpoche's teachings on the *Bodhicharyavatara*), and later as the shedra's khenpo. He stayed there for the next thirteen years, teaching, giving empowerments, and ordaining thousands of monks, as well as receiving many important transmissions.

The "experiential" instructions (*myong khrid*) that Lungtok Tenpai Nyima had received from Patrul Rinpoche and passed on to Khenpo Ngakchung became the tradition of Nyingtik practice at Kathog Monastery, and it was Lungtok Tenpai Nyima's Kathog followers who built the Nyoshul monastery in Derge, of which Khenpo Ngawang Pelzang became the first abbot. After his years at Kathog he traveled widely in east Tibet, establishing monasteries and shedras, giving teachings, practicing in retreat, and writing. The thirteen volumes of texts he composed include commentaries on Madhyamika treatises by Chandrakirti and Aryadeva, texts on sadhana practice, commentaries on Vajrayana, and works on the Great Perfection, many of which were teachings that he had received from Lungtok Tenpai Nyima. He was also responsible for propagating the teachings he received from Shenga Rinpoche on Nagarjuna's fundamental texts of the Madhyamika.

The visions, meditative experiences, and miraculous events that occur throughout Khenpo Ngakchung's life may seem to us almost the stuff of legend, yet some of them took place less than seventy years ago, and there are still one or two of his disciples living. The spiritual renaissance in eastern Tibet with which he was intimately connected is perhaps all the more remarkable for the fact that the region was not always an oasis of calm and often had its share of troubles and unrest. His activity in benefiting beings has extended to the West, where Buddhists practicing the Nyingtik teachings have been taught by masters who can trace their lineage back to him through his disciples, among them Nyoshul Shedrup Tenpai Nyima, Jamyang Khyentse Chökyi Lodrö, and Chatral Rinpoche. This, and the fact that the *Zintri* is now accessible to the English-speaking world, was perhaps foreseen in a dream Khenpo Ngakchung recounted to his teacher. In it he saw an immense stupa being destroyed and washed away by a river flowing west into the ocean, and he heard a voice from the sky saying that millions of beings in that ocean would be benefited. Lungtok Tenpai Nyima later explained that this dream foretold the destruction of the doctrine in the East and its spread to the West.

The Text

While the *Kunzang Lama'i Shelung* serves above all as a source of inspiration, Khenpo Ngakchung's text provides students with the theoretical background that serves as an essential foundation for the practice. To cite a few examples, where Patrul Rinpoche exhorts us in the chapter on refuge to have confidence in the Three Jewels, Khenpo Ngakchung in the corresponding chapter of his *Zintri* gives a detailed and lengthy description of the Three Jewels. In the chapter on bodhichitta, he provides an introduction to Madhyamika philosophy that is the basis of transcendent wisdom: an understanding of this is essential for anyone attempting to practice the Great Perfection. Patrul Rinpoche's insistence on the sincerity of one's confession in the Vajrasattva chapter is complemented by Khenpo Ngakchung's explanation of why negative actions hinder our progress on the path, together with an invaluable checklist of the negative actions one might need to confess. In the chapters on impermanence and the mandala offering, the *Zintri* completes Patrul Rinpoche's description of the Buddhist cosmology with a startling vision of the universe that forces us to revise our usual notions of time and space. And in the guru yoga chapter, the author compares the role of the teacher in the different vehicles, showing why the guru has such an important place in the practice of the Great Perfection.

On a more general level, Khenpo Ngakchung relates the stages of the practice to the Buddha's teachings on the Four Noble Truths and puts the practice of the Great Perfection into perspective with an interesting overview of the nine vehicles (*yana*s). Thus, starting with a general introduction as to how to approach the teachings, he goes through the *Kunzang Lama'i Shelung* chapter by chapter, filling in the background and putting each subject into greater perspective.

The *Zintri* is not all dry theory. There are occasional flashes of the pungent wit characteristic of Patrul Rinpoche's lineage: Khenpo Ngakchung does not mince words when he turns his attention to the false teacher and the blasé practitioner. There is plenty of thoroughly practical instruction too. The first chapter includes a section on how to organize the day into meditation sessions and how to divide up the time within each session. This is enlarged upon for each of the preliminary practices, providing students with a detailed schedule to follow from the moment they sit down on their meditation cushions to the moment they conclude the session. Particularly helpful is the step-by-step explanation in the bodhichitta chapter on how to train the mind in love and compassion.

Beginners may find this rich and dense text difficult in parts, and they should bear in mind that it includes instruction for experienced practitioners as well as those new to the Buddhist path. As a result, a number of passages, particularly those that refer to the generation and perfection phases or to the main practice of the Great Perfection, can be properly understood only by those who have received the corresponding instructions and gained some experience in practicing them. Teachings aimed in this way at such a diverse audience are not unusual. They contain all the instructions complete beginners might need, while showing how these practices relate to the main practice. At the same time, they serve as an essential reminder to practitioners who have advanced further along the path. For the preliminary practices are not simply an introductory course to be abandoned as soon as the student has qualified for the so-called main practice: they are the very foundation of the more advanced practices, so much so that many great masters have completed the preliminary practices not just once but several times. Once practitioners have completed each element of the preliminaries 100,000 times, they continue to go through the whole preliminary practice daily, if briefly, thus reinforcing the foundation on which all the other practices are based. This is by no means a necessary chore to be hastily executed before getting down to the real meat of the practice. At each stage along the path the preliminary practice takes on a further dimension. With new insights gained, the main practice nourishes the preliminary practice, while the latter provides an ever stronger foundation, an important insurance against the mistakes we can make on the path. Practitioners who think that they can leave the preliminaries behind risk encountering all sorts of difficulties.

Khenpo Ngakchung's text, as the author himself points out at the end, was compiled somewhat hurriedly from his own notes. Some sections are repeated in different chapters almost word for word, as might be expected in what was after all an oral teaching delivered on at least two separate occasions. At other points in the *Zintri* the line of thought seems to be so disjointed that one can only suppose that pages were perhaps missing from the pile of looseleaf notes when it was copied out for publication. The result is a work with no particularly consistent style, alternating outline-type lists with careful explanatory prose.

It would have been assumed by the author and all the subsequent lineage teachers that anyone studying the *Zintri* would be in possession of a copy of the *Kunzang Lama'i Shelung*, if not thoroughly familiar with its contents. The *Zintri* contains little repetition or duplication of the material in the *Kunzang Lama'i Shelung*, and while some passages could conceivably be read independently of Patrul Rinpoche's work, readers who do not have a copy of the latter may have difficulty understanding the numerous references to it found in the *Zintri*. The *Zintri* truly is a companion to Patrul Rinpoche's text, complementing it with important background information and detail.

Two complete English translations of the *Kunzang Lama'i Shelung* exist, one by Sonam Kazi bearing the same title as the Tibetan, and one by the Padmakara Translation Group under the title *The Words of My Perfect Teacher*. For the sake of consistency in translation, *The Words of My Perfect Teacher* has been taken as the reference.

The Translation

The *Guide* includes numerous references to local customs and considerable use of local dialect. As with *The Words of My Perfect Teacher*, Khenpo Ngakchung's audience consists of people born into nomadic families and familiar with a life of yaks to be milked, yak-hair tents, and the problems of louse infestation. In cases where it has been possible to render Tibetan sayings and ideas by English equivalents, the literal version is provided in a note. One section in particular, the explanation on how to avoid being distracted in meditation by sexual desire, was originally aimed at a male monastic audience and draws its arguments from traditional eighth-century Indian teachings, presenting ideas that modern Western readers might find inapplicable. We have taken the liberty of modifying this section slightly so that it continues to read convincingly.

Headings

Of the three Tibetan versions of the *Zintri* used by the translators, the Chengdu edition adds a number of headings. These have generally been kept in the translation and further headings have been added by the translators to orient the reader in the longer sections.

Headings that correspond with those in *The Words of My Perfect Teacher* have been numbered using the same system of uppercase Roman numerals (I, II, III) and Arabic numerals (1, 1.1, 1.2.3) to help readers keep their bearings between *The Words of My Perfect Teacher* and the *Guide*.

Khenpo Ngakchung's own headings tend to weave in and out of the outline structure in *The Words of My Perfect Teacher*. Where they do not correspond with the headings in the latter they follow a standard outline style of letters and numerals enclosed in parentheses: (A), (1), (a), and so on. A few headings that do not fit into the standard outline style have been left unnumbered.

Notes and Glossary

While the *Guide* goes a long way toward explaining points not dealt with in full in *The Words of My Perfect Teacher* and answers some fundamental questions that beginners might ask, it also introduces topics and notions that raise as many questions again. Even if it were within the translators' capacities to provide the answers to these, the number of notes that this might entail could easily fill another volume. Notes have therefore been kept to the minimum that would enable the student to know at least in which areas to pursue further study. At the same time, the importance of relying on the constant guidance of a qualified teacher when practicing the instructions explained in *The Words of My Perfect Teacher* and in the *Guide* cannot be overemphasized.

All references are to the second edition of *The Words of My Perfect Teacher*. References to the first edition are indicated where the page numbers differ between the two editions.

Footnotes are used to provide cross-references, both within this book and to *The Words of My Perfect Teacher*. Endnotes are used to explain terms or phrases or provide further information.

The *Guide* contains many technical terms and names with which the reader may not be familiar. Some of these have been italicized for clarity's sake. Where technical terms are not defined in the text itself or explained in specific endnotes, they may be found either in the glossary of *The Words of My Perfect Teacher* or in the glossary at the end of this book. Terms and names related to the five paths and to the different realms are presented in two charts. No attempt has been made to provide detailed explanations of terms relating to the main practice of the Great Perfection and other highly technical subjects that can only be appropriately commented on by qualified teachers.

Every effort has been made to maintain consistency in vocabulary between the *Guide* and *The Words of My Perfect Teacher*, but the problem remains of terms that have several different English equivalents in the numerous Buddhist translations that have appeared in recent decades. We have attempted to overcome the resulting confusion for readers by compiling a comparative glossary of some of the terms we have used along with their Tibetan and Sanskrit equivalents and a selection of alternative English translations. Obviously this list cannot pretend to be exhaustive.

Quotations

Khenpo Ngakchung quotes widely from different Buddhist works and in doing so often assumes in his readers an extensive knowledge of these. Indeed, many among his audience would have learned such works as the *Bodhicharyavatara* by heart from an early age and would be entirely familiar with the quotations he chooses. He does not therefore always make a point of identifying his sources. In one case he contents himself with referring to a particular topic by quoting no more than four syllables from Nagarjuna's *Letter to a Friend*. Few Western readers will possess sufficient knowledge to recognize many of these quotations, especially since universally accepted translations of the Buddhist classics do not yet exist in the English-speaking world. Whenever possible we have identified quotations and provided the reader with greater detail where appropriate.

Sources

The *Zintri* was translated from two editions, one published by Alak Zenkar Thubten Nyima Rinpoche (Chengdu, China: Minorities Publishing House) and the other by Chatral Rinpoche (Kathmandu, Nepal). The translators also used a computer file prepared from a copy supplied by Tulku

Pema Wangyal Rinpoche of Khenpo Ngakchung's original manuscript in Palyul Monastery.

A list of secondary sources is included in the bibliography at the end of this book.

Acknowledgments

This translation was made at the request of Alak Zenkar Thubten Nyima Rinpoche, who inspired and patiently supervised the project under the auspices of Dipamkara. He intended Dipamkara to be a sister organization to the Padmakara Translation Group, which produced *The Words of My Perfect Teacher*. It is to Rinpoche that we extend our gratitude first and foremost.

We are immensely grateful to the following masters who gave invaluable assistance in answering the the translators' and editors' innumerable questions: Tulku Pema Wangyal Rinpoche, Jigme Khyentse Rinpoche, Khenpo Pema Sherab, Dorzong Rinpoche, the late Khenpo Betse, Khenpo Chöga, Khenpo Losal, Khenpo Gyurme Tsultrim, and the late Khenpo Chadrel.

The work of translating this text would have been impossible without the patient and generous financial support of Patrick Godwin Naylor.

The chapters in the text were translated individually by Ani Jinba Palmo (E. De Jong), Anne Benson, Christian Bruyat, John Canti, Patrick Gaffney, and Peter Roberts. Their translations were subsequently reviewed and edited by Stephen Gethin assisted by Jennifer Kane, who also prepared the index. Sanskrit equivalents in the comparative glossary were provided by Patrick Carré.

We wish to express our thanks to our readers, Mike Gilmore, Judith Holder, and Barbara Gethin, for their invaluable suggestions; to Valérie Lhommelet, who prepared a computer printout from a copy of Khenpo Ngakchung's original manuscript; to E. Gene Smith for help in tracking down biographical sources; and to Vivian Kurz for her help in seeing this book published.

A Guide to
THE WORDS *of*
MY PERFECT TEACHER

Kunkhyen Longchen Rabjam (1308–63).

Introduction

Homage to the venerable master *endowed with the great compassion free from concepts.*

> Collect all your thoughts
> And listen with excellent motivation.
> To a forgetful mind the blessings of Vajrasattva
> And the other Buddhas of the three times will never come.

As this quotation from the *Vajra Pinnacle* tantra shows, whether we are listening to the holy Dharma, explaining it, or practicing it, we should first turn our thoughts inward and examine our own minds.

There are just three types of thoughts that one can have as a human being: negative thoughts related to attachment, aversion, or bewilderment; neutral thoughts; and positive thoughts of faith, determination to be free, and bodhichitta. If you have a negative thought, you should feel ashamed of yourself and quash it as it arises. As the saying goes:

> Clean the lamp while it is warm,
> Hit the pig on the snout with a pestle.[2]

In this manner, you should avoid negative thoughts, transform your neutral thoughts, and listen, teach, and practice with especially positive thoughts. Otherwise, if you only modify your outward conduct in the things you do and say, you will be a hypocrite, for as we find in the *Collection of Deliberate Sayings*:

> It is not with the hair, neither is it with the staff.[3]

The Buddha said:

> Bring your own mind under control.
> That is the Buddha's teaching.

He did not say:

> Change the appearance of your body and speech.
> That is the Buddha's teaching.

This is why we read in the sutras:

> When the mind is pure, the body will be pure;
> But purifying the body will not purify the mind.

Accordingly, since people go to monks for spiritual protection and often summon them to help the dead, monks should cure the sickness in their own minds. That which cures the mind's sickness, the disease of karma and negative emotions, is the sacred Dharma. Of the ten things that are called "dharma," this is the "sacred Dharma," or Dharma that is qualified as sacred. Its definition is as follows: just as medicine cures an illness, the Dharma transforms the mind, turning it away from the wrong path of nonvirtue. In this sense "Dharma," "cure," and "transformation" mean the same thing. You should have confidence in this cure, the Dharma. Once you know that the holy Dharma protects you from all the fears of samsara and the lower realms and is the source of benefit and happiness in this and future lives, and that the teachings of the sacred Dharma will therefore never let you down in this life, in future lives, or in the intermediate state, you have to have faith in it. It has been said:

> Day and night, apply the precious wheel of faith
> To the path of virtue.

and

> Faith comes before all else, like a mother it gives birth to all;
> The root of all Dharma is faith.

Who was it who taught this doctrine of the holy Dharma? It was:

The unsurpassable teacher, the precious Buddha . . .

—that is, the unsurpassable teacher, the incomparable, peerless King of the Shakyas. He is the Lion of the Shakyas who as the *dharmakaya* is Samantabhadra, as the *sambhogakaya* is the great Vajradhara, and in his *nirmanakaya* form is Shakyamuni the protector of beings.

Just as the Teacher is beyond compare, so was his aspiration as the brahmin minister's son Ocean Dust,[4] and so is his incomparable Teaching.

As we find in the *Seven Chapters*:

From the inconceivable, marvelous doctrine of the Buddhas
The supremely noble teaching will appear three times.

The Secret Mantra Vajrayana appeared more than ten million *kalpa*s ago when the Buddha Once Come King taught, during the kalpa called Complete Array. In the future kalpa Strewn Flowers, when the Buddha known as Manjushri will teach, the Secret Mantra will appear on a vast scale. At present, while the doctrine of the Buddha Shakyamuni endures, the Secret Mantra Vajrayana is taught extensively. These are the only three kalpas in which beings are suitable vessels for receiving the teachings of the Secret Mantrayana.

What then is meant by the following passage from the *Magical Net of Manjushri*?

The teachings of the past Buddhas
Will also be taught by future ones.

It refers to the Secret Mantrayana, which will not be proclaimed on a wide scale.

The realm of the present Buddha Shakyamuni, the one thousand million–fold Saha world, is called the "world of no fear" not because it is very good. Rather, it is so called for its great evil. Sentient beings here are not afraid of desire, they are not frightened by anger and they have no fear of ignorance, which is why it is called the realm of the Saha world.

That incomparable Teacher taught

> The unsurpassable protection, the precious sacred Dharma . . .

—that is, the 84,000 elements of the Dharma. When these are all put together they constitute the Twelve Branches of Excellent Speech, which again together constitute the Three Pitakas. The Tripitaka is what is called the Conqueror's precious doctrine of transmission and realization. The Tripitaka itself is known as the Dharma of transmission because, just as we use handles to carry an earthen pot or leather bag,[5] we use words to make the Dharma of realization unfold. The subject of the Tripitaka is the path of the superior threefold training, which is the Dharma of realization.

As to why this "path of superior training" is superior: non-Buddhist traditions have their own meditative concentrations and include ascetic practices in which one acts like a dog or an ox, but it is not possible to attain liberation and omniscience[6] by such paths. Through the Buddha's path of the superior training, Buddhists do attain the state of liberation and omniscience, which is why it is called the superior training.

There are no teachings belonging to the Sutrayana or Mantrayana that are not included in the Tripitaka and the threefold training. In the Basic Vehicle the subjects that are taught in the Three Pitakas—Vinaya, Sutras, and Abhidharma—are the three trainings: respectively, discipline, concentration, and wisdom.

In the Bodhisattva path, all the precepts that explain the root downfalls belong to the Vinaya Pitaka, and its whole subject is the training in discipline. All the sutras that teach the methods for developing concentration belong to the Sutra Pitaka; and its whole subject, the meditation on how difficult it is to find the freedoms and advantages and so forth, is the training in concentration. All the explanations of the sixteen or twenty kinds of emptiness belong to the Abhidharma Pitaka; and its whole subject is the training in wisdom.

The descriptions of the Secret Mantra Vajrayana *samaya*s belong to the Vinaya Pitaka, and its subject is the training in discipline. The explanations of the common generation and perfection phases belong to the Sutra Pitaka, and its subject is the training in concentration. The explanations on the Great Perfection belong to the Abhidharma Pitaka, and its subject is the training in wisdom.

To summarize, there are no texts and subjects belonging to these different vehicles that are not included in the Tripitaka and the threefold training.

Now, who is the holder of the Conqueror's precious doctrine of transmission and realization? It is:

The unsurpassable guide, the precious Sangha . . .

—that is to say, the doctrine is held exclusively by the members of the Sangha and not by beings such as gods, demons, Brahma, or the Lord of the Universe.[7]

The holders are the sublime members of the Sangha, and to hold the doctrine, they have to hold the Dharma of transmission by listening and explaining, and to hold the Dharma of realization by practice and accomplishment.

We should not look down like a dog, but look up like a bird,[8] counting ourselves as members of the Sangha. If we look down and behave like ordinary men and women, they will call us "corrupt monk, rotten monk!" A rotten monk is someone with shameful discipline, poor concentration, and a lack of wisdom. So instead we should look up and follow the Three Jewels: our teacher is the Buddha, the Bhagavan. That which shows us the path that leads to the state of liberation and omniscience is the sacred Dharma, the Conqueror's Dharma of transmission and realization. Those who accompany us on the way to the state of liberation and omniscience are the noble Manjushri and the spiritual friends attending this present teaching, whose conduct is equally pure. Since we count ourselves as members of the Sangha, we should hold the Dharma of transmission and realization and never be driven to demeaning it. This is what we mean by "members of the guiding Sangha."

Sangha, or "yearning for virtue," refers exclusively to those who yearn for the path of the superior threefold training. It does not refer to those who are fond of negative actions, of business, disputes, or fights.

"Guiding" means, having first been shown the path for liberating oneself and having attained liberation, showing ordinary lay people the path to liberation and guiding them on the path to liberation and omniscience as if leading them by the hand. This is why it is called the guiding Sangha.

Ordinary people have kings as their leaders, negative actions as their path, and people who act negatively as their companions—businessmen, thieves, hunters, friends whose mouths are full of empty oaths and lies, and those who destroy any virtue one might have. For this reason, you should think, "It is not right for me to follow such a path, so I shall never do so, for now I know the advantages of the Dharma and disadvantages of worldly paths."

These then are what we call the Three Jewels:

The unsurpassable teacher, the precious Buddha
The unsurpassable refuge, the precious sacred Dharma
The unsurpassable guide, the precious Sangha

—that is, the Three Rare and Supreme Ones. In this world precious things such as gold, silver, and wish-fulfilling gems are not all that rare. Sometimes old people with great merit find a precious wish-fulfilling gem. It is also possible that King Indrabhuti obtained one. But a wish-fulfilling gem can only be a source of food, clothes, somewhere to live, and possessions in this life; it does not dispel all the fears and sufferings of this and future lives. The Three Rare and Supreme Jewels remove all the fears and sufferings of this and future lives and give rise to all the benefits and happiness of this and future lives. Therefore, because the Three Rare and Supreme Ones are very rare in the world, they are called rare and supreme and not "abundant and supreme." You should understand that you need to have a thorough knowledge of the Three Rare and Supreme Jewels, so that whenever you listen to the holy Dharma, explain it, or practice it, you will never leave their protection.

Of these Three Jewels, the Buddha is the one who shows us the path to liberation and omniscience. As the Buddha said:

I have shown you the methods that lead to liberation,
But liberation depends on you, so exert yourselves.[9]

The Dharma is what protects us, and nothing else can do so. Even the Buddha cannot protect us. When Devadatta* seized the Tathagata's big toe and cried out in anguish, "Gautama, I burn, I am ablaze, I am consumed

---

*See WMPT page 189.

by fire!'" the Buddha could do no more than teach him the Dharma, saying:

> Devadatta, from the depth of your heart recite:
> "I go for refuge to the Buddha,
> I go for refuge to the Dharma, I go for refuge to the Sangha."

The Buddha is not a catapult that can shoot stones up to the level of liberation; no one can propel you to liberation if you do not practice the Dharma yourself.

Those who hold the Dharma are the members of the Sangha, and the Dharma they hold comprises 84,000 elements. Put together, these constitute the Twelve Branches of Excellent Speech, which in turn can be compiled as the Three Pitakas. The Three Pitakas together constitute the Buddha's two precious doctrines of transmission and realization.

If we divide the Dharma into vehicles, there are what we call the worldly vehicle, or vehicle of gods and humans, and the transcendent vehicle, or vehicle of complete liberation.

The worldly vehicle takes one from existence in the three lower realms to the level of gods and humans in the higher realms, and this is why it is called the worldly vehicle.

The transcendent vehicle comprises two vehicles: the Basic Vehicle, known as the Vehicle of Shravakas and Pratyekabuddhas, so called because it takes one to nirvana, the state of the Shravakas and Pratyekabuddhas; and the Great Vehicle, so called because it takes one to perfect buddhahood beyond the two extremes.

The texts that indicate these graded paths are the Buddha's own teachings[10] and the *shastra*s of his followers. These exist in the form of the vast Buddhist canon, a very large number of transmissions and widely dispersed pith instructions, so the subject matter is infinite, and in this decadent age when the span of life is short it is impossible to learn it all, let alone practice it. As Saraha said:

> Drink the cool, soothing nectar
> Of your master's instructions until you are replete,
> Else die exhausted in the plain of misery,
> Still thirsting for the teachings in a myriad shastras.

When these three vehicles are united into a single graded path, the worldly vehicle comprises the stage on the path for beings of lesser capacity; the Basic Vehicle or Vehicle of the Shravakas and Pratyekabuddhas is the stage on the path for beings of middling capacity; and the Great Vehicle is the stage on the path for beings of great capacity. Then there are the lower, middle, and higher stages on the path of the New Tradition, the Sakya teachings of the Three Appearances and the Three Streams, and the Nyingma's Great Perfection teaching on Resting in the Nature of Mind, and so on. To know these one has to rely on the teacher's pith instructions.

Furthermore, the graded path or vehicle for beings of great capacity can be divided into three: the long path of the Vehicle of Characteristics, the short path of the Vajrayana, and the swift path of the Radiant Great Perfection. Which one of these should we choose? With the long path one attains buddhahood at the end of a kalpa, which is too long. The short path of the Vajrayana can be subdivided into three: the long path, the short path, and the swift path. Through the three outer tantras—Kriya, Upa, and Yoga—buddhahood is attained within five, seven, or sixteen human lifetimes, but this again is too long a training to undertake. Through the short path of Mahayoga and Anuyoga it is possible to accomplish the state of union with one body in one lifetime, but if in the generation phase you cannot even clearly visualize a deity the size of a finger, and in the perfection phase you cannot master even one breathing cycle, it will be difficult to attain accomplishment. On the other hand, through the Radiant Great Perfection one can accomplish the state of union within years or months. So if you wish to attain accomplishment in a short time, you will have to rely on the master's instructions: without them you will not know how to practice. This is why Saraha said:

> The master's pith instructions are like sweet-tasting nectar.
> Integrate your mind with these and you'll need nothing more.

Practice, therefore, following the teacher's pith instructions.

The tantras of the Great Perfection number 6,400,000 and can be grouped together into three sections: the mind, space, and pith instruction sections. The pith instruction section contains four cycles: the outer, inner, and secret cycles and the unsurpassable most secret cycle. As it says in the *Great Array of Ati*:

> The outer cycle is like the body, extensively teaching conventional designations.

Regarding how to ascertain the trekchö based on primordial purity, the outer and inner cycles are more or less the same. However, as concerns ascertaining the thögal based on spontaneous presence, the outer cycle contains very extensive explanations of the ground, the primordial natural state, but does not explain how to practice the path, the visions that appear in the intermediate state, or how one is liberated as the ultimate result.

> The inner cycle is like the eyes; symbolic teachings for seeing.

Though in the inner cycle the path is explained simply by being introduced through analogies, meanings, and signs, neither the natural state that is the ground nor how one is liberated as the ultimate result is explained.

> The secret cycle is like the heart; recollection teachings.

The secret cycle teaches meditation on the special features of the path, but it does not explain the natural state that is the ground or how one is ultimately liberated.

The unsurpassable most secret cycle, however, is, according to the *Great Array of Ati*:

> Like someone whose body and organs are perfect and complete . . .

for it comprises a detailed explanation of the ground of the primordial natural state; the path of view, meditation, and action; and the result, how one is ultimately liberated.

This unsurpassable most secret cycle has seventeen tantras, plus the tantra of the wrathful female protector Ekajati, which makes eighteen. If these are condensed according to their essential meaning, they form two cycles: the vast cycle of the panditas and the profound cycle of the beggars.[11] The first of these includes Longchenpa's *Seven Treasures*. In the second there are Padmasambhava's Khandro Nyingtik and Vimalamitra's Sangwa Nyingtik, known as the two mothers, together with the Khandro Yangtik and the

Lama Yangtik, which are the two sons, and the quintessence of these two, the Zabmo Yangtik.[12]

The essential meanings of all these are combined in the *Heart Essence of the Vast Expanse from the Great Perfection*, which is divided into three: ground, path, and result. The path of the Great Perfection has two aspects: the maturing empowerments and the liberating instructions. Regarding these, provided one has received the maturing empowerments, one can receive the instructions, those on the preliminaries and those on the main practice. The instructions on the main practice comprise the instructions on the common practices of the generation and perfection phases and those on the extraordinary practices of trekchö based on primordial purity, the path by which lazy people may be liberated without effort, and thögal based on spontaneous presence, the strenuous path by which diligent people may be liberated.

The Words of My Perfect Teacher deals with the instructions on the preliminaries, divided into two parts: the ordinary preliminaries and extraordinary preliminaries.

Part One

The Ordinary or Outer Preliminaries

The preliminaries are so called for the following reason. In order to receive the main practice, we must first till the soil of our beings by training our minds with the ordinary preliminaries. Once we have prepared ourselves with the ordinary or outer preliminaries, we then proceed with planting the crop and so on until the final milling of the grain, practicing the extraordinary preliminaries from taking refuge onward. Then, when the barley is ready to eat, we receive the instructions for the main practice.

These are of two kinds: detailed instructions given according to the disciple's progress and general instructions given to inspire a general audience. As to the first, according to Vimalamitra's *Conch-Lettered Instructions*,[13] which are set out in great detail, there are two forms of instruction: pith instructions given step by step and those that are given in their totality. As an example of the first of these, we can cite the omniscient Dharma King Longchenpa who followed his master Kumaraja for six years. In their case, the teacher concluded the instructions and his disciple attained the final accomplishment of the path at exactly the same time. The Great Omniscient One attained the level of the exhaustion of phenomena in primordial purity and the level of the ultimate reach of awareness in spontaneous presence. We should do likewise.

In his description of the samayas, the *Ocean of Liberation*, Longchenpa left these parting words as his legacy: "Hereafter my followers should follow the teacher for a long, long time; for a long, long time they should receive the instructions."

The opposite of the detailed instructions given according to the disciple's progress are the instructions given to inspire a general audience, also called weeklong or monthlong instructions. While the teacher goes through the instructions like a horse in a race and believes he has given the teaching, his students consider that they have actually received the teaching, bearing out the proverb "Sticking your tongue out before the head is cooked,[14] stretching your legs out before the bed warms up."

The teacher has no time to take care of disciples, and the disciples have no time to serve the teacher but talk ambitiously about "the main practice, the main practice" without going through the preliminaries properly,[15] and one is reminded of the saying "If you tie your head up high your body will fall off."[16]

Nowadays people boast that they are Dharma practitioners, but what they say and what they do contradict each other. Their outer appearance and their inner attitudes are at odds, and their minds and the sacred Dharma go different ways. They adopt the right posture and stare with their eyes wide open, but this semblance of practice will not give rise to a mite of progress in their beings.

Here we are concerned with the detailed instructions taught according to the disciple's progress, given in their totality. They are divided into three sections: the ordinary or outer preliminaries; the extraordinary or inner preliminaries; and as part of the main practice, the swift path of transference.

To begin with, what is it that makes the ordinary preliminaries "ordinary" or "common"?[17] The way it is explained in the texts, what we meditate upon in these preliminaries is common to all vehicles, and so they are called the common outer preliminaries. The way it is explained in the pith instructions, what we meditate upon is common to all three kinds of beings. What then is extraordinary or uncommon about the extraordinary or inner preliminaries? As it is explained in the texts, the extraordinary preliminaries are extraordinary with respect to the worldly vehicle and the Basic Vehicle of the Shravakas and Pratyekabuddhas, while according to the pith instructions, they are extraordinary with respect to the beings of lesser and middling capacity. It is because what the being of great capacity meditates upon is extraordinary that we talk about the extraordinary or inner preliminaries.

As for transference, it is said: "Those without sufficient training can be received through transference." Those who do not have time to receive the main practice, and those who have received it but do not have signs of progress in the meditation practices related to birth, death, and the intermediate state,[18] and have not attained stability on the path, need to continue training on the path by relying on transference. This "sudden path of transference" is part of the main practice of the perfection phase and belongs to the six yogas.

Rigdzin Jigme Lingpa (1730–98).

CHAPTER ONE

The Difficulty of Finding the Freedoms and Advantages

THE ORDINARY or outer preliminaries are divided into six sections, of which the first four are the four thoughts that turn the mind from samsara, or four contemplations that give rise to disgust. We need to use these four thoughts to turn our minds away from the concerns of this and future lives, and to adopt the altruistic thought of enlightenment to turn our minds away from our own selfish preoccupations.

The reflections on the difficulty of finding the freedoms and advantages and on the impermanence of life turn our minds away from the concerns of this life, while the reflections on the defects of samsara and on actions (cause and effect) turn our minds away from our attitudes and conduct with respect to future lives. Along with these there is the need to turn the mind away from our attitudes and conduct with respect to our own selfish interests, which is a special feature of Longchenpa's lineage. So changing our attitudes and conduct applies to three things: the concerns of this life, those of future lives, and our own selfish concerns. Then we need to seek liberation and therefore to reflect on the benefits of liberation. And because the only one who can teach us the path to liberation is the authentic teacher or spiritual friend, and no one else we might happen to meet can do so, we need to know how to follow a spiritual friend.

In *The Words of My Perfect Teacher*, the main subject of the first chapter, the teaching on how difficult it is to find the freedoms and advantages, is preceded by an explanation of the proper way to listen to spiritual instruction.

I. THE PROPER WAY TO LISTEN TO SPIRITUAL TEACHING

This first section, on the proper way to listen to the teachings, applies equally to the proper way to practice and the proper way to meditate, and for all these there are two aspects: the right attitude, which combines the vast attitude of bodhichitta, the mind of enlightenment, and the vast skill in means of the Secret Mantrayana; and the right conduct. Right attitude has mainly to do with our thoughts, while right conduct refers mainly to what we do and say.

1. Attitude

The Tibetan word for "attitude"—literally, "causing to arise from all"—can be explained as follows. "All" is a word denoting multiplicity, so "attitude" means that of the many thoughts that one has, one may give rise to a particular thought. There are three types of attitudes: negative, neutral, and positive.

(A) NEGATIVE ATTITUDES

There are two sorts of negative attitudes: seeking protection from fear and wishing to better one's lot.

(1) *The Attitude of Seeking Protection from Fear*

If you practice the Dharma in order to be protected from the fear of being prey in this life to disease, negative spirits, being punished by the law, famine, and so forth, whether you follow the most basic practices of the Shravakas' Vehicle or the most advanced practices of the Radiant Great Perfection, you may well be protected from these fears, but apart from this there will be no beneficial result whatsoever. You should therefore avoid this sort of attitude.

(2) *The Attitude of Wishing to Better One's Lot*

From the start, being driven by the motivation to demean the Dharma and use it for your own ends, you may think, "I will request a teaching and receive the empowerments and the transmissions, and then, if I practice the sadhana in retreat, I'll gain something; people will praise me and I'll become famous." With these three—gain, praise, and a good reputation—you can obtain food, clothes, and other sources of happiness for this life. Gain, praise, fame, and pleasure, and their four opposites, which are the things we do not wish for, together constitute the eight ordinary concerns. If, motivated by these, you use the Dharma to provide for this life, then when business seems to go well you might acquire horses and *dzos*;[19] when the market is not so good you might come by poor-quality sheep or yak wool. But nothing on earth could be more shameful than using the Dharma to fulfill your worldly desires. Someone who does so, exchanging the priceless teachings of the sacred Dharma for worldly valuables and goods like food and clothes, is worse than an ordinary old man who gets rich hunting with a rifle.[20] The peerless Dagpo said:

> Unless you practice the Dharma according to the Dharma,
> Dharma itself becomes the cause of evil rebirths.

Those who are unable to use offerings properly will have to experience the burning of their monastic robes, the burning of their begging bowls, the blazing hammer, and the burning molten iron, and so on,[21] so avoid accepting offerings. It is said in the Sakya teaching *Parting from the Four Attachments*, "Those who are attached to this life are not practitioners of the Dharma." Such people are traders in the soul of the doctrine, people who demean the Three Jewels, mere collectors of monastic robes. You should avoid them like poison.

When you have this sort of motivation, hoping to better your lot, you might appear to be practicing the Dharma, whether the most basic Shravakas' Vehicle or the most advanced Great Perfection; you might lock yourself up in your hermitage[22] for many years; you might look as if you are diligently practicing sadhana in retreat; but, according to Apu, even if you acquire some wealth, praise, or a good reputation the only thing you will accomplish is being able to say, "It is because of my practice that I am rich, much-praised, and famous." You will not even sow the seed for liberation in the next life. Like the swindler who spread a deerskin over some donkey meat to sell it as venison, you will have covered the donkey meat of your own evil being with the deerskin of the sacred Dharma; you will have discredited the Dharma. Just as one says of an ordinary person who squanders his inheritance, "He's a hopeless businessman," people will say of you, "There is someone who has failed and discredited the Dharma."

(B) NEUTRAL ATTITUDES

People with neutral attitudes have no real purpose and simply think they will ask for some teaching because it is the custom, without really being interested, like a chimpanzee imitating a human, or a dog following someone who walks past. Or they have no appreciation of right and wrong, like someone who shoots an arrow into the air without aiming in any particular direction. According to Apu, with this sort of attitude too you will not even sow the seed for liberation. My own teacher said of neutral attitudes that even though our attitude may not be good, neither is it bad, so the seed for liberation will be sown.

(C) POSITIVE ATTITUDES

There are three sorts of positive attitude: those of beings of lesser, middling, and great capacity.

(1) The Attitude of Beings of Lesser Capacity

The lesser being wants to escape from the three lower realms and attain the state of a god or a human, just for himself or herself, and to that end may do various practices from those of the Shravakayana up to those of the Radiant Great Perfection. However, while these may be long, short, or swift paths to attaining higher rebirth, because of the person's intention, they do not enable him or her to proceed to attaining buddhahood. With this sort of attitude, though you may observe the 253 monastic rules of the *pratimoksha* and wear the three Dharma robes, your motivation will be no better than an old man's, and you will be simply an old monk or a well-disciplined old man. Similarly, if you visualize the peaceful deities of the generation phase in an ordinary way,[23] you will be reborn as a god in the world of desire; and if you visualize a wrathful deity in an ordinary way, you will be reborn as a demon or Rudra. As Apu said, "If you meditate on the deity with mouth agape and eyes wide open, you will return as an evil spirit."

Again, with this sort of attitude, you might meditate on the trekchö based on primordial purity and the thögal based on spontaneous presence, but you will be reborn in the four formless realms or the seventeen abodes of the world of form, provided, that is, that your practice has been sustained by accumulating merit and purifying obscurations; if it has not, then you can only take birth as a rat or bear or something similar. As Sakya Pandita said:

Fools who meditate on Mahamudra
Generally end up in the animal realm.

You should avoid this lesser being's attitude, for it is said, "While you are attached to samsara, there is no determination to be free."[24]

(2) The Attitude of Beings of Middling Capacity

Middling beings have seen the deeply miserable nature of the six realms of existence, which are an engine for suffering, like a pit of fire, an island of ogresses, or the edge of a razor; they seek to attain liberation for themselves from the six realms of samsara and to attain the nirvana of the Shravakas and Pratyekabuddhas. But whichever path they practice—long, short, or swift—it will only serve as the long, short, or swift path to attaining the level of a Shravaka Arhat or Pratyekabuddha Arhat and will not be a means for attaining buddhahood.

When the peerless Jowo Atisha was in Tibet, one morning after he had taken his breakfast he suddenly said, "Oh, dear!"

"What is it?" asked the Bodhisattva Drom Tönpa, who was with him.

"In India I have a student who practices Hevajra, and this morning he entered the Shravaka path of cessation."

Drom Tönpa asked how he could have entered the Shravaka path of cessation by practicing Hevajra. Atisha answered, "If, because of his motivation, a person does not know how to do the practice of the deity, by performing the Hevajra sadhana he can be thrown into the hell realms, the *preta* realms, or the animal realm. Whereas if he knows how to practice properly, he can be projected to the level of buddhahood. Therefore, rather than *what* you practice, it is your motivation, or *how* you practice, that is most important."

For this reason it is said, "While you are attached to your own interests, there is no bodhichitta."[25]

Nowadays people of all stations say, "I need a meditation so that at the time of death I will have no fear and no delusion." My teacher says that this is an entirely selfish attitude.[26]

(3) The Attitude of Beings of Great Capacity

The above four attitudes all boil down to the attitudes and conduct of people who are fulfilling their own desires, so you should think, "From now on I shall regard attitudes and activities that involve doing something for my own benefit as enemies, as defects, as bothersome irritants. Without thinking of myself, I shall free all sentient beings from suffering and the cause of suffering and make them attain the state of perfect buddhahood beyond the two extremes." This thought is the vast attitude of the bodhichitta, the mind of enlightenment.

For this to arise in our minds, it is essential to meditate on recognizing that all sentient beings have been our mothers, to remember their kindness, and so on. Otherwise, the teacher may appear to do so as he says, "Whatever is pervaded by space is pervaded by sentient beings," and so on, and the disciples may pretend to reflect on this, both with eyes wide open, murmuring, "How pitiful!" but for both of them what they are saying will be a meaningless show, entirely devoid of genuine feeling. This is the big danger nowadays, that people pretend to be teachers or disciples, but they do not even have a kind heart, let alone any of the other proper qualities. You must begin, therefore, by acknowledging that all sentient beings have been your mother, remembering their kindness, wishing to repay that kindness, and wishing to establish them in the omniscient state of buddhahood. Practice this meditation starting with your own old mother.

1.1 The Vast Attitude of the Bodhichitta

The essence of this is to arouse the mind turned toward enlightenment, which has two aspects or points. As Maitreya said:

> Bodhichitta is the wish to attain
> perfect buddhahood for the benefit of others.[27]

The first aspect, or point, is to focus with compassion on sentient beings, wishing that all beings be free from suffering and its causes. The second aspect, or point, is to focus with wisdom on perfect enlightenment with the intention of attaining perfect buddhahood. We must have both of these, and combine compassion and love, for though we may say "for the sake of sentient beings," if we do not develop the wish to establish them on the level of buddhahood, our bodhichitta will be no more than mere compassion. On the other hand, if we have the intention of attaining buddhahood without thinking that it is for the sake of beings, our bodhichitta will be no better than mere love. The vast attitude of bodhichitta is the wish that all beings may be free from suffering and its causes and attain perfect buddhahood.[28]

How should one meditate on this bodhichitta? Begin by meditating on your own mother. Then, gradually extend your meditation to include all beings filling the furthest reaches of space.

(A) FOCUSING WITH COMPASSION ON SENTIENT BEINGS
(1) Recognizing That All Sentient Beings Have Been Your Mother

First you should consider that whatever is pervaded by space is pervaded by sentient beings, and wherever there are sentient beings there are the karmic perceptions of suffering. Of all the beings who have karmic perceptions of suffering, there is not a single one from time without beginning who has not been your father and mother and friend. And of those there is not a single one who has not been a mother; and, when they were mothers, there is not a single being whom they did not care for with great kindness, and nothing but kindness. In this way, your present mother has been a mother an inconceivable number of times, and you have been wandering in samsara from beginningless time until now. There is not one place the size of your hand where you have not been born or died many, many times, and, except in the hells and most of the god realms, you have never taken birth without a mother. You cannot be certain how many times any single being has been a mother: the number of times all beings have been mothers is not just once but an inconceivable number of times, as we find in the verse "To count one's mother's lineage . . . ."[29] This is how to recognize that all sentient beings have been your mother.

(2) Remembering Their Kindness

Consider the kindness of your present mother in particular. From the moment that you, as the wandering consciousness of a *driza* on the point of seizing another body, entered the womb of this enormously kind person, she kept you there in her womb for nine months and ten days, disregarding all the negative actions she did and paying no heed to the hardship and criticism she had to endure.[30] Your mother's body fluids and nutrients passed through your navel so that your body could develop and grow. Later when she gave birth to you, this gentle mother of yours did not let you die, fragile little thing that you were, barely alive and unable to hold up your head. She did not let you fester and shrivel up, but felt the immense joy a mother feels at the birth of a child. She wiggled her ten fingers in front of your face to keep you amused, lovingly cared for you, looked at you with a smiling face, and called you with soft words. Your first food was the sweet milk from her breast, your first clothes the warmth of her body. She gave you the tastiest morsels of her food, dressed you with the best of her clothes, touched your belly to see whether you were hungry or full, chewed your food for you, wiped away your snot with her mouth, cleaned up your excrement with her hands, taught you how to eat when you did not know how to eat, taught you how to talk when you could not talk, showed you how to walk when you could not walk, fed you when you were hungry, and gave you possessions when you had none and clothes when you had nothing to wear. Reflect on how kind she was in bringing you up with such immense love, and remember her kindness in producing your body, giving you life, providing all your needs, and showing you the ways of the world. All this is remembering the worldly aspect of your mother's kindness.

From the point of view of the Dharma, it was your kind mother who gave birth to your precious human body endowed with the eighteen freedoms and advantages. Were it not for sentient beings who have been our mothers, it would be impossible initially to arouse the bodhichitta, impossible subsequently to train in the ways of the Bodhisattva, and in that case impossible finally to attain perfect buddhahood. For this reason, the arousing of bodhichitta in the beginning, the infinite practices of the Bodhisattva in the middle, and even the attainment of perfect buddhahood in the end are all due to your mothers' kindness. Furthermore, all the favorable conditions you have at present for practicing the Dharma, such as a place to practice, a bed, and other indispensable things, depend on beings who have been your mother. This is how to remember your mothers' kindness.

(3) *Wishing to Repay Their Kindness*

Your present and former mothers, in their kindness, have greatly helped you. They gave all they gained and achieved to their children and took all their losses and failures on themselves. They provided every material comfort and happiness for their children and endured all negative actions, hardships, and malicious talk by themselves. Now it is your turn, as their child, to consider the well-being of your old mothers. If you think about this, they all want happiness, from the temporary pleasure of a warm day to the bliss of perfect buddhahood, and yet they do not know how to accomplish the cause of happiness, which is virtue, nor the sublime path. They do not listen properly to the words of a spiritual friend or teacher. Beset by all sorts of afflictions, from the burn of a tiny spark upward, they wish for none of the sufferings of samsara, yet they unhesitatingly accomplish the causes of suffering—karma and negative emotions—and whatever they do goes counter to what they truly desire. As it is said:

> They long for joy, but in their ignorance
> Destroy it, as they would a hated enemy.[31]

Accordingly, since happiness is as rare as a star in the daytime, and beings are directly afflicted by the truth of suffering and indirectly afflicted by the truth of the origin of suffering, you should employ the three links:

- the link of the wish "Oh, that they could be free from the origin and cause of suffering—karma and negative emotions—and from all the resulting sufferings of the three worlds of samsara";
- the link of aspiration "May they be freed"; and
- the link of the commitment "I will free them."

With these three links, think that you are calling on the Three Jewels, the never-failing refuge, relying on them to free your old mothers from suffering and its causes, and recite the following prayers: "To the Master and Buddhas . . . ," followed by "Woe is me! Compassionate Three Jewels . . . ," and "Courageous One, you who possess . . ." and so on.*

All the above concerns the first aspect, focusing on sentient beings with compassion.

(B) FOCUSING ON PERFECT ENLIGHTENMENT WITH WISDOM

Now, we may wonder where, having freed beings from suffering and its causes, we should then take them, and for this we have a choice. Regarding the higher realms, our old mothers have attained the state of Brahma, Indra, and other gods numerous times in the past and even now, but since these

---

*See page 289 for the full texts of these prayers.

states do not transcend suffering and are impermanent, they constitute the extreme of samsara, so we should not take them there. As for the peaceful state of the Shravakas and Pratyekabuddhas, here one is completely freed from suffering and can never again return to samsara, like someone who has had smallpox.[32] However, this state has none of the Bodhisattva levels, neither any of the qualities of the Buddha Bhagavan (which are the result of the Bodhisattva path), and if we were to take beings there, this would constitute the extreme of nirvana, so we should not take them there either. Here we reflect on the need to establish beings in the state of perfect buddhahood, which is in neither of these two extremes.

With this second aspect, focusing on perfect enlightenment with wisdom, there are three degrees of courage: great, middling, and lesser.

When one has the great degree of courage, one thinks, "Before I get there, I will fulfill the good of all sentient beings."

The middling degree of courage involves thinking, "I will not go first, nor shall I be left behind; I shall attain buddhahood at the same time as the others."

The lesser degree of courage is like that of a crippled mother whose child is swept away in a river, and involves thinking, "Since I do not at present have the ability to liberate beings, and the one who has that ability is the Teacher, the Buddha Bhagavan, I shall first accomplish buddhahood and then liberate myself through realization and liberate other beings through compassion, teaching them the path of liberation. Until samsara is empty, I shall accomplish the infinitely vast benefit of beings, just as did the previous Buddhas of the three times and ten directions, Bodhisattvas, and Vidyadharas."

This is the second aspect, focusing on perfect enlightenment with wisdom.

This wisdom is the wisdom that accomplishes the good of others. Begin by developing it with respect to your mother, then apply it to your father, then to your brothers and sisters, your close friends, your father's friends and relations, your mother's friends and relations, and then to everyone in your country. Then gradually extend it during your session to encompass the whole of space. If you do not meditate in stages, you will only have a vague understanding, so it is very important to get used to this gradually, in stages.

◊ THE THREE SUPREME METHODS

Regarding the attitude of bodhichitta that has these two aspects or points, or what *The Words of My Perfect Teacher* refers to as "the supreme method, before beginning, of arousing the bodhichitta as a skillful means to make sure that the action becomes a source of good for the future," the Great Omniscient One, Longchenpa said:

> Begin with the thought of bodhichitta, do the main practice without concepts,
> Conclude by dedicating the merit. These, together and complete,
> Are the three vital supports for progressing on the path of liberation.

(A) PREPARATION

Before beginning, arouse the bodhichitta as a skillful means to make sure that the action becomes a source of good for the future. This involves thinking, "I will free all sentient beings from suffering and its causes and bring them to perfect buddhahood," and using this intention to bind the source of good for the future, like an iron hook holding together a bundle of straw.

(B) THE MAIN PART

While carrying out the action, you should avoid getting involved in any kind of conceptualization, so that the merit[33] cannot be destroyed by circumstances.

What are the circumstances that can destroy merit? If you fail to dedicate your merit in order to attain perfect buddhahood for others' sake, the happiness resulting from the positive action will be experienced once and then be exhausted.

As for what happens if you get angry, it is said:

> Good works gathered in a thousand ages,
> Such as deeds of generosity,
> Or offerings to the blissful ones—
> A single flash of anger shatters them.[34]

When anger arises in the mind, in that very instant all the virtuous deeds you have accumulated through generosity and discipline over a thousand great kalpas are destroyed.

If you regret your virtuous deeds, their potential for future good will be exhausted. You might make offerings to the Three Jewels and give generously to ordinary beings, but if you later have regrets and mentally withdraw your instructions with regard to the things you gave, thinking that you could just as well have offered half or a third as much, such regret leads to the merit of your positive actions being consumed.

Finally, showing off your positive actions leads to their merit being consumed. Whether or not you have been able to recite the Mani one hundred million times, you might thread a *dung*[35] onto your mala and swear that you have completed the hundred million, showing off your mala to everyone and getting in the way of people traveling on foot or standing in front of those on horseback to tell them all about the little virtue you have accomplished. In this way, positive actions are wasted.

To avoid these four causes of exhausting your store of merit, you need to realize the view of Madhyamika, which is the ground; of Mahamudra, the path; and of the Great Perfection, which is the result. My teacher said that you can give rise to something similar to this view by developing the conviction that the three concepts, though they appear, have no intrinsic existence, like a magical illusion, a dream, the city of the *gandharvas*,[36] or the reflection of the moon in water. This will do as a beginner's "main practice without conceptualization." For beginners in particular, it is difficult to be free from concepts in the main part of the practice right from the start; it seems as impossible as pulling one's nose to see whether it will go into one's mouth. This is why Shantideva declares:

> This mind I'll tether to that sturdy post, reflection on the Teaching,
> That it might never slip its bonds and flee.[37]

So when you meditate on the difficulty of finding the freedoms and advantages, and so on, it is very important to alternate periods of analytic meditation with periods of resting meditation.

(C) THE CONCLUSION

At the end, dedicate the merit of the positive action to ensure that it continually grows ever greater.

In the *Sutra Requested by Sagaramati* we read:

> Just as a drop of water that falls into the ocean
> Will never disappear until the ocean runs dry,
> Merit totally dedicated to enlightenment
> Will never disappear until enlightenment is reached.

Just as a single drop of water added to the ocean will not be consumed until the end of a great kalpa, positive actions dedicated to the great ocean of omniscience will not be destroyed or degenerate until we reach ultimate enlightenment. While they may result temporarily in our being reborn with all the breeding and virtues of the most supreme brahmin, the most supreme *kshatriya*, or the most supreme householder,[38] they can never be exhausted and will ultimately result in our attaining perfect buddhahood.

There are two sorts of dedication: unwholesome and wholesome.

◊ Unwholesome Dedication

It is said in the *Condensed Transcendent Wisdom*:

> Eating good food mixed with poison
> And practicing the virtuous way with concepts—
> These are the same, the Conqueror has said.

Just as good food mixed with a little poison tastes delicious when we eat it but gives rise to intense pain as we digest it, similarly, positive actions may result in rebirth in the higher realms but will not give liberation from samsara if you cling to the three concepts and consider that they are real. You should therefore avoid this sort of dedication.

◊ Wholesome Dedication

This refers to the pure dedication free from the three concepts, and such a dedication can be authentic or a surrogate.

Of the authentic wholesome dedication, the *Condensed Transcendent*

Wisdom has this to say: "The wisdom free from concepts performs all activities." In other words, this authentic dedication is the emptiness supreme in all aspects, which is the view that manifests as love, compassion, bodhichitta, dedication, prayer, and so on.

The surrogate dedication means dedicating the merit we have accumulated in the past, the merit we will accumulate in future, and the merit we are accumulating now, the untainted merit of the Buddhas and Bodhisattvas, and the tainted merit of all beings, mentally all gathered together and combined, so that all sentient beings may be free of suffering and its causes in the three worlds of samsara and attain perfect buddhahood.

◊ *How to Make the Dedication*

Recite the two verses below, thinking, "In the same way that the Buddhas and Bodhisattvas made a completely pure dedication free from the three concepts, I too will dedicate the merit."

> Emulating the hero Manjushri,
> Samantabhadra, and all those with knowledge,
> I too make a perfect dedication
> Of all acts that are positive.
> I totally dedicate all merit in the same way as the Buddhas of the past, present, and future.

This will do as an authentic pure dedication free from the three concepts.

There are no practices in the Mahayana sutra and mantra traditions that are not included in the three supreme methods, so to accomplish perfect buddhahood we need little more than these three methods. But we cannot do with anything less. When Arya Nagarjuna says:

> May we complete the accumulations of merit and wisdom
> And attain the two supreme kayas
> Which come from merit and wisdom[39]

it is because the three supreme methods are the epitome of the two accumulations or the two truths. The supreme preparation, arousing the bodhichitta, and the supreme conclusion, dedicating the merit, constitute the "apparent" accumulation of merit with concepts, while the supreme main part without conceptualization is the "nonapparent" accumulation of wisdom without concepts.[40]

The accumulation of merit with concepts creates the direct cause for attaining the *rupakaya* of the Buddha, and the accumulation of wisdom without concepts creates the supporting condition. The accumulation of wisdom without concepts creates the direct cause for attaining the dharmakaya of the Buddha, and the accumulation of merit with concepts creates the supporting condition. Therefore, to purify the two obscurations of the ground, perfect the two accumulations on the path, and attain the two kayas as the result, you need little more than the three supreme methods; but nothing less will do.

These three supreme methods are common to both Sutrayana and Mantrayana.

1.2 Vast Skill in Means: The Attitude of the Secret Vidyadhara Mantrayana

Whether we are studying or practicing the Secret Mantra Vajrayana teachings it is very important to have the Mantrayana attitude, and it is vital that from the start there be a sound connection between teacher and disciple. As we find in the *Torch of the Three Methods*:

> It has the same goal but is free from all confusion,
> It is rich in methods and without difficulties.
> It is for those with sharp faculties.
> The Mantra Vehicle is sublime.

Although the Sutrayana and Mantrayana both have as their ultimate goal the attainment of perfect buddhahood, the Mantrayana differs from the Sutrayana in the way that goal is attained. There are four distinguishing features that make it superior: the unobscured view, the many methods of meditation, the action that is without difficulty and the extremely sharp faculties of the individual.

First, the view of both Sutrayana and Mantrayana focuses on the absolute space, but the two views differ in nature: one sees as if with blurred vision, the other clearly. While in the Causal Vehicle of Characteristics the absolute truth, or absolute nature, is ascertained as being the Great

Emptiness free from the eight conceptual extremes, it is not possible to realize the nature of the union of the absolute space and primal wisdom. When this obscured aspect is eliminated, the nature of the union of the absolute space and primal wisdom is ascertained and the view of the absolute nature is unobscured.

In the Causal Vehicle of Characteristics, substantial relative phenomena are established as being interdependent, like magical illusions, but apart from this perception of ordinary, impure phenomena as illusion, one does not ascertain them as the kayas and wisdoms. It is this obscured aspect that becomes unobscured in the Secret Mantra Vajrayana, where the display of the kayas and wisdoms is ascertained as the great superior dharmakaya, the inseparability of the two truths, which is the meaning of the inseparability from the very beginning of the absolute space and primal wisdom.

Second, the meditation of the Secret Mantrayana is superior because it contains the generation phase, related to skillful means, and the perfection phase, related to wisdom.

Third, the action of the Secret Mantrayana is superior because it is without difficulty. Whereas in the Causal Vehicle of Characteristics there is no path taught for accomplishing enlightenment without giving up the five pleasures of the senses, in the Secret Mantrayana, where the mind is easily and quickly protected,[41] the five pleasures of the senses are not rejected but used as the path, and it is possible to accomplish the level of the union Vajradhara[42] in one lifetime and one body.

Fourth, the Secret Mantrayana is superior because the individuals who practice it have extremely sharp faculties. It is superior in general because these individuals possess the five powers; in particular these extremely sharp individuals have the power of the wisdom that is able to realize the profound view of the Secret Mantra Vajrayana, and the power of confidence, having no fear of living as outcasts.

❖ The Five Perfections

Whenever we study or practice this Secret Mantra Vajrayana, it is essential to keep in mind the five perfections. As Jigme Lingpa said:

> He who sees his teacher as a man
> Will receive the very lowest accomplishment.[43]

The teacher should perceive the disciples as Buddhas, and the disciples should perceive the teacher as Buddha. Otherwise they are no less than samaya breakers, for in the Secret Mantra Vajrayana the difference between someone who keeps the samaya and a samaya breaker is that the former perceives phenomena as deities, whereas the samaya breaker sees earth as earth, water as water, and so on.[44]

Therefore, the first of the five perfections is to realize that the *teacher* is the Buddha. There are two ways of establishing this: by scriptural authority and through natural reasoning.

First, that the teacher is the Buddha is mentioned in countless passages in the scriptures. Aryadeva, for example, says:

The genuinely accomplished Buddha,
The sole lord, the great deity
Gives the pith instructions directly.
For this reason the Vajra Master is supreme.

Elsewhere we find:

The teacher is the Buddha,
The teacher is the Dharma,
So too, the teacher is the Sangha.
The teacher is he who accomplishes everything,
The teacher is the glorious Vajradhara.

and again:

Master, Samantabhadra, think of me!

and:

Vajra master, glorious Buddha . . .

and so on.

That the teacher is the Buddha can also be established through reasoning. The teacher's vast wisdom mind is the dharmakaya. The expression of that primal wisdom is the rupakaya, and the essence of the rupakaya is the dharmakaya. The rupakaya is the expression of the dharmakaya and is inseparable from it as the vajra body. His vast wisdom mind appearing as form is the vajra body, appearance and emptiness inseparable. The great wisdom body resounding as speech is the vajra speech, sound and emptiness inseparable. The thoughts emanating as his mind are the vajra mind. Since its nature is these three vajras, his great wisdom mind appears as the rupakaya and the primal wisdom that is the essence of the rupakaya.[45] The inseparability of the rupakaya and the dharmakaya, the union Vajradhara, essence of all refuges, is the teacher.

The entire *assembly* also, whether each one in it realizes it or not, is pervaded by the Buddha nature, in the same way that sesame seeds are full of oil. They are Buddhas, as the quotation in *The Words of My Perfect Teacher* from the *Hevajra Tantra* clearly shows:

All beings are Buddhas,
But this is concealed by adventitious stains.
When their stains are purified, their buddhahood is revealed.

Their pure nature is the Buddha, their primordially pure essence is the Buddha, and their spontaneous qualities are the Buddha. Nevertheless, their buddhahood is not effective, for instead of being free of adventitious stains, they are obscured by them. But in truth they are Buddhas and should therefore be visualized as the *daka*s and *dakini*s of whichever Buddha family is appropriate.[46]

Both the teacher and the assembly being Buddhas, their *realm* too is pure and should be visualized as Akanishtha, "the Unexcelled," or another buddhafield.

The *teaching* is the Radiant Great Perfection. The *time* is the ever-revolving wheel of eternity, in which the teachings are transmitted from mouth to ear in an uninterrupted lineage from Samantabhadra down to your present root teacher.

These five perfections are "visualized" as they are,[47] and have been from the very beginning: we are simply visualizing the Buddhas who dwell in the ground of appearance and existence *manifesting* in the ground. We are not trying to say, for example, that a donkey is a horse or that coal is gold.

2. Conduct
There are two kinds of conduct: conduct to be avoided like poison and conduct to be adopted like medicine.

2.1 What to Avoid
2.1.1 The Three Defects of the Pot
The term "defect of the pot" is explained as follows. If nectar is poured into a pot containing poison, the nectar will itself become poisonous. Similarly, however much the Dharma is taught to students who are not fit vessels, not only will it not act as the antidote to their negative emotions, it will actually serve to reinforce these emotions.

Regarding the first of the three defects, if you do not actually listen, you will be like a pot turned upside down: even if liquid is poured over the pot, nothing goes in. Although your body is present at the teaching, your mind is not, and if you are not actually listening to the teacher's words, you will not understand anything he says. So you should use your ears and listen.

You may listen properly, but this is no use if you do not retain what you hear: you will not understand either the words or their meaning. So you must remember the teaching.

When your mind is full of negative emotions, you demean the Dharma. And if you give rise to attachment, hatred, and ignorance in the place where the teaching is being given you will accumulate bad karma. This is why listening to the teachings with your mind full of negative emotions is likened to a pot containing poison.

The antidotes to these three defects are indicated in the sutras: "Listen properly and well, and remember; then I'll teach you."

Indeed, the Tathagata said to Ananda, "Without adulterating your attitude with negative emotions, listen to the words and remember their meaning. Then I will teach you." He did not say, "If you develop an attitude full of attachment and hatred, and do not listen, and do not keep in mind what I say, I will teach you." So listen to the teachings with an attitude free from attachment and hatred, and never relinquish the thought of bodhichitta; truly listen to the words and remember their meaning.

2.1.2 The Six Stains

The Words of My Perfect Teacher lists the six stains in a quotation:

> Pride, lack of faith and lack of effort,
> Outward distraction, inward tension and discouragement;
> These are the six stains.

The first of these, pride, is the feeling of superiority that comes when one looks at one's inferiors. As soon as you become proud, you despise those who are inferior to you, feel jealous of those who are better than you, and develop rivalry with your peers. This is why it is said:

> Never will the water of good qualities
> Permeate the iron lump of pride.

The moment you feel proud, you fail to see your own faults and are blind to the good qualities in others. To remedy this you should always recognize your own shortcomings, lay bare your own hidden faults, keep a low profile, wear old, tattered clothes, and hold everyone in esteem, whatever their qualities.

When you lack faith, you have no confidence in the teaching or in the teacher. The antidote is to have a deep conviction that neither the teaching nor the teacher will ever let you down.

As for lack of effort, whether or not you have received Dharma teachings, if you are not interested in the Dharma, you will be no more motivated than a horse offered a bone or a dog presented with some grass. You should remedy this by thinking how difficult it is to come across the Dharma and how hard it is to find a spiritual friend, and by developing an insatiable interest in each and every word of Dharma and its meaning.

Outward distraction can give rise to negative emotions such as lust and should therefore be remedied by concentrating your thoughts.

On the other hand, concentrating too intently can make you dull and sleepy, so learn to listen properly relaxed.

With regard to getting discouraged when listening to the teachings, if you feel hungry and thirsty during a teaching that goes on too long, or have to put up with discomfort from sun and rain and so forth, there is a risk that you will want to leave the Dharma and the teacher. So before you accumulate the bad karma of giving up the Dharma, you should pray that you will meet the teacher and receive teachings again, and then leave the assembly. Indeed, it is important to listen to the teachings with joy, thinking: "In the past, I have wasted my life pointlessly, but now it is worth being ill, hungry, thirsty, and so on to hear the holy Dharma for the sake of all sentient beings. As I listen, in this world of Jambudvipa, this pure land of Buddha Shakyamuni in which I have had the fortune to be born, just the slight headache I have is purifying the numerous evil deeds of beings in other realms such as the vajra hell; I am exhausting an immeasurable amount of bad karma and accumulating incalculable merit. I have every reason to be joyful."

2.1.3 The Five Wrong Ways of Remembering

These refer to remembering the teaching in any way different from that taught in the Buddha's precious doctrine of transmission and realization.

The first is to remember nice-sounding stories and suchlike without thinking of their meaning, or else to concentrate only on getting the words right and remember them as a meaningless sequence.

Second, there are some who like to think they are great Nyingmapa meditators, saying, "The way the teaching is expressed is just a hollow series of words; the only thing you need to understand is the essence of mind." Pointing to their hearts, they claim they can grasp the essential naked meaning without bothering about the words.

The remedy for these two is to remember both the words and their meaning.

Third, to remember both but with no understanding is to apprehend the expedient meaning as the ultimate meaning,[48] to mix up the true intention and the indirect intention,[49] and to understand the opposite of what is meant by the four points of reliance.[50] To remedy this, you should rely on the teachings rather than individuals. However famous a person may be, if he does not act in accord with the Mahayana path and the teachings on cause and effect, he will not benefit you. And if he does practice the Mahayana teachings, no matter who he is, he too has to rely on the Dharma. Then, rather than relying on the words of the teachings, you should rely on their meaning. Of the expedient meaning and the ultimate meaning, you should rely on the ultimate meaning. And with regard to the ultimate meaning, you should rely not on intellectual knowledge but on wisdom.

Fourth, to remember the teachings incorrectly is to misunderstand what they mean. As a result you may think that as soon as you have received some teaching on the Secret Mantrayana, you can indulge in sex and alcohol and perform the practices of union and liberation. To avoid this mistake, the moment for practicing particular activities has to be well chosen. Your conduct should match your level of spiritual development; that is, you have obtained signs of progress in meditative concentration and have the ability to transform the color, smell, and taste of alcohol by reciting the three syllables or to kill beings through your enlightened activity and bring them back to life through your realization. If you do not know how to do these things and you recklessly indulge in the hidden secret practices without having attained realization of the profound secret truths,[51] there is no alternative to your ending up as a demon or Rudra.

Fifth, to remember the teachings out of order is to listen to or explain the main practice before receiving the teachings on the preliminaries, or to remember the ordinary or outer preliminaries and the inner preliminaries in the wrong order. To remedy this, you should remember the Perfect Buddha's teachings in their proper sequence, like the steps of a ladder.

2.2 What to Do

2.2.1 The Four Metaphors

In thinking of yourself as someone who is sick, you should recognize your own infirmity, namely that your mind has been stricken by the disease of the three poisons and their result, the three kinds of suffering. The other three metaphors are easy to understand.

2.2.2 The Six Transcendent Perfections

The six transcendent perfections concern both the person listening to the teaching and the teacher. How they concern the listener is explained in *The Words of My Perfect Teacher*. Here is how the six transcendent perfections apply to the teacher:

- Generosity involves explaining the teaching without hoping that one will gain anything or that one will be praised or become famous.
- Discipline involves not being sarcastic or scornful of others and so forth.
- Patience involves answering questions again and again without getting irritated.

- Diligence involves tirelessly teaching the Dharma day and night.
- Concentration involves focusing one's attention on the words and their meaning.
- Wisdom involves being free from the three concepts and inspiring disciples to study and reflect.

II. THE TEACHING ITSELF

This second part, the teaching itself, comprises the six chapters dealing with the difficulty of finding the freedoms and advantages and so on. The meaning of "teaching" (or Dharma) has been explained above; it is this teaching that we use to bring our minds under control. As it is said, "It is not with the hair, neither is it with the staff." So we should reflect on the freedoms and advantages and so forth again and again. The various names for these meditations—the four reflections that turn the mind from samsara, the four contemplations that give rise to disgust with samsara, the four meditations on determination to be free—all refer to the same thing.

First we need to turn our minds away from the concerns of this life by meditating on both the difficulty of finding the freedoms and advantages and the impermanence of life. As we read in *Parting from the Four Attachments*:

Those who are attached to this life are not practitioners of the Dharma.

The importance of the difficulty of finding the freedoms and advantages, which are

Like the udumbara flower, found once then rarely again,
Like the wish-fulfilling gem—to find which is of great consequence,

lies in the fact that the pivot on which your destiny[52] turns, like the bridle used to direct a horse, is this body that you have now. Moreover, because of impermanence, where there is birth, there is naturally death, so you should understand that achieving the things of this life, which are subject to impermanence and death, is hollow and pointless, and you should interest yourself in the next life. And to turn the mind away from samsaric concerns for your next life, you need to reflect on samsara and what causes samsara.

As to how one turns the mind in this way, beings of lesser capacity turn their minds from the three lower realms and aspire to be born in the higher realms, while beings of middling capacity turn their minds from the six realms of samsara and strive to attain liberation. Other teaching traditions mention only these two, but according to the tradition of Longchenpa and his followers, it is also necessary to turn our minds away from our own selfish concerns. When we reflect on the defects of samsara, we gain a lucid sadness and disillusionment, and thence gain the determination to be free as intention, but what use is it if we then attain liberation just for ourselves? Nothing could be more shameful than to leave behind those kind mothers who have lovingly cared for us throughout time without beginning and to attain liberation alone. You should think therefore, "I must make all sentient beings attain buddhahood," and develop the great renunciation, the determination to be free from the two extremes.

Determination to be free can be divided into four categories: simple renunciation which is the attitude of beings of lesser capacity; the two kinds of renunciation of the Shravakas and Pratyekabuddhas; and the great renunciation. Or we can talk about three kinds of determination to be free: the two kinds of renunciation of the Shravakas and Pratyekabuddhas, and the Bodhisattva's determination to be free.

Once we have the determination to be free from everything in samsara, we have to look for a place to which to escape, so we should strive to attain liberation and omniscience. The path of liberation is not something that we can know naturally, on our own, nor can our parents or relations teach it to us; even if they wanted to do so, they would not know how. We therefore need to look for a spiritual friend. However, not just anyone we happen to meet will do: we should follow a qualified teacher or spiritual friend and use the three ways of pleasing the teacher to serve him and learn from his realization and activities.

For the first of these six topics,* the teachings on the difficulty of finding the freedoms and advantages and so forth, there are both the detailed instructions given according to the disciple's progress, and general instructions given to inspire a general audience. Nowadays only the general inspirational instructions are given, for since the time of the Great Vidyadhara Jigme

---

*The six sections of the outer preliminaries, which Khenpo Ngakchung has just summarized and which make up part one of *The Words of My Perfect Teacher*.

Lingpa they have been substituted for the detailed instructions given according to progress. So we begin with the instructions on the difficulty of finding the freedoms and advantages, whose subject is our own body, for with this precious human body we have a choice of only two destinations.

Used well, this body is our raft to freedom.[53]

In other words, if we use our bodies to practice the sacred Dharma correctly, we can have the prospect of happiness and peace, and in the end we will attain liberation and omniscience. In particular, if we meditate on the Radiant Great Perfection, we will be liberated either in this life or in the intermediate state or in our next life.

Used badly, this body anchors us to samsara.

If we use our bodies to accomplish the worldly concerns of this present life, we can have the prospect of nothing but fear and suffering.
In this respect, "freedom" refers to our own body, because it constitutes the opportunity, free from adverse circumstances, to practice the Dharma. As the opposite of this freedom, we talk about the eight forms of lack of freedom, which are the eight states that provide no such opportunity. Of these eight, there are four nonhuman states and four human states where there is no opportunity to practice the Dharma.
Begin by meditating on the hell realms, which are one of the nonhuman states of no opportunity, and reflect again and again on whether or not they constitute a chance to practice the Dharma.
You should do this in sessions, with breaks between the sessions. There are many ways of dividing up the day, into two, three, four, or six sessions, and so on, but here we shall consider four sessions a day, two during the day and two during the hours of darkness, as this suits beginners quite well. Start the dawn session early in the morning, at cockcrow, and continue until it gets light. Then take a break from the end of the session until it begins to get warm. During this time carry out activities such as offering water *tormas* and the white burned offering, and do your daily *yidam* recitation. Then start the morning session and continue until noon, when the sun reaches its highest point. Conclude the session and then have lunch and study a little, relaxing until late afternoon, when the shadows start to lengthen. Begin the

afternoon session and conclude at sunset, after which you should make offerings to the Dharma protectors, recite any prayers of dedication and aspiration you know, and make the red burned offering. At dusk, the so-called dark faces time, when you can still see people but not recognize them, begin the evening session. End this session late in the evening.

Practicing in four sessions like this suits the mind well, and although beginners may try to meditate between sessions, the essential point will elude them, and in particular the flaws of drowsiness and distraction will occur more strongly. During the breaks, therefore, concentrate on reciting prayers and doing meritorious activities,[54] and let your meditation relax.

Each session should consist of the preliminary practice for each session, the main part, and the conclusion.

(A) THE SESSION PRELIMINARIES

The preliminary practice for each session is divided into the preliminary preparations and the actual preliminary practice.

(1) Preliminary Preparations

Blow your nose, wash, and complete any necessary chores.[55] In short, prepare things so you do not need to get up until the session is over. Then sit on your bed,[56] relax your body and mind, and rest. Make a firm resolve not to break the session and give in to delusion even if your kind old father were to appear, and promise not to abandon that resolution even if you are being tortured to death by having bits of flesh pincered from your body.

(2) The Actual Session Preliminaries

The essential point for the body is to sit in the seven-point posture of Vairochana: legs crossed in the vajra posture; hands in the gesture of equanimity; the spine straight like a stack of coins; shoulders stretched apart and relaxed; the neck slightly bent; tongue touching the palate; and the eyes gazing in the direction of the tip of the nose.

The essential point for the speech is to expel the stale breath. This is done nine times: in turn, three times through the right nostril, three times through the left, and three times through both. Alternatively you can expel the stale breath three times: once through the right nostril, once through the left, and once through both nostrils. Or you can exhale three times through both nostrils together. To expel the stale breath, make a vajra fist with your left hand and press it down on the great channel in your thigh. With your right hand in the three-pronged vajra mudra, block your right nostril. Slowly inhale through your left nostril and press the air down below. Imagine that all the karma, negative emotions, negative actions, obscurations, violations of samaya, and the three meditational faults—drowsiness, dullness, and oblivion—that you have accumulated throughout time without beginning in your series of lives in samsara turn into a black vapor that evaporates outside, and as you expel the breath, blow out in a manner resembling the tapering shape of a grain of barley,[57] gently at first, then with increasing force, and finally with full force. This practice is like rinsing a vessel.[58]

The essential point for the mind is to correct your attitude. Ask yourself, "Is my attitude in this session that I am beginning to seek protection from fear, with a desire to alleviate illness and so forth in this life, or is it to better my lot, to achieve gain or praise?" If you have either of these attitudes, you should shun them like poison. If your attitude is neutral, you should change it. The lesser being's attitude is the motivation of an ordinary old man: there is no intention to enter the path. The middling being's attitude is also motivated by selfish desires and should likewise be avoided. The great being's attitude is to think, "I shall meditate on the difficulty of finding the freedoms and advantages so that all sentient beings can be free from suffering and its cause and attain perfect buddhahood," and it is this perfectly pure attitude that you should develop.

Next pray to the teacher. Visualize on the crown of your head a white lotus with 100,000 petals, in full bloom. On its spreading orange anthers is a lion throne, piled high with fine silks, and on this sits your root teacher. Visualize him as he is, in the robes of a monk or tantrika, and, keeping in mind the five ways in which we should know him to be a Buddha,* recite the prayer "Essence of the Buddhas of the three times, precious master, think of me! . . ." and so on, and the supplicatory verses at the beginning and end of the section containing the four reflections that turn the mind from samsara. As you pray with sincere devotion, the teacher, with great compassion, melts into light and dissolves into you, and his mind merges completely with yours. In this state, rest in equanimity as long as you can

---

*These five are explained in the chapter on guru yoga, page 253.

without following past thoughts, welcoming future thoughts, or prolonging the flow of present thoughts.

All this is the preliminary practice for each session.

(B) THE MAIN PART OF THE SESSION

1. Reflecting on the Nature of Freedom

Begin by meditating on the eight freedoms, starting with the four nonhuman states with no opportunity. The first of these is the hells.

There are four topics of meditation: the place, body, sufferings, and span of life.

In the hot hells, the *place* is characterized by dense gloom and darkness; the ground everywhere is of red-hot iron, like the burning charcoal in a torch, and of ordinary earth there is not even a patch the size of a footprint. Dark red volcanoes a cubit high erupt, and glowing embers, burning rocks, and weapons rain down from above.

The *bodies* of hell beings are four times as big as those of the inhabitants of this world, and the color of boiled blood. Their skin is as delicate as that of a newborn prince, as fragile as gossamer-fine strands of wool. Their bodies are fully fleshed and tender, and exquisitely sensitive to touch, like the eye. Their hair swirls upward, their eyes are triangular, the hairs on their bodies stand on end, and they have big hands and feet and large bellies. The mere sight of these hell beings, like wrathful deities, would be enough to make a person from our world faint.

As regards their *suffering*, hell beings experience no leisure by day, nor do they sleep at night. For them there is no day and no night. Split open by sharp weapons, burned through from head to tail by a fiery rain of earth and rocks and so on, they suffer without a single second of relief.

The *span of life* that these beings have to endure cannot be counted in years: they live for periods like one intermediate kalpa.

The cold hells are snowy mountain ranges and glaciers where one is frozen by blizzards. The bodies of the beings there are similar to those in the hot hells. The suffering they experience is the torment of cold, and they have to live for infinite numbers of years.

Reflect again and again on this, asking yourself whether someone born in the hot or cold hells has any opportunity to practice the sacred Dharma. When you get tired of this analytic meditation and can take it no further, practice resting meditation, without fabricating anything; do not follow past thoughts, welcome future thoughts, or prolong the flow of present thoughts. When a thought starts to occur again, analyze, and when you do not feel like going on, again rest. In this way, practice analytic meditation and resting meditation alternately.

Second, meditate on the pretas. They live in places full of stones and pebbles, with many burned tree stumps and coarse, stiff, poisonous thorns scattered here and there. There are dry riverbeds, and the land is pitted with dried-up swamps.

The bodies of the pretas are like ages-old skeletons, dried mushrooms, or stiff butter bags.[59] Their heads are as big as Chinese pots, their throats as narrow as horsehairs, their stomachs as big as whole valleys, and their limbs as thin as coarse grass. When a preta goes by it makes as much noise as a five-hundred-wheeled wagon being dragged along, and from its joints red sparks crackle and spit.

As to how they suffer, in summer even moonlight feels hot, and in winter, even in the sun they are cold. Sometimes they see an orchard of fruit trees in the distance, but as soon as they approach the trees disappear. Sometimes they see the waves of a great lake shimmering like a string of crystal beads, but hardly have they seen it than it dries up and they become even more miserable and frustrated than before.

The longest these pretas live is ten thousand human years, while the shortest life span is not fixed.

Investigate whether there is any opportunity to practice Dharma when you are born in such a place, and alternate analytic and resting meditation.

Third, meditate on the animal realm. Animals mostly live between the continents, in darkness so deep that they cannot tell whether their own limbs are stretched out or bent in.

With regard to their bodies, some take the form of different kinds of fish and crocodiles, able to coil around Mount Meru three times, and so on. Others have tiny bodies, no bigger than particles of dust or the point of a needle.

They suffer in general from ignorance and stupidity, having no idea of right and wrong. In particular, they experience the infinite distress of being eaten: the smaller animals are swallowed whole by the larger ones, and the larger ones are pierced by the smaller ones, who bore through them and use them as dwellings and clothing.

The long-lived gods dwell in the city of the fourth concentration in the northeast, where tree stumps are jet black as if burned by fire.[60] Their bodies are mental, dreamlike bodies.[61] They have no perception of happiness and suffering or of positive and negative actions, as in a state of deep sleep. The explanation that they live in the fourth concentration follows the expedient meaning,[62] but in accordance with the line[63] "Why is it not the same as the place where they died?" wherever one dies, if one is in a mentally blank state with no perceptions, one remains like that for eighty great kalpas:[64] the light of the sacred Dharma is absent and there is no opportunity to practice it.

Reflect on all this properly, practicing both analytic and resting meditation.

Regarding the four human states with no opportunity, meditate in the same way as above, combining analytic and resting meditation.

(C) CONCLUSION TO THE SESSION

Beginning with the merit of the meditation you have done in this session, add together all the positive actions you have accumulated in the past, present, and future, and all the untainted positive actions of the Buddhas and Bodhisattvas and all the tainted positive actions of all sentient beings, and dedicate it so that all beings may be free from suffering and its cause and attain the precious state of perfect buddhahood.

To make the dedication, think, "In the same way that the Buddhas and Bodhisattvas made a completely pure dedication free from the three concepts, I too will dedicate the merit," and recite:

Emulating the hero Manjushri,
Samantabhadra, and all those with knowledge,
I too make a perfect dedication
Of all acts that are positive.

Then, instead of leaping straight up from the session, look back and ask yourself whether or not you have fallen into delusion and lapsed in the promise you made at the beginning of the session you have just done. If you have completed a perfect session without a single second's delusion you might feel pleased and proud, but you should break your pride by saying to yourself, "The fact that you have done such a good session now is simply due to the fleeting appearance of some frail merit. But it is nothing to be proud of. Let's see whether you do as well in the next session!"

If, on the other hand, your mind has strayed into delusion, you might feel depressed because you have not had a single good thought, and want to give up, thinking, "I am no good at anything." Encourage yourself by telling yourself, "It was not a good thing that you strayed into delusion just now, but why be depressed? You have been deluded from time without beginning until now, and even now you still need to practice in sessions with breaks between sessions. If it were not the case and you had not been deluded to start with, you would already be enlightened. Though you have been influenced by delusion now, you will definitely not wander off in the next session!" In this way, promise to do whatever you can.

Then take your time getting up from the session, and set about your usual between-session activities. However, if you do not reflect on each of these eight freedoms that you have meditated on in the sessions during the breaks, you will be like a piece of red-hot iron that becomes black again as soon as it is removed from the forge: your mind may change a little in the sessions, but between sessions you will get distracted by the mundane whims of this life, and there is a risk your mind will become impervious to the Dharma; whether or not you reflect on the freedoms and so on during the sessions will make no difference.

2. Reflecting on the Ten Particular Advantages Related to Dharma
2.1 and 2.2 The Five Individual and Five Circumstantial Advantages

Merely to have obtained the eight freedoms does not help: to practice the sacred Dharma, five factors need to be complete with regard to one's own circumstances and five with regard to circumstances other than one's own.

Of these ten advantages, if you have the first three individual advantages and the first three circumstantial advantages, meditating on them is simply a question of rejoicing. As for the last two individual advantages and the last two circumstantial advantages, you should investigate thoroughly and make every effort to ensure that you have them as well, dividing your practice into sessions and breaks, and alternating analytic and resting meditation, and so on.

2.3 THE EIGHT INTRUSIVE CIRCUMSTANCES THAT LEAVE NO FREEDOM TO PRACTICE THE DHARMA[65]

The eighteen freedoms and advantages can be compared to eighteen sheep, and the intrusive circumstances to a wolf that suddenly appears and kills one or two of the sheep, leaving only seventeen or sixteen sheep left. Even if you are not affected by any of these intrusive circumstances today, or in one particular session, or at the start of the session, they may appear tomorrow, in the following session, or at the end of the session. So examine yourself very carefully, and apply the appropriate remedy in each case.

Regarding the first, it is said that one should train by applying the remedy for the strongest of one's negative emotions. You should therefore meditate on ugliness as the antidote to attachment, on love as the antidote to aversion, and on the eighteen dhatus as the antidote to bewilderment.

The inability of very stupid beings to understand the words when they listen to the teachings, to fathom the meaning when they reflect, and to develop realization of the natural state when they meditate is an expression of their past negative actions and obscurations. The remedy therefore is to make a full confession that includes all the four powers, and to pray to the sublime Manjushri: of the Eight Great Close Sons or Bodhisattvas, each of whom has a special aspiration and activity, he is the one who helps beings to develop wisdom.

The remedy for being taken as a disciple by a false spiritual friend is to examine whether the spiritual friend is genuine. In this respect, do not consider outward signs like miraculous abilities or clairvoyance. You should look to see whether his mind contains the precious jewel of bodhichitta. If so, any connection made with him will be meaningful, and you should rejoice. If not, whether the split takes place well or badly, you should leave this sort of false spiritual friend or evil companion.

The remedy for being struck by bad karma is first to meet a spiritual friend, then to listen to the teachings and reflect on them, and finally, when obstacles come up during the meditation, to generate confidence in the infallible law of cause and effect and to regret your past negative actions, rather than thinking, "Why should this happen to me?" For as the *Vajra Cutter Sutra* states, "Bodhisattvas who practice transcendent wisdom will be tormented, indeed greatly tormented."

To counteract laziness, you should reflect deeply on death and impermanence and practice diligently, constantly, and enthusiastically.

The solution for being someone else's attendant or servant is, if you are forced to be a lama's or rich person's servant, to try to find the right way to procure your freedom.

If your motive for practicing the Dharma is to seek protection from danger, you should correct it by having the determination to be free from samsara and having genuine bodhichitta.

The remedy for hypocritical practice of the Dharma is to recognize the shortcomings of your worldly plans for success in this life and give them up.

2.4 The Eight Incompatible Propensities That Leave No Freedom to Practice the Dharma

Two explanations are given for the Tibetan name of the eight incompatible propensities. They are called either *ris chad* ("those that isolate us"), because they separate our minds from the paths of liberation and omniscience, or *rigs chad* ("those that cut us off from the family of enlightenment"), because when any one of them occurs it withers the fresh shoot of the three kinds of enlightenment and we are cut off from any sort of liberation.

The remedy for insufficient disillusionment is to recognize the defects of the three worlds of samsara and develop the determination to be free.

Lack of faith should be remedied by reflecting on the good qualities of the Dharma and the teacher. Develop irreversible faith.

The remedy for intense attachment is to bear in mind the defects summarized by the four ends of impermanence.

For evil conduct there is no distinct remedy.[66]

The remedy against breaking one's vows is to have a thorough knowledge of the four causes that lead to downfalls, and, even if you have broken one of the four root vows of the pratimoksha, you should keep the other three. It is said:

Better to regret greatly your broken vows
Than to be puffed up with pride about perfect observance.

In the best case, when you take vows and keep them without breaking them, you raise the victory banner of the Buddha's doctrine and tear down the battle standard of Mara. But failing that, should you happen to break any vows, proper confession also hoists the victory banner of the teachings and tears down Mara's standard, so it is important not to leave breaches unconfessed, thinking that they do not matter. Sincerely confess such breaches and resolve not to err again. Rejoice at others who keep their vows and you will become better able to keep vows yourself.

If you transgress the intention and application of bodhichitta and confess before daybreak, the transgression will not become a root downfall, so you must confess before the last watch of the night.[67]

If you break your Mantrayana vows, you should apply a remedy as for transgressions of bodhichitta. The Mantrayana vows can all be condensed into the samayas of body, speech, and mind. The body samaya is not to treat one's teacher and vajra brothers and sisters disrespectfully. The speech samaya is not to act contrary to what one's teacher and vajra brothers and sisters tell one. The best practitioners recite the mantra of their yidam like the flow of a river,[68] middling ones recite it on the six special days of the month, such as the days of the full moon and new moon, or at least once a month. At the very least, one should never fail to make the effort to do the recitation during the month of the New Year. The essence of the mind samaya is to keep the ten secrets and not to upset the teacher or vajra brothers and sisters.

3. Reflecting on Images That Show How Difficult It Is to Find the Freedoms and Advantages

According to the tradition of the pith instructions, we should first reflect on the difficulty of finding the freedoms and advantages by thinking of their causes. As Trakpa Gyaltsen says:

> This free and favored human existence
> Is not the result of your resourcefulness.
> It comes from the merit you have accumulated.

There are two aspects to this: general and particular.

In general, if you think about the positive actions you have accumulated in the past and those you are accumulating now, they may add up to a little bit of virtue, but you have also accumulated an inconceivable number of negative actions: to have obtained just the freedoms is already quite something; how could you possibly hope to obtain the advantages as well?

In particular, to obtain the freedoms, we need to observe pure discipline; to obtain the advantages, we need to gather a mighty store of merit through the practice of generosity and so on. Furthermore, in order to obtain the freedoms and advantages, these primary causes have to be linked by pure aspiration, which is a contributory cause.

First let us consider discipline, which is the primary cause for obtaining the freedoms. The pratimoksha vows comprise 253 precepts on things to be refrained from and 47 precepts on things that have to be taken up. If you examine yourself carefully, starting with the four root vows, you may not have been the target of scandal about having girlfriends, but apart from that can you be sure that you have nothing to be ashamed of, that you have kept the pratimoksha vows well enough to obtain the freedoms? It is by no means easy to have such perfect discipline.

As for the Bodhisattva vows, consider the vows in the tradition of the Profound View,[69] the twenty root downfalls (the eighteen root downfalls and the two precepts of intention and application) and eighty branch faults: these are even harder to observe than the pratimoksha vows. And according to the Vast Activity tradition,[70] there are the root downfalls, four attitudes, eight applications, and forty-six branch faults that have to be observed or avoided. It is extremely hard to rely on keeping these to obtain the freedoms.

In the Secret Mantra Vajrayana, to begin with there are the twenty-five yogas, then the common, outer, and inner vows of the five Buddha families, the fourteen root downfalls, and the eight lesser downfalls. In the Great Perfection, for those practitioners whose realization develops gradually, for whom there is something to be kept, there are twenty-seven root samayas to be observed with respect to the teacher's body, speech, and mind, and twenty-five branch samayas; for those practitioners of sudden realization for whom there is nothing to be kept, there are the four samayas of nonexistence, omnipresence,[71] unity, and spontaneous presence; and there are the 100,000 branch samayas. Think about it: if the cause for obtaining the freedoms depends on keeping all these samayas, it must be as rare as a star in the daytime.

While you might somehow manage to preserve pure discipline and thus have the cause for obtaining the freedoms, there is then the difficulty of achieving the cause for obtaining the advantages, namely virtuous practices such as generosity and so forth. Examine yourself and think how hard it is to be generous, whether in religious offerings to the Three Jewels or in mundane charity to beggars.

Now examine further: you may have kept all your vows and given generously, and so forth, but are these primary causes linked with the contributory cause, pure aspiration? They do not necessarily have to be linked by a specific aspiration to obtain the freedoms and advantages. When seed is sown with the specific purpose of harvesting the grain in autumn, the stalks and leaves automatically appear as well. In the same way, if you perform a genuine positive action such as keeping vows sustained by the jewel of bodhichitta with the aim of attaining omniscient buddhahood, you will meanwhile automatically accomplish an extraordinary rebirth as a human or god. In other words, you will in the meantime obtain numerous births as the most supreme brahmin, as the most supreme householder, or as the most supreme raja, and so on.

This is how you should reflect, analyzing in detail and alternating analytic and resting meditation.

The proper attitude is important. As it is said, "To see what you have done before, look at what you are now." It is as a result of the merit you accumulated through having the proper attitude in the past that you have obtained this extraordinary human body now. The saying continues: "To see where you are going to be born next, look at what you do now." If you have the proper attitude now, as Apu Rinpoche says, you will definitely not be reborn in a place where herdsmen drink curd and farmers eat bread.[72]

You should therefore reflect in this way on the difficulty of finding a precious human body in terms of its cause, and make full use of it.

Nowadays those who conduct village ceremonies recite rituals all day long without practicing the generation and perfection phases at all. Onto tormas thick with mold they sprinkle *amrita* and *rakta* green from corrosion. Rolling their eyes, they chant, "From that which is devoid of essence, I take the essence of accomplishment, *Kaya Siddhi Om* . . ." and so forth.

Nothing could be more meaningless. On the other hand, to put this precious human body characterized by thirty-six impure substances to proper use, using it to practice the sacred Dharma,[73] is the true *Kaya Siddhi Om, Waka Siddhi Ah,* and *Chitta Siddhi Hung*.[74]

This body that you have now, like the bridle used to direct a horse, is the pivot on which your destiny turns. It is now up to you to decide between happiness and suffering, just as one has to choose either the dzo or the salt.[75]

If you want happiness and you practice the Dharma and accomplish some virtue, the latter part of your life will be happier than the earlier part; in the intermediate state you will be happier than at the end of your life; in your next life you will be happier than in the intermediate state; and thereafter you will find increasing happiness. As we read in the *Way of the Bodhisattva*:

> For, mounted on the horse of bodhichitta,
> Who could ever be dejected,
> Riding such a steed from joy to joy?[76]

and,

> Merit is the true cause of the body's ease,
> While happiness of mind is brought about by training.
> What can sadden those who have compassion,
> Who linger in samsara for the sake of beings?[77]

Through the "apparent" accumulation of merit with concepts, you will gain bodily well-being; you will be born in a good family and have many excellent qualities. And with the wisdom that is the realization of no-self you will be happy: you will see all phenomena, in the absolute, as free from concepts and, in the relative, as being like magical illusions. As a result you will have no fear of any of the sufferings of samsara.

On the other hand, if you want suffering, again it is up to you. If your actions are exclusively negative, in the latter part of your life you will suffer more than in the earlier part; in the intermediate state you will suffer more than at the end of your life; in your next life you will suffer more than in the intermediate state; and subsequently there will be no end to the rebirths you have to take in the lower realms.

It is important therefore to make full use of this human body that you have now, that is, to practice the holy Dharma.

How does one realize the full potential of the precious human life? Beings of lesser capacity recognize the three lower realms as suffering and strive to attain rebirth as a god or human in the higher realms. In order to do this, they gather the merit that arises from discipline by avoiding the ten negative actions and practicing the ten positive actions; they gather the merit that arises from generosity by making religious offerings to the Three

Jewels and mundane gifts to beggars; and they gather the merit that arises from meditation by practicing the meditations of the four concentrations and four formless states. However, although they may realize the full potential of the lesser beings' way, it is only a prop for the path and not the actual path itself, and they do not realize the full potential of either the middling or superior ways.

Beings of middling capacity practice the precious threefold training, namely the training in the wisdom that is the realization of no-self, which is the principal aspect of the truth of the path, and the trainings in discipline and concentration, which are auxiliary aspects. However, while they may realize the full potential of this middling way, they do not realize that of the superior way.

You should therefore reflect on the need to realize the full potential of the freedoms and advantages through the great beings' way, on either the long path of the Vehicle of Characteristics or the short path of the Vajrayana, which is further divided into the long path of the three outer tantras (Kriya, Upa, and Yoga), the short path of two of the inner tantras (Mahayoga and Anuyoga), and the swift path of the Radiant Great Perfection.

In particular, you should think, "I must realize the full potential of the path of the Radiant Great Perfection, for through it I can attain the great transference rainbow body in a matter of months or years," and, alternating analytic and resting meditation, meditate again and again, dividing your practice into sessions and breaks.

In the example of the turtle, the ocean symbolizes the vastness and depth of the three lower realms and the endlessness of suffering. The blind turtle represents the beings in the lower realms who lack the eyes to distinguish right and wrong. The fact that it rises to the surface only once every hundred years illustrates the difficulty of escaping from the lower realms. The single hole in the yoke symbolizes how rare it is to be reborn as a god or human. The wind that drives the yoke to and fro represents the influence of circumstances, namely, positive actions.

Meditate on the significance of this image, alternating analytic and resting meditation.

CHAPTER TWO

The Impermanence of Life

YOU WILL NEVER realize the potential of the precious human body if you take your time, for you are always prey to impermanence and death. Here there are seven topics to reflect upon.

I. THE IMPERMANENCE OF THE OUTER UNIVERSE IN WHICH BEINGS LIVE

First, reflect on the formation of the outer universe in which beings live. Our world, the outer environment, was formed from the bottom upward, and the beings living in it came into existence from the top downward. Divide your meditation on this into sessions and breaks between sessions, as you did for the difficulty of finding the freedoms and advantages.

For the main part of the session, reflect as follows.

To begin with, before a universe like ours is formed there is a kalpa of destruction and then nothing but empty space, a state that lasts twenty intermediate kalpas. At the end of this the universe begins to take form. As a result of the common merit of the sentient beings in this kalpa, the base of the universe appears: this base is "pure mental space," space in the form of a deep blue triangle with an azure halo.

On top of it, where the eastern wind strikes the west, the western wind strikes the east, the southern wind strikes the north, and the northern wind strikes the south, there appears the mandala of wind in the form of a dark green crossed vajra with a dark green halo. Upon that rain falls from the cloud "the golden cored" to form the round, clear, white water mandala with a clear white halo. On top of that, the wind that separates off the best elements forms Mount Meru, the wind that separates off the second-best elements forms the seven golden mountains, and the wind that separates off the most inferior elements forms the four continents with the encircling range of iron coal-containing mountains.

The beings that live in this universe come into existence from the top downward, starting from the peak of existence and going down to the hell realms, gradually becoming more and more gross until, after twenty intermediate kalpas, the first hell being is born.

Then, at the beginning of the period of stability, when beings' life span is immeasurably long, there is a first long intermediate kalpa during which the life span decreases to ten years. Then the life span increases up to eighty thousand years, and decreases again to ten years, which makes up one cycle. After eighteen such cycles of increase and decrease, the life span increases until it is immeasurably long, after which it decreases again and the Buddha Infinite Aspiration[78] will come: the life span will then decrease to eighty thousand years. This is the final short intermediate kalpa, making twenty intermediate kalpas in all.

When the life span is eighty thousand years, the period of destruction begins, and no new hell beings are born in the hell realms of this universe; they are born in other hells in other universes and, as their karma lightens, take birth in higher states. Apart from a few beings underneath the Vajra Seat at Bodh Gaya[79] who have committed the five crimes with immediate retribution, given up the Dharma, or broken the Mantrayana samaya commitments with the vajra master, the hells are empty. Similarly the preta and animal realms then gradually become empty. Then someone in the human realm goes to a solitary place, attains the second concentration, and proclaims, "Oh, this is the joy and happiness that comes from leading the life of a hermit!" When all the other humans learn of this, they meditate and attain the second concentration, gradually transmigrating and taking birth in the Abode of Clear Light in the realm of the second concentration.

Then the gods in the realm of the Four Great Kings, in the Heaven of the Thirty-three and in the four sky abodes[80] one after another, like the humans, attain the second concentration and are all born in the realm of the second concentration. After that, the gods in the realm of the first concentration transmigrate to the second concentration, and from the realm of the second concentration down to the very bottom of the hells there is not a single living being.

As a result no rain falls, and all the plants and trees dry up.[81] One after the other, seven suns rise in the sky and burn Mount Meru, the four continents, and the celestial realms, transforming them into an immense, roaring mass of fire that blasts downward, burning up the empty lower realms. When it meets the fires of the hell realms, the hell fires first make the fire of the end of the kalpa blaze upward, and then, as a result of the immense power of karma, the fire of the end of the kalpa causes the hell fires to burn downward. The upper hells are consumed, and as the fire burns up the hell of Ultimate Torment, the beings in it are reborn in the twinkling of an eye in the hells of Ultimate Torment in other universes.

After that, the flames flare upward again and consume the abandoned celestial realms, leaving everything up to the realm of the second concentration empty. As it all turns into a single pile of ash, the beings in the realm of the second concentration transmigrate to the realm of the third concentration, and from the realm of the second concentration the "cloud with the core of water" forms: many huge raindrops as big as a yoke or plow fall, destroying this pile of ash and turning it into gruel. The beings in the realm of the third concentration attain the fourth concentration and transmigrate. The crossed vajra mandala of wind at the base of the universe rises with a roar, scattering everything up to the abode of the fourth concentration like dust and leaving nothing but empty space. All this takes twenty intermediate kalpas.

This is followed by twenty intermediate kalpas of nothing but empty space. The duration of these four periods of formation, stability, destruction, and emptiness is thus eighty intermediate kalpas, making what is known as a great kalpa.

This is how to meditate. There are also other explanations on this.[82]

II. THE IMPERMANENCE OF BEINGS LIVING IN THE UNIVERSE

Just as the outer universe and the beings that live in it are impermanent, so on the inner level are your own body (which is a vessel) and your consciousness (which, like the beings, is the content).

First, from conception until birth is the period of formation. From childhood until illness is the period of stability, and from the moment one becomes terminally ill until one dies is the period of destruction. At the time of the white path the water dissolves, at the time of the red path the fire dissolves, and at the time of the path of complete darkness the wind dissolves.[83] Losing consciousness corresponds to the period of emptiness.

Meditate in this way on the impermanence of the outer and inner aspects of the vessel and contents, alternating analytic and resting meditation, and dividing the practice into sessions and breaks.

Reflect that at the time of death the only thing that will help you is your positive actions and the only thing that can harm you is your negative actions. If you have committed negative actions that will harm you, confess them, for as Jetsun Mila said, "There is nothing good about negative actions—except that they can be purified through confession."

If you have not accumulated any positive actions, you should do whatever you can now. So starting from today, you must check your positive and negative actions. Otherwise, if you do so only as you are dying, and have only negative actions and no positive actions, you will have to set out on the highway to your next life deeply distressed, with your eyes full of tears and your breast pitted with the marks of your fingernails, as you think, "How stupid I've been, I never bothered to think . . . !" Convince yourself that apart from the true Dharma, nothing can help you at the moment of death, and reflect on this again and again.

VI. THE UNCERTAINTY OF THE CIRCUMSTANCES OF DEATH*

When you reflect on the uncertainty of the time of death, you should meditate (dividing your practice into sessions and breaks) on three points: that we are sure to die, that it is uncertain when we will die, and that when we die, there is absolutely nothing that can help us.

(A) THE CERTAINTY OF DEATH

Wherever there is birth, death is the natural consequence. With each moment that passes, each second that ticks by, our lives are running out, like the sun sinking toward the mountains in the west or an animal being led to the slaughterhouse. Take someone who is eighty years old today and a one-day-

---

*Khenpo Ngakchung jumps at this point to the sixth section of the chapter on impermanence in WMPT.

old baby born last night: in a hundred years' time, it will seem as if neither of them had ever existed; they are certain to die. This is easy to understand, but the trouble is it never occurs to us that when we will die is far from certain.

(B) THE UNCERTAINTY OF THE TIME OF DEATH

You may think you are young, but this is no guarantee that you will not die. You may think everything is all right, that you have food and clothes and so forth, but this is no assurance against dying. You may think you are in good health, but how can this make you confident you will not die?

The only way you could be sure that you will not die is if the Buddha in his omniscience were to predict that you would not die until a certain date, or if you were to know from your own unobstructed powers of clairvoyance that you would not die before a particular time, or if you were to meet the Lord of Death and make a friendly deal with him not to take you away until a particular day. Otherwise, there is no knowing how long this present life will be. Just as it is impossible to tell how far an arrow will fly or how long a lamp will burn, for they depend on the strength of the archer's finger and on how much oil is left, you cannot know whether your life will end today or tomorrow, in the second half of this month, next month, or next year. When you will die is quite uncertain.

When your allotted life span has run out and you are on the point of death, nothing can stop your dying, neither the Medicine Buddha giving you medicine, nor Amitayus conferring on you a long-life empowerment, nor Vajrapani standing guard over you.

Although there exist methods to prevent sudden death, sudden causes such as the 404 types of disease, the 80,000 negative forces, or the 360 types of accident induced by negative forces can unexpectedly cause sudden death, like the wind blowing out a lamp before the oil is used up; these make the duration of life on this earth quite unpredictable for us. Wherever you go you will die. Whoever you are with, you will die. No matter which country you live in, you will die. Whether you own wealth and property or possess nothing at all, you will die. Since you do not know whether your allotted life span will run out today, you cannot be certain when you will die. Even if it has not run its course, because of sudden causes of death, there can be no certainty when you will die. Examine this point deeply again and again.

(C) AT DEATH NOTHING CAN ACCOMPANY YOU

When you die, apart from the sacred Dharma nothing can help you: your food, clothes, home, bed, possessions, parents, relatives, friends, and partner are of no use to you. Even a lama with many thousands of monks cannot take a single monk with him. Even a head of state ruling millions of people is unable to take with him a single servant. The owner of all the wealth in the world is powerless to take with him even a needle and thread. You will have to depart leaving everything behind, even the body that you have cherished and cared for. You will sleep on your final bed, eat your last meal, wear your clothes for the last time, speak your last words, and your relatives and friends will gather round for the last time. And when the time has come to die, nothing will postpone it.

You will be powerless to stay. None of your relatives and possessions to which you are so attached[84] will be able to follow you, and as you set out on the road to the next life, naked and empty handed, you will not be able to assign the burden of all the negative actions you have accumulated for the sake of your parents, relatives, and friends to anyone else; you will have no choice but to shoulder it yourself and depart. At that time, only your own negative actions will be able harm you: not even the whole world, with the most hostile intent, will be able to shoot a single arrow at you. And even if you own all the wealth in the world, you will not be able to take anything with you apart from the sacred Dharma, not even a needle and thread. Then the Dharma will be a protector, a refuge, an island, a friend, a light, and a torch, so from now on you should practice teachings that will help you at the moment of death.

Regarding such teachings, beings of lesser capacity recognize the three lower realms as suffering, and with the intention of striving for rebirth as a god or human in the higher realms they accomplish the three kinds of merit. But though they may accomplish the instructions in preparation for death according to their own lesser beings' tradition, they do not accomplish those according to the tradition of either middling or greater beings.

Beings of middling capacity, on the other hand, recognize that the three worlds of samsara are suffering, and, desirous of liberation for themselves alone, they renounce the world accordingly and practice the precious threefold training of the superior path. But though they may accomplish the instructions in preparation for death for middling beings, they do not accomplish those for greater beings.

Beings of greater capacity have the attitude of bodhichitta and benefiting others, and by practicing instructions in preparation for death from either the long path of the Vehicle of Characteristics or the short path of the Vajrayana or the swift path of the Radiant Great Perfection, they accomplish the perfect instructions in preparation for death from their respective greater individuals' path.

Of these, if you practice in particular the perfect teachings in preparation for death from the path of the Radiant Great Perfection, the link between death and rebirth will fall away. So practice with two iron commitments, first vowing that whatever happens you will seize the citadel of genuine immortality, and second resolving never to give up this first promise.

For this, divide your practice into sessions and breaks, and alternate analytic and resting meditation.

VII. INTENSE AWARENESS OF IMPERMANENCE

The seventh section of this chapter in the root text refers to reflecting on impermanence between sessions.

CHAPTER THREE

The Defects of Samsara

Now, although death and impermanence may well happen like this, if it were all no different from a fire going out or water drying up, that would be the end of that. But, as Patrul Rinpoche says in *The Words of My Perfect Teacher*, after death we do not vanish into nothing; we are forced to take a new birth. After death there is nowhere else to go but here in samsara, so we need to reflect on the defects of samsara. By "samsara" we mean the three worlds, while "defects" refers to the three sufferings.*

Although you may obtain a precious human body endowed with the eighteen freedoms and advantages as already described, it is subject to death and impermanence, and you will be dogged by the sufferings of birth, old age, sickness, and death in this life, greeted by suffering in the intermediate state, and again yoked to suffering in your next life.

When you recover in the intermediate state from losing consciousness, you will not at first recognize that you are dead. But when you tell your weeping relatives and friends, "I'm not dead, look, I'm here," and they neither see nor hear you, you will wonder whether you are dead or not. Then you will check and find that you make no shadow in the sun, neither footprints in the sand nor reflection in water, and you will realize that you are truly dead. As you panic, you will hear four terrifying sounds: a sound like the whole universe shaking from the base, a sound like the whole cosmos of a billion universes raging with fire, a sound like the whole cosmos of a billion universes being devastated by wind, and a sound like the whole cosmos of a billion universes being swept away by water.

*See WMPT page 78.

And you will see three dreadful abysses: like the sky one generally sees at twilight, wherever you look, the natural radiance of desire will make everything appear as a diffuse red; then wherever you look, the natural radiance of anger will make everything appear as a flickering white; and then wherever you look the natural radiance of ignorance will make everything appear as oppressive darkness.[85]

At that time those with pure karma will be welcomed by dakas and dakinis and go straight up to liberation. Those who have committed any of the crimes with immediate retribution will perceive many infernal workers (as they are known in the Mantrayana; the sutras refer to them as Yama's henchmen); they will go straight down.

For anyone else, the stay in the intermediate state may be forty-nine days, three or four weeks, or an uncertain period of time. If you stay there forty-nine days, during the first half of this period you will perceive the body you had in the life you have just left, and during the second half you will perceive the body you are to have in your next life. If you are to be reborn in the hells or as a preta, you will feel as if you are moving around with your head pointing downward. If you are to be reborn as an animal, you will feel as if there are horns sprouting out of your head and you are moving about on all fours. If you are to take birth as a god or human, you will feel yourself walking around with your head held up and perceive your body as sunlight or moonlight. Thus the sufferings in the intermediate state act as a link, and it is in the intermediate state that the sufferings you are to experience in your next life will begin.

When the Tathagata taught the Four Noble Truths, he first said, "Recognize suffering." For this reason, although in other commentatorial traditions the instructions on actions, cause and effect, are explained first, here it is the suffering that is to be recognized (that is, the defects of samsara) that is taught first, and then the origin of suffering that is to be abandoned (that is, actions, cause and effect).

These are followed by the instructions on the spiritual path to be taken, namely the reflection on the benefits of liberation and how to follow a spiritual friend (which both act as links preparing one for the path), and the actual path, from taking refuge up to guru yoga. Finally, the instructions are given on the cessation of suffering that is to be realized, that is, the main practice of the Radiant Great Perfection. These are the teachings on trekchö based on primordial purity, the path through which lazy people may be liberated without effort; and thögal based on spontaneous presence, the effortful path through which diligent people may be liberated.

First, then, the defects of samsara, which are considered under two headings:

I. The defects of samsara in general
II. The particular defects of samsara in detail

I. THE DEFECTS OF SAMSARA IN GENERAL

This first section covers six aspects:

1. The place where beings circle[86]
2. The beings who are circling there
3. The time during which we circle there
4. The manner in which we circle there
5. The cause that makes us circle there
6. Similes that illustrate this circling

Meditate on these, alternating analytic and resting meditation.

People following the way of samsara put happiness first and end up with suffering, whereas those who adopt the Dharma start out with hardship and end up with happiness. This sort of general reflection on the sufferings of samsara should be enough to transform your attitude, but in case it does not, reflect on what follows.

II. THE PARTICULAR SUFFERINGS EXPERIENCED BY THE BEINGS OF EACH OF THE SIX REALMS

Now comes the reflection on the particular sufferings experienced by beings in each of the six realms.

For the hells, to imagine them as the eight stories of a metal building is a way of meditating on them. But more generally, "hell" is just a term covering an inconceivable number of different places and sufferings, which are described in the *Sutra of Sublime Dharma of Clear Recollection*. You should find out about them there. Indeed, for both the defects of samsara and the cause and effect of actions, you should repeatedly study the *Sutra of a Hundred Actions*, the *Sutra of Sublime Dharma of Clear Recollection*, and the *Hagiography of Purna*.

When you reflect on all the numerous different kinds of suffering, do not imagine someone else being cut or chopped up, as if you were just a spectator, but imagine that you yourself have really taken birth in this or that realm and are actually experiencing that suffering.

The way to reflect on these states is the same as when you reflect on the freedoms, that is, in terms of (1) the place; (2) the body that is the support; (3) the suffering; and (4) the life span.

The lucid sadness that you feel when you reflect in this way is called disillusionment, and the wish to be liberated from these states is called the determination to be free from samsara. Determination to be free has two aspects: determination to be free as a result[87] and determination to be free as an intention, and here it is the latter that is meant and will now be discussed.

Generally speaking, the cause that gives rise to birth in the hell realms is a major accumulation of any of the ten negative actions that are motivated by the three poisons. The most important of these are actions motivated by hatred, such as taking life. You have accumulated an incalculable number of such actions in your mindstream throughout time without beginning, so confess them completely using the four strengths as antidotes, and promise that you will never again commit any such action out of hatred—even if someone is torturing you to death by pincering pieces of flesh from your body.

Recognize that all the beings born in the hells have been your mother, remember their kindness, and give rise to the wish to repay their kindness. With the three links—(1) the link of the wish, thinking, "May they be free from these sufferings and their causes"; (2) the link of aspiration, thinking, "How good it would be if they were free from them"; and (3) the link of the commitment, thinking, "It is I who will free them from them"—pray insistently to the Three Jewels, the unfailing refuge, that they may all be free from both the causes of suffering and the sufferings that result, saying, "May all beings in the hells, my old mothers, be liberated from both suffering and its causes right now, immediately, on the spot, while I am sitting here."

In praying to the Three Jewels, recite the following prayers:

"Woe is me! Compassionate Three Jewels . . ."
"To the Master and Buddhas, guardians of wandering beings, who labor for the good of all that lives . . . ," and
"Courageous One, you who possess the power of compassion . . . ."*

It is said in the tradition of the Omniscient Father and Son[88] that saying these prayers is bound to make our self-centered preoccupations change by themselves.

The practice for the sufferings in the other five realms is similar in each case: reflect on all the details of place, body, sufferings, life span, and so forth; develop disillusionment and determination to be free; confess and resolve; recognize beings as having been your mother, remember their kindness, and so on, going through all the other stages.

---

*See pages 289–90.

CHAPTER FOUR

Actions: The Principle of Cause and Effect

As the second Noble Truth, the Buddha taught the origin of suffering, which is to be abandoned. Here therefore comes the explanation of cause and effect.

(A) GENERAL INTRODUCTION

In the six realms of samsaric existence, the different places and environments, the different kinds of bodies that support life, the different joys and sorrows, and the different durations of life all arise through the principle of cause and effect of actions.

This is set out in the "seal that marks the view of the transmitted teachings" taught by our Teacher, the Bhagavan, *Yedharma . . . sramana*.[89] This is usually said with *Om* at the beginning for auspiciousness and *Svaha* at the end to give stability: all the panditas have written it with these two elements to consecrate it and make it propitious. Translated, the *Yedharma* says:

All phenomena arise from causes;
Those causes and what puts an end to them
Have been proclaimed by the Tathagata himself.
He who truly speaks such words is the Great Shramana.[90]

To begin with, "all phenomena" is a plural expression, so what are the manifold phenomena referred to here? They include everything that can be known, all phenomena whatsoever, whether of samsara, nirvana, or the path.

The Buddhist tradition holds that all these phenomena arise from a cause, being produced via dependent arising and originating from causes and actions. Non-Buddhist traditions, however, comprise 360 wrong views holding that things are not produced by causes or that things arise in the absence of a cause. All of these can be included in one or other of the five *tarka,* or sophist, schools,[91] and these in turn can be summarized as being either of two: eternalist or nihilist.

First, according to the nihilists, both Gautama's[92] view and that of the eternalists are wrong because all phenomena just arise by their own nature. They would say that this present body of ours just appears, giving the similes of a rainbow arising in the sky or mushrooms springing up in a meadow. The body is like snow and the mind like the tracks left in it by a wolf; just as the wolf's tracks disappear when the snow melts, so also, apart from what we simply perceive in the present, nothing else, such as future lives, enlightenment, or liberation, can exist. At death, the body dissolves into the four elements, and the mind disappears with it and ceases to exist. As it says in the doctrine of Black Ishvara:

> The rising of the sun, the downhill flow of water,
> The roundness of peas, the bristling length and sharpness of thorns,
> The beauty of the iridescent eyes of peacocks' tails:
> No one created them; they all just naturally came to be.

In the view of eternalists, Gautama's tradition is wrong because, although there are past and future lives, they do not happen through cause and effect but are created by a creator other than ourselves. Who is this who created everything? A great, almighty God,[93] eternal, unique, and autonomous, created it all. And if we make offerings to him of a portion of our children and cattle, he is pleased and will bestow happiness on the world—while if he is not pleased he will bestow unhappiness on the world. Thus happiness and suffering are brought about by something other than ourselves.

Another group of eternalists believes in what is called "primal substance" or *prakriti,* the state of equilibrium between pleasure, pain and neutrality, or attachment, hatred, and ignorance.[94] From the prakriti's grain sack[95] of eternal space, an eternal being, the inner conscious principle, or purusha, causes particles to manifest and experiences them. When it finally recognizes them as the prakriti's manifestations, the prakriti is "embarrassed"[96] and flees. Thereupon, all modulations of the prakriti subside into the expanse of the prakriti, and when the purusha is free from such modulations, liberation is obtained. They believe that within the heart is an inconceivable, eternal self, about the size of a thumb, as if this body were a pot in which was a little bird, the consciousness. When the body disintegrates, they say, the consciousness is free and can go anywhere.

According to the Buddhist tradition, both of these beliefs, eternalist and nihilist, are mistaken. All phenomena included in samsara, nirvana, or the path arise from causes.

Now, just how phenomena arise from their causes is something that neither ordinary beings nor gods nor Brahma nor the Lord of the Paranirmitavasavartin realm, the king of the *maras* can know. Great monarchs, like King Bimbisara, King Ajatashatru, or Sharava, could not know it, nor could the six non-Buddhist teachers[97] and their kind. And among Buddhists, not even the Buddha's children, his regent Lord Maitreya and Manjushri, knew it except insofar as they taught according to the Buddha's words; the reason their knowledge was limited in this way is that they had not got rid of the obscurations of habitual tendencies. None of the Six Ornaments, Nagarjuna, Asanga, and the others, nor the Two Supreme Ones and so on, knew it. Nor did any of the Shravaka and Pratyekabuddha disciples.[98] None of their respective paths, except insofar as they follow the Buddha's words, could bring such knowledge.

For Shravakas, there are four reasons that something may be beyond their knowledge:

1. They may not know something because it is too remote in terms of space.
2. They may not know something because it is too remote in terms of time.
3. They may not identify an effect and its cause as such because of the absence of any contiguity between the two.
4. They cannot know all the very numerous qualities of a Buddha.

As the *Yedharma* says, then, "Those causes ... have been proclaimed by the Tathagata himself." Both samsara and nirvana arise from causes, and it is the Tathagata who taught what those causes are, as follows.

The ultimate nature of all phenomena is the absolute truth, the absolute expanse, the ultimate perfection, the flawless truth, that in which phenomena dwell. When the realization and meditation of that ultimate nature reach their culmination, it becomes manifest in its entirety, and this is the "primordial wisdom of knowing as it really is" the ultimate nature of all phenomena, absolute truth itself. Because of this realization of emptiness, every single phenomenon whatsoever included in samsara, nirvana, or the path can be known instantaneously, just like a reflection appearing in a mirror or a *kyurura* held in the palm of the hand; this is the "primordial wisdom of knowing each and every thing."

The latter can be subdivided into (1) knowledge of everything that can be known and (2) specific knowledge of what is truly important.

1. Knowledge of everything that can be known. To the Buddha, things that were completely obscure to Devadatta were all clearly evident: from dipping a piece of *kusha* grass in water and brushing it over a mixture of ashes, he could recognize whether the particles of ash adhering to the grass came from grains from a particular city or from trees in the forest on the sunny or shady sides of a valley. As it is said:

> Every single one of a peacock's brilliant hues
> Has causes that are distinct and of different kinds.
> To know these is to be omniscient;
> They cannot be known without the wisdom of omniscience.

Apart from its ability to inspire a certain confidence in disciples, this kind of knowledge need not concern us greatly here.

2. Specific knowledge of what is truly important. When one knows the causes and results of both samsara and nirvana—what causes samsara, the truth of the origin of suffering; its results, the truth of suffering; what causes nirvana beyond all suffering, the truth of the path; and what results from that, the truth of cessation—one knows in terms of the four truths exactly what needs to be done and what needs to be avoided.

Next, where the *Yedharma* speaks of "what puts an end to those causes," the way cessation is achieved is as follows.

Non-Buddhists believe that the result can be brought to an end without bringing its cause to an end. But that would be like bringing a disease to an end without ceasing to ingest the toxin causing it. In fact, it is impossible to stop a result. It is its cause that must be stopped. If one does not ingest the toxin, that disease will not be produced. Similarly, we have to put an end to the actions and negative emotions that are the causes of the next life and other lives to come. There are different ways of putting an end to those causes, corresponding to the three kinds of beings.

First of all, to practice the path leading to one of the three kinds of liberation or enlightenment, it is necessary to take a particular physical form as a support. So beings of lesser capacity, understanding that the three lower realms are suffering and motivated by the wish to be liberated from them, strive to achieve the states belonging to the higher realms—those of gods and humans. They give up the ten negative actions, undertake the ten positive ones, and may practice the unwavering actions[99] of the eight concentrations and formless absorptions as well. But although they thus attain the higher realms of gods and humans, they have only used positive actions to suspend the fruition of their negative actions; they have not been able to put an end to the negative emotions.

Beings of great or middling capacity have turned their minds away from all six realms of existence and must give up samsara and the cause of samsara, and take up nirvana and the cause of nirvana. These Four Truths, as is explained in the *Sutra Requested by Shrimaladevi Simhanada, daughter of King Prasenajit*, may be either (1) still unfinished or (2) completely finished.[100]

Beings of middling capacity know that the whole of samsara is suffering. For those who have attained either the Shravaka or Pratyekabuddha levels,[101] however, there is still the ignorance devoid of negative emotions,[102] and of innate ignorance and ignorance due to imputation, there is still innate ignorance; there is still the mental body, untainted karma, inconceivable death and transmigration,[103] and so forth. They have no knowledge of the sufferings that are due to these factors of subtle dependent arising. For them, therefore, the *suffering that is to be known* is still unfinished.

Regarding the *origin of suffering that is to be abandoned*, they have abandoned both karma and the negative emotions. However, because they have not abandoned their conceptual obscurations, for them the origin of suffering that is to be abandoned is also still unfinished.

On the *spiritual path that is to be taken* they have realized that there is no truly existent personal self and have partially realized that neither is there any truly existent entity in phenomena, for the full belief in a truly existing phenomenal entity has been broached. However, they have still not realized the views of the three great systems, and so their path too is still unfinished.

As for the result, they may have obtained the level of Arhat, but they still need to be aroused from this "cessation" by rays of light emanating from the Buddhas[104] and then to accomplish the state of buddhahood. So their *cessation* is also still unfinished.

Beings of middling capacity have understood the six realms of samsara to be suffering and are motivated by the wish to attain liberation for themselves from all of them. The causes from which the sufferings of samsara originate are karma and the negative emotions, and the root of those negative emotions is the belief in a self. The antidote, therefore, is the wisdom that realizes no-self. Such wisdom, however, cannot be cultivated in the mind from the outset. So, motivated by the determination to be free as an intention, they take pratimoksha ordination and bind their minds with perfectly pure discipline. In addition, they meditate on the eight concentrations and formless absorptions. Finally, they must give rise to wisdom, and to this end they investigate where a personal self, the so-called I, might dwell, whether it is one with or distinct from the five aggregates; and by meditating on the fact that it is neither one with nor distinct from them, they see truly that there is no self. This is the stage of Stream Enterer and is analogous to the path of seeing. The stages of Once Returner and Nonreturner are analogous to the path of meditation.

Since the root of karma is the negative emotions, and the root of the negative emotions is belief in an "I," when beings of middling capacity gain the realization that there is no such thing, they bring to an end both the karma and the emotions generated by that belief in an "I," just as killing an old magician naturally puts a stop to the whole machinery of his magic. Consequently they attain the result, the Arhat's nirvana, with and without residue. This is analogous to the path of no more learning.

Beings of the greatest capacity turn their minds away not only from the whole of samsara, but also from nirvana, the peace that Shravakas and Pratyekabuddhas take to be ultimate. From then on there is no other suffering to be known, so for them the *suffering that is to be known* is completely finished.

Since the *origin of suffering that is to be abandoned* is karma and negative emotions, together with the conceptual obscurations and those due to habitual tendencies, from then on there is no origin of suffering to abandon, so for them the origin of suffering that is to be abandoned is also completely finished.

As for the truth of the path, they realize the natural state of all phenomena, the absolute truth whose nature is the absence of the two kinds of independent existence. For them, therefore, the *spiritual path to be followed* is completely finished.

As the result, they attain the dharmakaya, buddhahood, and from then on there is nothing else to be attained, so their *cessation* is completely finished.

Beings of the greatest capacity, then, having turned their minds away from both samsara and nirvana, are motivated by a vast determination to be free. They practice discipline[105] keeping the vows of both sutras and tantras—the long path of the Vehicle of Characteristics and the rest. Their contemplation consists of the eight concentrations and formless absorptions and the generation and perfection phases of the Mantrayana. On top of that, their wisdom is the realization of the views of the three great systems. From the Shravakayana up to and including Anuyoga, conceptual ideas are overcome using conceptual ideas. In Atiyoga, by maintaining the true nature of the view of primordial purity free from elaborations, and by this alone, practitioners purify, liberate, destroy, and cut through all good and bad thoughts in the expanse of that vast primordial wisdom; having destroyed all the obscurations without exception—those due to karma, those due to the negative emotions, conceptual obscurations, and those of habitual tendencies—they attain buddhahood, the dharmakaya. Thence, through the unceasing rupakaya—the sambhogakaya and nirmanakaya—they bring about the welfare of beings.

This is how the Four Noble Truths were actually explained by the Teacher, the fully enlightened Bhagavan, the peerless Shakya King, Lion of the Shakyas.

All this my teacher taught as a general introduction.

(B) WHAT IS TO BE PRACTICED

Now, for what is to be practiced there are three sections:

I. Negative actions to be abandoned
II. Positive actions to be adopted
III. The all-determining quality of actions

I. NEGATIVE ACTIONS TO BE ABANDONED

1. Explanation of the Negative Actions to Be Abandoned

There is no end or limit to negative actions, but in terms of how they are accumulated they can all be condensed into three that are physical acts, and so forth,* making ten in all.

What motivates these actions are the three poisons. As the *Jewel Garland of the Middle Way* says:

> Desire, aversion, and stupidity:
> Actions arising from these three are negative.

The three poisons are negative by their very nature, and actions motivated by them are called "negative by congruence."

What activates the emotions, according to the treatises, is the mental event of mentation;[106] while according to the pith instructions, it is the conceptual mind.

When the negative emotions arise, they necessarily arise in relation to an object. Thus, it will be desire that arises in relation to a pleasant object, aversion in relation to an unpleasant object, and bewilderment in relation to an object that is neither pleasant nor unpleasant.

2. Explanation of Their Effects

The four kinds of karmic effects are described in *The Words of My Perfect Teacher*.†

---

*See WMPT page 102.
†See WMPT page 112.

II. POSITIVE ACTIONS TO BE ADOPTED

There is no end or limit to the positive actions to be adopted, which are inconceivable; but in terms of how they are accumulated they can be condensed into three that are physical acts, and so forth.

As for what motivates them, it is said:

> Absence of desire, absence of aversion, absence of stupidity:
> Actions that arise from these are positive.

To decide to desist from doing the ten negative actions, and to think, "From now on, even at the cost of my life, I will do none of the ten negative actions," is the "discipline of avoiding the ten negative actions."[107]

Specifically, the ten positive actions consist of abstaining from taking life and protecting it instead, and so forth.

Their effects are the four kinds of karmic effects.*

While meditating on all these negative and positive actions, it is important to reflect on the relationships between cause and effect.

III. THE ALL-DETERMINING QUALITY OF ACTIONS

As the sutra says,

> The joys and sorrows of beings
> All come from their actions . . .

Those actions can be (1) exclusively positive; (2) exclusively negative; or (3) a mixture of positive and negative.

1. For exclusively positive actions, both the intention and the act itself are entirely good. Their result is rebirth in the celestial and human realms experiencing the greatest happiness and prosperity.

2. For exclusively negative actions, both the intention and the act itself are bad, and they therefore cause rebirth in the three lower realms experiencing the greatest suffering.

*See WMPT page 118.

3. Mixed actions include:

(a) actions involving a negative act done with a positive intention, which is permitted in the case of Bodhisattvas who carry out one of the seven negative acts of body and speech without any selfish concern—like Captain Compassionate Heart killing Black Spearman;*

(b) actions involving a positive act done with a negative intention, such as a virtuous deed carried out with the motivation of wanting to achieve something for this life; and

(c) actions involving mixed intention and execution, where the intention and act may sometimes be positive and sometimes negative, thus resulting in birth among the humans on the four continents or else in the scattered god realms.[108]

If an action has not been done, its effect will not be experienced. But once an action has been done, its effect will never go to waste. The result accrues only to the person who carried out the action, not to his or her relatives and possessions. Likewise, the effects of an action will not ripen on the earth, nor will they ripen on a rock—they can only ripen on the aggregates held by that particular stream of consciousness.

There are three ways in which such ripening may happen: (1) the effect of the action will be experienced in this life; (2) the effect of the action will definitely be experienced in the next life; and (3) the effect of the action will be experienced in other subsequent lives.

1. Actions whose effect will be experienced in this life may be positive or negative. The ripening of negative actions in this way is exemplified by the kingdom of Aparantaka being buried under earth,† and that of positive actions by the story of Vajra, daughter of King Prasenajit.[109]

2. Actions whose effect will definitely be experienced in the next life are those with immediate retribution.‡

3. Actions whose effect will be experienced in other subsequent lives are negative actions such as murder or killing a horse.

---

*See WMPT page 125.
†See WMPT page 128.
‡ See WMPT glossary, Five crimes with immediate retribution.

The effects of actions do not go away by just decaying, decomposing, or drying up. They go away by being used up as they are experienced. Alternatively, for negative actions, the antidote of a full confession with all the four powers* by beings who are not yet Bodhisattvas can render the karmic effect more tenuous, in the same way that the sun reduces the thickness of snow. And for Bodhisattvas in whose minds the bodhichitta has taken birth, their negative actions, even without being confessed, will become purified on their own, in the same way that the sun dispels darkness.

The effect of positive actions too can be lost, namely through the four causes that exhaust one's store of merit.

Now for the ground where the karmic effects of these actions are stored. The Madhyamikas hold that there is no such ground. They say an action ceases in emptiness at the time it is done. Then, when its effect is experienced, that experience arises from emptiness through dependent arising. For the Chittamatrins, the ground is the ground of all. In the Mantrayana tradition it is said that in the impure state the persistence of impure energy and mind as the six seeds of the six realms provides the ground from which the effects of actions can manifest.

As for who experiences the effects of actions, no distinction in this respect can be made between Buddhas above and beings below. Buddhas, Bodhisattvas, their disciples, the assembly of Vidyadharas, and the rest—all of them have to experience the results of their actions.

The gravity of an action is a function of three aspects of the intention motivating it—constancy, compulsiveness, and absence of an antidote (all three of which apply to positive and negative actions in a similar way)—and of whether it is directed at those with good qualities, those who have helped us, or those who are suffering. The greatest benefit or detriment results from one of the ten positive or negative actions committed in relation to the Three Jewels and, particularly in the Vajrayana tradition, from any positive or negative actions directed at the teacher, since he is the very embodiment of all Three Jewels. Help or harm directed at our parents and anyone else from whom we have received help results in major benefit or detriment. And all positive or negative actions directed at those who are sick or otherwise suffering also result in major benefit or detriment.

---

*See WMPT page 265.

The time sequence in which the effects of these actions will be experienced is as follows:

Whichever actions carry the greatest effect,
Whichever are closest, whichever most habitual,
And whichever were done first—
These will be the very first to ripen.

Which of our actions, then, whether positive or negative, will be the first whose result we shall experience? The answer is that the first to be experienced will be (1) whichever action carries the greatest effect, whether positive or negative. If there are equally weighty actions, the first of those to be experienced will be (2) whichever is most closely related to our state of mind at the time of death. If there are actions equally closely related to our state of mind at the time of death, the first of those to be experienced will be (3) the one to which we had formerly been most strongly habituated. If there are actions to which we had been equally habituated in the past, the one that will be the very first to ripen will be (4) whichever one we carried out first, chronologically. It is important to know this.

Now, any such action—the ten positive actions, for example—may furthermore be either (1) an action that brings about existence in samsara or (2) an action that leads to the peace of nirvana. To know which of these two it will be, examine your own mind. If it is with the motivation of trying to reach the higher realms that you practice the ten positive actions and the eight concentrations and formless absorptions, these actions that bring the attainment of higher existences are (1) actions that bring about existence in samsara. On the other hand, if it is with the aim of freeing yourself from the six realms of existence and attaining liberation that you practice the ten positive actions, these are (2a) actions that lead to the peace of nirvana for beings of middling capacity—though this is only the means aspect; it must be applied with wisdom.[110] And if it is with the great beings' aim of attaining omniscience that you practice the ten positive actions, these will be (2b) actions that lead to the peace of nirvana for beings of great capacity—and they must be put into practice using the three supreme methods.

All these actions and their effects are interdependent. Depending on whether the cause is positive or negative, happiness or suffering arises as the consequent effect—this is dependent arising.

Moreover, as Nagarjuna says:

Apart from what arises dependently
There are no other phenomena.

Seeds are sown in springtime as a cause, for without such a cause no barley would appear in autumn as a result. So it is in dependence on that cause, the barley sown in spring, that the consequent effect arises.

Without wrong views, hatred, and so on as a cause, there would be no suffering as their result. It is in dependence on those causes—wrong views, hatred, and so on—that their consequent effects arise.

Without practicing the ten positive actions and so forth as a cause, one could not attain the state of celestial or human existence as their result. It is through the practice of the ten positive actions as the cause that the effect, attainment of the higher realms as a god or human, comes about through dependent arising.

In the same way, it is the paths corresponding to the three kinds of enlightenment as the cause that make the effect, attainment of those three states of enlightenment, come about through dependent arising.

In all of these cases, if things existed in the way that notional beliefs in the true existence of things hold them to exist, such truly existing things could never take part in the process of dependent arising. As Nagarjuna says:

Therefore, apart from emptiness
There are no other phenomena.

If causes—barley grains, for instance—were things that truly existed, existed by their own very nature, or existed by their own characteristics, the process of growing an autumn crop from them would be impossible. But because the cause, the barley grain, does not truly exist or exist by its own very nature, it can therefore take part in the process of developing into its result. As Nagarjuna says:

Only by things being empty
Can things be possible at all.

As the barley grain, the cause, disappears, the shoot is produced as a result. The shoot in its turn gradually develops into the stem, and so on. Now, if not only the cause but also the result, that autumn crop, were something that truly existed, existed by its own very nature, or existed by its own characteristics, it would have to be self-constituted, a result that existed regardless of any cause—and in that case there could be no process of cause and effect, of something that produces and something produced, as both would be completely indestructible and imperishable.

Similarly, if wrong views, hatred, and the other negative actions were things that truly existed, existed by their own very nature, or existed by their own characteristics, the problem would be that from the very start, wrong views and so on would have to be self-constituted, would exist regardless of any object, would never be interrupted by any other thought, and would not be able to give rise to suffering as a result. But that is not the case. All those negative actions such as wrong views and so forth, though they appear, have no true nature. If they are examined with absolute logic, they are in their very essence unborn—hence, as it is said, "action is empty." From the creative power of emptiness that cannot be qualified as anything, they emerge through dependent arising, by nature unceasing—hence "emptiness is action." They appear as emptiness and dependent arising, indivisible and mutually inclusive, their appearance being free of the extreme of existence and their emptiness free of the extreme of nonexistence in that they appear but without any true nature, like the moon reflected in water—and hence "there is no action other than emptiness, and there is no emptiness other than action." These four approaches to emptiness should be investigated by means of logical reasoning.

If faith and other causes that comprise the path of the three kinds of enlightenment were things that truly existed, existed by their own very essence, or existed by their own characteristics, then they would exist regardless of any object, could not be interrupted by anything else, and could not take part in any process through which enlightenment developed as their result. And if their results, the three different states of enlightenment, truly existed and so forth, they could never be developed as the effect brought about by some cause.

Thus, in all these cases, the two extreme views are disposed of in the following way: freedom from the extreme view of eternalism lies in the fact that the causes do not continue to be present in their results, and that everything is unborn; and freedom from the extreme view of nihilism lies in the fact that there is an unceasing arising of results that depend on preceding causes. It is important to prove for oneself that all these causes and results are empty, that they are empty dependent arising, that they are indivisibly and mutually inclusively both emptiness and dependent arising.

Who is it who accumulates all those actions? The Buddha said in the sutras:

They arise from thoughts, not from the absence of thoughts.

And the *Essay on the Mind of Enlightenment* says:

Deceptive appearances[111] arise from negative emotions and actions,
And actions arise from the mind.
The mind is collected habitual tendencies,
And being free of habitual tendencies is bliss;
That blissful mind is nirvana.

The *Sutra of the Descent to Lanka* says:

The consciousness that seizes[112] is profound and subtle,
A flow of all the seeds like the current of a river.
There is a danger that it might be thought of as a truly existing self,
So this is something of which I have not spoken to the immature.

And the Great Omniscient One speaks of, "The compounding of samsara and nirvana" . . . and so on.[113]

All Four Truths therefore are to do with dependent arising. And where does dependent arising arise from? It arises from absolute truth. How does it arise? All the relative phenomena of never-failing cause and effect arise from the truth that is the primordially pure essence of the *dharmata*—which is their cause, not through causation defined in terms of a producer and something produced, but their cause nevertheless in that without it they would never arise, in the same way that clouds arise from the sky, waves from water, and sunlight from the sun. Once you understand that relative truth and absolute truth are inseparable in this way, you should use this wisdom to keep your view pure.

You should understand also that from the perspective of delusion[114] there are causes and effects to be abandoned and adopted, and it is important to choose what to do and what to avoid in accordance with cause and effect. As the Great Master of Oddiyana said, "Although my view is higher than the sky, my attention to actions and their effects is finer than flour."

Avoiding or undertaking actions according to cause and effect, therefore, you should use skillful means to keep your actions pure.

In this way, by uniting the two accumulations or uniting the two truths, you will attain the level at which the two kayas are united.

Beginners should not think that the fact that nothing exists in the absolute means that nothing exists at all. It is necessary to take up good actions and reject negative ones. The way to do this is by means of mindfulness, vigilance, and carefulness.

- Mindfulness is not to forget what to do and what not to do. It is like a doorkeeper.
- Vigilance is to make oneself examine one's actions, words, and thoughts. It is like an overseer.
- Carefulness is to exercise the utmost prudence in doing what is right and avoiding what is wrong. It is like a bride.[115]

Use these three as a shepherd to watch over your actions, words, and thoughts. In particular, use them to examine your mind, whose thoughts may be positive, negative, or neutral, and, when a negative thought occurs, to flatten it, like hitting a pig on the snout with a pestle or extinguishing moxa with the tip of one's nail.

The foregoing concludes the chapter on the cause and effect of actions.

Now that we have turned our minds away from samsara in its entirety, it is important to consider where we wish to go. We should therefore reflect on the benefits of liberation.

CHAPTER FIVE
The Benefits of Liberation

HAVING USED the four thoughts to turn our minds away from the whole of samsara, we now reflect on the benefits of liberation, as follows.

Hitherto, because of thinking that samsara is happiness, we have not seen it as suffering. But now, having reflected on the defects of samsara, we think of the benefits of liberation. We think of the peacefulness, coolness, excellence, and all the qualities arising from riddance and realization that characterize the three levels of enlightenment. If we were to choose among the three, it is omniscience that we should try to accomplish.

Having reflected on how hard it is to find the freedoms and advantages, we think of their benefits that are so difficult to come by. Likewise for the other reflections. Then, similarly, we think of all the qualities of taking refuge and of all the other stages up to the main practice.

How to attain liberation, that is, one of the three levels of enlightenment, is summarized in the stages of the paths for the three kinds of beings, so it is important to remember these.

(A) THE STAGES OF THE PATH FOR BEINGS OF LESSER CAPACITY

The need to practice this path is related to the need to obtain an appropriate body as the support for the path to the three kinds of enlightenment. For that:

- the vehicle is the vehicle of the worldly;
- the motivation is the motivation of striving to attain higher rebirth;

- the sources of good are actions consistent with ordinary merit or actions that bring about existence in samsara; and
- the view is the correct view of worldly people.[116]

The sources of good here are, in brief, any sources of good, vast or small, that are accomplished without the determination to be free from samsara as an intention, without the view of emptiness, and without bodhichitta—these are the sources of good for beings of lesser capacity. Practicing the correct view of worldly people brings as its result the states of gods and humans.

(B) THE STAGES OF THE PATH FOR BEINGS OF MIDDLING CAPACITY

- The vehicle is beyond the worldly and is part of the Buddha's teaching.
- The motivation is thinking only of one's own aims.
- The sources of good are actions consistent with the liberation of the Basic Vehicle.
- The Dharma of transmission consists of the Tripitaka.
- The Dharma of realization consists of the threefold training:
  —the training in discipline and so forth as taught in the Vinaya;
  —the training in concentration, on what is repulsive and so forth, as taught in the Sutras; and
  —the training in wisdom, as taught in the Abhidharma. When one examines where the personal self, the so-called I, is located, if one checks whether it is identical with or distinct from the five aggregates, the six elements, and so forth, one realizes the absence of any truly existing personal self and realizes the absence of any gross truly existing entity in phenomena. By getting used to this training in wisdom over a long period—three human lives, or a thousand years, and so forth—one will obtain the result of the Arhat with or without residue.

For Pratyekabuddhas, the view, apart from some slight differences, is like that of the Shravakas.

The sources of good consistent with the liberation of the Basic Vehicle are, in brief, any sources of good, vast or small, that one accomplishes with determination to be free from samsara as intention, and with a limited realization of emptiness, but without bodhichitta.

***

"To know what you did in the past, look at your present body," it is said. Because you accomplished immense sources of good in a previous life, you have obtained this present body. The saying continues: "Where you will take birth next depends on your present actions." In other words, it depends on you. What you need to accomplish is not the higher realms or the Shravakas' and Pratyekabuddhas' paths; rather, you need to set out on the path of beings of greater capacity and attain buddhahood. To accomplish that you have to set about practicing the path of beings of greater capacity. This is the Greater Vehicle taught by the Buddha and is what follows.

(C) THE STAGES OF THE PATH FOR BEINGS OF GREATER CAPACITY

- The motivation is the bodhichitta.
- The sources of good are whatever is consistent with the liberation of the Greater Vehicle. These are, for the long path, the two accumulations; for the short path, the two phases of generation and perfection; and for the swift path, the trekchö based on primordial purity and thögal based on spontaneous presence.
- The view is that of the three great systems. Habituation to the realization of this view culminates in the result, the attainment of buddhahood according to the sutra tradition, and of the union level of Vajradhara according to the mantra tradition.

The sources of good consistent with the liberation of the Greater Vehicle are, in brief, any sources of good, vast or small, that one accomplishes with the determination to be free from samsara as intention, with the wisdom that realizes the absence of any truly existing self in the individual and of any truly existing entity in phenomena, and with bodhichitta.

If you were to choose among the long, short, and swift paths, it is the swift path of the Radiant Great Perfection that you should practice.

With the long path of the Vehicle of Characteristics, it takes three measureless kalpas to reach the far shore of a vast ocean of completion, maturation, and training. As is explained in the *Prayer of Good Actions,* there are infinite sentient beings to mature, infinite buddhafields to train, and, with infinite Buddhas to please by making offerings without ever disappointing them, an infinitude of the two accumulations to complete: unless one manages to do so, one will never attain buddhahood.

In the short path of the Vajrayana, on the other hand, one is matured through empowerment. In the first place, in Kriya, Upa, and Yoga tantras, one is matured by the common empowerment of the five families. One subsequently exercises discipline by keeping the specific samayas perfectly purely; and by practicing the yogas with and without images, one can accomplish buddhahood in three, five, or seven human lifetimes. In Mahayoga and Anuyoga, after the ripening factor or entrance or ritual for the vows,[117] one keeps discipline through perfectly pure samaya, and, having practiced the generation phase related to skillful means and the perfection phase related to wisdom, one can accomplish the level of Vajradhara in a single human lifetime.

In the tradition of the Radiant Great Perfection, however, obtaining the empowerments—elaborate, unelaborate, and so forth—keeping discipline through complete purity of the samayas, and practicing the trekchö based on primordial purity and thögal based on spontaneous presence, one can accomplish the Body of the Great Transference in a matter of years and months.

Therefore, of the long, short, and swift paths, it is the swift path that you should put into practice.

CHAPTER SIX

How to Follow a Spiritual Friend

IF WE ARE LOOKING for a teacher who can show us this path, no ordinary being, no god, nor demon, nor even the ruler of living beings, Brahma, is capable of teaching us. Neither are those who love us—our parents, relatives, loving friends, and so forth—capable of doing so.

Who then can show us this path? A teacher or spiritual friend, and since the spiritual teacher is the one who can benefit us, we must follow a spiritual teacher and spiritual companions. Without relying on these two, we can never know how to accomplish the levels of liberation and omniscience. Nowhere in any sutra, tantra, or shastra is it said that liberation and omniscience can be attained through one's own ingenuity and prowess without following these two.

Check whether or not you could accomplish the path of liberation on your own without relying on a spiritual teacher and spiritual companions: you will see that on your own it is impossible. You have to follow a spiritual friend. But it is not just anyone you happen to meet who can help you. If you take as your lama someone who teaches wrong views and actions and follow him, he will be a demonic friend. And if you take him as a spiritual companion and follow him, he will be a demonic companion. So try to find a spiritual friend who has the proper qualifications. For this you must first examine the teacher.

I. EXAMINING THE TEACHER

Examine the teacher from a distance by what you hear said about him, from close up by what you can see for yourself, and by such means as divination and mirror gazing. Especially, examine him in terms of the Dharma. A

Shravaka or Pratyekabuddha spiritual friend or preceptor endowed with the 105 virtues is one who has the qualities of a learned and disciplined monk, having taken pratimoksha ordination and kept the vows for ten years without giving rise to any degeneration of the discipline, and so forth. A Bodhisattva spiritual teacher is one possessing the ten virtues such as being peaceful, disciplined, and perfectly peaceful.* A Vajrayana spiritual teacher or lama is one who possesses the qualities explained in the texts of each of the different sections of tantra. In particular, in both Mahayoga and Anuyoga the lama is one who possesses the eight qualities: "He is a teacher, holds the treasury of the teachings, has perfected the stream of transmission," and the rest.[118]

You should examine more particularly a lama who teaches the pith instructions and check that he has all the following qualities:

- his mind has been matured by receiving the four empowerments specific to the path of the Great Perfection which are an amplification of the fourth empowerment in the lower tantras: the elaborate empowerment, unelaborate empowerment, and so forth;[119]
- he has practiced discipline by keeping the samayas purely, namely (1) those with something to be kept—the samayas for practitioners whose realization develops gradually, which are the twenty-seven categories of the root samayas related to the teacher's body, speech, and mind and the twenty-five branch samayas—and (2) those with nothing to be kept—the samayas for practitioners of sudden realization, which are nonexistence, omnipresence, and so forth—of which two, nonexistence and omnipresence, relate to primordial purity, and two, unity and spontaneous presence, relate to spontaneous presence;
- he has seen the absolute nature in reality through the liberating instructions on trekchö based on primordial purity and thögal based on spontaneous presence;
- he has understanding, experience, or realization, whichever the case may be, of the four visions as milestones on the path;
- he cares for disciples regardless of whether they are good or bad;
- he possesses the blessings of the lineage and is unsullied by any samaya breach in the lineage's golden chain; and

---

*See guru yoga chapter, page 253.

- he possesses the blessings of the lineage orally transmitted from one person to another, like a vessel filled to the brim with the blessings of past holders of the lineage.

There is one single criterion you should particularly check when examining a teacher: it is whether he has bodhichitta. If he has the bodhichitta, whatever sort of connection one makes with him will be meaningful. A good connection will bring buddhahood in one lifetime, and even a negative connection will eventually bring samsaric existence to an end.

An additional criterion to check for is whether he is someone with understanding, experience, and realization of the view of the three great systems.

II. FOLLOWING THE TEACHER

You should follow the teacher by serving him through the "three ways of pleasing him." While you are engaged in so following him, concentrate more on listening to his teachings and reflecting on them, rather than on trying to practice.

III. EMULATING THE TEACHER'S REALIZATION AND ACTIONS

When you come to emulate the teacher's realization and actions, you should first of all acquire in your own being the essence of his wisdom mind. It would be hypocritical to emulate the teacher's actions without attaining his realization; you should therefore acquire his realization, and only then emulate his actions.

Part Two

The Extraordinary or Inner Preliminaries

The extraordinary or inner preliminaries correspond to the last of the four ways of attracting beings, acting in accordance with what is taught. There are six chapters.

Jigme Gyalwai Nyugu (1765–1843), Jigme Lingpa's disciple and root teacher of Patrul Rinpoche.

CHAPTER ONE

Taking Refuge, the Foundation Stone of All Paths

WHY "THE foundation stone of all paths" rather than "of the path"? Because taking refuge is a necessary preliminary for every one of the paths of both the Sutrayana and Mantrayana. It has been said:

> Vows can be taken in any school,
> But without refuge they are not vows.[120]

It is perfectly possible for non-Buddhists to take different vows, but as they do not begin by taking refuge, their virtuous vows are not perfectly pure.

If we consider the truth of the path, the wisdom that realizes no-self depends on the mind and so depends on meditative concentration. And concentration, as we find in the following quotation, depends on keeping perfect discipline.

> Penetrative insight joined with calm abiding
> Utterly eradicates afflicted states.
> Knowing this, first search for calm abiding,
> Found by those who joyfully renounce the world.[121]

If, then, we are to take up discipline, there is no way we can take vows without first taking refuge.

The definition of "taking refuge" is as follows: it is a commitment, a resolution made to seek the protection of a special "object" through fear of one's own and others' suffering in samsara, in much the same way that a small child being chased by a dog runs to a grown-up for protection.

More specifically, in the Mahayana tradition we take refuge through fear of the two extremes, samsara and nirvana.

To begin with, just as taking refuge opens the gateway to all paths, it is faith that opens the gateway to taking refuge. Faith itself is of four kinds. The first is *vivid faith*: for this we do not have to be conscious of a particular reason for our faith; it can arise simply from seeing an object such as a Buddha image or statue, a volume of the scriptures, or even someone wearing the saffron-colored squares of cloth that make up the robes of a Buddhist monk or nun.

Eager faith is our eagerness, having recognized the defects of samsara and reflected on the benefits of liberation, to attain liberation.

Confident faith is confidence in the karmic law of cause and effect. This sort of faith does need to be reasoned: it is the faith that arises from knowing who the Buddha is, what the Dharma is, and what the Sangha is, and we therefore have to recognize the qualities of the Three Jewels:

Unsurpassable Teacher, precious Buddha,
Unsurpassable protection, precious and sacred Dharma,
Unsurpassable guide, precious Sangha . . .

Once we realize that the Three Jewels, and especially the teacher, will never fail us, confident faith arises in us.

A person who considers the refuge in this way is known as a triple-refuge-holder *upasaka*,[122] and it is to this that the above quotation from the *Seventy Stanzas on Refuge* refers when stating, "Vows can be taken in any school." If we do not first take refuge, there are no vows we can keep. Without vows, we cannot observe discipline, and if we do not observe discipline, there will be no way that we can accomplish all the teachings on the path. For this reason, of the four kinds of faith, confident faith, or *irreversible faith*, is considered fundamental. If for our part we have faith, then it does not matter whether the object we use to represent the refuge is something good or bad, as we can see from the example of the old lady who attained buddhahood by prostrating to a dog's tooth.*

---

*See WMPT pages 173–74.

I. APPROACHES TO TAKING REFUGE

There are three different approaches to taking refuge related to the three kinds of beings.

Beings of lesser capacity are distinguished by three things:

- by their motivation—they take refuge in order that they themselves may be freed from the three lower realms and obtain rebirth in the realms of the gods and humans;
- by the duration for which they take refuge—which is very short, ultimately until they obtain rebirth as a human or god and in the meantime for as long as they live; and
- by the object to which they go for refuge—which may simply be a statue of the Jewel of the Buddha, a stacked collection of volumes of the sacred Dharma, and the Sangha of ordinary beings who keep monastic vows (and not necessarily the Sangha of supreme beings). Their understanding of what refuge is may be quite simple.

These lesser beings are Buddhist lesser beings, who have taken refuge in the Three Jewels. They should be distinguished from non-Buddhist lesser beings who have not.

Beings of middling capacity include both Shravakas and Pratyekabuddhas, and they necessarily do have some understanding of what refuge is. Their particular motivation is the wish to obtain freedom for themselves alone from the six realms of existence, which they recognize as being nothing but suffering.

The duration for which they take refuge is ultimately until they attain the level of Arhat, and in the meanwhile for as long as they live.

As for the object to which they go for refuge, they consider the Buddha as no more than a Shravaka or Pratyekabuddha Arhat, not as someone who had already perfected the qualities arising from riddance and realization and gone beyond suffering to the state beyond the two extremes. For them the fact that he is superior to Shravakas and Pratyekabuddhas, being possessed of the wisdom of omniscience and adorned with the major and minor marks, is due to the merit he accumulated during three measureless kalpas and to his high birth, potentially as a universal monarch.

They do not take refuge in his physical person, which they consider to be an aggregate produced by the ripening of karma, an impure residue of the truth of suffering, formed from the semen of his father Shuddhodana and the ovum of his mother Mayadevi. They take refuge, rather, in the Buddha's mind of perfect cessation.

As for the Dharma, beings of middling capacity repudiate what we call the Great Vehicle, as they consider that it was not taught by the Buddha himself. For them the Dharma is the Tripitaka and the three trainings of the Basic Vehicle. Of the two aspects of this Dharma, the Dharma of transmission and the Dharma of realization, the object to which they go for refuge is the Dharma of realization. This also has two aspects, the truth of the path and the truth of cessation, and it is the truth of cessation to which beings of middling capacity go for refuge.

In terms of the Sangha, they take refuge not in the Sangha of ordinary beings but in the supreme Sangha made up of Stream Enterers, Once Returners, and Nonreturners. As the physical bodies of these Sangha members are considered to be fully ripened aggregates, residues of the truth of suffering and therefore impure, beings of middling capacity have to take refuge in the Sangha's perfect mind of cessation. They assert that the Buddha is an Arhat, and they therefore consider the Jewel of the Buddha to be their teacher. Regarding the manner in which they take refuge, as will be explained below, they take refuge in the Buddha as the teacher, the Dharma as the path, and the Sangha as the companions on the path.

Beings of great capacity have the particular motivation to attain buddhahood not for their own sake but for the sake of others. This intention is the supreme preparation, arousing bodhichitta.[123]

The duration for which they take refuge is from now until they attain the heart of enlightenment. One might wonder why it is no longer necessary to take refuge once one has attained enlightenment. When one attains enlightenment, one is strong and powerful, being endowed with the ten strengths and the ten powers, and one thus has no personal fears at all and moreover is able to protect others. For this reason, one no longer needs to take refuge.

Regarding the particular object to which great beings go for refuge, the ordinary or outer object of refuge is the Three Jewels: the Buddha, who is endowed with the four kayas and the five wisdoms; the Dharma, which is the Dharma of transmission and the Dharma of realization of the Great Vehicle; and the Sublime Sangha, which comprises the Bodhisattvas from the first level up to the final stage of the tenth level.

The extraordinary or inner object to which they go for refuge comprises the lama, who is the root of blessings; the yidam, who is the root of accomplishment; and the dakini, who is the root of activity.

The refuge according to the special, sublime method of the Vajra Essence comprises the fixed channels, the moving energies, and the structured bodhichitta.

The ultimate, infallible refuge is the indestructible natural state.

❧ Explanation of the Refuge Prayer

What is meant by "the Sugata . . . , the true Three Jewels,"[124] is that the Dharma and the Sangha are a temporary refuge, while the only ultimate refuge is the Buddha alone, for he embodies all the Three Jewels. As Maitreya said:

> Because it has to be discarded, because it is inconstant by nature,
> Because they do not have, because they are afraid,
> The Dharma in its two aspects and the Sangha
> Are not the ultimate refuge.

It is the meaning of the Dharma of transmission that has to be realized. Once the meaning has been realized, the words themselves are of little use and, like a boat that does not need to be carried once one has crossed the river, can be abandoned. The Dharma of realization is impermanent, for, as one progresses on the path, one can no longer rely on the earlier stages and dispenses with them. "Because they do not have" refers to the fact that the sublime Shravakas and Pratyekabuddhas do not possess the qualities of the sublime Bodhisattvas, and the sublime Bodhisattvas do not have those of the Buddha. Bodhisattvas who are ordinary beings still fear the lower realms. For all these four reasons, the Dharma and the Sangha are not the ultimate refuge.

On the other hand, the Buddha, who is the ultimate refuge, is the essence of the Three Jewels, as we can read:

> Because the Capable One is the corpus or embodiment of the teachings
> And is the ultimate nature of the Assembly.

The Capable One is the Teacher, the rare and supreme Buddha; the Dharma is both the corpus of the teaching that is realized and the corpus of the Dharma that is taught; that which has never separated and will never separate from the qualities contained in the Buddha's enlightened mind is the Sangha: in truth, the ultimate refuge is the Buddha alone.

The Three Roots and the channels, energies, and essences* will be explained later, but here it should be mentioned that the "essential nature, natural expression, and compassion"† constitute the refuge for the Great Perfection, and that the channels, essences, and energies are the support for the nature, the radiant primal wisdom that is the bodhichitta.

This can all be condensed into a single term, what the Sutrayana calls *sugatagarbha* and what the Mantrayana calls the single essence, the spontaneously arisen primal wisdom. If this is divided into two aspects, we speak of the wisdom of the primordially pure great emptiness and the wisdom of spontaneously accomplished phenomenal appearance. If we divide it into three aspects, we have the wisdom of the void essential nature, the wisdom of the radiant natural expression, and the wisdom of all-pervading compassion. This latter has two aspects, the outwardly radiating compassion and the inner luminous compassion, and of these the inner luminous compassion is appearance and emptiness inseparable, and this is the "great inseparability" of the three aspects: essential nature, natural expression, and compassion.

Regarding the particular duration for which we take refuge, according to the Causal Vehicle of Characteristics it is until we reach the outer "heart of enlightenment," when we sit under the Bodhi tree, or until we reach the inner "heart of enlightenment," when we realize sugatagarbha. According to the Mantrayana we take refuge until awareness is awakened in the wheel of the celestial gods.[125]

This refuge with its three particularities can again be divided into two: causal refuge and resultant refuge.

The causal refuge itself has two aspects: taking the refuge vow in name, and the genuine refuge of practicing the path. The first involves having some knowledge of the teacher, the path, and the companions on the path and reciting the refuge prayer one hundred thousand times or more, taking

---

*See line 2 of the refuge prayer, WMPT page 180.
†See line 3 of the refuge prayer, WMPT page 180.

refuge with the particular motivation, duration, and object in mind. Practicing the path entails actually adopting the Buddha as our teacher, the Dharma as the path, and the Sangha as the companions who are practicing the path, and making the refuge a living experience in accordance with the vow we have taken.

The resultant refuge, according to the Sutrayana, is the bodhichitta of intention or one's particular motivation at the time one takes refuge. According to the Mantrayana, the resultant refuge refers to the spontaneously arisen primal wisdom, the great inseparability of the essential nature, natural expression, and compassion. This is the natural state, and when we realize this natural state, we are protected in keeping with the definition of mantra—"that which protects the mind easily and swiftly":[126] all conceptual thoughts naturally disintegrate by themselves, free themselves, and cease, dissolve, and are purified by themselves in the space beyond concepts and characteristics. It is in this sense that it is the resultant refuge.

Again, the Vehicle of Characteristics calls the resultant refuge the promise one makes when one considers the qualities of the Three Jewels in the realization obtained by another person and wishes to attain them oneself. The Mantrayana makes the result the path: by making the two kayas the path, using the generation phase (the skillful means aspect) to make the rupakaya the path, and the perfection phase (the wisdom aspect) to make the dharmakaya the path, it makes the practices related to the three kayas[127] (that is, the result) the path. This is what is meant by the resultant refuge.

II. HOW TO TAKE REFUGE

Of the different ways these three kinds of being take refuge, here we are concerned with how great beings take refuge.

Their particular motivation is the selfless intention that all other sentient beings attain buddhahood, the quintessence of all the Three Jewels.

The particular duration for which they take refuge is from this very day until they attain total enlightenment.

The particular object to which they go for refuge is the Buddha and sublime beings who have full realization, and the Dharma contained in their minds.

Where *The Words of My Perfect Teacher* speaks of the "special, sublime method of the Vajra Essence,"* it is referring to the fact that though the gross causal channels, energies, and essences are complete in us and intrinsically pure, they are not fully manifest, and therefore in the Mantrayana tradition the object to which we go for refuge is the wisdom deity. Meditating on ourselves, with our gross causal channels, energies, and essences, as the samaya deity, and on the subtle wisdom channels, energies, and essences as the wisdom deity, we rely on these as the refuge object and accomplish pure, fully manifest buddhahood.

These channels are most commonly distinguished as the three main channels and the five wheels. The three main channels are *uma* (central), *roma* on the right, and *kyangma* on the left.[128] The five wheels are the wheel of great bliss in the head, the wheel of enjoyment in the throat, the wheel of Dharma in the heart, the wheel of manifestation in the navel, and the bliss-preserving wheel in the secret center.

One also refers to seven wheels: the above five wheels to which are added the wheel of blazing fire and the wheel of blaze-causing wind.

The Great Perfection tradition speaks of the wheel of the perfect array in the head with 360 radial channels, the taste collector in the throat with 16 radial channels, the wheel where all memories are structured in the heart with 8 radial channels, and the developing wheel in the navel which has 60 radial channels. These radial channels point alternately upward or downward like the bell of a *gyaling*.[129]

So what is known as the vajra body consists of the fixed channels and within them the circulating energies. These energies are essentially the subtle energies of the five elements, but one also refers to five principal energies and five branch energies. The five principal energies are the life-supporting energy, the upward-moving energy, the downward-moving energy, the fire-equalizing energy, and the pervading energy. The branch energies are the energies that circulate through the five physical sense organs.

Let us examine the energy circulation in detail. In a young, healthy person, in any twenty-four hour period there are 21,600 breaths in and out. Internally there are 120,600 moving energies that flow within the branches of the subtle channels.[130]

As for the essences that are carried by these energies, the structured bodhichitta comprises two essences, the white and red essences, and as they are

---

*See WMPT page 177.

carried by the energies they spread through all the channels, in the same way as oil pervades sesame seeds.

The refuge that is the "indestructible natural state" is this bodhichitta that is supported by this body comprising the channels, energies, and essences. How this is expressed as a single term, or divided into two or three aspects, has been explained above.

If we relate these channels, energies, and essences to their pure aspects, the channels in their pure aspect are the Jewel of the Sangha and the nirmanakaya; the energies in their pure aspect are the Jewel of the Dharma and the sambhogakaya; and the essences in their pure aspect are the Jewel of the Buddha and the dharmakaya. The void essential nature is the Buddha, the radiant natural expression is the Dharma, and all-pervading compassion, the primal wisdom that is the union of appearance and emptiness, is the unchangeable Sangha.[131]

All these—the Three Roots; the channels, energies, and essences; and the essential nature, natural expression, and compassion—that have been explained above, are included in the Three Jewels and never fall outside the scope of the Three Jewels. Let us therefore look at the Three Jewels in detail.

The Three Jewels can each be discussed under three headings: essence, divisions, and qualities.

(A) THE BUDDHA
(1) Essence

The essence of the Buddha is that he has reached the culmination of riddance and realization. One might wonder what this culmination is that he has reached.

Shravakas and Pratyekabuddhas have realized the no-self of the individual and destroyed gross belief in the self of phenomena, and they have thus got rid of karma and negative emotions, but they have not got rid of the conceptual obscurations or the obscurations of habitual tendencies.

Bodhisattvas on the first level have realized the truth of the absolute nature on the path of seeing and have at the same time got rid of the obscuration of imputative cognition. They meditate for five hundred great kalpas; in their postmeditation periods they rid themselves of the negative emotion of miserliness and they perfect transcendent generosity.

Subsequently, starting from the second level, they progress in stages from one level to the next, getting rid of the obscurations and achieving the realization particular to each level. As they progress and grow in realization, they get rid of emotional obscurations directly and, from the first level onward, indirectly weaken and reduce the conceptual obscurations, so that by the time they reach the seventh level, they have got rid of all remaining emotional obscurations completely.

Beginning on the three pure levels, they get rid of all the gross and subtle conceptual obscurations, and on the final stage of the tenth level, with the vajralike wisdom that is the antidote to the subtle habitual tendencies, they completely destroy the latter and realize all the different wisdoms. There is nothing more to be rid of, and no further realization to be gained, and so they have reached the culmination of riddance and realization. It is this that defines a Buddha.

(2) Divisions

There are three divisions: (1) the kayas that are the support; (2) the wisdoms they support; and (3) the activities that are performed.

(a) THE KAYAS

There are four kinds of kaya.

The *svabhavikakaya* of the Buddha is considered differently by the New Traditions and the Ancient Tradition. The New Traditions consider that it is the emptiness devoid of the five *skandha*s. They claim that such emptiness is mere nothingness and there cannot therefore be such a thing as the Buddha's wisdom of omniscience.[132] The Ancient Tradition considers that the svabhavikakaya is the union of space and wisdom, emptiness endowed with the essence of wisdom.

The dharmakaya is the wisdom of the radiant natural expression. The original meaning of the word *kaya* is "gathered together," so the dharmakaya is said to be that in which the twenty-one sets of immaculate dharmas are gathered together.

These two kayas represent the mind aspect of the Buddha, the wisdom of omniscience, and are therefore posited from the Buddha's own point of view. The sambhogakaya and nirmanakaya are posited from the point of view of others, that is, of the beings destined to be benefited, and these are of two kinds, pure and impure.

(i) Pure Beings

The sambhogakaya appears to pure beings through the power of the Buddha's natural compassion and prayers and the merit of those beings to be benefited, namely Bodhisattvas on the tenth level. It is endowed with five certainties.[133]

The certain place is the unexcelled buddhafield of the Dense Array.

The certain teacher comprises the Buddhas of the five families, the five Hemasagara Buddhas. Each of these is surrounded by an entourage of five subfamilies:[134] wherever there is space, it is pervaded by the dharmakaya, and whatever is pervaded by the dharmakaya is pervaded by the sambhogakaya for the purpose of benefiting the pure beings.

The certain teaching is that of the Great Vehicle, which cannot be expressed with sounds or words. *The certain assembly* consists of Bodhisattvas on the tenth level. *The certain time* is the ever-revolving wheel of eternity. Here it is not that time is permanent by nature but that the passing of time never ceases.[135]

(ii) Impure Beings

The Buddhas appear to impure beings in their supreme nirmanakaya form through the power of the sambhogakaya Buddhas' prayers and the merit of the beings they are to benefit.

There are four kinds of nirmanakaya: supreme nirmanakaya manifestations, nirmanakayas who manifest through birth, nirmanakayas who manifest in art, and diversified nirmanakaya manifestations.

(a) SUPREME NIRMANAKAYA MANIFESTATIONS

It is said that no one except those who are in the Dharma stream of the greater path of accumulating or on the four distinctly experienced stages of the path of joining can meet a supreme nirmanakaya manifestation. But one tradition states that when the Buddha came to this world even frogs and bats[136] were able to meet him. In any case, he who perfectly demonstrates the twelve deeds of a Buddha is a supreme nirmanakaya manifestation.

(b) NIRMANAKAYAS WHO MANIFEST THROUGH BIRTH

The Six Munis in the six realms and spiritual masters who guide beings on the path of virtue are nirmanakayas who manifest through birth. According to the *Nirvana Sutra,* in which we read:

Ananda, do not be sad,
Ananda, do not lament.
When five hundred years have passed,
I will return as spiritual friends
To act for your and others' sake

supreme spiritual masters are nirmanakayas who manifest through birth.

(c) NIRMANAKAYAS WHO MANIFEST IN ART

One tradition describes these as manifestations such as the King of Artists Vishvakarma.[137] Another says that they are artisans like masons and smiths, and also cast or sculpted statues and drawings and other merit-increasing items that can be purchased.[138]

(d) DIVERSIFIED NIRMANAKAYA MANIFESTATIONS

These may be anything that can bring benefit and happiness to beings, from boats, ships, bridges, and resting places to coolness when we are boiling hot and warmth when we are freezing cold.

(b) THE WISDOMS

Just as in one's ordinary mind there arise many different perceptions and thoughts, for the Buddha's wisdom too there are five aspects, the wisdom of the absolute space and so on.

The wisdom of the absolute space is the realization of the absolute truth, the natural state of all things.

Mirrorlike wisdom. In the same way that the clear surface of a mirror reflects everything, the surface of the wisdom of the absolute nature reflects all the phenomena of samsara and nirvana: this unobstructed, perfectly clear reflection is *mirrorlike wisdom.*

The wisdom of equality. Just as all the reflections in a mirror are the same in being simply reflections, without any concept of good or bad, *the wisdom of equality* is to regard samsara and nirvana as equal, as having a single mode and one taste.

Discriminating wisdom is the knowledge that while from the point of view of the absolute nature all phenomena are the same in being equal, from the point of view of the phenomena themselves all things in samsara and nirvana are distinct and not confounded.

All-accomplishing wisdom. Like a doctor who diagnoses a disease by taking the patient's pulse and then does all he can to treat and remedy the disease, the Buddhas, with their *all-accomplishing wisdom*, consider beings and the ways by which they might benefit them, and then appear spontaneously and effortlessly, without change or exertion, to benefit those beings.

These five wisdoms may be condensed into two: the *wisdom that knows the nature of all phenomena*, which comprises the wisdom of the absolute space, mirrorlike wisdom, and the wisdom of equality; and the *wisdom that knows the multiplicity of phenomena*, which comprises discriminating and all-accomplishing wisdom. They can all be condensed into a single wisdom, the *wisdom of omniscience*.

(c) THE ACTIVITIES THAT ARE PERFORMED

The Buddha establishes beings of the lower realms in the higher realms, he establishes beings in the higher realms on the paths of the three kinds of enlightenment, and finally he establishes the three kinds of beings on the level of buddhahood.

At first the Buddha can only establish these three kinds of beings—Shravakas, Pratyekabuddhas, and Bodhisattvas—on their own level of liberation and not on the level of buddhahood, and so he shows them the path that accords with their respective aspirations, and then he proceeds to establish them in ultimate buddhahood.

The activities the Buddha performs are superior to those of the Shravakas, Pratyekabuddhas, and Bodhisattvas in three respects: they are constant, they are all-pervasive, and they are spontaneous. With regard to the constant nature of his activities, it is not that he acted for the sake of beings in the past and does not do so now. In their all-pervasiveness, his activities pervade the whole of the ten directions and the three times: it is not that he performs his activities in the east and not in the south. And regarding their spontaneity, they are spontaneous in that they involve no deliberate effort.

(3) Qualities

The Buddha's qualities are divided into two, those of the dharmakaya and those of the rupakaya.

The qualities of the dharmakaya are the twenty-one sets of immaculate dharmas, such as the ten strengths, the four fearlessnesses, the eighteen distinctive qualities, and so on.

The qualities of the Buddha's rupakaya are the qualities of his body, the thirty major and eighty minor marks; those of his speech, the sixty branches of Brahma's melodious voice; and those of his mind: knowledge, love, and power.

The qualities of *knowledge* are: the wisdom that knows the nature of all phenomena, that clearly sees the absolute nature of everything in samsara and nirvana; and the wisdom that knows the multiplicity of all phenomena, that clearly sees all relative phenomena, without confounding them, like fresh kyurura seeds in the palm of the hand.

The Buddha's *love* is the compassion with which he looks night and day, throughout the six periods, to see who is flourishing and who is languishing, watching over all sentient beings impartially like a mother watching over her only child.

Of the Buddha's *power* to protect beings, it is said in the sutras:

Were it somehow possible that in the ocean, abode of serpents,
The ebb and flow of the tides fail to be on time,
Even then, for his children, the beings he must benefit,
The Buddha could never fail to act when the time was right.

Although the time may be right for Shravakas, Pratyekabuddhas, or Bodhisattvas to benefit beings, it may happen that, because of laziness or forgetfulness or for some other reason, they neglect the opportunity and fail to benefit them. But, even as he lay for the last time before passing into nirvana, the Tathagata still brought his human disciple Rabga the Wanderer and his nonhuman disciple Rabga the Gandharva to realization of the truth.

Long ago, five hundred merchants set out to sea in search of jewels. A sudden gust of wind drove their ship into the gaping mouth of a sea monster. The merchants all prayed to the mountain gods, forest gods, tree spirits, and so forth, but the captain, who was a Bodhisattva, said to them, "We must all take refuge in the Tathagata." So they all cried out, "We take refuge in the Buddha!" When it heard the name of the Tathagata, the monster was stricken with fear and sank back into the ocean. Thereafter it kept its mouth closed and as a result died of hunger, but because it had heard the name of the Buddha it was reborn as a god in the Heaven of the Thirty-three and subsequently attained realization of the truth. Such is the Buddha's activity that merely hearing the Tathagata's name protects one from the fears of samsara and the lower realms.

(B) THE DHARMA
(1) Essence

The essence of the sublime Dharma is to be rid of the obscurations of negative emotions, conceptual obscurations, and obscurations of habitual tendencies, or it is the means for getting rid of them. "To be rid of" refers to the perfect cessation which is the Shravakas', Pratyekabuddhas', and Bodhisattvas' state of being rid of negative emotions; and "getting rid of" refers to the truth of the path.

(2) Divisions

The Dharma is divided into the Dharma of transmission and the Dharma of realization.

(a) THE DHARMA OF TRANSMISSION

The Dharma of transmission can be divided into the eighty-four thousand elements of the Dharma. These can be condensed into the twelve branches of excellent speech, which can be further condensed into the Three Pitakas of the Doctrine.

The Causal Vehicle of Characteristics considers the Dharma of transmission to be only that which is in the minds of the members of the Sangha; the physical letters and books are merely the medium used for transmitting the Dharma.

The Secret Mantrayana considers three aspects: the Dharma that is written down in symbols, the Dharma that appears as symbols, and the Dharma that is voiced in symbols.

The Dharma written down in symbols is the Buddha's Excellent Words taking the form of books.

The Dharma that appears as symbols is the Dharma of transmission that appears in the minds of the Sangha.

The Dharma voiced in symbols is the words of the teachings articulated in speech.

In fact, when we talk of the two aspects of the Buddha's precious Dharma of transmission and realization, the Dharma of transmission is a firm understanding of the instructions on, for example, not taking life, while the Dharma of realization is the practical accomplishment of what those instructions mean.

(b) The Dharma of Realization

The Dharma of realization comprises the path of the precious superior threefold training.

In the Basic Vehicle it is the threefold training, which is the subject of the Shravakas' and Pratyekabuddhas' Tripitaka, their Dharma of transmission.

In the Mahayana it is the training in discipline, which includes the twenty root downfalls and so forth, as dealt with in the Mahayana Vinaya; the training in concentration, which includes love, concentration, and so on, as explained in the Mahayana Sutra Pitaka; and the training in wisdom, the Great Middle Way, explained in the Mahayana Abhidharma Pitaka, which includes the Extensive, Medium, and Abridged Prajnaparamita Sutras.

In the Mantrayana, all the rituals for empowerments and vows belong to the Vinaya, and their subject is the training in discipline, with the different levels of samaya. The four or six classes of tantra can be assigned to the Sutra Pitaka, and their subject is the training in concentration related to the common generation and perfection phases. The tantras of the Great Perfection belong to the Abhidharma, and their subject is the ultimate training in wisdom, the trekchö based on primordial purity and thögal based on spontaneous presence.

In short, everything that is words or explanation is the Dharma of transmission, and everything that is the meaning or subject is the Dharma of realization.

(3) Qualities

What is meant by "The qualities of the Dharma are inconceivable"[139] is that the holy Dharma dispels all the troubles and gives rise to all that is perfect and whole in samsara and nirvana.

(C) THE SANGHA
(1) Essence

The essence of the Sangha is that it possesses the two qualities of knowledge and liberation. Here "seeing," "knowledge," and "realization" are all different names for the same thing.

Members of the Sangha are thus those who, as Shravakas and Pratyekabuddhas, in attaining the four results one by one, see the nature of the four truths and are freed from the respective obscurations that have to be eliminated; and those who, as Bodhisattvas, see or realize the truth of the absolute nature on the path of seeing and are freed from their respective obscurations, and who subsequently, until the final stage of the tenth level, are freed from their respective emotional and conceptual obscurations and those of habitual tendencies.

(2) Divisions

The Sangha can be divided into two: the Basic Vehicle Sangha of Shravakas and Pratyekabuddhas, and the Mahayana Sangha of sublime beings.

A further classification speaks of first the common Sangha of Shravakas, Pratyekabuddhas, and Bodhisattvas, and second the extraordinary Sangha or Inner Sangha of Vidyadharas.

(a) THE COMMON SANGHA
(i) The Shravaka Sangha

The Shravaka Sangha consists of the Sangha of ordinary individuals and the Sangha of sublime beings.

(a) ORDINARY BEINGS

These are essentially those who, motivated by the determination to be free as intention, take the vows of the eight forms of pratimoksha ordination;[140] they observe pure discipline, train in meditative concentration, and give rise to wisdom, following the paths of accumulating and joining until they see the truth.[141]

(b) SUBLIME BEINGS

Stream Enterers have attained realization of the sixteen subdivisions (impermanence and so on) of the Four Noble Truths, and they then continue on the path.

Once Returners have not got rid of all the nine levels of emotional obscuration related to the world of desire on the path of meditation and have to take birth once more in the world of desire.

Nonreturners have completely eliminated all the emotional obscurations related to the world of desire and need never again take birth in the world of desire.

Arhats have conquered all the enemies, that is, the negative emotions related to the three worlds. Arhats are of two kinds, those with residues and those without.

(ii) The Pratyekabuddha Sangha

While they are training on the path, Pratyekabuddhas, like Shravakas, begin by accumulating merit for one hundred great kalpas. Then, in their final rebirth, as a result of the four prayers of aspiration they have made—namely that they will (1) be born in a world to which no Buddha has come and (2) attain enlightenment by themselves, without a teacher, and that (3) they will not teach the Dharma verbally but (4) inspire beings to gain merit through the miracles they display with their bodies—they are born in a world devoid of Buddhas or Shravakas, they bear a few of the major and minor marks, and they find no joy in the householder's life. Attracted as they are to lonely places, they go to charnel grounds where on account of the knowledge they have acquired from former lives they recognize the clothes they find there as the three Dharma robes, so they cut them, stitch them, and put them on.

When they look at the bones in the charnel grounds, they ask themselves, "How did these bones arise?" and understand that they arose through birth. "And what is the origin of birth? Becoming." And so on. Thus they work back through the twelve links of interdependent arising, taking them in reverse order, and understand that they originate from ignorance. Then they see that from ignorance come conditioning factors, and from conditioning factors comes consciousness, and so on, working through the twelve links of interdependent arising in the order of their arising up to old age and death. Next they ask, "What causes old age and death to cease?" and they see that stopping birth stops old age and death, and so on, working through the sequence of cessation in reverse order. Then they see that when ignorance ceases, conditioning factors cease, and so on, working through the twelve links of interdependent arising in the order of their arising up to the cessation of old age and death. By carefully investigating all this, they see the true nature of interdependence in the order of its arising and in the reverse order and subsequently, like the Shravaka Stream Enterers and so on, they attain the fourth concentration.

Some Pratyekabuddhas have sharp intellects and do not need to rely on companions but remain alone like rhinoceroses. Others with dull intellects need the company of friends and stay together in large groups, like parrots who fly around in flocks. Pratyekabuddha Arhats are of two kinds, those with residues and those without.

(iii) The Bodhisattva Sangha

The Sangha of Bodhisattvas also comprises the Sangha of ordinary individuals and the Sangha of sublime beings.

(A) Ordinary Beings

Ordinary Sangha members are those who, wishing that all beings may attain buddhahood, arouse the extraordinary bodhichitta and take the Bodhisattva vow according to either of the two traditions.[142] Subsequently they practice perfect discipline in keeping the vows of their respective traditions and train in the methods of completion, maturation, and training, which are included in the six transcendent perfections. These ordinary Bodhisattvas practice on the level of earnest aspiration that corresponds to the paths of accumulating and joining.

(B) Sublime Beings

The Sangha of sublime beings consists of Bodhisattvas on the path of seeing and higher paths who have seen the truth of the absolute nature directly on the path of seeing. Starting from the first level, they realize the lack of true existence of the two types of self; they get rid of the obscurations related to artificial imputation, which are the obscurations to be eliminated on the path of seeing; and they obtain twelve hundred qualities. These include the power to have a vision of one hundred Buddhas, to bring one hundred beings to spiritual maturity, visit one hundred buddhafields, illuminate one hundred worlds, miraculously shake one hundred worlds, attain one hundred kinds of concentration, and manifest one hundred likenesses of themselves, each of which manifests a retinue of one hundred attendants.[143]

Then from the second level up, they continue, and accustom themselves to, the meditation they experienced on the path of seeing. As a result they gradually get rid of the obscurations related to innate thought patterns, which are the obscurations to be eliminated on the path of meditation. The qualities they obtain number from twelve hundred thousand[144] up to inexpressible numbers as great as the number of atoms in the universe, at which point they can mature infinite sentient beings, purify infinite worlds, and, by pleasing infinite numbers of Buddhas and never displeasing them, complete the two accumulations on an infinite scale. In short, they gladden the hearts of beings and never upset them; they delight the hearts of the Buddhas and never displease them; and they accumulate merit and wisdom on an infinite scale and attain infinite kinds of concentration. It is beings invested with inconceivable qualities like these that make up the Sangha of sublime Bodhisattvas.

(b) THE EXTRAORDINARY INNER SANGHA OF VIDYADHARAS
(i) Kriyatantra

Kriyatantra is the first of the three outer tantras, Kriya, Upa, and Yoga, and for entering the door of Kriya, the ritual for the vows, the entrance, and the ripening factor are all the empowerment, for Kriya belongs to the Mantrayana. Kriya practitioners first receive the common empowerment of knowledge: the three empowerments with the water of Akshobya, the crown of Ratnasambhava, and the vajra of Amitabha together with the supplementary empowerment in which they are washed, brushed, and protected. They subsequently practice discipline, keeping the specific Kriya samayas perfectly. This is the ripening factor.

As for the practice of the liberating instructions, there are what are called the yogas with and without images, but Kriyatantra does not speak of the generation and perfection phases. For the first of these, the yoga with images, according to the Ancient Tradition one meditates on the four boundless qualities and then dissolves everything into emptiness with the *svabhava* mantra: from the union of emptiness and compassion one meditates on the six modes of the deity, visualizing oneself as the samaya deity with the wisdom deity as one's superior; in other words, one visualizes the samaya and wisdom deities as distinct. At the end one requests the wisdom deity to leave and dissolves the samaya deity into the state free from concepts. In the postmeditation period one eats the three white foods and three sweet foods and one emphasizes ablutions and purity in one's conduct.

Kriya practitioners remain ordinary beings until the day signs of accomplishment occur: as a result of this practice, the images used as supports for meditation smile, the butter lamps burn on their own, and the air is filled with the smell of incense. They then take the accomplishments and at that moment become Vidyadharas of the worlds of desire and form and have a vision of the deities of the three Buddha families. At the same time they obtain the supreme accomplishment and finally, after training on the path for up to sixteen human lifetimes, attain the state of Vajradhara of the three Buddha families. Individuals who follow this practice are known as tantric yogins or yoginis in the Inner Sangha of Vidyadharas.

(ii) Upatantra

The entrance for Upatantra is the three empowerments mentioned above, with in addition the bell empowerment of Amoghasiddhi and the name empowerment of Vairochana. Having received these, Upatantra practitioners subsequently practice discipline by keeping the specific Upatantra samayas. They then put the liberating instructions into practice, the meditation being similar to that in Yogatantra, in which the samaya deity and wisdom deity are seen as equals, like relatives or friends. Until they have a vision of the yidam deity, they remain ordinary tantric yogins and become Vidyadharas with celestial bodies and possessions equal to those of the gods in the worlds of desire and form. Then, on having a vision of the deity, they obtain the supreme accomplishment. From then on, until they finally attain the state of Vajradhara of the four Buddha families after seven human lifetimes training on the path, they are known as sublime tantric yogins and yoginis.

(iii) Yogatantra

The ripening factor or entrance for Yogatantra consists of the five common awareness empowerments of knowledge and the empowerment of the Vajra King's infinite command, together with the supplementary empowerment with the eight auspicious signs and eight auspicious objects. The practitioner practices discipline by keeping the Yogatantra samayas perfectly. The liberating instructions emphasize not ablutions and pure conduct but rather inner meditation: using the five masteries, Yogatantra practitioners meditate on the samaya deity and wisdom deity as being inseparable. When the image used as a support for the practice radiates light or smiles or other such signs appear, they take the accomplishment and become Vidyadharas of the worlds of desire and form. Subsequently they have a vision of the yidam deity and attain what the Sutrayana calls seeing the truth and what the Mantrayana calls the supreme accomplishment. From then on, until they finally attain the state of Vajradhara of the five Buddha families after five human lifetimes training on the path, they are known as ordinary and finally sublime yogins and yoginis.

This is the Inner Sangha of Vidyadharas of the three outer tantras.

According to the Ancient Tradition, Anuttarayoga includes three yogas: Maha, Anu, and Ati.

(iv) Mahayoga

The entrance, ripening factor, or ritual for the vows in Mahayoga is an empowerment such as that of the peaceful and wrathful deities from the tantra class or the empowerment of the Eight Herukas from the sadhana class. No other empowerment one might receive, such as the path empowerment, will serve as the ground empowerment.

According to the tantra class one must receive the ten outer empowerments that benefit, the five inner empowerments that confer ability, and the three profound secret empowerments. The teacher begins by maturing the disciple, starting from the preparation[145] and going through the empowerment ritual up to the vows of refuge and bodhichitta. This first stage can be illustrated by the analogy of brewing beer, where first the barley is cooked.

Next, in order to become a proper vessel for empowerment the disciple visualizes the deity, and in its three centers the three syllables appear as the three deities of body, speech, and mind. From them light rays emanate and fill the whole of space, and from the infinite buddhafields of the ten directions and in particular the Akanishtha buddhafield, the Unexcelled, the wisdom deities are invited, their body, speech, and mind arriving respectively in the form of particular deities, letters, and symbolic attributes and dissolving into the disciple. As a result, a disciple of superior faculties will realize the absolute primal wisdom from the empowerment. One of middling faculties has the experiences of bliss, clarity, and absence of thought. Even a disciple of inferior faculties should develop the firm conviction that the three doors are the three vajras. This stage is equivalent to adding the yeast to the cooked barley.

After this, the four empowerments are bestowed one after another, and one then concludes by making the promise that summarizes all the samayas: "Whatever the supreme master asks, I will do." This is equivalent to the beer fermenting.

However, if one subsequently fails to practice discipline by keeping pure samaya, which is what keeps the empowerment alive in one's being, the result will be similar to the beer going bad (despite the barley's being properly cooked, the yeast introduced, and the brew fermented) on account of negative forces associated with certain visitors or articles.[146]

The tantra *Vajrapani's True Empowerment* says:

What keeps the empowerment alive in one's being is the samaya:
If spoiled, it is like a seed burned by fire.

We may begin by receiving an authentic empowerment, but it will be of little use to us if we then fail to keep perfectly pure samaya. There is not a great difference between someone who keeps the samaya and one who spoils it: if you perceive earth as earth you are spoiling the samaya; to keep the samaya you have to perceive earth as Buddhalochana. These days, however, Mantrayana practitioners, to whom everything should appear as the natural display of deities, mantras, and wisdom, in fact perceive everything as ghosts and *gyalpo* spirits and upset both themselves and other people. There is not even a hint of Mantrayana about them. This is because, whereas the pratimoksha vows concern mainly one's external deeds and words and are therefore easy to keep, and the Bodhisattva vows depend simply on whether one's thoughts are good or bad and are therefore slightly more difficult to keep, in the Mantrayana the samayas all have to be based on primal wisdom and they are extremely hard to keep. But most people nowadays have got things completely back to front: they think the pratimoksha vows are difficult to keep and that they need pay little heed to the Mantrayana vows.[147]

Mahayoga practitioners, then, practice discipline by keeping the Mahayoga samayas, and to practice the liberating instructions they meditate mainly on the generation phase, the skillful means aspect, and part of the perfection phase, the wisdom aspect: of the two practices of the perfection phase related to the energies and essences they meditate on the energies.

(a) THE GENERATION PHASE

The generation phase related to skillful means is the antidote for ordinary, impure concepts. By practicing it one gains strength in the three kinds of meditational object, namely:

- the mental object, referring to the vivid visualization of one's yidam deity;
- the tangible object, referring to the stage at which the deity and deity's ornaments and attributes and so forth seem so solid one can touch them with one's own hands; and
- the object perceptible to the sense organs, perceptible even to other people, who say, "I can see the lama as the Great Glorious One," or as Vajra Bhairava or the deity in question.[148]

When one trains in the generation phase in this way until one attains the eight measures of clarity and stability and perfects the five experiences, one is able to correct and transform ordinary concepts into the deity.

However, if one is not free from clinging in one's perception of the deity, one may have strong attachment to the deity as something especially wonderful. This therefore has to be remedied with the perfection phase, the wisdom aspect.

(b) THE PERFECTION PHASE

There are two aspects to the perfection phase, that of the energies and that of the essences. If, to begin with, the energies are not in a suitable state, one will be unable to do the essences practice correctly. So having first properly completed the generation phase, one uses the stability thus gained in visualizing oneself not as an ordinary body but as the outer empty enclosure of the deity's body.[149] Simply breathing in and out serves no purpose in the perfection phase: it is very important to first gain stability in the generation phase. One then trains in the breathing practice of the vase exercise with its four features.[150]

As a result of this the mind and energy enter the central channel, remain in it, and dissolve into it, and this leads to four experiences of emptiness: as the energy gradually enters the central channel, there occur in the mind the experience of *emptiness* as the consciousnesses of the sense organs dissolve into the mental consciousness; the experience of *great emptiness* as the mental consciousness dissolves into the emotional consciousness; that of *extreme emptiness* as the emotional consciousness dissolves into the ground consciousness; and that of *total emptiness* when the ground consciousness dissolves into primal wisdom. These four experiences of emptiness give rise in the mind to the illustrative clear light that serves as a guide.

After that, through the clear light of the three appearances acting as the cause and the five light rays of the energies acting as the condition, one gains the ability to arise as the impure illusory body, the unfabricated, illusionlike body of the deity composed only of mind and energies, so that this illustrative primal wisdom introduces the absolute clear light.

This enhancing practice that develops our potential according to the Mahayoga path can follow two approaches: one where it is necessary to perform the six-month repeated group practice[151] and one where this is not necessary. In fact, as explained above, it is a requirement for such a gathering that all the participants—master and disciples—have achieved stability in the generation phase and in the energies practice; they should all have attained the wisdom of "warmth" on the path of joining and should be as many in number as there are deities in the mandala. All the articles and substances required for the accomplishment practice should be assembled—the three-story mandala palace, the weapons for repelling hostile forces, medicines for averting sickness, and food for nourishment. However, if there is in the assembly a single person who has spoiled the root samayas, the practice of all the others will be worthless and no one will attain the supreme accomplishment: a few ordinary siddhis might possibly be obtained, but the sadhana practice of the assembly as a whole will have been in vain. As Indrabodhi said:

> One degenerate yogi
> Spoils all the other yogis.
> A single frog infested with sores
> Infects all the other frogs around.

On the other hand, if only practitioners with pure samaya do a six-month repeated group ceremony and the additional practices or practices for making up deficiencies (whether or not these are necessary depends on the faculties of the practitioners), when the six months are completed, at dusk intertwined red and blue light rays radiate and the practitioners take the accomplishments from the deities. At midnight they take the accomplishments from the hostile forces, performing the practice of liberation with the three satisfactions[152] and taking the accomplishments. Then at dawn they make use of the path of mudra relying on another's body:[153] as the essence descends from above, the "substantial inborn wisdom," which is wisdom not separate from the experience of bliss, arises in the mind. At the end, when the essence ascends, the "natural inborn wisdom," the absolute wisdom devoid of all attachment to the experiences of bliss, clarity, and no thought, arises in the mind. At that moment the male consorts realize the wisdom of bliss and the female consorts realize the wisdom of emptiness.

Then, in the postmeditation they are able to arise as the unfabricated deity of the perfection phase, the pure illusory body that is the union level of the path of learning, the union of Buddha body and Buddha mind. Also practitioners on the path of accumulating progress to the path of joining, those on the path of joining progress to the path of seeing, and those on the path of seeing progress to the second level, and so on. If they have all kept the samaya, even the cocks, dogs, and cows will realize the level of Vidyadhara. Moreover, if the participants in the group sadhana have all previously achieved the level of "warmth," during the six months they will accomplish both the "peak" and "acceptance" levels, and when they take the accomplishments they will attain the wisdom of the last instant of the "supreme mundane level," and they will subsequently attain the path of seeing according to the Sutrayana or, according to the Mantrayana, the supreme accomplishment of Mahamudra.

According to the canonical lineage of Zur[154] and as we find in the *Stages on the Path*,

> As some have acquired power and others have not
> The path of seeing is divided into two

—those who have the ability to purify the ordinary body with the fire of concentration and transform it into a subtle body acquire the power of immortal life and are called Vidyadharas with mastery of the duration of life. Those who have not been able to purify their bodies but whose minds have ripened into the deity's body are known as apparently matured Vidyadharas. Those who are on the second to the ninth levels are Mahamudra Vidyadharas. Then, at the end of the path, at the moment buddhahood is reached, they are spontaneously accomplished Vidyadharas.

Kunkhyen ("Omniscient") Longchenpa, however, asserts that those at the end of the greater path of accumulating whose bodies have not been ripened as the deity's body but whose minds have ripened as the deity's body are apparently matured Vidyadharas. Practitioners on the path of seeing are Mahamudra Vidyadharas: some, who transform their bodies into subtle bodies and can control the duration of their lives, are Vidyadharas with mastery of the duration of life who have perfectly completed the sublime path; others, if they do not acquire mastery over the duration of life, reach the path of seeing in this life and in the intermediate state proceed to the second level and, having arisen into the postmeditation in the union level of the path of learning, remain Mahamudra Vidyadharas up to the final stage of the tenth level. Then, when they realize final buddhahood, they are spontaneously accomplished Vidyadharas.

Practitioners on these four Vidyadhara levels are known as dakas and dakinis of the Mahayoga tradition and constitute the Inner Sangha of Vidyadharas.

(v) Anuyoga

In Anuyoga the ripening empowerments comprise the outer empowerments known as the "ten rivers of the mindstream," the inner empowerments called the "eleven rivers of the elements," the accomplishment empowerments known as the "thirteen rivers of sound," and the secret empowerments called the "two rivers of perfection." Having received these thirty-six sublime root empowerments and practicing discipline by keeping the specific Anuyoga samayas, one proceeds to practice the liberating instructions. After first partially practicing the generation phase and then the perfection phase of the energies as one did for the perfection phase of Mahayoga, here one concentrates mainly on the perfection phase related to the essences: once one's own body is trained, that is, the channels are straightened, the energies properly directed, and the essences mastered, one relies on another's body on the path of the mudra. First one practices making the essence descend from above, and this leads to the substantial inborn wisdom. Then at the end when the essence ascends from below one achieves the natural inborn wisdom—at least, this is how it is said to be, but for beginners it is difficult to give rise to wisdom that is really free from attachment to experiences.

Then, if the illustrative wisdom dawns in one's mind, in the postmeditation one is able to arise into the postmeditation as what we call the impure illusory body, which in reality is the deity formed simply of mind and energy. If the absolute wisdom dawns in one's mind, one is able to arise as what is known as the pure illusory body, which is the deity that appears from the radiance of primal wisdom.

In Anuyoga, there are five Vidyadhara levels: aspiration and reflection, corresponding to the path of accumulating; the unfolding of great intellectual faculties, corresponding to the path of joining; the attainment of great indications, corresponding to the path of seeing; the great confirmation, corresponding to the path of meditation; and the perfection of great skill, corresponding to the path of no more learning. Practitioners on these five levels are Anuyoga dakas and dakinis and comprise the Inner Sangha of Vidyadharas.

(vi) Atiyoga

The ripening empowerment for Atiyoga is the fourth empowerment, the precious sacred word empowerment, which is distinguished from the empowerments for the two preceding yogas by being divided into four empowerments: elaborate, unelaborate, and so on.

Having received these four empowerments, one practices discipline by keeping the Atiyoga samayas. As for the liberating instructions, there are two that can be practiced: the trekchö based on primordial purity through which lazy people may be liberated without effort; and the spontaneous presence, the effortful path through which diligent people may be liberated.

According to the teachings, the vision of "dharmata actually appearing" occurs on the path of seeing. But in practice the vision of "dharmata actually appearing" occurs on the path of accumulating, the "increase of experiences and appearances" on the path of joining, and the "ultimate reach of awareness" on the path of seeing. As for "the exhaustion of phenomena beyond mind," the gradual exhaustion of the outer objects that are perceived, of the inner mind that perceives, and of the secret experiences that increase occurs on the supreme path of training, and their complete exhaustion corresponds to the path of no more learning. Beings on this path of the four visions comprise the Inner Sangha of Vidyadharas.

(3) Qualities

The Sangha possesses infinite inconceivable qualities, including discipline, concentration, wisdom, the power of memory, and courage and confidence.

These different sources of refuge are all embodied in the teacher; conversely they can be divided into the nine objects to which we go for refuge.[155] When we adopt these as our sources of refuge and take refuge in particular in the channels, energies, and essences that are complete in us, the channels are purified and one attains the nirmanakaya, and so on.

What is special about the great beings' attitude is that they take refuge in order to eliminate all the disadvantages of samsara and nirvana. Now according to the Causal Vehicle of Characteristics, this is not only a special attitude, it is also the resultant refuge. The causal refuge is taking refuge with the three special features.[156]

Here again there are two different doctrines. According to the Second Turning of the Wheel, the causal refuge is the cause for attaining the result, buddhahood, which is considered to be the resultant refuge. In this case there is a cause with characteristics that produces a result with characteristics.

The teachings of the Third Turning of the Wheel assert that the ground, or what is known as the wisdom of sugatagarbha, is the naturally arising wisdom that dwells as the ground in the minds of beings. This ground is constant, unchanging, and by nature empty, and in it all the qualities of the Buddha's three kayas are naturally present without being fabricated. However, this wisdom of sugatagarbha needs to be unveiled, for it has been obscured by adventitious stains, and means or conditions are therefore necessary to remove them, namely the two accumulations. But these are asserted to be secondary conditions for revealing the wisdom of sugatagarbha: the Third Turning does not talk about a cause with characteristics that leads to a result with characteristics.

Regarding the causal refuge mentioned first, there are two aspects: the promise one declares and to which one gives the name "refuge"; and the real refuge one subsequently accomplishes in following the path. The first involves considering the Buddha as the teacher, the Dharma as the path, and the Sangha as the companions on the path, and reciting the words of the refuge prayer one hundred thousand times or so. The second, the refuge one accomplishes in following the path, refers to all the various practices one engages in to gather the two accumulations.

As for that wisdom,[157] it is described as the cause without which nothing could happen. Beings, as long as they fail to recognize it, are beings; when they recognize it and make it revealed, they are Buddhas.

Starting from the first level, it is possible to have partial realization of this wisdom, and from this point on one gradually accustoms oneself to that realization until one finally reaches the end of the tenth level: this is the "Path Dharma of realization." Then on the final stage of the tenth level, with the adamantine antidote of wisdom one gets rid of all the obscurations to be eliminated, totally, and buddhahood is attained. This buddhahood, where the essential nature is doubly pure—primordially pure and pure by virtue of being freed from adventitious stains—is the "Result Dharma of realization." It is the profound and vast Dharma contained in the mind of such a Buddha.

Here one speaks of two kinds of cessation: conceptual cessation and nonconceptual cessation. Nonconceptual cessation is the wisdom of sugatagarbha existing in beings' minds as the primordially pure essential nature. Conceptual cessation is the dharmakaya Buddha which is the purity achieved by being freed of adventitious stains. In what way does this wisdom exist within beings' minds? It is covered by adventitious stains, like a sword in a scabbard or a precious gem covered with mud. What distinguishes the teachings of the Third Turning is that rather than proposing a causal refuge and resultant refuge they assert that the means for removing these adventitious stains are secondary conditions for realizing the cause.

In what way are the Three Roots, which are the extraordinary or inner refuge, the Three Jewels? According to the sutras, the Buddha is a supreme nirmanakaya manifestation. The Secret Mantrayana tradition considers the Buddha to be the sambhogakaya, and holds that the teacher is the Sangha, and both the inspirational deity and destined deity[158] are the Buddha. Another tradition states that the teacher is the Buddha, the yidam is the Jewel of the Dharma, and the other lineage teachers are the Inner Sangha of Vidyadharas.

How the teacher is the Buddha has to be established by scriptural authority and reason.

Our scriptural authority here is the *Five Stages:*

The naturally accomplished Buddha,
The sole lord, the great deity,
Gives the pith instructions directly.
For this reason the vajra master is supreme.

As for establishing this by reasoning: the teacher's mind is the great wisdom, and the expression of that wisdom appears to us as the teacher's Buddha body, resounds as his Buddha speech, and emanates thoughts as his Buddha mind. In this way the expression of the dharmakaya is the rupakaya, and the essence of the rupakaya is dharmakaya. The inseparability of these is the union Vajradhara.

How are the yidam deities the Jewel of the Dharma? In general there are four tantras common to the Ancient and New Traditions. The Yogatantra is divided into two, outer and inner yogas. The inner yoga comprises the three profound inner tantras for the Ancient Tradition and the three tantras of Chakrasamvara, Hevajra, and Guhyasamaja for the New Tradition.

For all these there are the Dharma of transmission and the Dharma of realization. The Dharma of transmission comprises the outer Mantrayana Dharma of transmission, the Dharma that is voiced in symbols, the Dharma that appears as symbols, and the Dharma that is written down in symbols, corresponding to the three outer tantras (Kriya, Upa, and Yoga). The Dharma of realization comprises the ripening empowerments and liberating instructions. The spiritual teacher who bestows the ripening empowerments and liberating instructions is the Buddha; the empowerments and instructions he gives are the Dharma; and the individuals who practice them form the Inner Sangha of Vidyadharas.

In the three inner tantras, the teacher who gives the entrance empowerments and the liberating instructions is the Buddha; the ripening empowerments and liberating instructions are the Jewel of the Dharma; and those who practice in accordance with these make up the Inner Sangha of Vidyadharas. Thus the Three Roots are by nature included in the Three Jewels. The latter can be divided up into nine sources of refuge, or on the other hand condensed into a single refuge, the teacher.

Once we have a little initial understanding of taking refuge, we can apply this understanding and put it into practice. Here we can talk about practice during the session and practice between sessions.

(A) PRACTICE DURING THE SESSION

However many sessions we do, whether four (two during the day and two during the hours of darkness) or eight, each session should consist of the session preliminaries, the main part, and the conclusion.

(1) The Preliminary Practice for Each Session

It is important to precede each session with four points, namely the three essential points for the body, speech, and mind, and prayer.

The essential point for the body is to sit in the seven-point posture of Vairochana or in the more relaxed seven-point posture of the path of liberation, or to sit cross-legged with the back straight.

The essential point for the speech is to expel the stale breath, blowing it out three times or nine times, according to preference. As you do so, imagine that you are blowing out all your own and others' negative karma accumulated in samsara throughout time without beginning; all the evil actions, downfalls, breaches, and degenerations; and everything that obstructs and interrupts our practice on the profound path, all in the form of black vapor.

The essential point for the mind is to form your attitude. First rid yourself of all negative attitudes. Change your neutral attitudes and form the attitude or motivation of the bodhichitta.

Prayer involves first visualizing your teacher above your head. Whether you visualize him transformed or untransformed[159] does not matter. Meditate that above the crown of your head is a lotus with one hundred thousand petals in full blossom, and in the center of its spreading orange anthers a moon disk. On top of this is a lion throne piled high with silken cushions, and on this is seated your teacher, wearing either monastic robes or the robes of a tantric yogin, whichever the case may be. Then with yearning devotion, perceiving him as the Buddha in person, pray to him to fulfill your wishes. When you are meditating on the difficulty of finding the freedoms and advantages, for example, you should pray that the teacher's own qualities and ability to make full use of the freedoms and advantages may take birth in you. After this meditate that the teacher melts into light and dissolves into you. Then rest in equanimity.

You should adapt this prayer and meditation to all your sessions: whether you are practicing the ordinary or extraordinary preliminaries, pray that the wisdom and qualities of the teacher's mind may arise in your being and then mingle the teacher's mind with yours and rest in equanimity.

(2) The Main Part of the Session

Of the three practices for Bodhisattvas—completion, maturation, and training—here we are concerned with training, purifying our environment, so visualize the entire ground as a ground of jewels, checkered with intricate designs. In front of you in the distance is a wish-fulfilling tree made of all kinds of precious gems. On the central one of its five boughs is a lion throne piled high with silken cushions, and upon this is seated your root teacher appearing in the form of the Precious Guru of Oddiyana. Above the crown of his head, inside circles of five-colored light, are the lamas of the lineage. Around the throne are the other teachers from whom you have received empowerment and teachings, and around them are the multitude of yidam deities of the four or six tantras.

On the right-hand branch are the Buddhas and so on,* and all around are the protectors. The male protectors all look outward: their activity is to prevent outer enemies and obstacle makers from coming in. The female protectors all look inward: their activity is to keep inner accomplishments from leaking out. They in turn are surrounded by the gods of wealth, treasure owners, and so forth.

All these are the manifold display of the teacher's great wisdom mind, beyond notions of good or bad, superior or inferior. They are all endowed with the omniscient mind of the Buddhas. They watch over beings with superhuman eyes, listen with superhuman ears, and think of them with superhuman minds. Meditate thinking of them as your leaders and guides.

As for the beings who are being given refuge, placing your father on your right and so on,† imagine them all as a great teeming crowd covering the surface of the earth, their clothes and ornaments of a shimmering brown hue.

Then recite the words of the refuge as if you were the *umdze*.[160] Here we do not do prostrations with the refuge practice,[161] so along with all the other beings show respect with your body by joining the palms of your hands together, express respect with your speech by reciting the refuge verse, and express respect with your mind by thinking from the depth of your heart: "From this day until we attain ultimate buddhahood, whether we find ourselves on the level of buddhahood above or in the hells below, whether things go well or badly, whether we are stung superficially or deeply hurt,

---

*See WMPT page 179 for the description of the four branches.
†See WMPT pages 179–80.

whether we are happy or miserable, we shall neither seek counsel from our father nor advice from our mother, nor decide on our own. You, our teacher and the Three Jewels, it is you who know best, it is you who think constantly of us, we seek no other refuge, no other hope than you! You alone will we accomplish, you alone will we approach, you alone will we follow."

With this sort of complete trust, recite the refuge prayer.

In particular, when you take refuge in the Buddha as the teacher, the Dharma as the path, and the Sangha as the companions on the path, first you should call, "Teacher, Buddha Bhagavan . . ." and so on. "From this year, this month, this day, from this very instant until I attain the essence of ultimate enlightenment, I take you as my teacher. I will not follow any other teacher but you!"

Again, call, "Teacher, Buddha Bhagavan," and say, "From this very day until I attain ultimate enlightenment, I vow to take as the path for accomplishing liberation and enlightenment the teachings you have given, the sacred Dharma that comprises transmission and realization. I will follow only the sacred Dharma, I will not rely on wrong, non-Buddhist paths."

And again, "Teacher, Buddha Bhagavan, I vow to take as companions accomplishing the path those guides, sublime beings of the Sangha who with the two wheels of study and practice hold your teaching, the sacred Dharma. I will rely on no other companions than these, neither on ordinary companions whose mouths are full of empty oaths and lies nor on those who practice negative actions."

The rest of this passage in *The Words of My Perfect Teacher*, "It is to you that I make my offerings . . ." and so on, is easy to understand.

(3) Conclusion

When it is time to conclude the session, red rays of light stream out from the refuge deities and touch you and all sentient beings, bringing about riddance and realization: all the obscurations of negative emotions, conceptual obscurations, and obscurations of habitual tendencies are purified, and the potential or nature of sugatagarbha present in the minds of beings is transformed and actualized as primal wisdom.

"Like a flock of birds scattered by a slingstone you all fly up . . ." and so on.* Finally the teacher too gradually dissolves, upward from his feet and

---

*See WMPT pages 181–82.

throne and downward from his crown, and vanishes into his heart. In that state rest in equanimity. This is the refuge of the absolute natural state. Meditate like this alternating analytic and resting meditation. Then when thoughts begin to occur again, continue into the postmeditation period by visualizing the field of merit as before. With a pure mind[162] dedicate the merit with the prayer "Through the merit of this practice . . . ," and so on, and recite wishing prayers.

(B) PRACTICE BETWEEN SESSIONS

Between sessions visualize the field of merit at all times—when you are eating, sleeping, moving around, or sitting, and so on as described in *The Words of My Perfect Teacher*.

When you return to the next session, first go to the toilet, blow your nose, wash, and properly finish everything you need to do outdoors or indoors. In short, complete any necessary chores and prepare things so that you do not need to get up until the session is over.

If you do not keep all trivial thoughts at bay during one session, you will not be able to interrupt them properly in the next. So make this resolve: "In this session I will absolutely not let my mind be influenced by delusion and negative emotions," and promise not to abandon it. Do not follow past thoughts, invite future thoughts, or prolong the flow of present thoughts, and rest in this state as long as you can. This is equivalent to banishing the obstacle makers and visualizing the protection circle when you practice the generation and perfection phases.

Next, adopt the essential point of the body and so on, in the same way as above.

After the session check whether you have managed to keep the resolution you made earlier. If you did keep your promise and had nothing but positive thoughts, you might feel pleased with yourself. You should remedy this and crush your pride, saying to yourself, "Look, this is simply due to the fleeting appearance of some frail merit. Let's see whether you do as well in the next session!"

If you did not manage to keep your promise and were carried away by deluded thoughts you might feel depressed and think, "I'll never make it." In this case, encourage yourself and renew your resolve: "Why are you getting depressed? If you had never had any deluded thoughts to start with, you would already be enlightened. This time you may well have fallen prey to delusion, but I swear I'm not going to let you be influenced by delusion and negative emotions in the next session."

So if you are going to do a session, either do it properly or not at all. And when you do it, make sure that the three supreme methods (preparation, main part, and conclusion) are in no way lacking.

When you rise in the morning, wake up with the confidence that you are your yidam deity. Imagine the whole sky filled with dakas and yoginis and that you have been woken up by the noise of their hand drums and bells and the spontaneous melody of the vowels and consonants. Then start the preliminary practice for the session and continue in the same way as described above.

III. PRECEPTS AND BENEFITS OF TAKING REFUGE
1. The Precepts of Taking Refuge

Put simply, the Dharma is to do no harm. This means that those who have taken the pratimoksha, Bodhisattva, and Mantrayana vows must all refrain from harming others and from the basis for doing harm. The Buddha never said, "You ought to harm others," so from the moment we become Buddhists we must avoid doing so. The pratimoksha vows too have this as their starting point. Furthermore, we need to avoid both thinking of harming other beings and actually doing so.

In the Mantrayana, the teacher embodies all refuges. You should therefore eschew any deeds, words, or thoughts that might violate his body, speech, or mind and seize on any deeds, words, or thoughts that accord with his body, speech, and mind. If you act in accord with his wishes, you will fulfill the wishes of the infinite sources of refuge. If you go against his wishes, you will upset the infinite sources of refuge: you might just as well cut someone's head off and expect to revive him. It is important therefore to refrain from doing anything that displeases the teacher.

If there is one practice that we should master in this one human life, it is the practice of refuge. Any one person, during one lifetime, experiences either suffering or happiness. There is no other alternative. Suffering itself has two aspects, result and cause.

◈ Suffering Experienced as a Result

If you find yourself in unwelcome situations such as being stricken by disease, seized by negative forces or paralyzed by a stroke, you must not think, "Why does this have to happen to me?" On the contrary, meditate as follows: "It is because of the Three Jewels' compassion that I have the opportunity to exhaust the effects of my negative actions. Thanks to their kindness the karma that I would normally have to experience in future lives can be experienced and exhausted right now. I have every reason to be happy."

◈ Causes of Suffering

When you have thoughts based on attachment, aversion, and bewilderment, which are causes of suffering, understand that these too are instances of the Three Jewels' compassion. How can this be? Because thanks to their kindness you are being warned of these negative emotions latent in your mind. You should see them as something to be happy about, as something necessary, and as something indispensable. Meditate with joy, thinking, "Three Jewels, through your infinite compassion may I never again have negative thoughts and deeds like these."

Happiness too can be understood from the point of view of cause and result.

◈ Causes of Happiness

Whenever you have a positive thought that is a cause of happiness, like devotion, determination to be free, or bodhichitta, work it thoroughly, as Apu used to say.[163] In other words, try to develop more and more thoughts of this kind, and even better. The *Way of the Bodhisattva* declares:

> As when a flash of lightning rends the night,
> And in its glare shows all the dark black clouds had hid,
> Likewise rarely, through the Buddhas' power,
> Virtuous thoughts rise, brief and transient, in the world.[164]

So it is important to pray to the teacher and the Three Jewels that thoughts of this kind may grow and flourish.

❧ Happiness Experienced as a Result

When everything is going well and you have plenty of food, clothes, and belongings, it is not because you are particularly great or special. You should understand that it is, rather, a mark of the Three Jewels' compassion and kindness and make every effort to repay this kindness by making all kinds of offerings.

These days most people, regardless of their standing or importance, think the first portion of what they eat and drink that they put aside in the offering vessel is an offering to ghosts and spirits. They do not realize that it is an offering intended for the Three Jewels.

Each time you put the first portion in the offering vessel, say the prayer, "To the unsurpassable teacher, the precious Buddha . . . ." This will ensure you do not miss making an offering on Buddhist festival days, and it is also the way to repay the Three Jewels' kindness. Moreover, you should also offer the Three Jewels your body and possessions and use all your influence and fortune to serve the Dharma, for it is important to accumulate merit. As the saying goes, "Better a single spark of merit than a mountain of effort."

The object through which we can accumulate merit is the Sangha. As we find in the teachings of the Kagyu lineage:

The living Buddha,
The living Dharma,
The living Sangha.[165]

When we acquire merit by making offerings to the Three Jewels, offerings made to the Buddha and Dharma enable us to acquire the merit of making the offering but not that of the offering being accepted. However, with offerings made to the Sangha we acquire the merit of both offering and acceptance. In particular, an offering made to our teacher is an offering to the Fourth Jewel, and the merit acquired thereby is boundless.

2. The Benefits of Taking Refuge

The benefits of taking refuge are twofold, temporary and ultimate. The temporary benefits are that in this life you will be protected from the eight and sixteen great dangers, including the danger of illness, negative forces, criminal punishment, and famine. And you will have all the happiness of the higher realms right up to the lasting happiness of liberation and omniscience.

The ultimate benefit is that as a result of taking refuge in the Buddha, you will attain buddhahood. As a result of taking refuge in the Dharma, you will be able to put into motion the three turnings of the Wheel of Dharma. As a result of taking refuge in the Sangha, you will become a teacher gathering around you a following of Shravakas and Bodhisattvas: a disciplined teacher with disciplined disciples, a peaceful teacher with peaceful disciples, a perfectly peaceful teacher with perfectly peaceful disciples.[166]

Patrul Rinpoche (1808–87).

CHAPTER TWO

Arousing Bodhichitta, the Root of the Great Vehicle

WHEN WE HAVE the vast attitude of bodhichitta, even if the Dharma we are practicing is that of the Lesser Vehicle, it will become the Dharma of the Great Vehicle. As far as beginners are concerned, the reason for designating a vehicle as "great" or "lesser" is whether it has the relative bodhichitta. Apart from this, there is nothing in the Dharma itself that makes it a great or a lesser vehicle, so relative bodhichitta is the most important factor, and it has to be accompanied by the view. According to the teachings of the ultimate meaning, to reach the final goal we need the absolute bodhichitta, as that ultimate result cannot be attained through relative bodhichitta alone.

Also, as beginners, we must have a good heart. It is said:

If the intention is good, the levels and paths are good.
If the intention is bad, the levels and paths are bad.

If we possess the intention of bodhichitta, then we will traverse the good levels, the ten Bodhisattva levels, and the good paths, the five paths. If our intentions are bad, then we have no choice but to depend on bad levels, the nine levels of the three worlds of samsara,[167] and follow bad paths, the paths of the five classes of living beings.[168]

This is why when we begin, everything depends on this intention of bodhichitta, on this and on nothing else. It does not depend on our view, nor does it depend on our meditation, for even Shravakas and Pratyekabuddhas have realization of the view, as the great Sakya Pandita points out:

Shravakas and Pratyekabuddhas meditate on emptiness,
And the result this brings is cessation.

It is through this intention of bodhichitta coupled with the accumulations of merit and wisdom that the result of buddhahood is obtained. In the New Tradition it is said that arousing the relative bodhichitta is the most important thing. According to the Ancient Tradition, which identifies (1) an expedient meaning; (2) a semidefinitive meaning; and (3) an ultimate meaning, from the point of view of the expedient meaning, we must have the relative bodhichitta. From the point of view of the semidefinitive meaning, we have to combine relative and absolute bodhichitta. And in this respect Shravakas and Pratyekabuddhas do not realize the views of the three great systems. In terms of the ultimate meaning, the ultimate and final goal is the absolute bodhichitta.

Nagarjuna says that bodhichitta is what makes the Mahayana vehicle great, and the glorious Chandrakirti, who asserts in his *Introduction to the Middle Way* that there is only one ultimate vehicle, maintains it is by virtue of absolute bodhichitta that there is a single ultimate vehicle and that it is impossible to assert one ultimate vehicle by means of relative bodhichitta.

This good intention of bodhichitta arises only in one who has a good heart, not in someone of ill will, and the way to make it arise falls into three sections:

   I. Training the mind in the four boundless qualities
  II. Arousing bodhichitta, the mind turned toward supreme enlightenment
 III. Training in the precepts of bodhichitta in aspiration and bodhichitta in action

I. TRAINING THE MIND IN THE FOUR BOUNDLESS QUALITIES

First we need to train our minds in the four boundless qualities. Without this training we will never give up all our schemes and efforts for achieving our own selfish ends, and from the point of view of both the Dharma and worldly life, we will never succeed in getting what we want. We have only to look around us to know this: the rulers of this world, the ministers and people of position and power who have exclusively their own selfish interests at heart, all in the end cannot but fall into states of misfortune, bringing ruin on themselves and others.

Then, from the point of view of the Dharma, the Shravakas and Pratyekabuddhas, who seek their own benefit, attain neither the qualities of the levels of the Bodhisattvas, children of the Buddhas, nor the qualities of the result, those of the Bhagavan Buddha, and all because of this self-centeredness. So it is not right to continue seeking to achieve our own selfish ends, and we must now arouse the attitude of bodhichitta within our minds.

Shantideva wrote:

May bodhichitta, precious and sublime,
Arise where it has not yet come to be;
And where it has arisen may it never fail
But grow and flourish ever more and more.

In the first place, "bodhichitta, precious and sublime" is the wish that all sentient beings attain buddhahood. The method for making it "arise where it has not yet come to be" is to train the mind in the four boundless qualities. The method for making it "never fail but grow and flourish ever more and more" is to arouse the supreme bodhichitta and to train in the precepts of bodhichitta. So we should practice these methods for making it arise where it has not yet come to be, for preventing it from declining where it has arisen, and for making it not fail but flourish more and more, either in a detailed way with the four boundless qualities, or in less detail with love and compassion, or simply with compassion alone.

◊ Boundless Qualities and States of Brahma

Regarding the four boundless qualities that are the means for making the bodhichitta arise where it has not arisen, we need to consider the four boundless qualities and the four Brahmaviharas. The four Brahmaviharas are "Priests of Brahma" and so on, and the cause for being born in these four is meditating on love, compassion, sympathetic joy, or impartiality, but in a limited way, without either the object or the mental attitude being boundless.

In what way are these four not boundless? Put briefly, they are love, compassion, sympathetic joy, and impartiality in which the determination to be free as intention is lacking, in which there is no bodhichitta, neither the view of emptiness, nor the wisdom that realizes no-self, and this is why they are known as "the four states of Brahma." The object on which they focus and the form they take are limited like those of a kind-hearted old lady, whose attitude is like that of a mother concerned for her child's happiness and well-being. But when taken onto the path of omniscience, these four become the four boundless qualities. While we are practicing on the path, the four boundless qualities constitute the first four of the thirty-seven elements of enlightenment,[169] and when we attain the result they are the four boundless qualities of a Buddha.[170] They are called boundless qualities because the object on which they focus is boundless, the form they take in the mind is boundless, and their result is boundless.

The order in which the four boundless qualities are explained in the texts puts love first. However, according to the tradition of the pith instructions, if we do not start by meditating on boundless impartiality, the others will simply turn into the brahma states. We should therefore meditate first on impartiality.

The wish that beings possess both happiness and its cause is the nature, definition, and form of *love*.

The wish that beings be free from suffering and its cause is the nature, definition, and form of *compassion*.

The wish that beings never part from happiness is the nature, definition, and form of *sympathetic joy*.

And the wish that beings be free from attachment and aversion is the nature, definition, and form of *impartiality*.

For these four boundless qualities there are "boundless qualities with concepts" and "boundless qualities without concepts." When you meditate on boundless qualities with concepts, the object on which you focus should be associated with the form of the meditation.

First, the object on which love focuses. When we say, "May all sentient beings, who have been my own mother, and who are as numerous as the sky is vast, enjoy happiness and the causes of happiness," the object on which we focus is beings who do not have happiness, and the form love takes in the mind is the wish that they have both the cause of happiness and the happiness that results.

With compassion, the object on which we focus is suffering beings, and the form compassion takes in the mind is the wish that they be free from both suffering and its causes. The object on which sympathetic joy focuses is beings who have both happiness and the causes of happiness, and the form it takes in the mind is the wish that they never be without happiness. With impartiality, the object on which we focus is both the attachment and aversion in our own minds and the attachment and aversion in others' minds. The form it takes is the wish to be even-minded, that is, the wish to still thoughts of attachment and aversion and to be of benefit to others. The way to meditate on these four boundless qualities is thus to match the object of meditation with the form of the meditation.

As for the boundless qualities without concepts, beginners should train the mind in the eight similes of illusion, seeing everything as a magical illusion, as a dream, and so on. Experienced, realized practitioners meditate with what is known as "all-accomplishing nonconceptual wisdom" on the love, compassion, and the like that arise as a natural result of their state of meditation.

1. Impartiality

Now we come to the actual meditation on the boundless qualities. If we do not begin by training in impartiality, then our love, compassion, and sympathetic joy will never become boundless. With regard to the ways of meditating, there are both analytic meditation and resting meditation: love and the samadhi of love, compassion and the samadhi of compassion, sympathetic joy and the samadhi of sympathetic joy, and impartiality and the samadhi of impartiality. Of the two sorts of meditation, sustained calm and profound insight, all these fall into the category of sustained calm meditation. And of the two traditions of meditation, that taught in the texts and that taught in the pith instructions, here we follow the latter. The preliminary practice for the session is the same in all cases.[171] Now we come to the main practice.

◊ Enemies and Friends

For the main practice, imagine your enemy on your right and a relative or friend on your left. Then begin by making a definite feeling of aversion arise toward your enemy and a feeling of attachment arise toward the person to whom you are close.

Next, you should think about the past, present, and future, as follows. Of our enemies and friends and ourselves, throughout the course of all our births and all our deaths, there is not one of them who has not been our father and mother and relative and close friend. At that time they helped us in countless ways, protected us from countless forms of harm. They were thus most beneficial friends.

◊ *Enemies*

Right now, we may think of somebody as being our enemy. However, we cannot be sure that he even conceives of us as an adversary. Even if he does see us as an enemy, and we fight one another, and he wins, it is likely to make him famous.[172] No longer will he even think of us as an enemy. Or if he has conceived of us as an enemy, a third person may show him how it has all been a misunderstanding, so that he turns into a friend, an even better friend than those we have already. Alternatively, we might say to each other, "Look, you were wrong, but then I was in the wrong as well. Now let's not behave as we did before." Or else, with gifts of some sort or with kind words, we might apologize and come to an agreement simply between ourselves, and so end up as friends.

Looking at it from the perspective of the Dharma, it is thanks to circumstances like being robbed or ruined by enemies that we first meet the Dharma. If you find yourself in such a situation, you should meditate and think: "Now I am a Bodhisattva, a child of the Buddhas, and as it is said, "Better than a hundred years of generosity is one day of maintaining discipline, and better than a hundred years of keeping discipline is one day of meditating on patience." All the major and minor marks of a Buddha are obtained through patience and for patience the object of meditation is enemies, so if I am able to meditate on patience, then this enemy is actually helping me, and is therefore not an enemy at all. In the future too, this enemy will become a friend and will help me."

At the same time, this enemy of ours, throughout all his beginningless lives, has been our enemy and inflicted harm on us. Even now he is an enemy and causes us harm, and in the future too he will act as an enemy and inflict harm on us. So this "enemy" of ours has both helped us and harmed us.

◆ *Friends*

Turn now to the friend. However much attachment we feel toward those to whom we feel close, when we think very carefully about them we are obliged to conclude that they are in fact our enemies. In previous lives, these relatives or friends have caused us harm: acting as our enemies, the number of times they have robbed us of our wealth, taken our lives, or cut off our head and limbs cannot be calculated. And in this life too, they have been an obstacle to our practicing the sacred Dharma. As children they have brought us, their parents, suffering. As parents they have harmed us, their children, marrying us off and tying us tightly down with the ropes of samsara. By teaching us how to get the better of our enemies and care for our families, and all sorts of negative activities like business and trickery, they have ruined us in ensuring that we will never be freed from samsara.

From the point of view of the Dharma also, regarding first of all meeting a true master, then engaging in religious activities,[173] and finally keeping discipline and so on, as long as we spend our time looking after the interests of our parents and family, thanks to them we will ruin our discipline, impair our concentration, and make our wisdom degenerate.

As a result of karmic debts incurred by our enemies in former lives, they are now friends or relatives. And because of debts incurred with those who are now close to us, in future lives they will be our enemies. So our friends in fact act as enemies in the past, in the present, and on into the future.[174] At the same time, this friend here has helped us throughout samsara which has no beginning in being our father and mother and the like. Now too he is our friend and helps us by giving us things like food, clothing, and somewhere to stay. And in the future as well he will be our friend and will help us. So this "friend" of ours has done us both good and wrong.

Now to sum up, the point about enemies and friends is that they both give help and both cause harm, and so when you see this, you will feel no desire to harm an enemy, nor any particular wish to help a friend. However, if you just leave it at that, this is "mindless impartiality," which brings neither harm nor benefit. Here what you must do is to see both enemies and friends as equal in having been your mothers, and to treat them as equal in both being objects to be helped. How does one meditate on this?

◆ Recognizing Beings as Our Mothers

Wherever there is space, it is filled with sentient beings. Wherever there are sentient beings, they are immersed in karmic perceptions and suffering. And of all these beings tormented by karmic perceptions and suffering, there is not a single one who throughout time without beginning has not been our father, mother, friend, and loved one. Of all of them it is our present mother who is dearest to us, and this enemy of ours is no different: he has been our mother too, not just once but an unimaginable number of times, for as it is said:

> To count one's mother's lineage with pills
> Just berry sized, the earth would ne'er suffice.[175]

Imagine that you and your mother, or you and your enemy, were seated before an omniscient Tathagata. He would tell you, "This enemy and you in your last life were human beings, and he was your mother. In the life before that when you were gods he was your mother," and so on, one after the other, life after life. Even if you were to take this great earth and roll it into little balls the size of juniper berries and count them, you would run out of earth, but you would never finish counting the number of times this one enemy had been your mother. Why is this? Throughout samsaric existence, from time without beginning until now we have been going around in circles, and there is nowhere, not even a piece of ground the size of a hand, where we have not been born or have not died an inconceivable number of times. With the exception of gods and hell beings, who usually take miraculous birth, most beings are born from a womb, and if they are born from a womb, they cannot be born without a mother. It is not as though one being has been our mother and that is all: all sentient beings have been one another's mothers an inconceivable number of times, and so this enemy has been our mother many, many times. To reflect in this way is to "recognize beings as our mothers."

◆ Remembering Their Kindness

Next we need to remember our mothers' kindness, for a mother is only ever kind; there is no such thing as a mother who is not. Even among the most ferocious wild beasts, like hawks and wolves, the females kill other animals to feed their offspring, and they care for them with kindness. One need hardly mention children born in a rich family, who have everything like food and clothing; even when the mother is a poor beggar she will look after her child with immense love and kindness. She will stay up long into the night with only the stars to cover her head; she will get up before dawn with only the frost for her shoes, hurrying along, the folds of her skirt whipping the backs of her legs, blood from her feet lying spattered on the ground, blood from her hands spilled on the stones; she will beg without shame or embarrassment, letting the dogs tear at her calves; and then, if there is just a small morsel of fat in the few poor scraps she gets, for which she has both suffered and caused harmful actions, she will give it to her child. From the one and only blanket she has, torn and tattered, she will find a piece that is thicker, and make her child's clothes or patch the ones it has.

When this present enemy of yours was in the process of becoming your mother, you were a driza, a consciousness on the point of seizing another body, wandering in the intermediate state, roaming in search of the odor of food. Then, because of the conjunction of cause and condition, namely your past karma and your parents' having sexual intercourse, you entered the womb. For nine months and ten days your mother kept you in her womb. She endured hardship and put up with having to commit negative acts. She had to suffer and weep, alone and in secret silence. Her whole body felt as if it was being shaken and churned like milk for butter. She cared nothing for negative actions, her own suffering, or people's spiteful remarks. All the goodness in the food eaten by your mother and all the vital force in her body was channeled through her child's navel and provided the nourishment for its life, enabling its body to grow. All this constitutes *the kindness of producing your body.*

Next, when she had given birth, one might have said you were alive, but you could not even lift your head up; or one might have said you were dead, but there you were, breathing. You were just this tiny, tender, pudgy thing, which your mother, with all her kindness, managed to keep from dying when it could so easily die, and to keep from drying out when it could so easily desiccate and putrefy. And yet a mother feels the most tremendous delight and joy to think she has given birth to a child. Looking after you with a mind full of love, her face always beaming, calling to you in a sweet voice, with infinite care she lifted you onto her lap on the tips of her ten fingers. This is *the kindness of giving life without letting you die.*

Then, as a consciousness wandering in the intermediate state with no food in your mouth, no money in your hands, and no clothes on your back, you arrived in a home where you knew no one and no one knew you. This mother, so kind, gave you your first nourishment, her sweet breast milk: the essential goodness in this milk went into your eyes and at the moment of death will trickle from your eyes as teardrops. The grosser, nonnutritious part of your mother's milk stayed within your body and is what now allows you to absorb all the nutrition in the food you eat. Having enabled your body to grow, at the time of death this "vital force of the body" will be vomited out or else excreted.

Your first clothing was the warmth of your mother's body as she held you close to her. Then, when you could eat a little food, she gave you the very best of her food, the cream of the milk, the curds of the yogurt, the tenderest and freshest pieces of meat, whatever was delicious and good to eat, and lots of it, chewing all the solid food herself before she put it in your mouth.

With her hand she wiped up all your excrement and dribble, with her hand she touched your belly to test whether you were hungry or full, and with her fingers she checked whether your food was too hot or too cold before she gave it to you to eat. She dressed her child in the best clothes, finding whatever she could that was soft and warm.

And yet your mother was stingy about making offerings to the Three Jewels above or giving to the needy below; she was stingy about making offerings for the dead and stingy with food and clothing for the living. And all of this without a care for her negative actions, her suffering, or the bad things people said about her. All the possessions and money she had amassed exclusively through negative actions and through craft and deceit she gave to her child. And still, even if she saw her child crowned in the kingdom of a Universal Ruler, she would never think it was good enough; if her child wanted food in his mouth, she would give him food; if he wanted money, she would give him money; and if he lacked clothes on his back, she would give him clothes. Without the slightest stinginess or second thoughts, your mother gave everything she had to you, her child. This is *the kindness of providing material needs.*

Later, when you could eat and crawl a little, she showed you how to eat properly, how to get dressed, how to put on your clothes the right way, how to adjust your belt, how to tie your shoelaces, how to walk when you did not know how, and how to talk when you did not know how, teaching you words like "Mummy" and "Daddy" and so on, teaching you all the right words you need in everyday life. So dear, so very precious was this little child to its mother that when she lay you down to sleep in your cot, for her it was as if she was tearing out her own heart, red and beating, from her chest and abandoning it in a field. From then she brought you up until you could stand up straight and finally became an adult.[176] This is *the kindness of teaching you the ways of the world.*

These four—producing your body, giving life, providing material needs, and teaching you the ways of the world—are the four sorts of kindness from the worldly point of view that you should remember.

From the point of view of the sacred Dharma, even this precious human body, with the eighteen freedoms and advantages, was brought into being by this mother of yours, who is so very kind. All the favorable conditions for practicing and attaining enlightenment—food, clothing, somewhere to stay, and material needs—not one of them could you acquire by yourself without mother beings. Remember that these things are due to their kindness.

At the beginning of the Bodhisattvas' path, without mother beings as the object it would be quite impossible to arouse the supreme bodhichitta. In the middle, again without mother beings as the object there would be nobody on which to train in the infinite Bodhisattva activities. And in the end, without there having been an object for arousing bodhichitta nor anyone on whom to train, there would be no perfect buddhahood. So from the Dharma point of view too, mother beings are extraordinarily kind.

So remembering their kindness involves remembering their kindness from both points of view—Dharma and worldly life.

❖ Wishing to Repay their Kindness

Next say to yourself, "Now, this mother of mine, who is so kind, who has such exceptional kindness, has always given the gain and victory to her child, both in the present and in the past. She has taken all the loss and defeat upon herself and looked after me with her tremendous kindness. Now I have met with the teachings of the Mahayana, I have been accepted as a disciple by a spiritual teacher and I know what is the right path and what is the wrong. So now it is my turn. My mother concerned herself with my well-being in the past, and now it is time for me, as her child, to concern myself with her welfare." This is wishing to repay their kindness, giving rise to the longing to repay your mothers' kindness.

When you have recognized your enemy as your mother, remembered her kindness, and aroused a longing to repay that kindness, then do the same with your own mother and father, your relatives, your brothers and sisters, and so on, until toward the end of the session you see all beings as equal, without any attachment to friends or aversion to enemies, because they have all been your mother. This is the meditation on boundless impartiality.

When you meditate by analyzing things like this, you may grow weary and feel disinclined to continue. Then, without following the past, without anticipating the future, and without prolonging the present thought, simply leave the mind just as it is, without any manipulation or meddling. This is the samadhi of impartiality.

If you wish to meditate with elaborations once more, then analyze again. In this way alternate analyzing and resting, and so practice the meditation of sustained calm.

The conclusion of the session is as usual.

In the breaks between sessions, focus on any beings who have attachment or aversion and recognize them as your mother, remember their kindness, and so on, as before. Say to yourself, "May their minds be free from attachment and aversion. If only they could be free from it. I myself shall be the one to free them." And pray to the Three Jewels that they find such freedom.

Next meditate on impartiality without concepts. Our body and all others' bodies are composed of minute particles, and our minds are simply a continuous succession of instants arising and ceasing and not lasting as long as the next instant: in absolute truth none of them has any inherent existence. Yet on the conventional level, out of this emptiness that cannot be qualified as anything there arises the whole variety of interdependent phenomena, unceasingly. So we are led to the conviction that emptiness and interdependent arising are both *equal* in their ceaselessness. To rest in that state, without any manipulation or meddling, is the way to develop profound insight. Furthermore, in all the breaks between sessions consider beings who quarrel on account of their attachment and aversion, and reflect on the four links again and again:

- the link of aspiration:[177] "May they be free from the attachment and aversion in their minds, at all times and in all situations";
- the link of the wish: "If only they could be free";

- the link of the commitment: "I myself shall be the one to free them"; and
- with these three links, prayer to the Three Jewels (the fourth link).

When you have meditated properly on impartiality like this during the sessions themselves, your mind may start to change a little. But if you do not continue to reflect in the breaks between sessions, you will revert to your former bad habits, like iron that glows red when heated in the fire but turns dull and black when it is pulled from the flames and left on the ground. So it is even more important to meditate in the breaks than in the sessions themselves. After meditating like this on impartiality, give up aversion toward enemies in the postmeditation as well, give up attachment to relatives and friends, and consider everyone equal, all of them being your mothers and fathers.

2. Love

With impartiality, we have quelled attachment and aversion and developed an even-minded attitude toward everyone, by virtue of their having been our mothers and fathers. Now we need to meditate on love. At the beginning of a session, we meditate by focusing on individual beings, one by one, and by the end of the session we should meditate on all sentient beings.

First of all, imagine that your real mother is actually in front of you, just the same, in every respect, as when she was alive.[178] This mother of yours has not only been your mother on this one occasion but an inconceivable number of times. Reflecting on the countless times she has been your mother, recognize that all beings have been your mothers, as we find in the verse "To count one's mother's lineage . . . ."

Now remember her kindness. You did not drop out of the sky like a thunderbolt or sprout from the ground like a flower. Your mother conceived and nurtured your body, keeping you in her womb for nine months and ten days, and so on. All the goodness in the food she ate, like an extra piece added to the wick in a butter lamp, passed through your navel. So remember her kindness in producing your body.

Then, when giving birth, apart from her jaws, every joint in her body was stretched open. For at least a week afterward she suffered, and even the idea of making love filled her with fear. You, her child, suffered as if you were being pulled through a hole in a drawplate. When you were born you were as good as dead, apart from the fact that you were still breathing, as has been described above. You could not tell which of the six realms you had come from, nor did you know where you had landed. If at this point this woman, in all her kindness, had not cared for you, you surely would have died. First, she separated you from the placenta, washed you with a warm stream of milk, cut the umbilical cord, and when you could so easily have died, she did not allow you to die, and so on. So remember her kindness in giving life.

Next, think about how she gave you your first food, her sweet breast milk, and so on, and remember her kindness in providing all your material needs.

After that, your mother was always around you, her mind so full of love for you it was as if she had left her own heart on the ground. She looked after you, thinking only of helping you, and cared for you until you knew and could understand things properly. So remember her kindness in teaching you the ways of the world.

Next, reflect on your mother's kindness from the Dharma point of view. In providing you with a place to live and all your material needs, she is a "field of benefit." In being your extraordinarily kind mother, she is a "field for meditating on love." These are the sorts of benefits she has brought you.

Yet in the past you did not give her the same sort of help. Whenever your dear old mother gave you advice about everyday things, telling you what to do and what not to do, you did not see fit to listen to her. "You ugly, sunburned old crisp," you would say, "why don't you just drop dead?" It was as if you were smashing her kindly hands with a rock,[179] and this kind of thing was all due to your failing to remember her kindness.

Now, after remembering our mother's kindness, we come to repaying that kindness. If you think about what it is that this mother of yours really wants, it is to be happy, to have every kind of happiness: a comfortable existence with plenty of food and clothes, somewhere to live, and everything else she might need in this life; all the happiness of rebirth in the higher realms as a god or human being; even the simple pleasure of a warm sunny day or a good cup of tea. She does not want to suffer. Yet she possesses neither the causes of happiness—faith, the determination to be free, and bodhichitta—nor the happiness that results, from the happiness of the higher realms of gods and humans up to the bliss of buddhahood, and she continuously indulges in the causes of suffering. This extraordinarily kind mother of yours, who has neither happiness nor the causes of happiness, is the object on which you should focus, while the form love takes in your mind is to think, "In this life and throughout all her series of lives, may this mother of mine have these three—faith, determination to be free, and the precious bodhichitta—which are the causes of happiness. If only she could have these. I shall be the one to ensure she has them," and to pray to the Three Precious Jewels that she may have them.

Also think, "May she have the resulting happiness, from that of the higher realms of gods and humans up to the bliss of perfect buddhahood. If only she could have such happiness. I shall be the one to help her have it," and pray to the Three Jewels that she may be happy, reciting prayers like: "Woe is me! Compassionate Three Jewels . . .," "To the Master and Buddhas, guardians of wandering beings . . . ," and "Courageous One, you who possess the power of compassion . . . ."*

When you feel permeated with happiness and bliss in this way, leave the mind as it is, without trying to stop thoughts and without following them.

Regarding the above, confidence in the law of cause and effect is the cause of being born in the higher realms, determination to be free is the cause of liberation, and bodhichitta is the cause of perfect buddhahood.

All this, from recognizing beings as one's mother up to wishing that she possess happiness and its causes, is the analytic meditation. Leaving the mind without blocking thoughts or following them is the samadhi of love.

In the breaks between sessions, you should constantly practice loving deeds and words. Have loving thoughts, thinking, "I must bring these old mothers every temporary and ultimate happiness." Act lovingly toward the older generation and even your domestic animals, and avoid hitting them or mistreating them; talk to them lovingly, not harshly or with unpleasant words. As for loving thoughts, as much as you wish all possible temporary happiness and ultimate bliss for beings, you should actually do everything you can to achieve it.

To practice love without concepts is to arrive at a certainty and conviction that although subject, object, and action may well appear, they are without any intrinsic existence.

---

*See pages 289–90.

3. Compassion

In meditating on compassion, the approach of Apu and Lord Atisha is to begin by meditating on your present mother. According to Rigdzin Jigme Lingpa, you meditate by concentrating on a sentient being on the point of being killed, such as a sheep going to the slaughter, or on someone who is sick or suffering, and then considering that they are either you or your old mother. Whichever way you choose will do.

Let us suppose that as a beginner you start by meditating on your own mother. Picture this old mother of yours in front of you, clearly, exactly as she is. Begin by acknowledging that she has been your mother not only once but many times over. Then remember her kindness—in giving you your body, in providing your material needs, in putting up with all manner of difficulties and hardship and fondly looking after you, in watching over you by day and guarding you all through the night. And her kindness in teaching you the ways of the world: she taught you to talk when you did not know how to talk, how to walk when you could not walk, how to eat when you did not know how, and how to put on your clothes when you did not know how to get dressed; she cared for you from childhood to youth and from youth to adulthood, until you could really know and understand things. Then remember her kindness from the Dharma point of view, how the freedoms and advantages are all due to her, and so on, as before.

Next, give rise to a wish to repay her kindness. What is it such a kind mother as this would want? What she wants is to be happy, and yet she does not know how to achieve by herself the causes of happiness, namely faith, the determination to be free, and bodhichitta. She does not have a teacher, a spiritual friend, and even if she did have one, she would not carry out his instructions. It is just as the *Way of the Bodhisattva* says:

> They long for joy, but in their ignorance
> Destroy it, as they would a hated enemy.[180]

She destroys the very causes of happiness, positive actions, as if she had seen her greatest enemy. Though she has no wish to suffer, she indulges unhesitatingly in negative acts, the very causes of suffering:

> Beings long to free themselves from misery,
> But misery itself they follow and pursue.

She does not want any of the sufferings of the three worlds of samsara, not even the paltry discomfort of being struck by a tiny spark from a fire or pricked by a thorn. And yet she creates the very cause of suffering, negative actions: when she performs physical actions, they are unvirtuous; when she talks, her words are unvirtuous; and when she thinks, her thoughts are unvirtuous. So what she truly desires and what she does are completely at odds, and she is harmed directly on account of the truth of suffering and harmed indirectly on account of the truth of the origin of suffering. She has both the cause of suffering and the suffering that results: the suffering of this life sends her on her way, the suffering of the next life waits to greet her, and the suffering of the intermediate state helps her across.

And that is not all, for when the negative actions she has committed just for her child's sake alone are fully ripened—quarreling and disputing with people, fighting off dogs, and even just crushing a single head louse—she will have to wander amid the infinite sufferings of the hell realms. She does not even recognize the danger of negative acts and see that they are the cause of suffering; she does not recognize the benefits of positive actions; and so day and night, without a break, she surrounds herself continuously with suffering. When you think, "Poor thing, how terrible," it is this very kind mother who is the object of your compassion.

So think, "May she be free from the suffering that results, the suffering of the three worlds of samsaric existence. If only she could be free. I shall be the one to free her," and pray, "Precious Three Jewels, our unfailing refuge, let her be freed from this suffering; show her your greatest compassion and power."

Then think, "May she be freed from the cause of suffering, all her karma and negative emotions. If only she were free. I shall be the one to free her," and pray to the Buddha, Dharma, and Sangha.

Meditate in this way, alternating analytic and resting meditation. Then meditate one after another on your father and sister and so on, and then on the relatives on your father's side, your brothers, and uncles, and the rest. At the end, destroy the three types of suffering of all beings who fill the whole of space.

Then consider the suffering upon suffering in the three lower realms, the suffering of change in the two higher realms of gods and humans, and the all-pervading suffering of everything composite in the two higher worlds.[181] Consider the specific human sufferings: the fear of meeting hated enemies;

the fear of losing loved ones; the suffering of not getting what one wants; the suffering of encountering what one does not want; and the sufferings of birth, old age, sickness, and death, and so on. Consider how beings are dogged by these sufferings in this life, greeted by suffering in the next life and bounded by suffering in the intermediate state, and think, "May they be free from these sufferings and their causes. If only they could be free. I shall be the one to free them," and pray to the Buddha, Dharma, and Sangha.

Then establish the certainty that in all this, though subject, object, and action appear, they have no intrinsic existence.

In between sessions, meditate with compassion for any beings you see.

4. Sympathetic Joy

The training in sympathetic joy also begins by focusing on one's own mother. Acknowledge her as your mother, reflect on her kindness, long to repay that kindness, and meditate on both love, the wish that she possess happiness, and compassion, the wish that she be free from suffering. Then meditate on joy.

Imagine that this old mother of yours has obtained food, clothing, somewhere to stay, wealth, possessions, and influence; she has good qualities, a good family, a good name, happiness, and well-being. Whatever little she has of each of these, she is the object or focus, while the mental attitude or form this takes is to consider how much these things make her happy, to consider how much she needs them, and to consider how indispensable they are to her. This is meditating on joy. Think, "Whatever well-being and its cause—virtue—however small, my old mother may have, may these never decline nor be lost but go on increasing more and more. And may the causes of happiness—positive actions—and the resultant happiness never leave her. If only they would never leave her. I shall be the one to make sure they do not leave her," and pray to the Three Jewels.

Think, "May this happiness and the causes of happiness she has obtained never leave her but increase more and more. May they increase so much that she attains temporarily the higher realms of gods and humans, and ultimately the lasting happiness of liberation and omniscience. If only these would increase. I shall be the one to make them increase," and pray to the Three Jewels that the causes of happiness and the happiness that results increase.

Meditate in this way, alternating analytic and resting meditation. This will lead to the certainty that although subject, object, and action may appear, they have no intrinsic existence.

In between sessions, at all times and in all situations, whenever beings are happy and well, instead of being jealous, train in being joyful. With regard to your Dharma brothers and sisters who are engaged in study, reflection, and meditation, think, "May they never be separated from the happiness and good qualities that come from these. May these never leave them but go on increasing more and more; oh, that these things may never leave them." If you meditate on sympathetic joy like this, there can never be any loss or decline in your own study, reflection, and meditation.

As the child of one's mother, it is one's duty to do everything to make her happy. So once you have the thought "All sentient beings are my mothers, and I am their child," if they do manage to achieve some happiness on their own without your having to do anything about it, be glad. Meditating like this, there is no way you can go on and on being jealous.

II. AROUSING BODHICHITTA, THE MIND OF SUPREME ENLIGHTENMENT

Arousing bodhichitta comes under three headings: (1) its essence; (2) its classification; and (3) how to arouse bodhichitta.

(A) ESSENCE

Arousing the bodhichitta has two aspects or points. The regent Maitreya says:

> Bodhichitta is the wish to attain perfect buddhahood for the benefit of others.[182]

The first aspect, or point, is to focus on sentient beings with compassion, thinking how all beings may be parted from both suffering and the causes of suffering.

The second aspect, or point, is to focus on complete enlightenment with wisdom, thinking how to attain the precious level of perfect buddhahood, which is free from both suffering and the causes of suffering.

Neither of these two aspects should be lacking. If we think of freeing sentient beings from suffering without focusing on the wish to attain buddhahood, this is only compassion; if we think of attaining buddhahood without having focused on suffering, this is only love. So we must have both aspects or points.

(B) CLASSIFICATION

1. Classification Based on the Three Degrees of Courage

The classification of the arousing of bodhichitta based on the three degrees of courage applies not to the first aspect, the compassion that focuses on sentient beings, but to the second, as follows.

The wish "I shall accomplish buddhahood first" is known as "arousing bodhichitta with the great wish," or "the king's way of arousing bodhichitta."

The wish "Sentient beings and I will attain buddhahood at the same time: I shall not go first, leaving beings behind, but we will accomplish buddhahood together" is "the boatman's way of arousing bodhichitta," or "arousing bodhichitta with sacred wisdom."

"Throughout time without beginning I have acted out of a desire to achieve my own selfish ends, and as a result I have wandered until now. Even now, if I continue to do the same, I shall have to go on wandering, endlessly. So now, whatever happens to me, I shall first set all beings on the level of perfect buddhahood, and then after that, whether I attain buddhahood or not does not matter." When we think like this, we subdue the demon of our self-centeredness with the precious bodhichitta. This wish for other beings to attain buddhahood is known as "the arousing of bodhichitta beyond compare," or "the shepherd's way of arousing bodhichitta."

These similes are simple to understand. Accordingly, a person of ordinary faculties will attain buddhahood in thirty-three measureless kalpas, one of higher faculties in seven, and someone of very sharp faculties in three.

2. Classification According to the Bodhisattva Levels

On the paths of accumulating and joining, arousing bodhichitta is known as "arousing bodhichitta with earnest aspiration" because even though the genuine relative bodhichitta may arise within the mind, apart from having an abstract notion or gaining just a taste of it, the absolute bodhichitta is not directly realized. Hence it is known as "arousing bodhichitta with earnest aspiration."

From the first Bodhisattva level up to and including the seventh, it is called "arousing bodhichitta through excellent and pure intention." In meditation the emotional consciousness is brought to cessation, and in the postmeditation, even though subtle grasping at an "I" may arise, it does not become an obstacle on the path, and so this is called "arousing bodhichitta through excellent and pure intention."

On the three pure levels, arousing the bodhichitta is known as "arousing fully matured bodhichitta." This is because all the prayers of aspiration we made earlier when we were on the paths of accumulating and joining are now fulfilled, just like the harvest ripening in autumn, and it is at this time that we accomplish vast waves of benefit for others.

On the level of buddhahood, what is called "arousing bodhichitta free from all obscurations" refers to the fact that the two obscurations and the habitual tendencies have all been eliminated. The promise we formerly made in relative bodhichitta, "until we reach the heart of enlightenment," no longer applies, but we still refer to "arousing bodhichitta" because absolute bodhichitta has been attained, complete and undiminishing, and this marks the beginning of the enlightened mind directed toward limitless numbers of other sentient beings.

Again, on the paths of accumulating and joining, while we may well arouse perfectly pure relative bodhichitta, as regards the absolute bodhichitta, on the path of accumulating we gain some understanding of it, and on the path of joining we experience a taste of it. At this stage, of the view reached by direct perception and the view derived through inference, this is the view derived through inference, and so we refer to "arousing bodhichitta with earnest aspiration."

The path of joining culminates in "supreme mundane realization" and what is termed the "instant primal wisdom of supreme mundane realization on the path of joining" joins us to the path of seeing, for the very next instant after it arises in the mind *is* the path of seeing. In the case of it taking three measureless kalpas to accomplish buddhahood, from the path of accumulating up until the path of seeing will require one measureless kalpa.

On the path of seeing is the first Bodhisattva level, called Perfect Joy, where the truth of dharmata is seen. Here, primal wisdom is realized directly, accomplishing our own benefit, and for the benefit of others we master meditative concentration and the power of miraculous transformation. By gaining miraculous powers such as expanding an instant into a kalpa and reducing a kalpa to an instant, we bring vast benefit to beings, and this is why this level is called Perfect Joy.

On the seven impure levels like this one, emotional obscurations are directly eliminated and conceptual obscurations are indirectly weakened. They are termed the seven impure levels because up to and including the seventh level the emotional consciousness is not eliminated. During the state of postmeditation, subtle self-centered thoughts may arise, but they are naturally purified or dissolved, and so selfish intentions are never acted out. This is why we talk about the "excellent and pure intention."

Next, what are termed the "three pure levels" are so called because the buddhafield and the activities are pure. On these three pure levels, emotional obscurations have already been completely eliminated from the seventh level onward, and it is during the course of these three levels that all the gross and subtle conceptual obscurations are removed. Then at the very end of the tenth level, the obscurations of habitual tendencies are also eliminated without a trace. This is why the bodhichitta on the three pure levels is called "fully matured."

At this point, as the first instant the bodhichitta completely eliminates the obscurations of habitual tendencies with the antidote of vajralike primal wisdom, and as the second instant it becomes the primal wisdom of omniscience. This is "arousing bodhichitta free from all obscurations." Here the term "instant" is used to signify not two points in time but rather two different ways of acting on the object.

The way our tradition interprets the two obscurations follows the *Sublime Continuum*:

> All thoughts such as miserliness and so on
> Are held to be emotional obscurations.
> All thoughts of "subject," "object," and "action"
> Are held to be conceptual obscurations.

We accept that negative emotions such as attachment are the emotional obscurations, and that considering subject, object, and action to be true constitutes the conceptual obscurations. However, the new schools assert that the emotional obscurations and the conceptual obscurations share a common ground, because considering things to truly exist is held to be an emotional obscuration. They maintain that as the emotional obscurations get more and more subtle, they become the conceptual obscurations, and as these get subtler still, they become the obscurations of habitual tendencies. They compare them to the smell of musk, which lingers in a container in which it has been kept, growing gradually fainter and fainter.

3. Classification According to the Nature of Bodhichitta

When we classify the arousing of bodhichitta according to its nature, it falls into two: relative bodhichitta and absolute bodhichitta. It is said:

> Divided into relative and absolute,
> Bodhichitta is of two kinds.

Relative bodhichitta is aroused and dissolves with our thoughts, whereas absolute bodhichitta is that state of primal wisdom in which all the movements that are conceptual thought have subsided into the absolute space.

Relative bodhichitta has two aspects: intention and application. Bodhichitta in intention is to pledge ourselves to the result. Bodhichitta in application is to pledge ourselves to the cause, that is, to wish to accomplish the six transcendent perfections that are the cause or means for attaining that result. Each of these two pledges, my teacher said, must be backed by a second iron resolution.

(C) HOW TO AROUSE BODHICHITTA

To make the relative bodhichitta arise requires a ritual. Although in the Secret Mantrayana it is taught that the absolute bodhichitta can arise by means of a ritual, this is not genuine absolute bodhichitta but merely making aspiration the path. Genuine absolute bodhichitta can only arise through the power of meditation, relying on three supreme factors. The *Ornament of the Mahayana Sutras* explains these as follows:

> The perfect Buddhas have been gladdened,
> The accumulations of merit and wisdom perfectly gathered,
> Primal wisdom free from conceptual thought regarding phenomena arises,
> This is why they are stated to be supreme.

The "supreme tutors" are both outer and inner. The outer tutors are the many masters and fully enlightened Buddhas whom we, from the path of accumulating up until the path of seeing, do our best to please and to avoid disappointing. The inner tutors are compassion and wisdom, which hold and support us.

The "supreme practice" is the gathering of the accumulations: the "apparent" accumulation of merit with concepts, and the "nonapparent" accumulation of wisdom without concepts.

The "supreme realization" occurs when, as the climax to these, the nonconceptual primal wisdom arises: it is the realization of the wisdom of the path of seeing.

Genuine absolute bodhichitta, then, has to arise through the power of meditation. In other words, it has to arise by relying on these three: the supreme tutors, supreme practice, and supreme realization.

As for relative bodhichitta, it must be aroused with the support of a ritual, and whether we employ the ritual of the Madhyamika or Profound View tradition or that of the Chittamatra or Vast Activity tradition, there are three parts: (1) the preliminary preparation; (2) the main part, the vow itself; and (3) the conclusion, rejoicing on the part of ourselves and others.

(1) The Preparation

The preliminary preparation consists of gathering the accumulations, training the mind, and, in addition—following the approach of Shantideva—giving away the three possessions.[183]

While the Madhyamikas hold that bodhichitta arises through gathering the accumulations, the Chittamatrins assert that it arises from a perfectly clear mind.[184] Here we accumulate merit and wisdom by offering the seven branches, after which we train the mind in the four boundless qualities. Then comes giving away the three possessions. This is both a Chö practice, because it cuts through our clinging to the three possessions, and, as taught here, a form of mind training.

(2) The Main Part: The Actual Vow

Before beginning the prayer "Think of me . . . ," meditate as you did before, thinking, "Wherever there is space it is filled with sentient beings," and so on, recognizing beings as your mothers, remembering their kindness, wishing to repay their kindness, and focusing with compassion on beings and with wisdom on perfect enlightenment, ensuring that neither of these last two is in any way lacking. In short, you should think, "So that all beings may be free from suffering and its causes, and attain the precious level of perfect buddhahood, I will arouse the supreme bodhichitta in intention. And for the bodhichitta in application I shall do my utmost to train in the six transcendent perfections."

Then begin by reciting three times:

> All you Buddhas who dwell in the ten directions
> All you Bodhisattvas on the ten levels,
> All you great teachers, the vajra holders,
> Think of me, I pray,

praying that the Buddhas, the Bodhisattvas, and the spiritual teachers, great vajra holders, turn their minds toward you. Next, lay the ground, which is to take refuge with the three special features,[185] reciting three times:

> Until the essence of enlightenment is reached,
> I go for refuge to the Buddhas,
> Also I take refuge in the Doctrine
> And all the host of Bodhisattvas.[186]

These two form the preparation. The main part consists of taking the vow three times:

> Just as all the Buddhas of the past
> Embraced the awakened attitude of mind
> And in the precepts of the Bodhisattvas
> Step by step abode and trained,
>
> Just so, and for the benefit of beings,
> I will also have this attitude of mind,
> And in those precepts, step by step,
> I will abide and train myself.[187]

The first two lines refer to how the Buddhas and Bodhisattvas formerly aroused the bodhichitta of intention, and the second two lines describe how they aroused the bodhichitta of application. This verse therefore indicates who it is whose example we are following.

Then, with the second verse, you should think, "Now I too will follow in the footsteps of the Buddhas and Bodhisattvas: I will arouse the bodhichitta of intention, and I will do my best to train progressively in the six transcendent perfections, the cause of supreme enlightenment."

Recite these verses three times, and at the end of the third recitation imagine that the Buddhas and Bodhisattvas exclaim, "It is the way!" and that you reply, "Yes, how wonderful!" at which point the vow is established in your mind and you know that you have received it. As for the exact point when we receive the vow, it is said, "The point when you receive it is at the conclusion of the third recitation." So the moment you have finished the third recitation, the bodhichitta is born in you.

(3) *The Conclusion*

The conclusion consists of rejoicing on the part of oneself and of others:

> Today my life has given fruit.
> This human state has now been well assumed.
> Today I take my birth in Buddha's line
> And have become the Buddhas' child and heir.[188]

As you recite this (and the following verses), reflect and rejoice on your own behalf: "Today I have made this support, the human body that I have obtained, fruitful and meaningful. Why? Because now this human existence I have is not badly obtained but well obtained. How? Today the nature of the Buddhas—the jewel-like bodhichitta—has been born within my mind, and I have become a child of the Buddhas: the physical representative of their line, keeper of the treasure of their speech, and holder of the secrets of their mind. And as their child who will take care of all remaining beings who need to be benefited, I have become a Bodhisattva."

> In every way, then, I will undertake
> Activities befitting such a rank.
> And I will do no act to mar
> Or compromise this high and faultless lineage.[189]

"From now on, whatever happens, even if my life is in danger, I shall be without the fault of wanting anything for myself; I shall have only the noble qualities befitting this family, like a pure and perfect queen who always remains loyal to her king. I must act without ever staining this family by marring it with evil, selfish thoughts, and I must undertake deeds that befit this sacred family, the activities of a Bodhisattva."

> For I am like a blind man who has found
> A precious gem within a mound of filth.
> Exactly so, as if by some strange chance,
> The enlightened mind has come to birth in me.[190]

"How, I wonder, has this bodhichitta come to be born in me? It is as if I were a blind man who finds a precious jewel in a heap of rubbish. It is as if by some coincidence, some good fortune, that this gemlike bodhichitta has arisen in my mind."

Inciting others to rejoice:

> And so, within the sight of all protectors,
> I summon every being, calling them to buddhahood—
> And till that state is reached, to every earthly joy.
> May gods and demigods, and all the rest, rejoice.[191]

As you recite this, reflect as follows: "Today, at __o'clock on the __th of the month, in the year____, in the presence of all the protectors—the Buddhas and Bodhisattvas—I have invited all beings to the temporary happiness of gods and humans, and to the ultimate bliss of perfect buddhahood. So rejoice, all you gods and asuras, humans and nonhumans, all you beings throughout the six realms."

Then imagine that you hear all the gods from the mountain gods, tree gods, and gods of the groves up to the gods of the Akanishtha heaven, the Unexcelled, proclaim one by one: "In such and such a place, so and so has said that they will set us all temporarily on the level of gods and humans, and ultimately on the level of perfect buddhahood, so let us rejoice." Later, if you are ever tempted to commit some downfall or other, these words will serve to remind you of a sense of shame and decency.

Once we have aroused the supreme bodhichitta in this way, and as long as we do not commit the root downfall of giving up the bodhichitta, our name will have changed, and we will be called Bodhisattvas, children of the Buddhas.[192] And our whole raison d'être will have changed, and we will become worthy of the homage and offerings not only of all beings, including the gods and Brahma, but even of our teacher, the Lord Buddha. The Bodhisattva Vajrapani will be always at our side, and all the guardians of virtue, such as Brahma, the gods of the pure celestial abodes,[193] the seventy glorious protectors, and all the rest, will guard and protect us. Every wonderful quality will be ours, such as the power to relieve illness and poverty wherever we set foot.

This bodhichitta may be easy enough to arouse, but it is quite difficult for it really to be born in our being, and this is why we must meditate constantly and earnestly on the four boundless qualities, or on love and compassion, or simply on compassion. Why such a need? If we break our promise, it is not as though we are deceiving the five or six people who are our preceptor and instructors, as is the case when we do not keep the pratimoksha vows. If our bodhichitta fails, then all four "black dharmas" will occur in our minds at once: in deceiving those who are worthy of respect we deceive the Buddhas and Bodhisattvas, every single one of them; and in cheating beings, it is each and every sentient being that we are cheating. In short, we are duping both samsara and nirvana, and so we are committing an extremely heavy negative action.

❖ The Benefits of Bodhichitta

> Have it, and it is all that's needed to attain buddhahood
> Without it, all chance of attaining buddhahood is ruined:
> May this unfailing seed for attaining buddhahood,
> The real supreme bodhichitta, arise within us.

To have bodhichitta is quite sufficient on its own to attain buddhahood, but without it, nothing is of any use. The seed that is referred to here has a "naturally existing potential" and a "developable potential." The former is the primal wisdom of the Buddha nature that is present within the mind of each and every sentient being. The developable potential is the relative bodhichitta. The naturally existing potential is the cause for attaining buddhahood, and the developable potential is the contributory condition, and therefore these two are like a seed.

When the thought of bodhichitta arises in the mind, as explained above, it brings three benefits:

- our name and purpose change;
- all our sources of good will embody the Mahayana, bearing fruit and growing unceasingly; and
- they will be far superior to all positive actions done without bodhichitta, where the happy results are experienced only once and then exhausted, like the plantain tree that bears fruit once and then dies.

To give some examples:

1. Even though you offer nothing more than a single butter lamp, if you do so while directing your mind toward the state of buddhahood, then your merits will go on and on increasing, to equal the number of great qualities of the Buddhas above and the number of beings below.

2. If the precious bodhichitta has arisen in the mind of someone who has accumulated negative acts with a definite outcome, like one of the crimes with immediate retribution, the person will suffer no more than a flash experience of the lower realms.[194] Negative actions of uncertain outcome, and in fact all other negative acts, like killing people and slaughtering their horses, or burning down houses and the people inside, are erased the instant that bodhichitta arises in the mind, like dry grass consumed in the fires at the end of time.

3. As a result the obscurations of karma and negative emotions are eradicated, and the conceptual obscurations are completely banished.

Benefits such as these are described in detail in the *Avatamsaka Sutra*, at medium length in the first chapter of the *Way of the Bodhisattva*, and briefly summarized in this verse from the *Prayer of Maitreya*:

Turning us from the road to the lower realms,
It shows us the road to the higher realms
And leads to where there is no old age and death:
To this bodhichitta, in homage I bow.

If we remind ourselves constantly and in all situations of the benefits of bodhichitta, our bodhichitta will never degenerate, and root downfalls and the like will never occur. How should we do this? We should remind ourselves of this before beginning and again at the end, before rejoicing on behalf of ourselves and others.

III. TRAINING IN THE BODHICHITTA PRECEPTS

We now come to the methods for preventing this bodhichitta from declining once it has arisen and for making it grow more and more. These entail training in the precepts of the bodhichitta of aspiration and training in the precepts of the bodhichitta of application.

1. Training in the Precepts of the Bodhichitta of Aspiration

The method for preventing the bodhichitta from declining once it has arisen is the bodhichitta of aspiration. There are two causes that make bodhichitta decline: a self-centered attitude and its partner, anger. These two are responsible for our bodhichitta waning and failing to increase. How do they make it decline? When either of the two aspects of the bodhichitta of aspiration fails, it is as if the roots of a tree have been cut: the branches are all drained of their strength and wilt. Avoiding the branch downfalls will not help once you have fully committed a root downfall. Once the root is damaged, it is difficult to repair, whereas if the branches are damaged, it is easy to restore them.

So how can the two aspects of bodhichitta be damaged? By forsaking sentient beings and by abandoning omniscience.

(A) FORSAKING SENTIENT BEINGS

Whenever someone wrongs us, for example, by murdering our father, or even if we simply provoke someone we dislike, saying, "*What* did you say?" then our ingrained attitude of self-centeredness is aroused and we fly into a fit of rage. When this happens, we are forsaking one another, and this is how our self-centeredness and anger cause "focusing on sentient beings with compassion" to decline. Imagine binding a lot of sticks together tightly in a bundle, and then pulling one out. All the others automatically fall loose. Even if we only forsake one sentient being and do not forsake the others, it will not do any good, for we will have committed a root downfall.

(B) ABANDONING OMNISCIENCE

Abandoning omniscience can be illustrated with a single example, that of generosity. The objects Bodhisattvas give when practicing generosity are their head and arms and legs; the recipients are all sentient beings; the duration is for as long as samsara endures; and the number of times they give their head and arms and legs to each individual being is as incalculable as the number of atoms in the universe. Bodhisattvas have to practice discipline and each of the other transcendent perfections in exactly the same way. If our teacher the Buddha, before the Bodhi tree, could give away his head and arms and legs so that they surpassed the number of atoms in the whole world, one hardly need mention the extent to which he had trained in all the six transcendent perfections. When we follow in his footsteps and accumulate merit and wisdom, then the obstacles created by Mara while we are on the paths of accumulating and joining can cause us to lose heart, and we might think, "I will never be able to accomplish such a great task. Wouldn't it be better for me to follow the path of the Shravakas or Pratyekabuddhas and try to attain the state of Arhat?" When we think like this, we are abandoning omniscience, because we have not mastered the view of all phenomena as magical illusions, which is realized on the path of seeing.

◊ The Dangers of Self-Centeredness

Furthermore, from the outset on the paths of accumulating and joining we have thought and acted for our own selfish ends, and it is these self-centered considerations that make us lose both the pratimoksha and Bodhisattva vows of the sutra system. Equally our impairment of the Mantrayana vows, when we fall into conflict with the master or our vajra brothers and sisters, is entirely due to this thinking and acting for our own selfish benefit. This is why we need to bear in mind the disadvantages of self-centeredness and the benefits of the gemlike bodhichitta, as explained above.

Shantideva sums this up:

Is there need for lengthy explanation?
Childish beings look out for themselves,
While Buddhas labor for the good of others:
See the difference that divides them.[195]

The Capable Ones, perfectly enlightened Buddhas who have vanquished the maras, who possess all the qualities of realization and have gone beyond samsara and nirvana, attain this state of perfect buddhahood by striving for the benefit of others. The childish have from time without beginning acted solely in their own interests, those of the so-called I. As long as they continue to work for their own benefit, for this "I," they will go around and around in samsara, endlessly. So if there is any happiness and well-being in samsara and nirvana, it all stems from the benefits of helping others and of bodhichitta. Chandrakirti explains:

The Shravakas and Pratyekabuddhas are born from the Mighty Sage,
And Buddhas take their birth from Bodhisattva heroes.
Compassion, nonduality, the wish for buddhahood for others' sake
Are causes of the children of the Conqueror.[196]

All the suffering in this life and the next, all the suffering, gross and subtle, of the three worlds of samsara, is due to this thinking and acting to achieve our own ends. So, this self-centeredness richly deserves to be given the name "demon." If a *dri*[197] that will not give milk can cause its owner to curse, putting all the blame on a demon, then surely no less a demon is this attitude of self-interest that cuts us off from all the temporary qualities of the Bodhisattva levels and all the ultimate qualities of the result of omniscience. And as bodhichitta is what drives it out, it is called "the ritual for exorcising the demon."

How is this demon to be exorcised?

1. By considering others as equal to oneself
2. By exchanging oneself and others
3. By considering others more important than oneself

When we train our mind in these three, the bodhichitta will not decline, and we are able to banish this demon of self-obsession.

1.1 Considering Others as Equal to Oneself

Throughout time without beginning we have never looked upon ourselves and others as equal; we have always been attached to ourselves and everything concerning us and have loathed our enemies and anything to do with them. So now we need to give up our attachment to our self and our side, and give up our aversion to others and their side. Both these are due to our self-centered thoughts and actions, so now that we have realized the fault in this we must refuse to behave as before and bring ourselves and others together to make them into one family.

How do we meditate on this? Think, "Sentient beings fill the whole of space; each one of them is my mother. I am her child. Because she is my one mother and I am her only child, the well-being of both of us, mother and child, is one and the same." When you reflect like this, your self-centered attitude will disappear and be stilled.

◊ Achieving Happiness Together

"All beings are my family. Both they and I are the same in wanting happiness; we are the same in not wanting suffering." With great love, think that you will accomplish happiness for yourself and all beings together. And as much as you think of achieving happiness together, so must you act to achieve happiness together.

"Although what all beings want is happiness, they do not know that the sources of happiness are positive actions and following the correct path. They do not have a spiritual friend to show them the right way to act, and even if they did, they would not follow his instructions. But I am supposed to be a practitioner, someone who has met a spiritual friend, who has encountered the teachings of the Mahayana, who is always in the company of a master—the spiritual friend who knows the crucial points of what to do or not to do—and who is surrounded by virtuous friends: I should be bringing about the happiness of all sentient beings."

Meditate therefore on the four links:

- the link of aspiration: "May all sentient beings have happiness, from the happiness of the higher realms of gods and humans up to the bliss of perfect buddhahood, and may they have the causes that result in such happiness: faith, determination to be free, and the precious bodhichitta.

May they possess both the causes of happiness and the happiness that results";
- the link of the wish: "If only they could possess them";
- the link of the commitment: "I shall be the one to ensure that they do"; and
- prayer, praying to the Three Jewels (the fourth link).

Meditate on these three links and prayer, focusing first on the higher realms and so on (that is, happiness as the result), and then on faith and so on (that is, the causes of happiness). And say to yourself, "From this day on, both in my thoughts and in my actions I must help them all equally. As much as I think about us all attaining the level of buddhahood together, I must do everything I can to achieve this."

❖ Dispelling Suffering Together

We also need to dispel suffering: "Wherever there is space, it is filled with sentient beings, and wherever there are sentient beings, they are immersed in karmic perceptions and suffering. Of all these beings, who have been tormented throughout time without beginning by karmic perceptions and suffering, there are none who have not been my mother, my father, and so on. And among them, there is not a single one who has not been the dearest to my heart, my own mother. She has not been my mother just this once; the number of times she has been my mother is inconceivable, and were we to take this whole earth and use it to roll balls the size of juniper berries, we would run out of earth before there was any end to the number of times one sentient being had been the mother of another. And all the while, as our mothers, they devoted themselves exclusively to caring for us with kindness."

Then remember their kindness while they have been your mothers: first, the kindness of producing your body; second, the kindness of giving you life; third, the kindness of providing all your material needs; and fourth, the kindness of teaching you the ways of the world.

Next arouse the wish to repay that kindness. All that these beings want is happiness and yet they do not realize that its very causes are positive actions and following the correct path. They do not have a teacher, and they would not properly carry out what a spiritual friend told them anyway. They do not have any happiness, neither the happiness of the higher realms of gods and humans nor the bliss of perfect buddhahood. They do not want suffering, and yet they are harmed directly by suffering—the three sufferings of the three worlds of samsara—and indirectly by the causes of suffering—karma and negative emotions.

Focusing on these beings and seeing them all as equal in that they are our mothers, meditate on impartiality. Focusing on their lack of happiness and wishing for them both happiness and its causes, meditate on love. Focusing on their having both suffering and its causes and wishing for them freedom from both suffering and its causes, meditate on compassion. Since we are mother and child, and children should be concerned for their mothers' well-being, meditate on sympathetic joy: when mother beings do manage to achieve some happiness for themselves without our needing to get involved, how could we possibly be jealous and fail to rejoice? Be joyful, considering how delighted they are, how much they need it, and how they cannot do without it.

You should meditate on the four boundless qualities like this both during meditation and in the postmeditation period and include each of the stages, recognizing beings as our mothers, remembering their kindness, and the rest.

Reflect now as follows: "Beings' suffering is my suffering. When I have a headache, for example, it is the suffering of the gods. When I get a sore throat, it is the suffering of the asuras. If I have a sharp pain in my heart, it is the suffering of human beings. An ache in my stomach or below is the suffering of beings in the three lower realms. I must dispel their suffering, just as my hands should act to remove a pain in my foot. What sentient beings long for is happiness; they do not want to suffer. But their deepest desires and their actions are completely at odds, and they are like blind people wandering without a guide in a vast, deserted plain. I have met a Mahayana master and the Mahayana teachings, and I know what is profitable and what is detrimental. So, may all beings be freed from suffering and its causes. If only they were free from them. May I be the one to set them free. I pray to the Buddha, Dharma, and Sangha that they find freedom."

As much as you think in this way about dispelling the suffering of yourself and others together, that much must you act to dispel your and others' suffering together. For whenever a sentient being has even a headache, a Bodhisattva should feel pain in his or her mind.

Here is an example of how to put equalizing into action. Two of us have to go out in the snow; I have a pair of boots, the other person does not. If we each put on one boot, we will be able to proceed. Two of our feet will suffer together, and two will be comfortable together.

So we must actually bring about the happiness of sentient beings. We must remove their suffering. When they are happy on their own account without your needing to do anything, meditate on joy. Rejoice when beings are experiencing the happiness that results from their past actions without your having to make any effort yourself—rejoice as if it were your youngest child enjoying the happiness of the higher realms, your middle child experiencing the happiness of a Shravaka or Pratyekabuddha, and your eldest child experiencing the bliss of buddhahood. Rejoice when they obtain the causes of happiness—faith and so on. In your thoughts, rejoice: "If only this kind of happiness and bliss could never be spoiled or lost, if only it would go on and on increasing." And in your actions too, do all you can to achieve happiness together.

If you practice this in detail, meditate on all the four boundless qualities; if more briefly, on love and compassion or else simply on compassion, wishing to free beings from suffering. All this is relative bodhichitta. The absolute bodhichitta is the certainty and conviction we arrive at through repeated analysis that although subject, object, and action may appear, they are devoid of any intrinsic existence.

To sum up, as Apu Rinpoche used to say:

When there's happiness, stick together like brightly colored magpies.
When there's misery, stick together like dark ravens.
Seek out one another's happiness together;
Get rid of one another's suffering together.

While we are on the path, this practice of considering others as equal to oneself is the method for treating ourselves and others as equal both in our thoughts and in our actions. At the moment of fruition, it is the method for realizing the sameness of all the phenomena of self and others: ourselves and all others are the same from the point of view of emptiness, dharmata. We are the same from the point of view of appearances arising from emptiness. We are the same on the level of relative appearances. We are the same from the point of view of the union of appearance and emptiness. This is the meditation on equality or sameness according to the sutra tradition.

1.2 Exchanging Oneself and Others

Once we have become thoroughly familiar with the equality of oneself and others, we should meditate on bodhichitta by exchanging oneself and others.

Here is what Apu used to say about exchanging oneself and others: "Imagine that you were one of a group of herdsmen, with only a single raincoat between you. To put yourself in the middle and let the others huddle under the raincoat would be like the stage of considering others as equal to oneself. To make sure that the raincoat covered everybody else first, so that you got left out in the rain, would be like the stage of exchanging oneself and others."

Indeed, if there is a shortcoming in the meditation of wishing to achieve happiness together and to remove suffering together, it is that we are meditating on ourselves as if we were at the center of things. So now we have to drive out this demon of self-grasping, and when we reflect on exchanging ourselves and others, this is rightly called a "ritual for exorcising the demon."

For this meditation, first of all begin by going thoroughly through the practices of recognizing beings as your mothers, appreciating their kindness, and thinking of repaying their kindness.

Now, this mother of ours may have nothing to wear herself, but if she finds a scrap of clothing, she gives it to her child. She may have no food, but if she finds even a little of something good to eat, she gives it to her child. All her money and possessions she gives unstintingly to her child, and even if she were to see him enthroned as a Universal Ruler, she would never reckon this was good enough but surround the child with anything and everything for his happiness and comfort. Every kind of suffering—misery, negative actions, and spiteful rumors—our mother takes upon herself. All loss and defeat she takes upon herself; all gain and victory she gives to her child. So it is now our turn, as her child, to get rid of our old mother's suffering, and we should therefore do the practice of "taking with great compassion."

◊ Taking with Great Compassion

Ask yourself, "Is this mother of mine happy? Does she suffer?" The answer is that she is not happy, and she is always suffering, because she is propelled along by the sufferings of this life—birth, old age, sickness, and death; the suffering of the intermediate state provides the connection; and the suffering of rebirth and the next life waits to greet her. She is tormented continuously by the three sufferings, their causes—attachment, aversion, and bewilderment—and the ten unvirtuous actions that these causes give rise to. So pray, "May she be free from all these sufferings and their causes. If only she were free. I shall be the one to free her." And pray to the Buddha, Dharma, and Sangha that she might be freed from suffering and the causes of suffering, using the following prayers that our wishes might be fulfilled: "Woe is me! Compassionate Three Jewels . . . ," "To the Master and Buddhas, guardians of wandering beings . . . ," "Courageous One, you who possess the power of compassion . . ."*

Yet, like the transference of consciousness done from a distance, all this may not be of very much help. So pray: "May my kind mother's sufferings and their causes land on me, at this very moment, as quickly as possible, right here where I am, here where I'm sitting. If only they would land on me. May I be the one to make them land on me. I pray to you, Buddha, Dharma, and Sangha, my unfailing sources of refuge, that they do land on me. Show me now all the force of your compassion and power.

"May all my happiness ripen within the mind of this mother who is so kind, right now, as quickly as possible, wherever she is, wherever she's sitting, from the little happiness I have at present, through the temporary happiness of the Bodhisattvas, right up to the ultimate bliss of perfect buddhahood. If only it could ripen in her. May I be the one to make it ripen in her. I pray to the Three Jewels that it may all ripen in her."

From time to time, in order to make it easier to get used to this idea, "mount her sufferings upon your breath." Imagine that this old mother of yours breathes out her suffering and its causes in the form of a stream of black vapor, and at the same time you inhale and it enters through your nostrils, so that now you have her suffering and its causes and she is freed of it all, just like the sun emerging from an eclipse.

Reflect like this again and again, thinking, "I must take my mother's suffering upon myself: whatever I think, I must think about taking on my mother's suffering, and whatever I do, I must act in order to remove her suffering."

---

*See pages 289–90.

◊ Giving with Great Love

We come now to the practice of "giving with great love." Think, "May my mother possess every happiness, from that of the higher realms right up to the lasting happiness of liberation and omniscience. If only she could have it. May I be the one to enable her to have it." And pray that she may have every happiness.

Think, "May she have the causes of happiness—faith, determination to be free, and the precious bodhichitta. If only she had them. May I be the one to enable her to have them." Then pray that she may have the causes of happiness.

Yet this on its own may not help much. Every happiness and every cause of happiness, that is, all your physical and mental happiness, the happiness of the higher realms up to the lasting happiness of liberation and omniscience, and their three causes—faith, determination to be free, and the precious bodhichitta—must be given to this elderly mother of yours, must be dedicated to her. So imagine your mother receiving this gift from her child, and in order to do this mount the happiness upon your breath. Imagine that as you exhale, your longevity, merit, good fortune, influence, body and wealth, your happiness and well-being, and every source and kind of happiness are all expelled through your nostrils in the form of a stream of white vapor like incense smoke[198] and that simultaneously your mother inhales it as she breathes in. Now you are parted from your happiness and its causes, and your elderly mother has them all, receiving them as if she has put on a new set of clothes.

As much as you think about bringing your old mother happiness and its causes, so you must put it into practice and provide her with even the smallest thing to make her happy.

◊ Universalizing the Practice

Next, gradually extend your meditation on love to your father, your brothers, sisters, and so on. Wish that they may possess happiness, from the temporary happiness of the higher realms up to the ultimate and lasting happiness of liberation and omniscience, praying, "May they possess its causes—faith, determination to be free, and the precious bodhichitta," and so on, and meditate on giving them all your body, possessions, and sources of good for the future.

* * *

At the end of the session, wish, "May all the physical pains of beings, who pervade the whole of space, all the anguish in their minds, all the obstacles to their wishes, all their negative actions and downfalls, and all their obscurations ripen within my being this very instant, as quickly as possible," and so on, applying the three links and the prayer to the Three Jewels. Then inhale all beings' negative actions and downfalls through your nostrils in the form of black vapor. Imagine that they melt and dissolve into the demon of self-cherishing inside your heart, like dye soaking into wool, and that you possess both their suffering and its causes.

Consider how dear all these sentient beings are, see how precious they are to you, what a deep empathy you feel with them, see how fond you are of them, how necessary they are, how indispensable. After that, to make it easier to get used to this notion, do the practice of mounting upon the breath as before.

Meditate on sympathetic joy. With regard to your attitude, we are all mother and child; it is impossible for a child to be jealous of its mother being happy, so rejoice. From the point of view of actual practice, it is out of the question to act out of jealousy and make others suffer rather than making them happy, so you must do all you can to bring about their happiness.

In all our thoughts and deeds for achieving our own ends lies the reason for not cherishing others, not regarding them as precious, feeling no empathy with them; in it lies our dislike for them and our disregard for them. This demon of planning and acting for our sole benefit is the demon we have to drive out.

After meditating on the three links ("May all sentient beings have happiness" and so on) and the link of prayer, imagine in addition that your longevity, merits, good fortune and influence, body and possessions, your happiness and well-being, and every kind and source of happiness you have, all of it you dedicate, you hand over, you give it all away to all beings: "May it be theirs," and so on. Again, mount this upon your breath. You should carry this out both in thought and in deed.

The root of "exchanging ourselves and others" can be summed up as offering gain and victory to sentient beings and taking loss and defeat for oneself.[199] This is the awakened mind of bodhichitta, and neither of its two aspects should be lacking. Taking with great compassion is the first aspect:

focusing with compassion on sentient beings. Giving with great love is the second aspect: focusing with wisdom on perfect enlightenment.

There are four kinds of exchanges taking place here.[200] First, there is the exchange of our way of apprehending things. When we say, "All sentient beings are me," it means that we should consider the three higher realms as being the upper part of our body and the three lower realms as being the lower part of our body: they are "me." Alternatively, when we say, "All sentient beings are my mother; I am their child," "all sentient beings are my mother" means that we should regard them as "mine."

Second, there is the exchange of what is cherished. We have given up our former attitude of cherishing ourselves, and we now consider all beings as dear, we regard them all as precious, we look on all of them fondly, we see them as necessary, we see them as indispensable.

Third, there is the exchange of happiness for suffering. Up until now, we kept all gain and victory exclusively for ourselves and reserved all loss and defeat for others. All the warmth we took for ourselves, and the bitter cold we gave to everyone else. But now, from this day on, we will offer all gain and victory to others, and take all loss and defeat upon ourselves. We will give other people all the warmth and keep all the cold for ourselves. In brief, we will give every kind of happiness and well-being to other beings and take all their sufferings upon ourselves. As before, we do this by mounting them on our breath.

This grasping at a self where there is no self, this grasping at an "I" where there is no "I" is quite senseless. Our mind is just a wanderer, a consciousness that has taken birth before as a god, or whatever. If we think about the origin of this body of ours, the positive and negative deeds we have done in our previous lives are the main cause, and the contributory condition is the consciousness inserting itself between our parents' sperm and ovum. So this mind is the mind of another, and this body is the body of others, and yet they are what we conceive of as "I." From time without beginning we have habituated ourselves to conceiving of this "I" as existing in the past, the present, and the future, and because of this we have tried to get for ourselves gain, praise, good reputation, and fame—the four advantageous aspects of the eight ordinary concerns—reserving all gain and victory for ourselves. We have given all loss and defeat to others, and we have steered loss, criticism, infamy, and obscurity—the four disadvantageous aspects of the eight ordinary concerns—toward others. As a result of this error we have been wandering in samsara up until the present.*

Now we see the error in seeking our own selfish ends and that it is not right to act in such a way. We understand that we are others, and that others are us, so we put ourselves in the place of others and consider others as ourselves. Now we cannot but give all gain and victory to others and take all loss and defeat onto ourselves. If we do this, then thanks to the kindness of these beings, in all our future lives we will obtain a human body with its eighteen freedoms and advantages and finally attain perfect buddhahood.

By habituating ourselves to this obsession with our selfish desires, we commit an error that has caused us to wander through our series of lives from time without beginning until now, and which will force us to go on wandering, endlessly. So contemplate the respective faults and advantages of cherishing oneself and cherishing others. Train yourself by making use of verses such as these:

> When happy, I dedicate my happiness to all:
> Let good and happiness fill the universe.
> When in pain, I will bear the suffering of others:
> Let the ocean of suffering run dry.

and

> Living beings, numerous as the sky is vast—
> May their suffering and emotions leave them and ripen in me.
> Let all my happiness and my merits, without exception,
> Go to mother beings, and may all attain buddhahood.

In all your everyday activities, whether eating, sleeping, walking, or sitting, you should train yourself with verses.

Here is another: "Three objects, three poisons, and three roots of virtue."[201] Whenever things like happiness and its causes, suffering and its causes, and especially breaches of samaya happen to you, you should not treat these as undesirable but know how to use the skillful means of the Bod-

---

*The eight ordinary concerns are more usually given as gain and loss, pleasure and pain, praise and criticism, and fame and infamy (or obscurity).

hisattva to carry everything onto the path. Again, when you are happy or do something that will cause happiness, as the essence of bodhichitta carry this onto the path and with great love practice *giving* your happiness and merits. When you are stricken by suffering or do something that will cause suffering, practice *taking* with great compassion and there will be no obstacle to the path to enlightenment. In this way, make every effort to apply the skillful means that transforms happiness and suffering into the essence of the path.

Furthermore, seeing that you are giving happiness and its causes to all beings, you should give away the four advantageous aspects of the eight ordinary concerns. And seeing that you are taking upon yourself their suffering and its causes, you should take upon yourself the four disadvantageous concerns.

◊ Countering Difficulties

Whenever you have any slight pain or suffering, even something as trivial as a headache, draw into it all the suffering of all beings in the three worlds of samsara and think, "May this headache of mine take the place of the suffering experienced by all beings. If I am ill, let it take the place of beings' illnesses; if I am in pain, let my pain take the place of beings' pain; if I am dying, let my dying take the place of that of sentient beings." This is how to deal with suffering itself.

When the causes of suffering occur, namely thoughts related to attachment, aversion and bewilderment, infuse them with bodhichitta and so give them meaning. First, think of a thought, attachment for example, and make it surface. Then say to yourself: "May this thought of mine arising from attachment, aversion, or bewilderment take the place of all the negative thoughts related to attachment and so on that motivate beings' negative actions and are the causes of their suffering. May all beings' thoughts arising from attachment ripen in me. May their thoughts arising from aversion and bewilderment take the place of these thoughts of mine. May they all ripen in me. May all sentient beings be freed from suffering and from its causes—attachment, aversion, and bewilderment—and may they all land on me."

With such words, put to proper use the suffering and causes of suffering of all beings and take them upon yourself, thinking, "Let my sickness take the place of their sickness; let my pain take the place of their pain; let my dying take the place of their dying; let my misery take the place of their misery."

◈ Making Connections

Any connection with a Bodhisattva is a meaningful one. Those who make a good connection will attain buddhahood in one lifetime, while even for those who make a bad connection, their wandering in samsara is bound to come to an end. For this reason, in addition to practicing "giving and taking" (*tonglen*) as explained above, you should give away the three possessions so as to provide all beings with the necessities for obtaining happiness and the conditions for removing suffering.

(A) GIVING AWAY ONE'S BODY

It is important to have the following aspiration: "All my bodies in this and former lives I have uselessly squandered, so now, from this day until ultimately I attain the level of perfect buddhahood, no matter what kind of body I take in the meanwhile, whether as great as Brahma or Indra or as tiny as an ant, and regardless of whether beings have a good connection with me based on faith and pure perception or a bad one because of attachment, aversion, or ignorance, for all those who see my form with their eyes, hear my voice with their ears, or even smell my rotting corpse, touch my body, or think of me, for all of them may this have the power to cure their sickness, to pacify the negative forces that possess them, and to ease their physical pain, their mental anguish, the frustration of their wishes; in short, may I be able to ease all their suffering in the three worlds of existence. And may I be able to still all the negative emotions—attachment, aversion, and bewilderment—and the negative actions these emotions provoke, all these things that cause their suffering."

In short, pray that you may be able to free these beings from suffering and the causes of suffering.

Again, make a prayer of aspiration that there arise in the minds of all those who see you, hear you, think of you, or touch you every happiness, from that of the higher realms of gods and humans right up to the bliss of perfect buddhahood, and the causes of that happiness—faith, determination to be free, and the precious bodhichitta.

(B) GIVING AWAY ONE'S WEALTH

The wealth too that you have had in the past has all been wasted and squandered to no useful purpose, so now pray as follows: "Now, from this day on, whether I am a humble beggar clutching his staff or owner of the whole treasury of space, whether I have many possessions or few, whether the connections beings have with my possessions through their six senses (seeing, hearing, and so on) are good (based on faith and pure vision) or bad (on account of attachment, aversion, or ignorance), may all these beings thereby have their suffering and the causes of their suffering allayed. May those who are sick be cured; may those who are possessed have their negative forces pacified; may all their physical pain be soothed and their mental anguish and the frustration of their wishes eased. May the causes of their suffering, thoughts related to attachment, aversion, and bewilderment, be stilled. May they obtain all happiness, from the happiness of the higher realms up to the bliss of buddhahood, and may its causes—faith, determination to be free, and the precious bodhichitta—be born in their minds."

Make a wish that your possessions may give liberation when seen, liberate when heard of, and liberate when touched. And invoke the truth of the Buddha, Dharma, and Sangha that this may happen.

(C) GIVING AWAY ONE'S MERIT

The same applies to your merits, sources of good for the future, gathered over the three times. As before, pray with the following aspiration and appeal to the truth of the Three Jewels: "May the connections I make with beings through their seeing my positive actions (or otherwise perceiving them through any of their six senses) all be meaningful, whether these connections are good (based on faith and pure perception) or bad (due to attachment, aversion, or ignorance), and whether these actions are the most minor positive acts that give rise to a little ordinary merit or the infinite untainted virtue of ultimate omniscience."

All this is the practice of exchanging oneself and others.

1.3 Considering Others More Important than Oneself

Once you have trained and accustomed yourself to exchanging yourself and others mentally, you need to consider others more important than yourself, actually putting this into practice.

Considering others more important than oneself is possible even for ordinary individuals, as was the case for the master Maitriyogi.* It comes about as a result of having trained the mind in relative bodhichitta. But the genuine ability to treat others as more important than oneself comes with the realization of the wisdom of the path of seeing and the simultaneous realization of the "four equalities:"

- realization of the equality of ourselves and others on the level of absolute truth, free from all concepts;
- realization of the equality of ourselves and others on the relative level, as simply like magical illusions;
- realization of the equality of Buddhas and beings; and
- realization of the equality of oneself and the Buddhas.

At this point we at last begin to be able to truly benefit others, for when someone can cut off our head and carry it away and we think of it as no different from a stone or clod of earth, we then have the capacity to make others more important than ourselves. As beginners, however, we have to practice thinking of others as more important than ourselves by training the mind in relative bodhichitta.

There are two ways to destroy ego-clinging, with skillful means and with wisdom.

First we have to destroy it with skillful means, cutting through our self-centeredness by equalizing ourselves and others, exchanging ourselves and others, and considering others more important than ourselves. Then, with the wisdom that realizes the absolute truth, which arises as a result of practicing these skillful means, it is uprooted and destroyed. We should therefore begin by firmly establishing the relative bodhichitta, meditating on it over and over again, and then train principally in the absolute bodhichitta. The former gets rid of self-centeredness by crushing it and the latter by uprooting it altogether.

This practice of bodhichitta should be quite sufficient for a single human lifetime, so it is important to know how to bring whatever happens to you, happiness or suffering, on the path. After all, no one is constantly happy or constantly unhappy: sometimes you are happy, sometimes you are unhappy;

---

*See WMPT page 228.

you suffer and are happy in turn. So when any happiness or suffering you go through becomes the path to enlightenment and suffering is not an obstacle to the path, you will be a Bodhisattva expert in skillful means. As a Bodhisattva, when you are happy, you should see it as nothing to be excited about; neither is it right to cling to the causes of happiness—faith, determination to be free, and the precious bodhichitta—when they arise in your mind. Indeed, since these may be consumed when you get angry, you should give them to sentient beings before this can happen.

As for suffering, whenever any kind of misfortune befalls you, such as being plagued by illnesses like leprosy or smallpox, falling under the influence of negative forces, or being paralyzed by a stroke, you should recognize, as in the refuge practice, that such things are the compassion of the Three Jewels and reflect as follows:

"Because of the compassion of the Three Jewels, the karma that I am due to experience in my future lives as the result of the negative actions that I have accumulated in all my births throughout my whole series of lives is maturing now, in this life. And with it, all the suffering experienced by all beings who fill the entire expanse of space is being transferred to me alone."

Whenever causes of suffering—attachment, aversion, and so on—arise in your mind, think, "This is a warning, thanks to the Three Jewels' compassion. So may this attachment or aversion take the place of all the attachment and other negative emotions of all beings. And may all the karma and attachment and other negative emotions of all beings ripen in me."

By taking all the suffering and causes of suffering we encounter on the path like this, we make them allies on our journey to enlightenment; we purify the negative actions of countless kalpas and complete the accumulations of merit and wisdom.

Whenever you see people acting wrongly, breaking their vows or the like, practice tonglen—giving and taking—for them. As for keeping your own vows, it is important to apply the antidotes. Just as a crow will never dare to try eating a snake that is not dead, provided that you have not lost the antidotes of mindfulness, vigilance, and carefulness, you can never commit a fault that leads to a serious downfall. However, when it comes across a dead snake, even a crow can act like an eagle; similarly, if you do not have the antidotes, even the smallest wrongdoing will lead to a downfall. It is therefore important to build up the strength of these antidotes. As Bodhisattvas, followers of the Conqueror, the perfect Buddha Baghavan who is like a lion, we should be like young lion cubs and muster all our courage and strength to stand firm in everything that works against downfalls. But however well we keep our vows and cause others to do so, if self-righteousness, pride, or gross attachment are involved, this is the work of Mara and must be avoided.

When we have mentally exchanged ourselves and others again and again, our minds acquire the capacity of "equal taste" with regard to obtaining or rejecting the eight ordinary concerns, and we can then meditate on considering others more important than ourselves. For this we should reflect as follows:

"From this day on, even if I do not attain liberation, it does not matter. I shall take upon myself and bear the suffering of the six realms, those of the hells, pretas, animals, and so on. And I shall give all my physical and mental happiness and everything that makes me happy to all sentient beings."

Recognize all beings as your mothers, from those on the Peak of Existence at the top to those in the hell of Ultimate Torment at the bottom. Think of their kindness, and arouse the wish to repay that kindness. And as you wish them to be free from suffering, say to yourself, "May all these beings be freed from the three types of suffering and from their causes—the negative emotions like attachment, aversion, and bewilderment, and the acts they motivate: the ten negative actions, the five crimes with immediate retribution, the five crimes that are almost as grave, the four serious faults, the eight perverse acts, and the like. If only they were free. Let me be the one to set them free." Then pray to the Three Jewels.

Yet this on its own is not enough: you must think, "This very instant, as quickly as possible, may all these sufferings and their causes land on me" and take them onto yourself both in your imagination and in actual practice. "If they really could mature in me, may I replace the flesh, the blood, the bones, and the sickness and dying of all sentient beings. And even if I go to the hell realms, let me experience the sufferings of all the beings in hell." Or else think, "However many times I have to multiply my body for each sentient being, I shall take each one's place and experience and bear all their suffering." Or imagine that your body becomes so huge that it entirely fills the six realms in the three worlds of samsara. Imagine the upper part experiences the sufferings of the higher realms, mainly the all-pervasive suffering of everything composite and the suffering of change, so that all the beings in the higher realms are freed from suffering. Imagine that the lower part of this body experiences the suffering of the three lower realms, mainly the suffering upon suffering, so that all the beings in the lower realms are freed from suffering and attain happiness.

Reflect thoroughly on each of the different individual sufferings in the hells and other realms, and take them all onto yourself. Imagine that your mothers, the beings who live there, are freed from all their suffering and so enjoy all kinds of happiness, from the level of the higher realms of gods and humans up to perfect buddhahood, and that every single being attains buddhahood.

At the end think, "If all beings have become Buddhas, they have attained buddhahood because of my merits, sources of good; what joy that fills me with." At the same time, reflect, "This is not just for a brief span of time; even for the sake of one single being, I must bear this for as many kalpas as there are grains of sand in the river Ganges."

"So, as much as I wish in my mind for the suffering of all beings to fall on me, I must put it into action as well, and may I only need to think of it or aspire to it for the suffering of all beings actually to land on me. May all the karma and negative emotions that are its causes also come onto me. All my happiness and well-being, physical and mental, and everything that makes me happy I dedicate and give for the benefit of sentient beings."

And for giving with great love: "From this day onward, there is no being to whom I shall not give all my bodies, possessions, and merits gathered in the past, present, and future. I shall give and dedicate with generous longing, in numbers myriad as the dusts of the earth. And with all that I have given, there will be no taking anything back. They can put a bridle in my mouth or a saddle on my back, but whatever wrong beings may inflict on this body of mine, it will be all right: it is entirely up to them. Besides, to think of things as substantial, as 'my body' and so on, is not the way of a Bodhisattva. So if I give my bodies, possessions, and merits to all beings, without attachment or regret, it will directly help sentient beings and indirectly benefit me as well."

All these were the methods for preventing the bodhichitta of intention from declining.

2. Training in the Precepts of the Bodhichitta of Application

It is the training in the six transcendent perfections that prevents the bodhichitta of application from declining. Once we have aroused the bodhichitta of aspiration and of application, it is necessary to train in the precepts of aspiration and application. The precepts of aspiration have already been explained, so we come now to the precepts of application.

The activities of the Bodhisattvas, infinite though they are, can all be condensed into the six transcendent perfections. These six can be further condensed into the accumulation of merit with concepts, or the skillful activity aspect, comprising the first five transcendent perfections (generosity, discipline, patience, diligence, and concentration); and the accumulation of wisdom without concepts, or the view aspect, comprising the last perfection, transcendent wisdom.

The definition of the term "transcendent perfection" is as follows: it is transcendent perfection because it is a means for "reaching the other side," the state beyond misery. Here the other side beyond misery that is reached refers both to the peace attained by the Shravakas and Pratyekabuddhas and to the state of perfect buddhahood.

These six transcendent perfections are supported by the determination to be free as intention and by the wisdom that is the realization of selflessness. If they lack the view of emptiness, they are limited transcendent perfections that lead to the attainment of the Shravakas' and Pratyekabuddhas' state of peace. Buddhahood is that which does not dwell in either of the two extremes, and therefore the means for attaining it are to overcome the extreme of samsara with the view and to overcome the extreme of nirvana with compassion; in other words, they are the six transcendent perfections, for they cause one to reach the "other side" that dwells in neither of the extremes of samsara or nirvana.

Here, skillful means and wisdom should be treated as a pair. When the skillful means of great compassion is conjoined with the wisdom of emptiness, skillful means suppresses the extreme of nirvana, and wisdom suppresses the extreme of samsara. This means that for those who have set out on the path of earnest aspiration and are training in the six transcendent perfections, the latter are transcendent perfections in name only. Practitioners at this stage do not have the capacity actually to make a gift of their head or of their arms and legs and the like; they may give them away mentally, but in practice they take care of them. Apart from having some general understanding of emptiness, they have not had a direct vision of emptiness, and therefore at this stage they only give their head and so on mentally and in practice they protect them. Otherwise, if they were actually to give them away, this would lead to a downfall. So they practice simply with the aspiration to practice generosity, discipline, patience, diligence, concentration, and wisdom, and these are therefore transcendent perfections only in name.

From the moment one realizes what is to be realized on the path of seeing (that is, from the moment one sees the truth of dharmata, or sees reality directly with wisdom, or has a vision of thusness, or realizes the ultimate perfection—all these being different terms for the same thing) and until the final stage of the tenth level, in meditation one is free from conceptual fabrication and in the postmeditation period one has to complete the ten transcendent perfections, practicing generosity on the first level, and so on. At this point one is truly able to give away one's head and arms and legs. Because everything is the emptiness supreme in all aspects, one's meditation is devoid of solid perceptions and in the postmeditation one experiences things as the eight similes of illusion, and in this way the transcendent perfections are perfected. At this point, generosity and the other perfections are not merely a question of the things one is giving; their essential nature is emptiness, but on the level of appearance they take the form of generosity, discipline, and the rest. They are the activity of emptiness, the manifold display of emptiness, arising as emptiness supreme in all aspects. They thus lead to the perfection of the result, from the temporary result of the ten levels up to the result of perfect buddhahood, and this is why, from the first level to the tenth, all the transcendent perfections are genuine transcendent perfections: when the two accumulations are united, the meditation is devoid of appearances and the postmeditation experience is an illusionlike display—that is genuine transcendent perfection.

By training in the six transcendent perfections on the long path, the short path, or the swift path, we should perfect three practices: completion, maturation, and training. By means of the six transcendent perfections we fully complete the infinite accumulations of merit and wisdom. With the six transcendent perfections we establish sentient beings on the paths to the three kinds of enlightenment and bring infinite beings to maturation. And by relying on the six transcendent perfections we should train in our perception of infinite worlds, both pure and impure, in accordance with our wishes: "By this merit gained from practicing the six transcendent perfections, in the future may any world, pure or impure, that I wish to train in come into being." Here our merit is the primary cause and our prayers of aspiration the contributory conditions. Examples of pure worlds are the buddhafield of Manjushri and the Pure Land of Sukhavati, while impure worlds are those such as this world of ours, the buddhafield of our teacher the Buddha.

2.1 Generosity

As beginner Bodhisattvas, whatever we are doing—walking, sitting, or engaging in general activities—we should train again and again in our attitude, never straying from generosity or whichever transcendent perfection it may be. In our deeds, we should train ourselves in generosity by giving as much as we are able, starting with small gifts. Stingy people in particular will need to take an object and pass it from their right hand to their left, working on the attitude of giving and getting used to this by degrees. Then they can progress to giving someone a real object, like a green vegetable or cooked dish, gradually getting used to this until in the end they can give their head or arms and legs.

A Bodhisattva on the first level up to the tenth has to train in the transcendent perfections mainly in deed rather than in mental attitude. For beginners, though, the view is of paramount importance and the reason it is so necessary is that it is this grasping at "me" and "mine" that has kept us shackled to samsaric existence. The antidote to this grasping at "me" and "mine" is the path of the three trainings, and the most important thing on the path is the truth of the path, the wisdom that realizes no-self. By using this wisdom to examine whether the "self" of the individual is the same as, or different from, the five aggregates, we come to understand that the notion of an individual has no basis. Then, by investigating the five aggregates—the basis on which a self is designated—as being made up of particles and instants of consciousness, we should arrive at the conclusion that the five aggregates have no intrinsic existence. This kind of analytic meditation, which investigates the no-self of the individual and the no-self of phenomena, is what we should concentrate on.

It is through the view directly experienced on the path of seeing that we realize suchness, and from the path of meditation onward we familiarize ourselves with the continuity of this view. So at the beginners' stage, the view is all-important.

These six transcendent perfections have two aspects: their nature and their classification. Here, we meditate on their nature, which is the subject of meditation, and we reflect on their different categories in the intervals between sessions.

First of all, dividing your practice into sessions and breaks between sessions, do the preliminary to the session as usual. When you do the prayer, imagine that all the wonderful qualities of the transcendent perfection of generosity (or whichever transcendent perfection you are meditating on) that are present in the wisdom mind of the teacher now arise in your own mind. His or her wisdom mind merges with your mind; rest in equanimity, maintaining this state of mind as much as you can.

For the main practice, meditate on the attitude of giving freely. The things to be given are your body, your possessions, and whatever merits you now possess and those accumulated in the past, present, and future. Begin by recognizing sentient beings as your mothers, recalling their kindness, and giving rise to a wish to repay that kindness: "Gathering and adding together my present body and everything I have with me in this little retreat cell, and all the bodies, possessions, and merits I shall have until I attain ultimate buddhahood, I give it, hand it over, and dedicate it to mother beings[202] to help them achieve temporary happiness and ultimate bliss and their causes, and to help remove all their suffering."

To whom should you give? To all sentient beings.

What should you give? Your bodies, possessions, and merits.

Why do you give? So that they may attain temporarily the higher realms and ultimately the state of buddhahood.

How should you give? You should give without expecting anything in return in this life or any results that may ripen in your future lives.

Then pray that all your connections with others may be meaningful, whether they have a bad connection based on attachment, aversion, and ignorance and they physically beat or strike you, harbor evil intentions, or behave roughly toward you, or whether they have a good connection with you based on faith and pure perception.

In the sessions themselves therefore it is in your mind that you should repeatedly get used to the attitude of giving freely. In between sessions, when you actually put this into practice, train by starting with small gifts and gradually making them bigger and bigger.

Transcendent generosity includes both offering and giving.

◊ GIVING

Take the example of material giving. When you see a beggar approaching, as a Bodhisattva you should be thrilled, and when the beggar calls out, "Spare us something, please," rather than getting annoyed you should find something to give him, even if it is something you are already eating. At this point a feeling of stinginess may well up, and you should therefore remind yourself of the drawbacks of miserliness:

> The miserly are reborn in the realm of the pretas;
> Even if born among humans, they are paupers.

Generosity then becomes the antidote to stinginess. Regarding the food—or whatever it is—that you intend to give, if you have both good and bad food and you give the bad you are breaking the discipline of generosity, so regardless of how much you give, you must give the good, with a completely pure attitude. Put as much as you can afford in a vessel that is not cracked or chipped, and reflect, "At the moment I do not have anything else to give, but from now on I must give my bodies, my possessions, and my merits to sentient beings, starting with this beggar." With this, thinking of him as your mother and yourself as his child, give him a welcoming smile and then hold out your gift in both hands and give it to him. If he keeps on begging do not get irritated, but if you have anything, give him as much as you have. If you have nothing, then apologize politely and explain that you do not have anything else to give. Then dedicate your act of generosity and its resulting merits (like a cow followed by its calf) for the benefit of all beings, starting with the recipient of your gift, and make prayers of aspiration.

◊ OFFERING

When you make an offering, you should consider that the support for your practice, even if it is just an image of Buddha, is in reality all the infinite sources of refuge, and while the offering itself may be only a single butter lamp, the way in which you offer it must include the preparation, main part, and conclusion.

In the main part of the practice, you should arrive at a certainty that although the three concepts—the one to whom you give, the things given, and the purpose of giving—all appear, they are empty and devoid of intrinsic existence. You must offer or give these things without expecting anything in return in this life or any karmic reward in lives to come. Then, with a mind full of love and compassion, take your leave with sweet-sounding words of gratitude.

Ordinary material giving, acting as an antidote to miserliness and practiced without expecting anything in return or any future karmic reward, belongs to the path of accumulating. "Great giving" belongs to the path of joining, and "exceptionally great giving" to the path of seeing. As a beginner you should give your body mentally, but in practice you should take care of it. Of your possessions you should give as much as you can, to counteract your stinginess. Your merits you must give completely, along with their results.

The point at which one can start "giving the Dharma" and truly benefit sentient beings is from the first Bodhisattva level onward. Until then, since you will not really be able to benefit beings, you can go somewhere like the top of a high mountain and, creating a very pure attitude with verses like "Namo Arya Dampa: Homage, noble ones . . . ," recite the sutras. Then make the incense offering, the burned offering, and the offering of the body, and conclude with prayers for giving the Dharma.* Consider that as a result of this the minds of infinite *jungpo* spirits are liberated. For beginners this is a suitable substitute for "giving the Dharma."

2.2 Discipline
2.2.1 Avoiding Negative Actions

Discipline is something one should practice all the time, without making any distinction between sessions and breaks between sessions. It is said to be a continuous attitude of giving up negative actions together with its seed.[203] As long as we have this attitude of avoidance in our minds from the beginning when we go through the session preliminaries, there is discipline. If we do not have the attitude of avoidance in our minds, even if we give up the ten negative actions, for example, there is no discipline. So whether we have discipline depends on whether we have the attitude of avoidance in our minds, and it is therefore essential to be guided by the attitude of rejection and a second iron resolution, the promise not to give it up.

*See WMPT page 238: "Abandon evil-doing . . . ."

In the main part of the session, from the ten negative actions up to the samayas of the Great Perfection, in each instance we must have first the attitude of avoidance—to refrain from committing a wrong action—and second the iron resolution whereby we say to ourselves, "I have made this pledge and I will never go back on it."

Begin by recognizing that all sentient beings are your mothers, reflecting on their kindness, and arousing the wish to repay their kindness. This applies also to all the other practices below.

First, think, "All beings must attain the level of perfect buddhahood. To bring that about, from this day onward until I attain perfect buddhahood I'd rather die than take the life of a single sentient being. I'd rather die than induce another person to kill. I'd rather die than rejoice at killing." This is the attitude of avoidance. Then say to yourself, "Even if my very life is at stake, I swear I shall never go back on this pledge." This is the second resolution, and you must have these two each time. This same principle applies to all that follows. Here, related to the discipline of avoiding killing is that of saving lives.

Again, make the following promises: "Even if I'm dying of starvation, I shall never take what has not been given. I shall never make someone else steal," and "Never will I rejoice when others steal things."

Next, resolve, "I shall never indulge in impure conduct," and, related to this, practice celibacy.[204]

Avoid lying and tell the truth instead. When you are talking with someone else, examine your mind carefully, and when you realize you are about to tell a lie, you must tell the truth. Or else, when you recognize that you have already told a lie, promise, "From now on, I'd rather cut my tongue out than tell a lie."

Again, give up sowing discord and reconcile differences between people. Promise, "I'd rather die than let my divisive words make two friends fall out." Whenever you feel the urge to say anything that sows discord, or are about to do so, stop yourself by slapping yourself on the face, or punching yourself in the chest.

Avoid harsh words and speak pleasantly.

Give up worthless chatter and devote yourself instead to reciting mantras. To expand on this point, when you take part in village ceremonies and so on it is important to avoid gossiping and to do the rituals properly.[205] If you correctly practice the confession in four sections and the fulfillment with the four essential elements, the sponsor's accumulations[206] will be completed and your own obscurations caused by misusing offerings made to the Three Jewels will be purified. The four sections are as follows: the section for the body is performing prostrations, that for the speech is the recitation of the hundred-syllable mantra, that for the mind is confession, and the section for the three doors together is confession within the expanse of the view. The four essential elements are the four essential elements of the body: the channels, the white essence, the red essence, and the energies. These correspond to the offerings of amrita, rakta, torma, and lamps. You should put all your efforts into this practice of confession and fulfillment and keep your senses under control, refrain from speaking and not let your mind get distracted thinking of other things.[207]

Next, make this resolve: "Even if my heart were torn still beating from my body, I would rather die than have covetous thoughts about other people's things or the property of the Buddha, Dharma, and Sangha." Along with this, meditate on generosity.

Promise, "I'd rather die than think of harming beings, treat them violently, or harbor evil intentions!" and meditate on compassion.

Then resolve, "I'd rather die than have wrong views concerning the true teaching on cause and effect," and exercise faith and confidence in the law of karma.

By now you will already have received the upasaka vows when you took refuge (as explained above). You should therefore make five promises not to break the five vows—the four root vows and the injunction against intoxicants—and back them up with the five iron resolves never to give up these promises.

As for the point when shramaneras, fully ordained monks and nuns, Bodhisattvas, and tantric yogins can drink alcohol: when they have attained the "heat" of samadhi, and thence the power to transform the color, smell, taste, and effect of alcohol by reciting the three syllables, and when they can transform the color, smell, taste, and potency of even the deadly black aconite and eat it with no ill effects, then they may drink alcohol and the like without harm. Otherwise, if a shramanera or *bhikshu* or anyone craves the smell or taste of alcohol and then drinks it, according to our teacher the Buddha, the link between teacher and student is severed:

Whoever drinks alcohol is no disciple of mine;
Neither am I his teacher.

Accordingly, shramaneras should make a pledge for each of the four root precepts and the fifth against alcohol, thinking, "Even if my life is at stake, I shall not commit this." They also make the thirty pledges against committing the thirty detailed branch faults.

The fully ordained monk makes 4 pledges for the 4 radical defeats, 13 pledges for the 13 residual faults, 30 pledges for the 30 downfalls requiring rejection, 90 pledges for the 90 "mere downfalls," 4 pledges for the 4 faults to be specifically confessed, and 112 decisions to avoid the 112 wrong actions.

The Bodhisattvas' tradition of the Profound View includes 20 decisions to avoid the 20 root downfalls, and 80 decisions to avoid the 80 branch faults. The Vast Activity tradition has 4 decisions to avoid the 4 root downfalls, and 46 decisions to avoid the 46 branch faults. In both of these traditions the crucial points are the two aspects of bodhichitta, intention and application, so make the double resolution,[208] "Better my head were cut off: *never* shall I abandon sentient beings," and the double resolution for the bodhichitta of application, "I'd rather die than fail to guard the six transcendent perfections," and the double resolution, "I'd rather die than fail to reject their six opposites."

As for the Vajrayana samayas, in Mahayoga there are 5 decisions to avoid the 5 root downfalls and 10 decisions not to transgress the 10 branches. In Anuyoga there are 3 pledges for the 3 root samayas of body, speech, and mind and 25 decisions not to transgress the 25 branches. In the Great Perfection, for practitioners whose realization develops gradually and for whom there is something to be kept, there are 27 decisions not to transgress the 27 divisions of the root samayas relating to the teacher's body, speech, and mind, and 25 decisions not to transgress the 25 branch samayas. For those of sudden realization for whom there is nothing to be kept, there are 4 decisions not to transgress the 4 samayas.

At the end of the session one should arrive at the conviction that although the samaya that has to be kept like this, the person keeping it, and the benefits of keeping it all appear, they lack intrinsic existence.

After that, it is in the breaks between sessions that one practices the three forms of transcendent discipline: avoiding negative actions, undertaking positive actions, and bringing benefit to others.

In the Bodhisattva tradition, there are two sets of vows: the pratimoksha vows and the two aspects of bodhichitta. Now, although the pratimoksha vows can be absorbed upwardly, within the higher vows, the Vajrayana vows must never be included downwardly, within the lower. An individual who has taken all three kinds of vows must refrain from all the wrongdoings proscribed in these three: pratimoksha, Bodhisattva, and Vajrayana.

If we summarize these vows, the pratimoksha is to refrain from harming others and from the underlying wish to harm. The Bodhisattva vow is to bring about the benefit of others, and the underlying wish to help. The Mantrayana vow is to regard the body, speech, and mind as being the three vajras.

So to refrain from physical violence, harsh and offensive speech, and all intention to hurt—in short, to refrain from the slightest harm perpetrated by body, speech, and mind—is to avoid negative actions.

2.2.2 Undertaking Positive Actions

"Undertaking positive actions" is in fact the training in the six transcendent perfections. For beginners, however, undertaking positive actions means making every effort to do even the smallest positive actions of body, speech, and mind. Whether we simply remove our hat when we see an image of a Buddha or a stupa, offer a solitary prostration with our body, recite the confession of downfalls with the speech, or arouse just a momentary positive thought in our mind, every effort we make toward wholesome actions is the discipline of undertaking positive actions.

2.2.3 Bringing Benefit to Others

The point at which we can truly bring benefit to beings is when we have realized the truth of dharmata on the path of seeing and, having gathered disciples by means of the four ways of attracting beings, we establish beings on the paths of ripening and liberation.

All of these aspects of discipline can be illustrated by the case of a single louse. When one picks up the louse, to think, "Now, so that all beings as numerous as space is vast can attain the level of buddhahood, I will not kill this louse" is the discipline of avoiding negative actions. Having avoided killing it, to make its life safe is the discipline of bringing benefit to beings. And to dedicate the merit of this to the welfare of others is the discipline of undertaking positive actions.

In short, as much as you can, refrain from the ten negative actions, help others and develop the attitude behind doing so, and regard your body, speech, and mind as the three vajras.

Throughout the postmeditation period, in your thoughts, words, and deeds avoid any kind of negative action and undertake all kinds of positive action. And in all this apply the three supreme methods. You should arrive at the conviction that although all these things appear, they have no intrinsic existence whatsoever.

2.3 PATIENCE

The definition of patience is not getting upset. Being upset is a mental event, whereas anger is its expression in physical behavior or words. There is a proverb: "All the merit accumulated over a thousand kalpas is destroyed in a single surge of anger." And the *Way of the Bodhisattva* says:

> Good works gathered in a thousand ages,
> Such as deeds of generosity
> Or offerings to the blissful ones—
> A single flash of anger shatters them.[209]

What is it that burns? It is anger that burns. What is it that is burned? The sources of good for the future consistent with ordinary merit. It is claimed that sources of good that are undertaken with the three supreme methods cannot be burned. Worldly sources of good are said to be burned even if one is angry with just a piece of charred wood. Positive actions consistent with liberation in the Basic Vehicle are all burned when Shravakas and Pratyekabuddhas get angry with one another, but if Shravakas and Pratyekabuddhas get angry with ordinary people, the merits of their positive actions are not burned but weakened. If a Bodhisattva gets angry with a Shravaka or Pratyekabuddha, it will only weaken the merit of his or her positive actions but cannot burn it, just as a piece of turf has no effect in cutting iron. However, if a Bodhisattva gets angry with another Bodhisattva, all his or her merits will be destroyed, like iron smashing through iron. If a Bodhisattva still on the paths of accumulating and joining gets angry with one who has attained the Bodhisattva levels, then every one of his or her sources of good will be consumed without a trace. So from the very beginning of the path of accumulating it is important to arouse the bodhichitta. This is why it is said:

No evil is there similar to anger,
No austerity to be compared with patience.
Steep yourself, therefore, in patience—
In all ways, urgently, with zeal.[210]

What, you may wonder, does anger consume? It destroys the merits from acts of generosity and discipline accumulated over a thousand kalpas. The *Introduction to the Middle Way* explains that all the merits of generosity and discipline gathered over a hundred kalpas are burned up.[211] The bodhichitta is banished and eradicated without a trace.

Just as one cannot put fire and water together in the same container, if you have hatred, you cannot have bodhichitta; if you have bodhichitta, you cannot have hatred. The specific result of hatred is that ultimately one will go to the hell realms; the specific result of patience is that ultimately one will attain buddhahood. For this reason, once you have understood the benefits of patience and the dangers of hatred it is important to meditate on patience.

The meaning of "No austerity to be compared with patience" is that patience is the greatest of all hardships. To meditate on patience we have first to starve hatred to death, so whenever the food of dissatisfaction is provided we must use every possible means to meditate on patience.

In the breaks between sessions, meditate on the three categories of patience: patience when wronged, patience to bear hardships for the Dharma, and patience to face the profound truth without fear. Whenever you meet with the food of dissatisfaction, that is the moment to meditate on patience.

2.4 Diligence

For diligence there are two topics: essence and classification.

(A) ESSENCE

> Heroic perseverance means delight in virtue.[212]

The significance of "virtue" here is that since delighting in negative, worldly actions is laziness, so to delight in virtue is diligence (or heroic perseverance). "Delight" refers to the fact that diligence concerns not the lesser positive actions of body and speech but the mental state, a supreme delight in positive actions.

How can we make diligence come about? By thinking of the benefits of positive actions and the drawbacks of negative actions. These benefits can be found in the *Sutra Designed like a Jewel Chest*; they include such benefits as purifying crimes with immediate retribution and not being overwhelmed by anger, the benefits of taking refuge, and the benefits of bodhichitta.

Arousing bodhichitta completely changes one's name and purpose. It is like a brave bodyguard, for it overcomes the effects of negative actions with a definite outcome. Like the inferno at the end of time, it eradicates the effects of negative actions of uncertain outcome. As illustrated by the fruit of the wish-fulfilling tree, the benefit of the bodhichitta of intention is that its results are inexhaustible, and the benefit of the bodhichitta of application is that not only do the results increase but the cause keeps growing. Reflect on all of these benefits and apply yourself with diligence.

(B) CLASSIFICATION

Diligence is of three kinds: armorlike diligence, diligence in application, and diligence that cannot be stopped.

2.4.1 Armorlike Diligence

For armorlike diligence, it is necessary to arouse a vastness of attitude such as no ordinary person could ever conceive. Imagine gathering together all the infinite activities of completion, maturation, and training that the Buddhas and Bodhisattvas have accomplished over as many great kalpas as there are grains of sand in the river Ganges. To think, "That is what I will accomplish in every instant" is the "great armor." Then say to yourself, "All acts are imitation, so I shall follow in the footsteps of the Buddhas and Bodhisattvas, completing, maturing, and training, just as they have done." When you hear the life stories of the Vidyadharas of the past, with all the hardships they endured, you should think, "Even if I cannot do better than they, I must certainly not do less. Until all beings have attained buddhahood, I shall explain the Mahayana teachings to each and every one and help them arouse the bodhichitta. Even if I must strive for kalpas in the various methods for putting the precepts of the Bodhisattvas into practice, never, even for an instant, will I let myself feel weary." This is the antidote to the kind of laziness where one loses courage and feels inadequate.[213]

All this is summarized in the various "infinities" listed in the *Sutra of the Prayer of Good Actions*,[214] where we also find:

> As I wander through all the states of samsaric existence,
> May I gather inexhaustible merit and wisdom
> And so become an inexhaustible treasury of noble qualities—
> Of skill and wisdom, concentration and liberation.

Such is this wish to benefit all sentient beings. Its reach and range stretch to the very edge of space, and it endures until the whole of samsara is emptied. If you wonder, "Do I really have the capacity to enact this 'until samsara is emptied'?" the answer is, "You can. There is no suffering involved." For Shantideva said:

> When their bodies are happy because of their merit,
> And their minds are happy because of their wisdom,
> Even if they stay on in samsara for the benefit of others,
> Why would the compassionate ones ever be miserable?[215]

As a result of the "apparent" accumulation of merit with concepts, we will temporarily attain birth in a noble family in the higher realms, like the highest birth in a royal lineage or the best among brahmins or householders, along with all their splendor and wealth. Physically we will be free from suffering and attain the samadhi that can transform suffering into happiness. And when, with the wisdom that is the realization of no-self, we see that in absolute truth the three worlds are devoid of all conceptual fabrication and that in relative truth all birth and death, happiness and misery are like a magical illusion, there will be no suffering as such in our minds. Then, even if we do have to stay on in samsara to benefit others, it will never occur to us to be weary.

2.4.2 Diligence in Application[216]

Until one attains ultimate buddhahood, there is always something more to be realized and something more to be discarded. That is why one has to train in the six transcendent perfections. Accordingly, in both your thoughts and your actions you must constantly apply yourself to virtue, neither taking it easy during the day nor sleeping at night nor leaving the body, speech, or mind for even an instant in a state without Dharma.

With regard to "devoted application," you should develop devotion and a sense of joy and enthusiasm toward your outer tutor, the master and spiritual friend; to the Mayahana teachings he imparts; and to the bodhichitta within your own mind. The word "application" here has the sense of "never separating from."

Furthermore, if one grows weary when teaching the Dharma, then of the four forces—the force of devoted interest, the force of steadfastness, the force of joy, and the force of moderation—it is necessary to exercise the force of moderation. Moderation is of two kinds, pausing for a while and stopping altogether, and here it is a question of pausing for a short while. Stopping altogether implies that a particular task has been completed, for example, teaching the Dharma. In this case, the teacher has finished teaching, but the students' work is not finished since they must now begin practicing what has been taught.

2.4.3 Diligence That Cannot Be Stopped

You must never feel satisfied with your practice of generosity and the other transcendent perfections, for until you reach the level of buddhahood there are obscurations to be progressively eliminated and good qualities to be progressively developed, and as long as that is the case you will need to put in a great deal of energy, practicing diligence over a long period of time.

2.5 Concentration

2.5.1 Giving Up Distractions

In order to practice concentration, we first have to pursue the two kinds of seclusion, which are prerequisites for concentration. What are these two? Physical seclusion from crowds and bustle and mental seclusion from thoughts.

Physical seclusion means to leave behind all the "important" things of this worldly life, to get rid of all the trivial ones, and so to abandon all the affairs of this life totally. Mental seclusion from thoughts means to give up all our plans and activities for achieving things in this worldly life and not to think about anything except the Dharma, not to reflect on anything but Dharma, not to do anything but Dharma, and not to accomplish anything but Dharma, so that there is only one thing to think about: the Dharma.

These two kinds of seclusion are those of the common vehicle. In the extraordinary vehicle of the Bodhisattvas, seclusion is seclusion from one's self-centeredness. If you do not isolate yourself from thinking about your own selfish desires, you will be as the *Condensed Transcendent Wisdom* describes:

Though they stay many millions of years
On lonely snake-infested mountains, five hundred miles around,
Bodhisattvas who know not this seclusion
Remain superior and proud.

Finding physical seclusion from crowds and bustle and mental seclusion from thoughts takes the form of (1) abandoning worldly things and (2) letting go of discursive thinking.

(A) ABANDONING WORLDLY THINGS

This has two aspects: (1) giving up attachment to material things and (2) giving up attachment to sentient beings.

(1) Attachment to Material Things

Begin by thinking about the shortcomings of material things. The way to do this is to remember the drawbacks of the three ruinations, or acquiring, protecting, and increasing.

In the first place, there are two ways to accumulate wealth: the Dharma way and the worldly way. The worldly way is that of people who spend their summers as bandits and their winters as petty thieves, getting rich through suffering and negative actions. As for the Dharma way, as soon as a child has learned the alphabet and can read his letters, people will say, "Now he can earn his living"; and with his sights set firmly on this life, as a lama or monk he will do his utmost to trade the Dharma for prized possessions, thus accomplishing entirely worldly ends.

Next, to keep our gains, we have to keep them safe from enemies, thieves, and wild animals, with men to guard them by day, and dogs by night.

Then, think about all the trouble we go through trying to increase our property, worrying about whether we can manage to turn one into ten, or ten into one hundred, or one hundred into one thousand.

(2) Attachment to Sentient Beings

For giving up attachment to sentient beings, use the detailed way, meditating on the four thoughts that turn the mind from samsara, or the briefer meditation on the four ends of impermanence.

Begin by thinking about yourself. When you were born, you were born alone. Nothing, out of all your possessions and wealth, came with you from your past life. In your next life everybody, all your friends and relatives and so on, will be left behind: not a single one of them will follow. So if you have to arrive alone at the beginning when you are born and depart alone at the end when you die, now too you need to be alone, in a solitary place.

Having thus given up your attachment to material objects and to sentient beings, you should seek the seclusion of an isolated place of retreat. When you go into isolated retreat you must avoid falling into either of the two extremes connected with provisions. Do not fall into the extreme where luxury spoils one's merit: make do with staying somewhere simple and small like a cave, with a little plain food and clothing that is easily got by begging, and wear clothes that someone has thrown out. At the same time, avoid the extreme of getting too tired and exhausted, and the kinds of severe austerities that might become an obstacle to your physical health or life.

(B) LETTING GO OF DISCURSIVE THINKING

Once we have gone to a lonely place of retreat, it is important give up discursive thinking. In general, we should rid ourselves of all distracting thoughts. In particular, of all the desires that characterize the desire realm, in which there is attachment and clinging to the pleasures of the five senses, the one that distracts our minds and never lets them rest is attachment to sexual pleasure, and this is therefore the main one we have to give up.[217]

Let us examine the drawbacks of sexual desire. Once we fall under the influence of a sexual partner, it is impossible to break free, hence the Tibetan word for "partner," "no escape." Another word used is "black one" because, like a hail of red-hot iron blasting a field of miraculous rice, a partner can black out and destroy the positive actions that lead us to enlightenment. To counter our desire for this person to whom we are so attracted, this "no escape" or "black one," there are three points to be understood: the cause, which is difficult to come by; the essential nature, which is unclean; and the result, which is a great deal of harm.

First, the cause. In Tibet you would not find a spouse without paying a price. If you were even slightly well-off you could never get a wife without handing over a lot of horses and dzos. Even a monk would have to hand over everything, his *damaru* and bell and his robes, to the woman's family.

As for the essence of your desired one, on whose account you may have to commit negative actions and suffering, it is unclean, consisting as it does of thirty-six impure substances. Right now, you might not be able to take your eyes off him or her, and yet if you really look closely, the source of his white complexion is lymph, the cause for her rosy glow is blood: in reality the person is a bag of skin full of lymph, blood, and other filth. If you are wondering how this can be, then take this person, the object of all your attachment, and use the scalpel of wisdom to slice him or her open from head to toe. It is all filth: the person smells revolting, the insides make the stomach turn, and the brains in the skull, the snot oozing from the nostrils, and the tears from the eyes all look disgusting. The sole reason for lusting after this person is improper thinking, which results in clinging to three features: his or her shape and complexion and physical contact with the person.

The antidote to attachment to your lover's shape is to meditate on his body as being chunks of leftover meat that have been chewed up by wild animals. The antidote to attachment to her complexion is to meditate that she is completely raw and red, or a corpse bloated from putrefaction or green with mold, or a mushy mass crawling with worms. Alternatively, imagine that the head and limbs and everything have been burned by fire.

The antidote to desire for physical contact is to be found in the *Treasury of the Abhidharma*:

> Whatever I desire is skeleton,
> Bones spreading as far as the ocean's edge,
> And then gathering back again,
> First, from the feet, till half the skull.
> Thus the training is taught.
> By fixing the mind between the eyebrows,
> This is the way to train.

In this case, consider that either your own body or that of the desired one is a skeleton and, apart from the ligaments in the limb joints, is stripped of all skin and flesh. Alternatively, imagine that between the eyebrows there first appears a little sore the size of a thumbprint, with pure white bone in the middle, surrounded by pus and lymph, and then everything gradually peels away to reveal a skeleton. Then, step by step imagine that this same sore spreads to the entire universe and all the beings in it until at the end everything on dry land takes the form of skeletons. After that, from the edge of the oceans, the whole world and all the beings in it are gradually restored to their former condition. Then half of the person's body, or alternatively half the skull, recovers its flesh, and half remains bone. Concentrate on the body, half fully fleshed and half shining white skeleton.

This meditation can also be applied to your own body. All this is the antidote to desire employed in the tradition of the lower vehicles.

The Bodhisattvas' approach is to cultivate the idea that all those to whom we are sexually attracted and who are older than we are are our fathers or mothers, those of our same age are our brothers or sisters, and all those younger are our sons or daughters. These can be combined by simply meditating on the idea that all beings are our parents. This is the meditation followed by beginner Bodhisattvas.

In the Vajrayana, all beings are visualized as male and female deities, and it is out of the question to feel desire toward the play of the kayas and wisdoms.

If you do not meditate in one of these ways, you will simply find yourself proving the saying,

Lovers bring destruction and ruin,
Destruction in this life, and destruction in all lives.

By familiarizing yourself with this, you should isolate your mind from attachment and rely on a lonely retreat. Whenever you cannot bear being alone in retreat, you need to reflect on the benefits that seclusion brings.

The moment one arrives in a solitary place, there is an absence of sensory objects such as sexually desirable people, and all the negative emotions that their presence would provoke are therefore automatically stilled. "Birds and wild deer are easy companions . . . ."* It was only by taking to lonely her-

---

*See WMPT page 250.

mitages that the Buddhas, Bodhisattvas, and Vidyadharas of the past were able to attain the result.

Those who follow the extraordinary path of the Bodhisattvas should isolate themselves from self-centered attitudes. Once you take to solitude and come to practice concentration, you should keep very pure discipline, where there is nothing you need regret, for as it is said, "Everything comes from having discipline." Then you should practice concentration, which is the source of an undistracted mind:

> Penetrative insight joined with calm abiding
> Utterly eradicates afflicted states.
> Knowing this, first search for calm abiding,
> Found by those who joyfully renounce the world.[218]

Having first taken up discipline, then as long as there is no impairment you will be tearing down the standard of Mara and raising the victory banner of the Buddha's doctrine. However, if any breach occurs you must never ignore it, thinking it does not matter, but arouse regret at your previous actions, confess in accordance with the teachings, and so repair your vow. By so doing, you will be casting down the standard of Mara and hoisting the victory banner of the teachings. In addition, when you practice the generation and perfection phases you must maintain a rock-solid samaya and practice concentration keeping the three vows perfectly purely, adopting or rejecting whatever is permitted or forbidden in accordance with these three vows.

2.5.2 Actual Concentration

The definition of concentration is an absence of distraction. In everything you do, whether walking, sitting, eating, or sleeping, practice with your mind bound fast by the rope of mindfulness:

> This mind I'll tether to that sturdy post, reflection on the Teaching,
> That it might never slip its bonds and flee.[219]

Just as you would use a rope to tether an animal to a stake or post, use mindfulness to bind the mind to the object on which you are concentrating, never forgetting what you should be doing or not doing, nor distracted elsewhere. Then you should use vigilance as an overseer to check whether the mind stays where it should. And with carefulness you should be ever attentive, like a newlywed bride, as to what you should be doing and what you should be avoiding, so that if the mind is distracted it is brought back and placed again on its original object.

Beginners should alternate between analytic and resting meditation, meditating on love and the samadhi of love without letting themselves be distracted by external objects, tethering their minds with the rope of mindfulness, and using vigilance to spy and keep a lookout.

To begin with, you will need a meditation cushion, a yard square,[220] higher at the back and sloping slightly toward the front. Alternatively, you can arrange your bed in a similar fashion. Then sit on it and assume the seven-point posture of Vairochana. When you are practicing sustained calm, your body should be relaxed and at ease and your mind untroubled.

Sustained calm is divided into sustained calm with concepts and sustained calm without concepts. In sustained calm with concepts, concentrate on positive thoughts such as love and the samadhi of love, and use the support of mindfulness, vigilance, and care. Avoid being distracted inwardly: do not follow past thoughts, invite future thoughts, or be distracted by present thoughts concerning objects of the six senses.

As for how taut or relaxed your mind should be, this is a question of finding your own individual balance to suit your particular disposition. Once you get it right, then just settle the mind without meddling or interfering.

In sustained calm without concepts we do not concentrate on a single object such as love: without manipulating or altering the mind in any way, simply leave it as it is, calm, spacious, and at ease. From time to time, bring mindfulness, vigilance, and care to bear.

As the mind settles like this and becomes more and more still, different kinds of concentration are to be distinguished.

(A) THE CONCENTRATION PRACTICED BY ORDINARY BEINGS

To meditate on the samadhi of love and the like is called the concentration practiced by ordinary beings.[221] Here one becomes increasingly attached to meditative experiences, namely:

- the experience of bliss, in which one feels a sense of euphoria even though there is no reason to be joyous;
- the experience of clarity, in which the murkiness caused by thoughts has cleared and one feels like a building that is transparent; and
- the experience of the absence of thoughts, in which, when one checks whether any thoughts are arising in the mind, one has the impression there are none to arise.

It is because they are only states in sustained calm meditation that these experiences of bliss, clarity and nonthought are accompanied by clinging, and this is why it is the concentration practiced by ordinary beings. As a result of the clinging to bliss, clarity, and nonthought, this kind of concentration cannot serve as a means for attaining liberation. Indeed it is quite the opposite of the cause of liberation, namely the realization of no-self, since both the belief in a personal self (the notion of "*my* bliss," "*my* clarity," "*my* nonthought") and the belief in the substantiality of phenomena (clinging to the actual experiences of bliss and so forth) are still present in the mind.

As one familiarizes oneself with the practice, one goes through the different concentrations, along with their branches, and the formless absorptions, and with these stages of meditation one obtains the five eyes, the six clairvoyances, miraculous powers, and the like, which are the special qualities attained through meditative concentration.

(B) CLEARLY DISCERNING CONCENTRATION

In clearly discerning concentration, following on from the previous concentration, one uses reasoning to examine the self of the individual and the substantiality of phenomena, and so becomes practiced in uniting emptiness and sustained calm, like mixing water and milk. Now one's mode of apprehension will have shifted, and while the clinging one had earlier to bliss, clarity, and nonthought no longer occurs, one is unable to let go of clinging to emptiness as an antidote. The concentration practiced by ordinary beings thus belongs to the path of accumulating, whereas clearly discerning concentration is the principal meditation on the path of joining.

(C) THE EXCELLENT CONCENTRATION OF THE TATHAGATAS

The excellent concentration of the Tathagatas is similar to "the concentration of the Tathagatas." It is the concentration attained on the path of seeing: when sustained calm and profound insight have become indistinguishable and one is freed from clinging to substantiality and clinging to emptiness, one arrives at the natural state where one sees just how things are and one has no conceptual position.

2.6 WISDOM

In essence, wisdom is the perfect discrimination of phenomena. "Phenomena" here is a collective term meaning everything that can be known in samsara, in nirvana, and on the path. The noble Nagarjuna establishes these as follows:

> All dharmas taught by the Buddhas
> Are entirely subsumed in the two truths:
> Worldly, relative truth
> And absolute truth.[222]

The basis for classification, then, is anything in general that can be known, and this is classified into two categories: the two truths.

◆ RELATIVE TRUTH

There are a number of synonyms for relative truth: "all-concealing," "complete fiction," "total falsehood." For whom then is relative truth true? It appears as true to the deluded minds of naive, ordinary people and is therefore known as "the infallible truth of cause and effect, of the conditioned." Apu defines relative truth as a deluded mind and its object, while Lama Mipham says, "to be the object of knowledge, expression, or implementation is the definition of relative truth." So in our tradition, anything that can be known as an object of the mind, expressed in speech, or undertaken as physical action is defined as relative truth.

According to the New Tradition, whatever can be found through analysis by a valid cognition that distinguishes conventional designations is defined as relative truth.

◆ Absolute Truth

Synonyms for the absolute truth include the absolute, absolute space, that-ness, the natural state of things or the way things are, the ultimate perfection, emptiness, and thusness. For whom is absolute truth true? It is true, or undeceiving, for sublime beings as the object of self-cognizing wisdom, and so it is called the truth of the absolute. Apu defines absolute truth as that which transcends the mind, which is inexpressible and inconceivable. And according to Lama Mipham, "That which is beyond being an object of knowledge, expression, or implementation is the definition of absolute truth." Because it cannot be known by the conceptual mind, and so cannot be expressed by speech nor undertaken as physical activity, it is held to be the absolute truth.

Who then, you might ask, is able to know it? The sublime beings, who see it with their self-cognizing wisdom, while being free from the duality of subject and object. The glorious Chandrakirti says of this, "not seeing is the great seeing, not beholding is the great beholding." And in the *Introduction to the Middle Way*, he explains,

If the uncreated is suchness, mind too is uncreated.[223]

Concerning this question of a mind that is unproduced reflecting the form of an object that is unproduced, or a mind free of all concepts reflecting an object free of all concepts, when we talk about "seeing the intrinsic nature (as an object)," this is a way of demonstrating this seeing in an affirmative sense, as if there were a subject and an object, whereas when we say "not seeing object and subject as distinct," it is a way of demonstrating this with the accent on negation. However, ultimately the "seeing" here is seeing without seeing any conceptual characteristics whatsoever.

According to the New Tradition, whatever is found through analysis by a valid cognition determining an absolute nature is defined as absolute truth. They maintain that to say that the absolute is beyond being an object of the two types of valid cognition means that it cannot be known at all, and this is tantamount to inventing something unimaginable and nonexistent, which is the view of Hashang.[224]

This topic of the two truths has to be taught by an authentic spiritual master, teaching disciples with the right qualifications, who study each of the different presentations of the two truths. While the subjects of these different presentations—establishing the two truths—are one and the same, they differ in the degree to which different individuals of varying mental acumen have realized the essence of the two truths, just as racehorses may differ in speed even though they are running the same course.

(A) THE TWO TRUTHS ACCORDING TO THE SHRAVAKAS[225]

Relative truth refers to all phenomena, such as the gross five aggregates. The absolute truth is realized when, on examining whether the personal self is the same as or different from the five aggregates, one fails to find any such self, and when, as regards any truly existent entity in phenomena, on dividing the gross phenomena into parts, one concludes that there are subtle partless particles and indivisible moments of consciousness.

(B) THE TWO TRUTHS ACCORDING TO THE SAUTRANTIKAS

What the Sautrantikas call the "absolute truth that both appears and is able to perform a function" consists of all those entities that are "specifically characterized" objects and can perform a function. Things that cannot perform a function and are "generally characterized" are held to be relative truth.

(C) THE TWO TRUTHS ACCORDING TO THE CHITTAMATRINS

The Chittamatrins condense all phenomena into three categories: imputed, dependent, and truly existent. They hold that the imputed and the dependent are relative truths, and that the truly existent is absolute truth.

First, the imputed is divided into "the imputed lacking identity" and "the nominally imputed." Examples of the former include the horns of a rabbit, the child of a barren woman, and flowers in the sky. The latter includes such things as pillars and vases.

The dependent is divided into the "pure dependent" and the "impure dependent." The impure dependent consists of deluded perceptions caused by distorted thinking, the perception of the universe and its inhabitants as they appear to beings.

The pure dependent is what appears in the form of illusions and dreams in the postmeditation state of sublime beings and is called the "mere relative of the postmeditation." Dependent phenomena consist of mind and mental factors, and they come about on account of the interdependence of causes and conditions. The essential nature of the dependent is the awareness that is self-knowing, self-illuminating consciousness and is the absolute truth of "the truly existent, possessing the real nature."

The truly existent is as follows: when free from the duality of the imputed and possessing the three doors of perfect liberation, this self-knowing, self-illuminating consciousness, the essential nature of the dependent, is held to be the *subject*: self-cognizing wisdom. Its emptiness aspect, where the essence of the dependent is devoid of the duality of the imputed, is held to be the *object*: the absolute space, or dharmata.

(D) THE TWO TRUTHS ACCORDING TO THE MADHYAMIKAS

The Madhyamikas fall into two schools: the Svatantrikas and the Prasangikas.

(1) Svatantrika Madhyamikas

The Svatantrikas emphasize a "nominal absolute" that during the postmeditation involves assertions, whereas regarding the "nonnominal absolute," they agree with the Prasangikas. The Prasangikas from the very outset establish this to be the absolute space, in which all conceptual elaborations are dissolved, a freedom from any assertions, as in the wisdom of the meditation of the three kinds of sublime beings. Whereas the distinction between Prasangika and the Svatantrika was well known in the sacred land of India, *Rangtong* and *Shentong*[226] are terms designated by Tibetan masters and were unknown in India.

The basic texts of Madhyamika are the noble Nagarjuna's *Five Treatises on the Middle Way*, in which he comments on the Buddha's seventeen "mother and son sutras" of the Prajnaparamita as explicitly introducing emptiness. Then their hidden meaning is elucidated as what can be realized on the path by the regent Maitreya in his *Ornament of Clear Realization*. Most important are Nagarjuna's *Treatises* and Aryadeva's *Four Hundred Verses on Madhyamaka*, which give no cause for contention from either the Prasangikas or Svantantrikas and are known as the "original Madhyamika," having become the basic authoritative sources for both Prasangikas and Svatantrikas that can be understood either way.

The master Buddhapalita, a brahmin by birth, interprets Nagarjuna's *Fundamental Treatise on the Middle Way* from the Prasangika point of view and does not make use of the terms "inherently" or "truly." The master Bhavaviveka, who was a *kshatriya*, commenting on Nagarjuna's text from the Svatantrika point of view, refuses to accept this absence of the use of terms like "inherently" or "truly" on the grounds that we would have to say "an eye exists at the same time as it does not exist," whereas he holds that we should say "the eye has no inherent existence," "it is not truly existent," or "it is not ultimately existent."

The Svatantrikas are divided into upper and lower schools. The latter includes the master Shri Gupta and others, who hold that though ultimately everything is like a magical illusion, reasoning shows that magical illusions do exist, inasmuch as they are magical illusions. The upper school includes Jnanagarbha, Shantarakshita, and Kamalashila,[227] who were renowned as the "three Svatantrika preceptors from the East." Our discussion here should follow the views of these masters.

Their understanding of the two truths is as follows. The text the *Two Truths* says:

> Though in appearance they may be the same,
> According to whether they are able or unable to perform a function,
> Relative truths are divided
> Into rational and irrational.

Relative truths are objects that, from the point of view of their own characteristics, do not deceive the mind. Things that have an incontrovertible function, such as fire to heat or water to quench thirst, all specifically characterized things that are capable of functioning nondeceptively from the object's own side are held to be the rational relative. Everything that only appears but is not capable of performing a function—as for example when two moons are perceived in the sky or a butter lamp is drawn in a picture—is held to be the "irrational relative, incapable of performing a function."

As for absolute truths, the nominal absolute is as follows. All phenomena, from form up to omniscience, are neither one nor many, therefore "form is emptiness." This statement dispels the extreme of a perceived existence. The statement "emptiness is form," refers to the fact that phenomena arise interdependently and unobstructedly out of the emptiness that cannot be qualified as anything, and dispels the extreme of a void nonexistence. "Form is not other than emptiness" and "emptiness is not other than form" establish emptiness and dependent arising as being indistinguishable and mutually inclusive. So in this way beginners refute the four extremes one after another and are then led all at once to certain conviction.

Nowadays, people claim that noninherent existence is specifically the thinking of the Prasangikas, but in fact this kind of view is not all that much better than the Svatantrikas' nominal truth, and so, needless to say, it is not the nonnominal absolute truth.

As for the nonnominal absolute truth, the *Ornament of the Middle Way* says:

> Ultimately, from all the different kinds
> Of mental constructs, it is free.

When, one day, our meditation practice has gathered strength and our self-cognizing primordial wisdom sees its object, the absolute space, directly, then we are free from the four or eight conceptual extremes such as existence, nonexistence, both existence and nonexistence, and neither existence nor nonexistence;[228] this is held to be the nonnominal absolute truth. All positions such as existence or nonexistence are but the work of the mind, and here the activities of the dualistic mind have stopped altogether, so that even the concept of just freedom from conceptual elaboration has completely dissolved, and this falls into exactly the same point of view as the Prasangikas.

(2) Prasangika Madhyamikas

Now for the two truths in the system of the Prasangika Madhyamikas. Chandrakirti says in his *Introduction to the Middle Way*:

> The nature of phenomena, enshrouded by our ignorance is "all-concealed."
> And what this ignorance contrives is a delusion.
> Therefore the Buddha spoke of "all-concealing truth."[229]

All those things that are fabricated by ignorance, clinging to relative entities just as they appear, are said to be relative truths. Here, asserting relative truths to be mistaken or unmistaken is not based, as with the Svatantrikas, on whether or not they are deceptive from the object's own side, but mainly based on whether or not the mind is impaired. So the objects of the six sense consciousnesses of an unimpaired mind are asserted to be the real relative, and what appears to a consciousness deluded on account of something like a phlegm disorder, in other words an impaired mind, is asserted to be the unreal relative.

As for absolute truth, it is not divided, as with the Svatantrikas, into nominal and nonnominal absolute truths, but from the very beginning it is established as being primal wisdom, compatible with the meditation of the three sublime kinds of beings. That wisdom, free from all extremes, is therefore concluded to be the true nature of things, totally beyond all positions. This is why Nagarjuna says:

Because I have no position,
I can only be without fault.[230]

It is not that he is simply not taking a position out of fear of being criticized for having a thesis of existence or nonexistence. The very nature of things is devoid of any position or thesis. So in this school, the two truths are asserted to be different only in the sense of their not being the same. The upper Svatantrikas claim that the two truths are different in being one entity but different isolates, and the lower Svatantrikas assert that the two truths are different entities.

◊ Meditation on the No-Self of Persons and Phenomena

With the above we have given a general idea of the two truths. Now, when we come to the meditation practice, we should divide our time into sessions and breaks between sessions. Go through the preliminary practice for the session and then concentrate on the main meditation.

Here, when we speak of "all phenomena," we mean all things that can be known, and these can be condensed into the five aggregates. These can be further condensed into matter and consciousness, and we therefore need to meditate on both the no-self of the individual and the no-self of phenomena.

To do so, we first have to be clear about what it is we are refuting, which is the nature as it appears.[231] So what we refer to as an individual is a continuity, and what we call a phenomenon is something that has characteristics. Thus when we focus on the continuity of the aggregates, thinking, "From a point with no beginning I have arrived at this point, and from here I shall continue further to the next point," this concept of "I" is the self of the individual. The way we apprehend this self varies. Sometimes, when we say "I am sick," we are thinking of the aggregates as "I." But if someone asks us, "What is the trouble?" and we reply, "My head aches," we are thinking of the aggregates as "mine."

So focusing on the continuity is the belief in the self of the individual, and the object of that belief is the individual. The basis for designating the individual is the five aggregates, which are the objects of the belief in the substantiality of phenomena, and the belief that they truly exist is the belief in the substantiality of phenomena.

When we believe in the personal self, we are clinging to it as something permanent, single, and independent. So, begin by examining whether this so-called individual self is the same as, or different from, the five aggregates. If it is the same, then just as the self is permanent, single, and independent, so too must the aggregates be permanent, single, and independent. On the other hand, if the aggregates are impermanent, multiple, and dependent, then it follows that this self must also be impermanent, multiple, and dependent. When you investigate in this way, you will find that the self and the aggregates cannot be the same.

If the self is something other than the aggregates, you should be able to observe that the self and aggregates, which are not separate in terms of place, time, or appearance, are distinct. Since this is not what one sees, you have to conclude that there is no basis for a self.

You might think then, "Well, even though the self does not exist, the aggregates still do." But if you analyze them, you will find they do not exist either. Starting from the premise that the body is the phenomenon of form, you should conclude that it is no more than a collection of particles and that its nature is that of indivisible atoms.

◊ Analyzing External Phenomena

It is necessary now to examine the things you perceive outside: mountains, walls, rocks, and houses. Start by analyzing something like a house. In the beginning we conceive of this thing that we call "house" as a single whole; this is because we have not analyzed it. But when we do, we find that this so-called house actually consists of a combination of many things, such as stones and bricks, compressed mud walls, masonry, earthen bricks, and wooden beams. When we break this agglomeration down, bit by bit, we will have dismantled our concept of it as a house, and we will then conceive of it as stones and earth and the like. These again are collections of many particles, and if we take one stone, for example, and divide it into four pieces we will have done away with our concept of it as a single unit. Then, if we further split these quarters into four parts, this will remove our concept of them as single pieces. As we continue to split one of these sections into conceptual parts, we will end up with conceptual particles that have no intrinsic existence. This is why the *Heart Sutra* says, "Form is emptiness."

It is when we fail to investigate and analyze like this that we perceive things in the form of houses and so on. The fact that dependently arising phenomena arise ceaselessly out of emptiness that cannot be qualified as anything is "Emptiness is form." These two lines dispel the extreme of apparent existence and of empty nothingness. With "Emptiness is not other than form, form is not other than emptiness," we see that emptiness and interdependence are indistinguishable and mutually inclusive. Meditate on this until definite conviction dawns.

Consider also something like your own tent. You may begin by thinking of it as a single thing called "tent," but when you dismantle the door and sides, the notion of it as a single unit changes. Then although you may have the concepts "This is the door," "These are the sides," once you take apart the strips of woven yak-hair cloth, the concepts of door and sides disintegrate and you are left with the concept of strips of cloth. If you reduce even these pieces of cloth to threads, the concept of strips of cloth is upset, and there is a concept of threads. If you divide even the threads into strands, you destroy the concept of thread and are left with single hairs. This hair too can be split into conceptual particles. When you conclude that the conceptual particles do not themselves have any inherent existence, this sort of analysis will lead you to certainty regarding the oneness of appearances and emptiness, through the "reasoning that unites the four emptinesses": "Form is empty; emptiness is form; form is not other than emptiness and emptiness is not other than form."

This is how to examine the outside world, from mountains and continents, ranges and forests, up to the golden mountains, the seas of enjoyment, and Mount Meru.

❖ Analyzing the Internal Phenomena of One's Own Aggregates

Now examine inside, looking at your own aggregates. What you call "this one body I have now" you conceive of as being single, permanent, and independent, and so this is what you need to analyze and investigate.

You might think, "This body of mine is permanent," but it is not. It is impermanent in the gross changes it goes through from the beginning, from when we are the sperm and ovum of our parents and a tenth the size of a white mustard seed, then growing bigger and bigger, going through all the stages of development one after another till the body is fully formed, and through birth and childhood right up until old age. And it is impermanent in the changes from one instant to the next that are the natural subtle workings of impermanence, like the flow of a river.

Ask yourself now whether the body is a single entity. It is not. It is flesh and skin and blood and lymph and bone and mucus and phlegm and tendon. To take just one of these, of bones the body contains 360 in all, and these again consist of many molecules. Moreover, the body has 30 teeth, 21,000 hairs on the head, 30,000,000 hairs on the body, and so on: it is by nature multiple and manifold.*

You might think then, "This body of mine is independent." But it is not. It is dependent on karma and negative emotions: it is dependent in that the body's ailments, its pleasure and pain, its beauty, and its ugliness all depend on karma.

Although you may think of your body as a single whole, if you cut it up and divide it into five sides, you destroy your concept of "body," and you are left with a concept of "side." By dissecting one of these sides into shoulder blade, upper arm, forearm, and hand, you destroy the concept of "side" and

---

*The figures mentioned here reflect the point of view of Tibetan medicine.

are left conceiving of its various joints. These too you can divide up into flesh and skin, blood and bones, and the like, thus destroying the concept of "joint" and being left with the concepts of flesh, skin, and so on. Now split the flesh, skin, and the rest into conceptual parts. As you continue to analyze the conceptual parts and find they have no intrinsic existence, you will say to yourself, "The body is emptiness." It will seem like space.

Since interdependent phenomena arise ceaselessly out of emptiness, which cannot be qualified as anything, "emptiness is the body." "Emptiness is not other than the body, the body is not other than emptiness." Thus the extreme of apparent existence is dispelled, for although the body appears, it is nonexistent; and the extreme of an empty nothingness is dispelled, for emptiness has the potential to appear as dependent arising. Emptiness and dependent arising are thus established as indivisible. As Prince Könchok Pang said:

> Form and sound themselves are free from mental constructs,
> Yet freedom from constructs itself arises as form and sound.
> As something separate from form and sound
> Freedom from constructs is not separately observed;
> As something separate from freedom from constructs,
> Form and sound are not separately observed.

This is how, with what is called "the wisdom that mentally analyzes all outer and inner phenomena," we turn outward and analyze things objectively until we reach a state of conviction. We call this "the wisdom arrived at through intellectual analysis" or "the view arrived at through mental analysis."

In the Great Perfection and Mahamudra, the view is established by first cultivating the view arrived at through mental analysis and then resting in equanimity, turning the mind inwardly and examining the natural state of the subjective mind with what is called "self-cognizing wisdom." This is called "the view of primal wisdom arrived at through resting in equanimity." So the first of these involves the thinking mind, and the second is primal wisdom that transcends mind altogether. The difference between them is greater than that between earth and sky.

When you have gone through this analytic meditation and you do not feel like going further, simply rest, leaving the mind just as it is, without any manipulating or meddling, in something akin to the view of meditation. When thoughts arise again, practice analytic meditation and then rest again, thus alternating analytic and resting meditation. Through meditating like this, the mind becomes well trained, flexible, and fully functional.

❧ Analyzing the Mind

Next, look inside and analyze your own mind. Here again, we tend to think of the mind as being permanent, single, and independent, but close scrutiny does not bear this out. It is not permanent, for its very nature is to create an endless succession of thoughts arising and ceasing: like the flow of a river, it is impermanent. Neither is the mind single. It can have any number of negative thoughts such as attachment, aversion, bewilderment, pride, jealousy, and miserliness; many different positive thoughts like faith, determination to be free, and bodhichitta; and numerous neutral thoughts, memories of things that have happened in the past, or things we have said or heard. And besides, its nature is multiple inasmuch as there are eight consciousnesses, fifty-one mental factors, and so on.

As for whether or not it is independent, it is not, for it depends on its object. When it comes into contact with a pleasing object, desire is aroused; when it comes into contact with something displeasing, aversion grows; and when it comes into contact with something that is neither, a state of bewildered indifference occurs. And in states such as determination to be free and faith, the mind again depends on an object: it is determined to be free *from* samsara and has faith *in* nirvana.

Again look at your past thoughts: since you cannot say that they are still stored somewhere, they cannot exist. Look at your present thought: it dissolves instantaneously by itself without leaving any trace, so it cannot exist either. And though you may think your future thoughts are getting ready to come from somewhere, you will never find them; they have not arisen, you have not yet had them, so they cannot exist.

When those with superior faculties investigate the past, present, and future in this way and do not find anything, they gain a definite certainty that the mind has no intrinsic existence. But although beings with duller faculties also find nothing through this sort of analysis, they still think, "Even if the mind does not exist, I cannot help having all sorts of thoughts, so somehow it must exist." They therefore need to examine how the mind comes, stays, and goes.

◊ Coming, Staying, and Going

You might think, "To begin with there may not be any thoughts like attachment, but suddenly one springs up from somewhere, so it must exist." In this case, first of all, investigate where the mind is born, where it comes from, where it arises.

If a thought has arisen,[232] it must have come from the six sense objects outside, or from the six sense organs inside, or from somewhere in between: there is nowhere else from which it could arise. So start by investigating the six sense objects: form, the object of the eye consciousness; sound, the object of the ear consciousness; smell, the object of the nose consciousness; taste, the object of the tongue consciousness; touch, the object of the body consciousness; and, based on these, the objects of the mental consciousness, that is, the *dhatu* of mental phenomena.

Begin with forms, which are the objects of your eye consciousness: using the wisdom of mental analysis, split them up into conceptual parts and then break them down into atoms, conceptual particles without inherent existence. Since these have no inherent existence, there cannot exist an object from which a consciousness could arise.

In the same way, since sounds and the other sense objects are all material phenomena made up of atoms, use the wisdom of mental analysis to dissect all such phenomena into four parts. Then analyze these quarters further, dividing each of them into four parts, and so on, until you have split them into minute particles, one-fortieth the size of a medium-sized speck of dust seen in a shaft of sunlight, which is what is said to be the "partless particle." Yet even this "partless" particle can be divided into a top and bottom and four sides, so it is something that has no intrinsic existence, a phenomenon of emptiness, devoid of any origin or basis. Apart from these nonexistent atoms, there is no object from which a mind could arise.

You may wonder then how the mind can arise. Since the ceaseless interdependent arising is the great ornament of the appearance and manifestation of the power of emptiness, a certainty will dawn in you of what emptiness and dependent arising really are. And as the six outer objects have no intrinsic existence, it is impossible for a mind to arise from them, as impossible as for a child to be born without a mother.

In that case, you may ask, do thoughts arise from the six inner sense organs? No, they do not. Of the six sense organs, five—the eye, the ear, the nose, the tongue, and the body[233]—control the apprehension of their respective objects, hence the Tibetan term for organ, "ruler." Of the sixth, it is said,

> The consciousness of the six that have just ceased—
> What is it? It is the mind.

When the initial consciousnesses of the five organs have ceased, this provides the opportunity for the arising of a nonconceptual mind consciousness, and as soon as this sixth, the nonconceptual mind, has ceased it causes the conceptual mind consciousness to arise, which is why it is termed an organ.

Analyze the five physical sense organs using the same method as when you analyzed the body. The atoms of which they are composed have no intrinsic existence, so for the mind to arise from the inner sense organs is impossible, as impossible as for a child to be born without a father.

You may now wonder whether mind arises from somewhere in between the sense organs and their objects, but this is not the case. In the space between the sense organs and their objects there is also nothing but particles—light particles by day and darkness particles by night. Apart from these light particles and darkness particles, which are by nature partless particles, there is nowhere from which the mind could arise.

When you investigate the mind like this, it would seem to be nonexistent. "Nevertheless," you might say, "once a thought has arisen, there is a an instant during which it is present, so there must be somewhere the mind stays." But such a location does not exist either. Take the example of the child of a barren woman: if it cannot be born in the first place, there cannot be anywhere for it to stay subsequently. So it is pointless to investigate something like this.

"Still," you might argue, "there *is* a mind!" Investigate it, then. Analyze the six sense objects outside and the six sense organs inside and the space between them, as you did before, and you will find there is nowhere the mind can stay.

There is thus for the mind neither arising nor staying, but all the same you may think, "At the end, there is somewhere the mind ceases to be." Again, take the example of the barren woman's child: since there was no one in the first place who was born, and no one in the meantime who stayed, there is no one at the end who can die. Similarly, by analyzing the six objects oustide, the six sense organs inside, and the space in between, and splitting them into subtle conceptual particles, you will find they have no inherent existence, and so again there is nowhere there for the mind to cease to be.

When you look in this way for a mind that comes, stays, and goes, you will not find anything, but still a thought may suddenly spring up and you might think, "Aha! This is something that exists." But it is not, because if there were some *thing* to the mind, it would have to have shape and color: there cannot be anything that does not have these two. If you examine the mind's shape and look to see whether it is round, square, semicircular, triangular, long, short, oblong, smooth, or bumpy, you will find it has no shape. If you examine its color to see whether it is white, yellow, red, green, and so on, you will find it has no color. When you examine to see whether or not it has a form— that of a man, a woman, a person of no specific gender, a horse, an elephant, or whatever—you will find it does not exist as a form.

"Still," you insist, "there is *something* there." Then look at the sense objects outside, the sense organs inside, and everywhere outside and inside the body: is there a mind you can see? Mind has no form that you can see. And if you listen with your ears, mind has no sound that you can hear. So how can the mind be intrinsically existent? Even perfectly ordinary people, when they cannot see something with their eyes or hear something with their ears, would never say, "There's something there"; they would say, "There's nothing there!"

But even now, you might still wonder: "Does mind have a smell that can be sensed with the nose? Does it have a flavor that can be tasted with the tongue?" You might look everywhere inside and outside the body to see if mind is something you can touch with your hands. But there is nothing. For this reason, it is said, "Mind is empty."

At the same time, left unexamined and unanalyzed, mind does indeed appear, out of the emptiness that cannot be qualified as anything, as the ceaseless working of interdependent arising; and therefore it is said, "Emptiness is mind."

Like the moon and its reflection in water, emptiness and interdependence cannot be dissociated: "Emptiness is not other than mind; mind is not other than emptiness." With this you will develop an unshakable realization of the unity of the four emptinesses, one that can never be taken away.

Subsequently you should reach the conviction that the nature of phenomena (for which nothing can be found by analysis and yet which, unanalyzed, arise ceaselessly and interdependently) is that of the eight similes of illusion. Seven of these are easy to understand, but the simile of the magical illusion needs to be illustrated by the allegory of the magician Longbeard of Khyungpo. When he recites his magic spell, the incantation *Om Tibi Tibi Svaha*, over the twigs and pebbles he uses as props, he tricks our eyes into perceiving what appear to be the horses and elephants of the illusion. Then, when he wishes to break the spell, he dissolves the illusion by reciting the incantation *Om Miti Miti Svaha* and the twigs and pebbles reappear. In the same way, the magician, this "old man" ignorance, recites his spell (the condition, karma and negative emotions) over the cause (dualistic grasping), and, like the illusions in a display of magic, there arise all the various perceptions of the six realms, from the peak of samsara down to the vajra hell.

However, in this example there are two points when the appearances of the illusion do not exist: at the start before the spell has been recited over the twigs and pebbles, and at the end when it is all dissolved by the final incantation. It is only in between that they appear, because of the interaction of the particular conditions. It is the same with the nature of mind, our Buddha nature; there are two points when deluded illusionlike perceptions do not exist: at the very beginning when the ground is undeluded, and at the end when perfect buddhahood is attained. Nevertheless, because of adventitious delusions, we are deluded as if by the perceptions in a show of magic.

For this reason, use the eight similes (the magical illusion and the others) to reflect on these deluded perceptions, and meditate again and again, alternating analytic and resting meditation.

Conclude the session as usual. In between sessions, read about the different categories of wisdom and reflect on them carefully.

This completes the training in the precepts of the bodhichitta of application.

Nyoshul Lungtok Tenpai Nyima (1829–1901/2), Patrul Rinpoche's disciple, who transmitted The Words of My Perfect Teacher *to Khenpo Ngawang Pelzang.*

CHAPTER THREE

Meditating on the Teacher as Vajrasattva and Reciting His Mantra so as to Cleanse All Adverse Circumstances, Negative Actions, and Obscurations

I. HOW NEGATIVE ACTIONS CAN BE PURIFIED THROUGH CONFESSION

The obstacles that prevent the extraordinary experiences and realization of the profound path from arising are negative actions and obscurations, so it is important for beginners to concentrate on purifying mainly karmic obscurations.

The term "negative actions and obscurations" is used here in a general sense; it refers to the four kinds of obscuration, namely (1) karmic obscurations; (2) the obscurations of negative emotions; (3) conceptual obscurations; and (4) the obscurations of habitual tendencies.

(A) KARMIC OBSCURATIONS

There are two kinds of negative actions: naturally negative acts and downfalls that violate edicts.

Naturally negative actions are acts such as killing, which are not negative simply because the Buddha proscribed them. From the moment they are committed, they are in themselves productive of negative karma.

Downfalls that violate edicts are acts that are not negative when committed by ordinary folk but become so when committed by ordained persons. One example is that of cutting grass.

Naturally negative acts, those acts that are negative independent of the Buddha's edicts, therefore include the ten negative actions, the five crimes with immediate retribution, and so on.

An act that is both a naturally negative act and a downfall in violation of an edict is the root downfall of killing. It is naturally negative in that one has taken life, and it is a downfall in violation of an edict in that it breaks a root vow.

An act that is only a downfall in violation of an edict is cutting grass. When a lay person mows the lawn, this will not produce negative karma. But if a fully ordained monk who follows the Buddha's edicts does so, this constitutes a downfall, and it is as great a negative act for a monk to cut grass as it is for an ordinary person to kill an animal.

Thus downfalls that violate the Buddha's edicts include all transgressions of the outer pratimoksha vows, the inner Bodhisattva vows, and the secret samayas of the Mantrayana.

The higher the level of the vow, the more serious the downfall. For example, if an ordinary person kills a louse, this constitutes the negative action of taking life. If a Bodhisattva kills a louse, it constitutes not only the negative action of taking life but also the crime of killing one's mother. You might think that in that case a Bodhisattva who kills a louse commits one of the crimes with immediate retribution, but it is not so: only if you kill the mother who has given birth to your present body do you commit a crime with immediate retribution. If a mantra practitioner kills a louse, in addition to the negative action of taking life and the crime of killing one's mother, there is the crime of slaying the glorious Vajrasattva and with it the negative karma of killing the forty-two deities that are the louse's aggregates, elements, and *ayatanas*.[234]

In this way, negative acts increase in strength from one level to the next. A monk who fails to wear the lower robe, the *shamtab*, correctly commits one of the wrong actions of the pratimoksha,[235] which stipulates that the shamtab must not be worn unevenly. On the other hand, since these wrong actions fall within the Bodhisattvas' discipline of avoiding negative actions, a monk who has taken the Bodhisattva vow and who does not wear his shamtab in the correct manner is transgressing the discipline of avoiding negative actions, and therefore committing a root downfall. And for a mantra practitioner who is a monk, this same wrong action constitutes the root downfall of transgressing the Sugata's edict.[236]

All transgressions, therefore, whether naturally negative or violations of the Buddha's edicts, are karmic obscurations. What is it that they obscure? They obscure the attainment of the states of gods and humans in the higher realms.

(B) THE OBSCURATIONS OF NEGATIVE EMOTIONS

These are the thoughts that impel the above actions, namely the 84,000 negative emotions and the five or three poisons that include all these. They can all be summed up as wrong thoughts.[237]

What do they obscure? They obscure the attainment of the Shravakas' and Pratyekabuddhas' state of liberation.

(C) CONCEPTUAL OBSCURATIONS

Conceptual obscurations are the thoughts that involve the belief that subject, object, and action are real.

(D) THE OBSCURATIONS OF HABITUAL TENDENCIES

According to the sutras, the obscurations of habitual tendencies are a very subtle form of conceptual obscuration, while according to the tantras they are what are called the habitual tendencies associated with the changes of the three perceptions. The very subtle obscurations are:

- the habitual tendency of the white aspect, the cause or seed that gives rise to the gross body that is dependent upon the subtle mental body;
- the habitual tendency of the red aspect, the cause that gives rise to the gross speech; and
- the habitual tendency of the very subtle movement of energy or the black path, the aspect that unites the white and red elements and is the cause or seed that gives rise to the mind.

What is it that these last two obscure? They obscure the attainment of the wisdom of omniscience.

All these obscurations thus obscure attainment of the higher realms, liberation and omniscience in particular, and in general obscure thusness, the natural state of all phenomena. If one were to give a name to that natural state, it can be called dharmata, thusness, the only true state, the ultimate perfection, the absolute space, the faultless absolute nature of all phenomena, the Buddha nature, and so on. These names are common to both the Sutrayana and Mantrayana.

In the Mantrayana it is called the natural pure buddhahood, the buddhahood of the primordially pure essence, the buddhahood of the spontaneously present ground.

The *Heruka Galpo* speaks of it as:

The natural state, the ground of the nature as it is,
The supreme dharmakaya, beyond bondage and freedom

—referring to the way the mind settles or the way it naturally is or the way it simply dwells: the absolute space and primal wisdom are inseparable, and this natural state has never been affected by the stains of karma and negative emotions. Like the orb of the sky or of the sun, all the qualities of the three kayas of the Conqueror are perfect from the very beginning, without having to be sought. At the time of the ground, when one is an ordinary being, there is no worsening; the qualities do not diminish. And at the time of the result, when one is a Buddha, there is no improvement; the qualities do not increase. Free from any increase or diminution in qualities, it is unaffected by adventitious stains; its own essence is thus pure from the beginning, and this primal wisdom whose nature is the primordially pure essence, and which from the very beginning is beyond bondage and liberation, is known as "the natural state, the ground of the nature as it is," or "the universal ground of the primordial meaning."

When one realizes this so-called ground, it is the true ground, the producer of nirvana and the product itself. When one does not realize it, it is the ground without which none of the phenomena of samsara could arise, and this is why it is called the ground.

Simply having this nature of primal buddhahood does not mean one is actually a Buddha. As we find in the *Hevajra Tantra*:

All beings are Buddhas,
But this is concealed by adventitious stains.

The reason we are not actually Buddhas is that the ground nature is obscured by the adventitious stains of dualistic delusion. These adventitious stains can be categorized into the eighty-four thousand negative emotions and so on, but they can all be summarized as the five aggregates, which can further be condensed into this obdurate succession of thoughts that is the mind. This is what we call "the ground of labeling through delusion," and it is the true cause, the producer and product, of all the phenomena of samsara, of all deluded perceptions.

For this reason, in order that realization can arise like a reflection in the mirror of the ground of all, we have to purify our obscurations, for as it is said, "When obscurations are purified, realization dawns by itself." Accordingly, beginners should concentrate mainly on purifying the obscurations of karma.

As for the methods of purification, for those who have taken the pratimoksha vows, the Buddha, with his skill in means and great compassion, explained how to repair radical defeats, residual faults, and so on, according to each individual case. For Bodhisattvas there is the *Sutra in Three Parts*, so named for its three sections of homage, confession of negative deeds, and rejoicing or dedication. And there are other confessions such as the confession ritual from the *Sutra of Great Liberation*. In short, all positive, virtuous practices are simply means for confessing negative actions.

A genuine pratimoksha confession can thus purify all downfalls of the pratimoksha and free one from both causal downfalls and resultant downfalls,[238] but it does not purify downfalls related to the Bodhisattva vows. Bodhisattva and Mantrayana confessions not only free one from the causal and resultant downfalls related to their respective vows but also have the power to free one from the resultant downfalls related to the lower levels of vow.

So of the many methods of confession of negative actions in the sutra and mantra traditions, this meditation and recitation on the teacher Vajrasattva is by far the best. When Vajrasattva was on the path of learning, he prayed, "In the future, may the negative actions and downfalls of all who hold my name be purified. As long as they are not, may I not attain buddhahood." He gathered an immeasurable accumulation of merit and wisdom and made prayers of aspiration. All his prayers were accomplished and Guru Vajrasattva became a Buddha. Therefore, since the teacher emanates and embodies all the mandalas, rather than making efforts to confess in the presence of each of the Buddhas in the ten directions, you should make your confession meditating on your teacher and Vajrasattva as inseparable. This is much better than the above methods of confession.

Here the way we meditate is that of the "the jewel which includes all."*

II. HOW TO CONFESS NEGATIVE ACTIONS

Every confession should be a complete confession, including as antidotes all the four powers. As Shantideva explains:

> What is to be purified? The six doors of negative action.
> What does the purifying? The antidotes, the four powers.
> How do they purify? With the three supreme methods.

1. The Power of Support

The support for confessing negative actions, or the object to which they are confessed, is for the pratimoksha the preceptor together with the Sangha; for the Bodhisattva vows it is one's teacher or spiritual friend, or a fellow Dharma practitioner,[239] or the thirty-five Buddhas of confession, or the Buddhas of the ten directions referred to in the *Sutra of Great Liberation*, and so on. And in the Mantrayana, it is the teacher and deities of the mandala. In this case it is the teacher as Vajrasattva.

The power of support in fact has two aspects: the outer power of support and the inner power of support. In this context the outer power of support is meditation on the teacher as Vajrasattva. The inner power of support is taking refuge, arousing the mind turned toward supreme enlightenment, and especially developing great compassion. It is therefore most important in this practice to form the correct attitude, and in this respect the essence of the outer power of support is faith.

---

*See WMPT, note 199 (note 185, 1st edition).

2. The Power of Regret
The essence of the power of regret is remorse.

3. The Power of Resolution
The essence of the power of restoration[240] is the vow not to do negative actions in the future.

4. The Power of Action as an Antidote
The antidote in the "power of action as an antidote" is in essence to develop a real wish to practice the Dharma.

III. THE ACTUAL MEDITATION AND RECITATION ON VAJRASATTVA

Start by meditating on the power of support. For this there exist practices in which one visualizes Vajrasattva on the crown of one's body visualized as a deity, or on the crown of one's own body considered without attachment, but in this practice you are someone with bad karma, an old sinner, a seasoned offender. On the whorl of hair on the crown of your head is set the stem of a lotus, four finger-widths high, its flower a white lotus with one hundred thousand open petals. Its spreading orange anthers are two-thirds covered by a moondisk, whole and perfect. Upon it is your glorious root teacher, that incomparable mine of compassion, in the form of a white syllable *Hum* a finger's width in size. Concentrate on this, visualizing the *Hum* pointing forward toward the breast, and pray fervently to the teacher keeping in mind the five ways in which one should know him to be a Buddha.*
As a result of your prayer, the teacher's mind, that syllable *hum*, is overwhelmed by great compassion and, in a state of great bliss, seems to tremble, In the manner of a fish leaping from water,[241] it transforms into the Guru Vajrasattva, "like a snow peak lit up by the brilliance of one hundred thousand suns." The rest of the description is easy to understand.†

Imagine him thus, gazing with superhuman eyes, listening with superhuman ears, thinking with the superhuman mind of omniscience: his face is

---
*See chapter on guru yoga, page 259.
†See WMPT, page 267.

turned toward you; he is listening to you and thinking of you. Imagine moreover that Vajrasattva, your teacher, seems displeased and is looking gloomy.

It is of the greatest importance to develop faith, believing that the teacher knows what is best, and to arouse the sublime bodhichitta. So rather than the outer power of support, concentrate on developing the inner power of support—faith, taking refuge, and arousing bodhichitta.

The power of regret concerns what is to be purified, namely the *six doors of negative action*.

The first of these is the *door of time*. Your confession should take the following form: "All the negative actions I have accumulated in samsara from time without beginning until now; and those acts, naturally negative or in violation of edicts, that I can remember committing in this life; and negative acts that I have committed in such-and-such a year, in such-and-such a month, on such-and-such a day, at such-and-such a time: negative acts such as these I have committed, I have incited others to commit, and I have rejoiced at their being done. All these I confess, keeping nothing secret in my mind, hiding nothing with my body, and openly declaring them with my speech."

Do not think, though, that since no one has seen the faults you have committed, the Buddhas have not seen them either, for it is said:

> Your evil deeds, unseen, or so it seemed,
> Will ne'er escape the perfect sight
> Of rishis, gods, and yogins.

Or as Apu said:

> The poison of your evil thoughts lies hidden in your body,
> But when you are on the point of death, nothing will prevent it being revealed.

So, since the Buddhas and Bodhisattvas, like hundreds of sighted people standing around a blind person, cannot but see your negative actions, declare all those that you can remember and confess them with shame, dread, and remorse, along with all the negative actions you cannot remember but that are perceptible to the Buddhas' and Bodhisattvas' all-knowing wisdom.

The second door is the *door of motivation* and refers to all negative actions motivated by bewilderment, attachment, and aversion.

The third door is the *door of wandering*, or the *door of accumulation*, and refers to all the negative actions you have gathered with your body, speech, and mind.

The fourth door is the *door of the nature*. It refers to all your naturally negative actions such as the ten negative actions and the five crimes with immediate retribution, and all the downfalls in violation of edicts, namely transgressions of the outer pratimoksha vows, the inner Bodhisattva vows, and the secret Vidyadhara's commitments of the Mantrayana.

The fifth door is the *door of the object*, which refers to all the negative actions you have accumulated in relation to the two objects, namely samsara and nirvana.

The sixth door is the *door of function*. It refers to all the negative actions and downfalls that in this life cause a short life, frequent illness, poverty, fear of hostility, and so on, and in future lives lead to endless wandering in the lower realms and existences.

Stricken with remorse for all these, as if they were some deadly poison inside you, make your confession, thinking, "Lama Vajrasattva, turn your gaze on me, listen to my prayer, keep me in your thoughts! I have nothing good to tell you today. All the negative actions that I have accumulated throughout time without beginning until now I repent and regret, openly confessing them in your presence, hiding nothing and holding nothing back."

Your confession should be a matter of desperation: "You who know! Purify my negative actions this very moment, instantly, in this very place, on this very seat." If there are people who can pester you desperately for something as worthless as half a penny, then why should you be any less desperate when you purify and confess your negative actions?

The third power, the power of restoration, entails using confession to restore broken pratimoksha, Bodhisattva, or Mantrayana vows (rather as one would repair a dilapidated wall), and then promising not to break them again even if it costs you your life.

Once we have taken all the pratimoksha, Bodhisattva, and Mantrayana vows, it is impossible to be completely free of infractions, but nothing comes from emptily declaring, "Henceforth I shall do this no more!" Monks and lamas these days recite from the *Confession of Downfalls*: "Nothing do I hide, nothing do I hold back; I vow to stop from now on." But in the meantime they seem to do nothing but negative acts.

First, therefore, if it is just for a single thing—taking life, for example—you should vow, "I shall not take the life of those I cannot kill." This way you will keep the discipline of refraining from taking life and obtain the benefits of that. If, on the other hand, you do not make such a promise, apart from naturally not committing a negative action, you will not have had the opportunity to acquire the merit of refraining from killing. So if you are a lay person and you promise not to kill lions, dragons, elephants, and other animals you cannot possibly kill, you will acquire merit.[242] Ordained persons too should first make a similar resolution—"Even if my life is at stake, I shall never kill a lion"—and back it with a second iron commitment: "Even if it costs me my life, I will never give up my promise." And for each such promise not to kill a particular type of being, there should be a corresponding second iron commitment to keep that promise.

In the same way, promise not to commit the other nine negative actions, taking what is not given, and so on, and back each such promise with a second iron commitment: "Even if I am tortured to death with flesh being pincered from my body, I would rather die than give up my promise." Likewise, you can take five vows not to commit the five crimes with immediate retribution; five vows not to commit the five crimes that are almost as grave, and four vows not to commit the four serious faults.

The four serious faults are stated to be:

The serious fault of taking the head of the row of scholars,[243]
The serious fault of appropriating a tantrika's wealth,
The serious fault of accepting the homage of a fully ordained monk,
The serious fault of eating the practitioner's food.

The fourth refers not to the food in general of anyone who is a practitioner, but to a situation where eating the provisions of a practitioner who is short of food and who has decided, "With this amount of food I can practice x number of months," will make his or her food run out prematurely.

The eight perverse acts are cited as:

Maligning the good, praising the bad,
Stopping the virtuous accumulating merit,

Disturbing the minds of the faithful,
Forsaking the teacher, the deity, and Dharma kindred,
Separating from the sacred mandala, these are the eight.

These, then, are: (1) maligning those who are on the white side, who practice virtue; (2) praising those who are on the black side, who practice evil; (3) creating obstacles and preventing the virtuous from accumulating merit and wisdom; (4) speaking unpleasantly to those who have faith and are practicing positive actions, and thus upsetting them; and (5–8) the last four occur when a mandala of the Secret Mantra Vajrayana has been revealed and subsequently there are fights, quarrels, and disputes among the practitioners of that mandala, so that they become separated from the teacher, the deity, the vajra brothers and sisters, and the sacred mandala.

There are thus eight vows you can take not to commit these eight perverse acts.

Then, related to the precepts of the outer pratimoksha, there are first, for upasakas, 5 promises not to break the 4 root vows and the fifth vow that proscribes the drinking of alcohol. For shramaneras there are the respective promises not to transgress the 10 basic vows and the 30 details thereof. For bhikshus there are, to begin with, 4 promises not to break the 4 root vows against committing the 4 radical defeats, even if your life is at stake. Then there are 13 promises not to commit the 13 residual faults; and the respective promises not to commit the 30 downfalls requiring rejection, the 90 "mere downfalls," the 4 faults to be specifically confessed, and the 112 wrong actions. In each case your promise should be backed by the second iron commitment not to break that promise.[244]

Next, for Bodhisattvas who follow the tradition of the Profound View, there are 20 vows not to commit the 18 root downfalls or transgress the precepts of aspiration and application (making twenty in all), nor commit the 80 faults; and for those who follow the tradition of the Vast Activity there are relevant promises concerning the 4 attitudes, the 8 applications, and the 46 branch faults.

In the Mantrayana, you should make promises not to transgress the 25 yogas, the common[245] outer and inner vows of the outer and inner 5 Buddha families, the 14 root downfalls, and the 8 lesser downfalls; and, in the Great Perfection, the 27 root samayas, the 25 branches, and the 4 samayas of nonexistence, omnipresence, unity, and spontaneous presence. And in each case it is important to seal your promise with a second iron commitment not to break it even if your life is at stake.

So think, "I promise not to break those vows that I am able to keep, and I will do my best to keep those that I am unable to keep: Guru Vajrasattva, bless me that I may be completely purified." As you make each of these promises, you will become more and more pure.

On the other hand, nothing at all will come of reciting abstractedly, "I vow to stop from now on."

Concerning the power of action as an antidote, although any positive action can act as an antidote for negative actions, in this case the power of action as an antidote refers to visualizing the nectar flowing down and cleansing you.

When you do the dharmakaya recitation that benefits yourself, develop extraordinary confident faith in the Buddhas and Bodhisattvas and then practice the emanation of light rays. When you do the rupakaya recitation that benefits others, meditate on beings, recognizing them as your mothers, remembering their kindness, and so on, and arouse unbearably intense compassion, then practice the emanation and reabsorption of light rays.*

---

*See WMPT pages 271–72.

CHAPTER FOUR

Offering the Mandala to Accumulate Merit and Wisdom

IT IS NOT ENOUGH simply to have purified adverse conditions, namely negative actions and obscurations. It is also necessary to gather favorable conditions, that is, the accumulations of merit and wisdom. Just as on the path of the Causal Vehicle of Characteristics we have to practice accumulation and purification for one measureless kalpa before we finally see the truth of the absolute nature on the path of seeing, here too, in order to give rise in our minds to the extraordinary realization of the profound path, our practice of both purification and accumulation has to be complete.

We have already seen how to purify negative actions in the chapter on Vajrasattva, and we come now to the accumulation of merit and wisdom.

I. THE NEED FOR THE TWO ACCUMULATIONS

Although the Bodhisattvas' activities in accumulating merit and wisdom seem infinite, here we can speak of two accumulations: the "apparent" accumulation of merit with concepts and the "nonapparent" accumulation of wisdom without concepts.

The "apparent" accumulation of merit with concepts comprises the five transcendent perfections (from generosity to concentration) related to the practice of skillful means. Transcendent wisdom is the accumulation of wisdom.

The result of these two accumulations is the attainment of the two kayas. How this actually happens is explained in the New Tradition as follows. The

233

accumulation of merit with concepts creates the direct cause, and the accumulation of wisdom without concepts creates the supporting condition for attaining the rupakaya of the Buddha. On the other hand, the accumulation of wisdom without concepts creates the direct cause and the accumulation of merit with concepts creates the supporting condition for attaining the dharmakaya of ultimate buddhahood.

According to the Ancient Tradition, however, in the state of buddhahood, the primordially pure essential nature, all the qualities of the Conqueror's three kayas are perfect and complete from the very beginning, without having to be sought, but they do not manifest clearly unless one relies on the two accumulations as contributory conditions. They are compared to the sun and its rays in the sky: the rays are naturally there with the sun, but when the sun is obscured by clouds its rays are no longer visible; it is necessary for the wind to get up for the clouds to be blown away. Now although the wind is the cause that dispels the clouds, it is not the real cause that produces the sun. Similarly, without accumulating merit and wisdom one cannot ultimately obtain the result, the two kayas, but these two accumulations are not the real causes that give rise to the two kayas. They are, rather, contributory conditions that we term causes.

None of the levels of fruition, therefore, from those of the Shravakas and Pratyekabuddhas up to the perfect great enlightenment, can be attained without accumulating merit and wisdom. Nevertheless, the methods for gathering the two accumulations are not all completely the same. For Shravakas and Pratyekabuddhas the accumulation of merit with concepts comprises the practices of discipline and concentration, and the accumulation of wisdom without concepts comprises the realization of the no-self of the individual and of only the "gross" no-self of phenomena. For them the indivisible atoms of perceived phenomena and the indivisible instants of the perceiver constitute the absolute truth. This is not because Shravakas and Pratyekabuddhas are incapable of logical analysis but because they do not dare go further. They argue that if the indivisible atoms in perceived phenomena did not exist, there would be nothing from which the universe and its inhabitants could be formed. And if there were no indivisible instants making up a perceiver, there would be no basis for karma (cause and effect) and samsara. So they assert that these things exist.

For Bodhisattvas the accumulation of merit with concepts comprises the five transcendent perfections, which are related to the practice of skillful means; the accumulation of wisdom without concepts is the perfection of transcendent wisdom. Alternatively, we can say that for each of the transcendent perfections, generosity and so forth, there is what from the means-appearance aspect is called the apparent accumulation of merit, and what from the wisdom-emptiness aspect is called the nonapparent accumulation of wisdom.

For beginners the two accumulations are dealt with separately and cannot be practiced together, but for those who have attained the Bodhisattva levels the emptiness supreme in all aspects arises in the form of the six transcendent perfections, so that from the appearance point of view such Bodhisattvas are accumulating merit, and from the emptiness point of view, being free from the three concepts, they are accumulating wisdom.

You might wonder whether the two accumulations gathered by these three kinds of beings—Shravakas, Pratyekabuddhas, and Bodhisattvas—are the same, but they are quite unalike. In terms of the cause or motivation, the practice one concentrates on, and the result that is attained, there is a very great difference between them.

As for the Mantrayana, in the three outer tantras all the yogas with images are the accumulation of merit with concepts, and the yogas without images are the accumulation of wisdom without concepts. Of the inner tantras, in Mahayoga everything in the generation phase related to skillful means is the accumulation of merit with concepts, and the perfection phase related to wisdom is the accumulation of wisdom without concepts. In Anuyoga, just the generation phase part and all the active control of the yogic exercises in which one concentrates on the channels, energies, and essences, and the arising as the illusionlike body of the deity in the postmeditation period constitute the accumulation of merit with concepts, while the primal wisdom brought about by the four joys that arise through these skillful practices constitutes the accumulation of wisdom without concepts. As for Atiyoga, in the trekchö based on primordial purity it is not incorrect to apply the term "accumulation of merit" to the wisdom of the essential nature and the term "accumulation of wisdom" to the wisdom of the natural expression that is clarity. Another way of classifying these is to say that the four visions related to spontaneous presence constitute the accumulation of merit, and the trekchö based on primordial purity constitutes the accumulation of wisdom. In this case they are classified according to their relative importance in ultimately bringing about the attainment of the two kayas.

It is possible, nevertheless, for beginners to develop something akin to the union of the two accumulations. In the vehicle of the six transcendent perfections,[246] for each of the six, one first goes through much repeated analysis and then meditates using the eight similes of illusion. In the three outer tantras, one practices the union of the two accumulations, in this case the yoga with images and the yoga without images, whose result is the deities of the three families. According to Mahayoga, one meditates on the essential nature that is emptiness, the radiant aspect that is great compassion and the form aspect that is the seed syllable, and by transforming these one creates the mandala of the palace and deity.[247] In Anuyoga one practices the two accumulations together in arising as the deity, as the pure or impure illusory body, this being the union of Buddha body (the illusory body) and Buddha mind (the illustrative clear light and absolute clear light). In Atiyoga, (1) the inseparability in the trekchö based on primordial purity of the wisdom of the void essential nature and the wisdom of the radiant natural expression, which is the inner luminous compassion, and (2) the union in the thögal based on spontaneous presence of the absolute space and primal wisdom (that is, of the radiance of primal purity and of its essential nature, the great primordially pure emptiness) constitute the union of the two accumulations. Genuine union, however, does not come until one reaches the Bodhisattva levels.

The accumulation of merit and wisdom on the Sutrayana and Mantrayana paths thus takes many forms, such as the seven branches, and while these paths are all essentially means for gathering the two accumulations, the offering of the mandala taught here includes them all; it is simple to perform, very effective, and easy for beginners to practice. Moreover, like a string tied around one's finger, the mandala serves as a reminder of the ways in which the three-kaya realms of the Conquerors are arranged, so you should offer it imagining the whole cosmography of the buddhafields of the three kayas. Apu and Khenpo Pema Dorje[248] speak of this as follows:

> The nature as it appears is the nirmanakaya mandala,
> The nature as it is is the sambhogakaya mandala,
> The all-pervading aspect is the dharmakaya mandala.

(A) THE ORDINARY MANDALA OF THE NIRMANAKAYA

Inside the alms bowl that Vairochana-Hemasagara holds in his hands in the gesture of meditation are twenty-five lotus flowers tiered one above the other and reaching up to his crown protuberance, the thirteenth being level with his heart, and in the middle of the latter's fresh pistil is the Saha universe of a hundred times ten million worlds, that is, a thousand million worlds.

Counting the four continents, Mount Meru, and the gods' realms as one world, a thousand of such worlds is called "a first-order universe of one thousand worlds." It is encircled by a single ring of iron mountains as high as the Heaven without Fighting.

Taking this first-order universe as the unit of calculation, a thousand such first-order universes make a "second-order intermediate universe of one thousand times one thousand worlds." It is encircled by a single ring of iron mountains of the same height as the realm of the first concentration.

A thousand of these second-order universes make a "third-order great universal system of one thousand million worlds." It is encircled by a single ring of iron mountains as high as the realm of the fourth concentration, and it constitutes the dominion of a single nirmanakaya Buddha.

This is just one example of five such Hemasagara Buddhas, or, if subdivided into families, twenty-five, and in each atom of the petals and anthers of the lotuses before them there appear an inconceivable number of distinct buddhafields. Even in something as small as the tip of a hair there are unimaginable numbers of nirmanakaya buddhafields, numerous as the atoms therein. And to take just one of those buddhafields, in every microscopic droplet of scented water that comes from each pore of the body of the Buddha in that buddhafield, there is again an array of infinite numbers of such buddhafields. Imagine the whole array of buddhafields of all these nirmanakaya Buddhas, and all the splendor and possessions of the celestial and human realms, and offer it all, adding to it everything that you cherish most, your life, good fortune, power, and strength. This is the offering of the ordinary mandala of the nirmanakaya.

(B) THE EXTRAORDINARY MANDALA OF THE SAMBHOGAKAYA

The pure nature as it is of all these impure nirmanakaya buddhafields is the sambhogakaya buddhafields endowed with the five certainties.

1. The certain place is the array of buddhafields such as the unexcelled buddhafield of the Dense Array, which is the spontaneous vision of the supreme primal wisdom:[249] as it is beyond measure it is especially exalted.

2. The certain teacher comprises the Buddhas of the five families: Vairochana-Hemasagara in the center, Vajrasattva-Hemasagara in the east, Ratnasambhava-Hemasagara in the south, Amitabha-Hemasagara in the west, and Amoghasiddhi-Hemasagara in the north. Alternatively, by further dividing them into subfamilies, we can speak of twenty-five Hemasagara Buddhas: in the center, the five Buddhas of the Body family, in the east the five Buddhas of the Vajra family, in the south the five Buddhas of the Quality family, in the west the five Buddhas of the Lotus family, and in the north the five Buddhas of the Karma family.

3. The certain assembly is composed of Bodhisattvas on the tenth level.

4. The certain teaching is that of the Great Vehicle.

5. The certain time is the ever-revolving wheel of eternity.

Taking this example of how the sambhogakaya of one Buddha is endowed with the five certainties, imagine how the buddhafields of the sambhogakaya of all the Buddhas in the three times and ten directions are arrayed and endowed with the five certainties; imagine the ground, materials, ornaments, and layout of their measureless palaces; imagine the Lady of Beauty and other goddesses who offer the delights of the senses, bearing billowing clouds of innumerable inconceivable offerings; imagine them all in their different forms, one for each of the five Buddha families,[250] and offer them all. And on top of that, make the inner offering of the pure channels, energies, and essences in your own vajra body, which are the natural expression of primal wisdom. This is the offering of the sambhogakaya mandala.

(C) THE SPECIAL ALL-PERVADING MANDALA OF THE DHARMAKAYA

What pervades these nirmanakaya buddhafields that appear impure and sambhogakaya buddhafields that are pure is the dharmakaya mandala. Moreover, the dharmakaya is the primal wisdom that makes no distinction whatsoever between samsara and nirvana, and that does not fall into the bias of existence or nonexistence. Imagine the whole display of the great unfolding power of that wisdom, all the impure phenomena of samsara and the pure phenomena of the path and of nirvana, and in particular the four visions of the spontaneous presence, not set out as piles of offerings but existing perfectly since the very beginning. Offer it all and add the whole array of thoughts that arise as the unceasing display of your own unborn mind, not to be rejected but arising as wisdom. This is the dharmakaya mandala.

Mount Meru, the four continents, and the other features of the ordinary mandala of the nirmanakaya are explained in detail in the mandala section of the *Detailed Commentary on the Condensed Meaning*, and *The Words of My Perfect Teacher* goes no further than advising one to read this text.

Now when you perform the mandala offering, to accumulate merit and wisdom begin by sweeping and cleaning the room and sprinkling it with saffron water. Then, since it is important that the offerings be complete, for as long as you are practicing the mandala make sure you always have a full set of offerings—water offerings, *shelze*,* lamps, incense, and so forth, depending on what you can afford.

II. THE ACCOMPLISHMENT MANDALA

For the accomplishment mandala, the way the piles are set out and the visualization of the field of merit are similar to those in the refuge practice. In particular, take (if necessary, borrow) a statue or painting to represent the Buddha's body, the *Abridged Prajnaparamita*, or the root text of the *Guhyagarbha Tantra* to represent his speech, and a stupa such as the Kadam Stupa[251] to represent his mind, and set them out on a table or shelf covered with a cloth.

---

*See WMPT note 214 (note 199, 1st edition).

III. THE OFFERING MANDALA

The offering mandala and the offering materials you arrange in piles on it should reflect your resources and not be tainted by stinginess. Here you are purifying your environment,[252] so make sure the offering of barley is clean and of good quality, free from stones, chaff, straw, bird droppings, and the like, and without broken bits of grain. Saturate it with scented water.

Divide your practice into sessions and breaks between sessions. Go through the preliminaries for the session. Then for the main practice, according to Tshampa Tshang's[253] and Apu's way of practicing, do the detailed recitation of the preliminaries once in each session. If you are following Tulku Shabdrung's[254] method, recite the long version of the preliminaries in the dawn session and in the later sessions use the *Mindroling Prayer Book* version, meditating briefly on each of the four contemplations that turn the mind away from samsara, from "With these freedoms and advantages so hard to find . . ." to "like bees caught in a jar."*

Then practice the refuge, bodhichitta, and Vajrasattva as much as you can. Here again you need to know which sections can be added or omitted, so that in different situations, depending on the practice you are doing, you can precede it by meditating briefly on practices like the four contemplations and doing a little in the later sessions too. Up until the mandala, therefore, simply go through the basic sequence of the practices, from the four contemplations through to Vajrasattva.

Then recite the *Sutra Remembering the Three Jewels*, and the prayer beginning, "Turning us from the road to the lower realms,"† and continue with the practice as in the *Mindroling Prayer Book* from the blessing of the ground up to the invitation and offering of a throne.

Next, depending on your inclination, recite the praises the *Twelve Deeds of the Buddha*, the *Single Verse*, and the *Two Verses*. After that recite the *Prayer of Good Actions* from "To all the Tathagatas, Lions of men" until "To all the Sugatas I sing praises."‡

At this point recite the hundred-syllable mantra while rubbing the mandala with the point on your wrist where the channel that gives rise to wis-

---

*See the prayer on page 291.
†From the *Prayer of Maitreya*; see page 161.
‡See page 292.

dom runs, three times clockwise and three times counterclockwise. As you do so, consider that with the truth of the path, the wisdom that is the realization of no-self, you are wiping away and completely purifying all the deluded, ignorant perceptions of the ground staining the mandala of the ground, which is the unborn absolute space.

Next, recite:

To the Buddhas, those thus gone,
And to the sacred Law immaculate, supreme, and rare,
And to the Buddha's offspring, oceans of good qualities,
That I might gain this precious attitude, I make a perfect offering.[255]

In other words, in order to hold within us the jewel of the precious bodhichitta, that pure attitude that is quite unlike the worldly attitude of seeking protection from fear or wishing to better our lot in this life, we are making a perfect offering—perfect in that it consists of pure constituents offered to pure objects, namely to the Three Precious Jewels and not to non-Buddhist teachers and the like. Here "pure constituents" refers to three aspects: substance, quality, and arrangement.

(A) SUBSTANCE

If you have both gold and silver, for example, the better substance is gold, and it is this you should offer to the Three Jewels. In other words, offer the best of whatever you possess.

(B) QUALITY

If you have both eighteen-carat and fourteen-carat gold,[256] it is the eighteen-carat gold that is purer, so you should offer that to the Three Jewels. Similarly, you should offer to the Three Jewels fresh butter, fresh vegetables, and sweet cheese, and not rancid butter, withered vegetables, and moldy cheese.

(C) ARRANGEMENT

Whether you have a shrine with several tiers or simply a wooden plank as a shrine, clean it thoroughly and carefully set out first the shelze, then the flower offering, and after that the water offerings. The latter should be disposed in a straight line, not crooked and higgledy-piggledy. With a set of seven large offering bowls, the bowls should be a finger's width apart, while with a set of small bowls leave enough room between them to place two grains of barley side by side. They should be neither too full nor half-empty, and should not spill over onto the offering table. Next set out the lamp offering and then the incense sticks, arranged in a lattice. In short, arrange the offerings beginning from your left (the shrine's right), avoiding the heat from the lamp offering melting the butter ornaments on the shelze or ashes from the incense dirtying the water offerings. When you undo the water offerings, empty the bowls beginning from your right (the shrine's left).

All this—setting out the offerings and removing them—must be done carefully, with a sense of modesty, awe, and respect. If it is de rigueur nowadays to serve tea to important lamas with the cups and vessels borne above the head, why should things like respect be any less necessary when making offerings to the Buddhas and Bodhisattvas?

Now hold the mandala base, placing the offering piles on it, and offer the detailed thirty-seven-element mandala. Then do a full thirty thousand recitations of "*Om Ah Hum* The cosmos of a billion universes . . . ,"[257] holding the mandala in your left hand and with your right hand counting the recitations on your mala and offering the piles with each recitation.

After that, make the offering seventy thousand times (together with the supplement for making up errors and omissions) with the following prayer by Tulku Shabdrung:

> All the wealth and positive actions, both mine and others', gathered in the three times,
> And all the mass of offerings in the infinite realms of the three kayas,
> I imagine and offer to the glorious teacher:
> Accept them and bestow the supreme and common accomplishments.
> Om Guru Buddha Bodhisattva Ratna Mandala Puja Megha Samudra Sapharana Samaya Ah Hung

When it is time to conclude the session, recite the mandala verses by Ngari Panchen that begin:

Namo, the measureless palace of the Great Powerful One . . .
The jeweled array of body and mind . . .
The precious mandala of gold and turquoise . . .
The ground is purified with perfumed water . . .
The excellent and pleasing mandala . . .

Then, continue the *Prayer of Good Actions* with "To the Conquerors I make offerings of the loveliest flowers,"* and do the ritual of the Bodhisattva vow. After that, complete the practice by going through the kusali's accumulation up to the guru yoga. All sessions conclude in the same way.

---

*See page 292.

CHAPTER FIVE

The Kusali's Accumulation: Destroying the Four Demons at a Single Stroke

THOSE WHO HAVE renounced the concerns of this life and whose ordinary activities are limited to eating, sleeping, urinating, and defecating, who wander the mountains as solitary hermits—such yogis have nothing outside they can use to accumulate merit and wisdom. They have to do so by giving up cherishing their own aggregates inside. For as we find in the *Condensed Transcendent Wisdom*:

> A Bodhisattva with the four causes who is skillful and strong—
> Hard it is for the four demons to stand up to him, impossible to move him:
> He dwells in emptiness, never losing compassion.
> He acts by the teachings and is blessed by the Sugatas.

The whole of the profound Chö is set forth and explained in this verse. "The four demons" refers to what has to be destroyed: the four demons outside and inside. "Emptiness" and "compassion" refer to the two ways in which the demon of conceit, the belief in an "I," is eradicated, namely by wisdom and by skillful means. They also indicate that the demons are subjugated by great compassion and overawed by wisdom.

"He acts by the teachings" refers to all the activities of the preparation, main part, and conclusion in the practice of the profound Chö, and also to the different levels of samaya.

"Is blessed by the Sugatas" refers to all the ripening empowerments of the profound Chö: these have to be received directly from a teacher who holds the lineage of the profound Chö.

(A) GIVING ONE'S BODY[258]

At this point in *The Words of My Perfect Teacher* only the visualization sequences for giving away the body are described, so here is a brief explanation of the basic principles.

In fact, what we have to destroy are the four demons. According to the Causal Vehicle of Characteristics, these are the demon of the aggregates, which is that which dies; the demon of negative emotions, which is what makes it die; the demon of the Lord of Death, which is death itself; and the demon of the sons of the gods, which prevents us from attaining the state of deathless peace.

What we call "demon" is not something with gaping jaws and glaring eyes: rather it is that which creates all the afflictions of samsara and prevents the attainment of liberation, the state of nirvana. In short, it is anything that harms (or afflicts) one's body and mind.

Where do all the sufferings of samsara come from? If the five inner aggregates did not exist there would be no location, or ground or vessel or support, for suffering. However, from the moment this body comes into being, it is, as it were, the location, ground, vessel, and support from which all suffering arises, and thus it is we have the *demon of the aggregates.*

Regarding the negative emotions, there are eight-four thousand of them, and they can all be included within the five or three poisons. These can be summarized as wrong mental activity, which is to consider the aggregates as pure, blissful, self, and permanent. Driven by this improper mental activity, the view of a self, we give rise to thoughts that are the negative emotions of attachment, aversion, and bewilderment. Then, motivated by these negative emotions, we accumulate negative actions, and because of our actions we cannot help subsequently taking birth and dying in samsara. So what makes us die is the *demon of negative emotions.*

As for the demon of death, it is death itself. On the gross level, if there is birth, then naturally there is death, and thus sentient beings are powerless to avoid being afflicted and distressed by death. On the subtle level there is natural impermanence; every instant things are changing, and the nature of impermanence is by definition suffering. So we speak of the *demon of the Lord of Death.*

The *demon of the sons of the gods*, the distraction that prevents our attaining the peace beyond death, refers to the distracting thoughts that divert the consciousness toward outer objects and obstruct the path to liberation and omniscience. Because of these there is, constantly shadowing us, what the Causal Vehicle of Characteristics calls the Wicked Black Demon with his henchmen, and what the Mantrayana refers to as the Lord of Supreme Joy. Although the latter is a god of the world of form, because of his attachment to objects of desire, he dwells in the Joyous Realm of Tushita, some distance from the city.[259]

(B) THE MEANING OF CHÖ

In the Mantrayana, the four demons are identified thus:

The tangible demon, the intangible demon,
The demon of exultation, and the demon of conceit:
All are included in the demon of conceit.

The *tangible demon* represents external dangers: fires, floods, precipices, lightning, savage beings, enemies, robbers and thieves, vipers and carnivorous beasts, flesh-eating spirits, and any other frightening things that can harm our bodies and minds.

The *intangible demon* refers to inner attachment, aversion, bewilderment, and the other eight-four thousand negative emotions, which give rise to all the sufferings of samsara.

The *demon of exultation* is the exultation that comes when one is wandering in haunted places,[260] in the mountains, and so on, and one thinks, "My teacher is not like other teachers, his teachings are not like other teachings, there are no practices quite like mine, my vajra brothers and sisters are much better than anybody else's." In short, the demon of exultation is the attachment and infatuation one feels when one achieves the slightest inner warmth or power in one's concentration.

The *demon of conceit* is the root of the preceding three demons. It is the conceited belief in "I" and "me" that makes one think that the five aggregates are "me" or "mine." If one eradicates this inner demon, all the outer demons will automatically be destroyed. For example, when one cuts a tree at the root, all the branches and leaves are brought down in the process. Similarly, since the root of the demons described here is contained in this inner demon of self-centered conceit, it is this that we have to destroy.

There are two ways in which we can do this: destroying it with skillful means and destroying it with wisdom.

Shravakas and Pratyekabuddhas, with their limited means and wisdom, overcome the gross demons and thus attain liberation, but they do not overcome the subtle four demons, such as the subtle state of ignorance and habitual tendencies, the mental body, untainted karma, and the inconceivable death and transmigration.

Bodhisattvas, on the other hand, have to destroy both the gross and subtle demons. Bodhisattvas who have entered the Mantrayana as Vidyadharas[261] also have to overcome all the gross and subtle demons, but there is a very great difference in the means used to destroy them.

(1) Cutting through the Belief in a Self with Skillful Means

Throughout time without beginning the belief in an "I" has given rise to all the suffering experienced until now, and if it is not eliminated it will continue to wreak endless harm; so the defects of this belief in a self have to be recognized. At the same time as recognizing these defects, you need to understand the qualities that are obtained through the jewel-like bodhichitta: temporarily the attainment of the higher realms and the qualities of the Bodhisattva levels, and ultimately the state of omniscience.

To make the precious, jewel-like bodhichitta take birth, meditate on the four boundless qualities and on the bodhichitta practices of considering others as equal to oneself and exchanging oneself and others, practicing until you have uprooted your self-centeredness. Thinking of all sentient beings as your mother and yourself as their child, in order to help them achieve temporary and ultimate happiness give away the three possessions, namely your body, your wealth, and your positive actions accumulated in the past, present, and future. If you can thus destroy attachment to these three possessions, then there will be no other basis for ego-clinging.

Training the mind in this way and destroying the demon of self-infatuation is what we call Chö. You do not have to rattle a damaru, tinkle a bell, blow a thigh-bone trumpet, sport matted locks on your head, or carry a skull cup in your hands. With the jewel of bodhichitta you can banish and obliterate this inner conceit, this belief in a self, while doing nothing at all. Someone who can do this is termed "the best, recumbent-cow sort of Chö practitioner."

Quite the opposite are the sort who have no idea that it is the demon of conceit inside that they need to eradicate: they see ghosts and *gyelgong*s[262] in everything that happens and brag about what they have to destroy as if it were something outside themselves. With cries of "P'et!" and angry glares they blast away on their thigh-bone trumpets and drub their damarus, upsetting people, making dogs cower in fear, and pitting themselves against spirits as if they were bitter rivals. Such Chöpas are "the worst, yapping-dog type of Chö practitioners," and it is to them that Machik Labdrön was referring when she prophesied the emergence of "false doctrines of Chö, the teachings of the demons."* They are the Chö "adepts" with matted locks we see nowadays, boasting they have seen gods when they have not, that they have seen demons when they have seen none, and that they have attained accomplishment, though they have attained nothing of the sort. They give their time to horse racing, archery, drinking, and womanizing, and with their performance of a semblance of the practice they fool themselves and others alike into having faith and believing they are *siddha*s. These Chöpas create a stone that drags themselves and others down to the depths of the hells. They are emanations of the demons of false Chö practices, the Ninefold Black Chö; they are counselors in evil,[263] spirits who lead one astray. Keep away from them.

(2) Cutting through the Belief in a Self with Wisdom

The belief in an "I," this inner conceit concerning our own aggregates, has to be destroyed, and its destruction involves realizing the meaning of Prajnaparamita, preserving the natural state of that view through meditation, and enhancing it through action. Here, however, to make things easier to understand, we will consider the aggregates: it is the belief that they are "me" and "mine" that is the demon we have to destroy.

In order to establish conclusively that they are devoid of any basis or origin, we should examine whether the personal self, the so-called I, is the same as or different from the five aggregates. If we do so, we will come to the conclusion that it does not exist as anything, being neither the same nor different, that there is no basis for a self, that it is like space. Furthermore, the five aggregates, which we use as a base on which to stick the label "I," can be split into their gross parts, and these can be divided into subtle particles, each

---

*See WMPT pages 302–3.

with their different conceptual parts, and into different instants of time,[264] having moments when they come into being and moments when they cease to exist. And when we examine their shape, particular features, color, and so forth, we will find there is nothing there, and we will come to a definite conclusion as to the way all material things are: inconceivable and inexpressible, like space, free from concepts, vast, and mind-transcending, by nature the Mother, Transcendent Wisdom.

(C) THE ACTUAL PRACTICE OF OFFERING THE BODY

Having reached this conclusion, one preserves the flow of the wisdom of this realization and accustoms oneself to it. Practitioners who have received empowerment, kept pure samaya, and achieved a little warmth in the view and meditation, or have at least been through the approach[265] and obtained a bit of stability in the generation phase, may then fearlessly throw themselves into taking on obstacles and unfavorable circumstances. Practicing taking obstacles as accomplishments and bad omens as good signs, they wander in haunted spots, in the mountains, and like places. There they make use of outer spirits (those they can actually see or whose presence they can feel) to frighten themselves. When this happens, they are so petrified they simply stop thinking. In that empty state where all thoughts cease, there is left the natural state of the mind, transcendent wisdom, arising naked, stripped of thoughts. That is what has to be recognized. If they have not yet done so, it is vitally important for their own benefit that Chö practitioners give birth to this realization and, if they have done so, that they further it. Then, for others' benefit, they think of all gods and demons with love, compassion, and bodhichitta, considering them as their mothers. In order to repay their kindness they give their own bodies to them as food. In this way they benefit intangible beings such as spirits who can be turned to the Dharma. For untamed spirits who cannot be brought into service for the Dharma in this way, Chö practitioners engage in the activity of subduing them by wrathful means, with the wrathful form of compassion, like a mother who, having failed to induce good behavior in her children by giving them sweets and other treats, puts on a compassionate show of anger and gives them a good smack.

Thus, as a yogi who has severed the inner demon of conceit at the root, you should gather gods and demons under your power with great compassion and overawe them with wisdom. First you should recognize that these spirits have been your mothers, remember their kindness, and wish to repay that kindness. Developing an almost physically unbearable compassion from your desire to free them all from suffering and its causes, visualize yourself as Vajra Yogini (or a similar deity), who is the manifest radiance of that compassion, and bring them under your control. Then with the view of transcendent wisdom, the Absolute Mother, dissolve everything—yourself, the place, and the spirits—into the absolute space free of the three concepts and remain in equanimity, relaxed and at ease in the expanse of emptiness free from concepts that excludes nothing (neither the phenomena of samsaric existence nor those of nirvanic peace), never has excluded anything, and never will. In this way all dualistic perceptions will be awed into submission in the absolute space, in the same way as a king's subjects are overawed by the king sitting on his throne.

Next, without stinginess or attachment, give your body to the gods and demons in whatever form they might want, banishing all clinging to the aggregates. You should think, "Even if you spirits were not to harm this useless old body of mine, even if you were to protect it, one day nobody, not even I, will be able to protect it. So whichever of you wants it, take it, carry off all you need. Whatever is going to happen, let it happen. If something unpleasant is to befall me, let everything else nasty be added on top."

In complete contrast to this, there are those who recklessly bully gods and demons while running after fame and the other seven ordinary concerns. Thinking, "Don't cut short my longevity and sever my life force, don't take away my life spirit," they make a mere show of offering the body, a pretense at exorcising haunted places, a masquerade as "visitors of a hundred springs."[266] They go through the recitation of wrathful mantras, visualization of the protection circle, and prayers to the teacher, thinking that if they meditate on compassion it has to be wrathful and that if they meditate on emptiness it has to be wrathful. Such people, rather than destroying the demon of conceit, have truly been carried away by demons. Whether one lives in a village or is wandering in haunted places, it is this inner demon of conceit that has to be destroyed. So the ultimate point of the practice of the profound Chö must be to destroy "I" and "me" with the emptiness whose essence is compassion.

When we practice offering the body, we have to bring to the fore our latent infatuation with our body. All the food, clothes, dwellings, and possessions we have in this worldly life are accumulated through negative actions and suffering—with this body our chief concern. More than anything else, it is our body that we value and cherish most. So after fully exposing this infatuation, think of all beings, and principally gods and demons, recognizing them as your mothers, remembering their kindness, and wishing to repay their kindness. And in order to repay that kindness, make an offering and gift of your body to the four guests.

When you are accumulating offerings of the mandala, for example, you should perform the white feast at daybreak, the variegated feast at noon, and the red feast at dusk. Alternatively you can offer the three great feasts in each session.

In particular, in cases of illness due to powerful negative forces, and for those spirits who are not appeased by the white feast and who crave flesh and blood, it is necessary to perform the red feast. The black feast should be used when these feasts are not effective in appeasing the spirits, or if they are only partially effective, or if they seem to be working but it is taking too long for the full effect to be felt. Never perform it, though, if it is because you are feeling impatient or vexed at trifles, for this would be quite contrary to the path of bodhichitta. Although Patrul Rinpoche did teach the visualization for the black feast occasionally, he did not write it down.

Khenpo Ngawang Pelzang (1879–1941).

CHAPTER SIX

The Profound Guru Yoga, the Ultimate Method for Arousing the Wisdom of Realization in One's Mind

I. THE REASON FOR GURU YOGA: A COMPARISON OF THE ROLE OF THE TEACHER IN THE NINE YANAS

In every one of the nine vehicles of the path that leads to total liberation, the important thing is to attain the result by generating the wisdom of realization in one's mind. According to the New Tradition—"Shravakas too meditate on emptiness, and the result of it is cessation"—there are no such things as high and low views. But according to the Ancient Tradition of the Mantrayana, there *are* high and low views. Even though Shravakas and Pratyekabuddhas are not without wisdom, their wisdom is limited. Bodhisattvas, on the other hand, have realized the view of transcendent wisdom, and so their wisdom is not limited but immense; in other words, theirs is a lofty view. There is thus an enormous difference between the Shravakas' and Pratyekabuddhas' wisdom on the one hand and that of the Bodhisattvas on the other.

◈ THE BASIC VEHICLE

Shravakas and Pratyekabuddhas begin by looking for an abbot or a teacher who has all the proper qualifications. Then, motivated by the determination to be free as intention, they take the pratimoksha vows. If they subsequently practice the superior and precious threefold training, they attain the level of liberation. For them the main part or essence of all paths is wisdom, with discipline and concentration as accessory supports, and so they are said to practice the truth of the path and its accessory supports; but nowhere is it said that Shravakas and Pratyekabuddhas attain the level of Arhat merely through faith in the teacher or abbot.

You might argue that since the Buddha, in a sutra, tells Shariputra, "It is through faith that absolute truth is realized," no-self can be realized merely through faith. But this is not the case: the point of this quotation is that without faith there is no way to enter the path and that, since it is faith that opens the door to the whole Dharma, we must begin by having faith. It does not mean that we can realize the absolute through faith alone.

If we dispute with the abbot or teacher who gave us the vows, this will create an obstacle on the path, so it is necessary to have faith. But we cannot attain the Shravakas' or Pratyekabuddhas' state of Arhat through faith alone; we must also meditate on the path of the Four Noble Truths.

◊ The Bodhisattva Vehicle

As for Bodhisattvas, if they do not rely on a spiritual teacher as their outer tutor and train their minds in love, compassion, and bodhichitta as their inner tutor, they will not see the truth of dharmata on the path of seeing. For this reason it is said:

> Take as a teacher someone peaceful, disciplined, perfectly peaceful,
> Possessed of superior qualities and knowledge of the texts;[267]
> Who understands them fully, is skilled at explaining them,
> Is full of love, and never tires of teaching.

Bodhisattvas follow a teacher who has these ten qualities,[268] or at least a spiritual friend who has trained his mind in love, compassion, and bodhichitta, relying on him with devotion and arousing the mind turned toward supreme enlightenment. Nowhere is it said that they see the truth of dharmata on the path of seeing merely through faith, without their first having trained in the infinite activities of completion, maturation, and training that constitute the Bodhisattva path, in short, the six transcendent perfections.

If they harm the teacher and develop negative views toward him, they will accumulate very negative karma:

Those who harbor evil in their minds
Against such lords of generosity, the Buddha's heirs,
Will stay in hell, the Mighty One has said,
For ages equal to the moments of their malice.[269]

All the sources of good they had previously accumulated will be destroyed, like iron cut by iron.

Bodhisattvas have to begin by accumulating merit, from the lesser path of accumulating onward, and no one would say that Bodhisattvas can develop the wisdom of realization by praying to the teacher with devotion, seeing him as a Buddha—though this may certainly result in accumulating immense merit:

Yet if someone generates perfect faith
He will reap even superior fruit.[270]

❧ THE THREE OUTER TANTRAS[271]

Bodhisattvas who have entered the Mantrayana as Vidyadharas first receive from an authentic vajra master the ripening empowerments of the three outer tantras, namely the five common empowerments of awareness:[272] the introduction to the Buddha families through the water empowerment, crown empowerment, and so on, and the permission empowerments. They observe discipline by keeping the samaya perfectly, and they practice the path, meditating on the two types of yoga—with and without images. As a result, the objects they use as supports for their accomplishment manifest signs of warmth in the practice: butter lamps start to burn by themselves, rainbows appear, and so on. When this happens, they take the accomplishments of their practice[273] and thereby attain the ordinary accomplishment and become equal in fortune to the gods of the desire and form realms. Then, without discarding their bodies they depart miraculously to a buddhafield such as the Potala Mountain. There they meet Avalokiteshvara, or Manjushri or some other deity, and immediately attain the supreme accomplishment. Subsequently, after five, seven, or sixteen human lifetimes, they reach the level of vajra holder of the three, four, or five Buddha families.

If such practitioners enter into conflict with their vajra masters, this will prevent them from attaining accomplishment. On the other hand, it is not generally stated that by avoiding all conflict with their teacher and praying to him, seeing him as a Buddha, they will develop the wisdom of realization, even though this is not entirely impossible. So attaining the supreme accomplishment merely through devotion to the teacher without practicing the vajra master's teachings, namely the yogas with and without images, is not something that is taught in the three outer tantras.

◆ THE THREE INNER YOGAS
Mahayoga

In the three inner yogas of Vajrayana, practitioners first receive the empowerments that constitute the entrance to Mahayoga, the ten outer empowerments that benefit, and so on. Having completely received the four empowerments, they observe discipline by keeping perfectly pure samaya. They then practice the path, which is twofold, consisting of the generation phase and perfection phase. Through their practicing the generation phase and mainly the energies aspect of the perfection phase, the illustrative clear light heralded by the four experiences of emptiness arises in their minds. In the postmeditation period, through the clear light of the three appearances acting as the cause and the five light rays of the energies acting as the condition, they arise as the illusory body of the deity. Then, when the time has come to realize the absolute clear light, they perform the group practice. Having done so, at dusk they take the accomplishments from the deity, at midnight they take them from the hostile forces, and at dawn from the consort, as a result of which the absolute clear light arises in their minds. In the postmeditation period they arise as the union deity on the path of learning.

In this tradition, any conflict with the vajra master renders any accomplishment as impossible as bringing back to life someone whose head has been cut off. Moreover, in the present life many undesirable things—premature death, frequent illness, and so on—will happen to one. And in the next life one will be reborn and suffer in the vajra hell, from which it is hard to escape. On the other hand, practitioners who pray to the vajra master, seeing him as a Buddha, will achieve the supreme accomplishment, which is the wisdom of realization. But this is not a point that is emphasized in the Mahayoga texts. What they teach, rather, is that the activity that boosts accomplishment is mainly the performance of the group practice followed by constant application in the mudra practice relying on another's body.

◊ *Anuyoga*

In Anuyoga, practitioners first receive all the ripening empowerments—outer, inner and secret—from a qualified teacher and subsequently keep discipline with perfectly pure samaya. For the practice on the path, they practice the generation phase only partially and concentrate mainly on the perfection stage related to the essences. As the channels are straightened, the energies properly directed, and the essences mastered, the illustrative wisdom dawns in their minds, heralded by the four joys. Then in the postmeditation period they arise as the impure illusory body of the deity. By constant application to the unelaborated mudra practice relying on another's body, which is the activity that boosts realization of the absolute clear light, they realize it, and in the postmeditation period they arise as the union body on the path of learning.

Here again, the Anuyoga texts say that in order to come to realization of the absolute wisdom, one meditates mainly on the perfection stage and uses the mudra practice as a means to progress, but nowhere is it taught that one can attain the supreme accomplishment solely through devotion to the teacher.

However, when the masters of the inner Mantrayana say, "It is taught that accomplishments depend on the lama," this means that accomplishments depend on the lama rather than on the yidam or the dakini, but this is a question of the minds of individuals: some beings have faith in the lama, some in the yidam, and others in the dakini. If we have such devotion to the teacher that we see him as a Buddha, the wisdom of realization will arise in the mind without our meditating on the generation and perfection phases. This opinion is shared by the New Tradition. Nevertheless, both Mahayoga and Anuyoga teach that the main meditations are the generation and perfection phases.

That being the case, if one enters into conflict with the teacher and vajra brothers and sisters, one will confirm the saying

> Channels go awry, energies go awry, all sorts of things go wrong,
> Gaping and glaring, meditating on the deity one becomes, instead, a ghost.

If, on the other hand, one meditates on the teacher as being essentially the deity, with no conflict with one's teacher and vajra brothers and sisters, then accomplishments will be close and blessings swift.

◈ *Atiyoga*

In the special tradition of Atiyoga, practitioners first receive from an authentic lama the four types of empowerment of the Great Perfection: elaborate, unelaborate, very unelaborate, and extremely unelaborate. They then observe discipline by keeping the samayas perfectly. For those whose realization develops gradually, for whom there is something to be kept, there are the twenty-seven root samayas to be observed with respect to the teacher's body, speech, and mind, and the twenty-five branch samayas. For those of sudden realization, for whom there is nothing to be kept, there are the samayas of nonexistence, omnipresence, unity, and spontaneous presence.

The practice consists of two paths: the trekchö based on primordial purity and the thögal based on spontaneous presence. In Atiyoga, however, whether it is practiced by beings who rely on mental references or by those in whom awareness arises by itself, it is not taught (as it is in the preceding vehicle) that the boosting activity for initially bringing about realization, preventing it from declining, and further making it grow is mainly the group practice and constant application to the mudra practice, using someone else's body. What then is the most important thing here? It is to pray to the teacher with such devotion that we see him as a Buddha. If we do so, the wisdom of realization will take birth in our minds:

> With six months of unwavering devotion,
> You will reach the level of Vajradhara.

Also:

> Through devotion to the teacher, even the graded levels and paths
> Are accomplished within months or years.

So we must see the teacher as Buddha. How? In the pratimoksha tradition, whether or not the teacher is a sublime Shravaka or Pratyekabuddha, it is sufficient to see him as an ordinary person with good qualities. In the Bodhisattva tradition, it is enough to see the teacher as someone with

Bodhisattva qualities, whether he is on one of the sublime Bodhisattva levels or a nirmanakaya Buddha or simply someone on the greater path of accumulating. In the tradition of the Great Perfection, seeing one's teacher as an ordinary pandit, a sublime Arhat, a sublime Bodhisattva, a nirmanakaya Buddha, or even a sambhogakaya Buddha will not do: you have to see him as the dharmakaya Buddha. If you are able to do so and pray to him thus with unwavering devotion, the wisdom of realization can arise in your mind without your having to rely on any other factor as a path. This manner of realization has been borne out in many cases: in the noble land of India, those of Naropa, Nagabodhi, and the master Ghandhapa; and in Tibet, those of Sogpo Lhapel,[274] the Great Omniscient Longchenpa, the Vidyadhara Jigme Lingpa, and others.

In order to see the teacher as a Buddha, there are five things you should know: (1) that he is a Buddha; (2) that everything he does is the activity of a Buddha; (3) that for us he is even kinder than all the Buddhas; (4) that this immensely kind teacher is the embodiment of all the refuges; and (5) that if you pray to him with all this in mind, the wisdom of realization will take birth in your being without your having to depend on any other factors as a path.

(A) KNOWING THAT THE TEACHER IS A BUDDHA

We can know this from the point of view of the expedient meaning and from that of the ultimate meaning.

(1) The Expedient Meaning

According to the expedient meaning, the lama is actually a nirmanakaya Buddha. Here you should know that in response to the minds of others, the Buddhas temporarily compound the rupakaya for the sake of beings to be helped, in order to benefit them in ways appropriate to their needs. They appear interdependently, like the moon reflected in water, through the power of their compassion and prayers of aspiration on the one hand, and the merit of beings on the other. Having understood this, if you pray with devotion it is natural that the Buddhas' blessings will enter you. But if, because of a lack of wisdom, you still take the teacher to be a "form body" in the sense of something solid and real—if you cling to impure perceptions and consider the teacher as an ordinary individual—such prayer will not be the perfect means for developing primal wisdom. As the Buddha said:

> Those who see me as a form,
> Or think of me as words
> Are on the wrong path.
> They are not seeing me.

Nevertheless, it is taught that the teacher is a manifestation of the Buddha. How can this be explained?

> Ananda, do not be sad.
> Ananda, do not lament.
> In the final five hundred years,[275]
> I will return as spiritual friends
> And act for your and others' sake.

This is how the common tradition of the sutras and tantras sees the accomplishment of the teacher, perceiving him as a Buddha.

(2) The Ultimate Meaning

According to the extraordinary ultimate meaning, however, the lama is the dharmakaya in reality. This can be shown by reasoning and by scriptural authority.

(a) DEMONSTRATING THIS BY REASONING

The teacher's mind is the wisdom present in the ground nature, which is profundity and clarity inseparable.[276] Whether or not we understand that, its essence is the primordially pure buddhahood, the eternal, constant, unchanging, and uncompounded Buddha dharmakaya. As it is said:

> Recognize the Buddhas as dharmata;
> The guides are the dharmakaya.

The manifesting power or display of the Buddha dharmakaya, in which ground and result are inseparable, is the rupakaya, an empty form appearing as the "mandala of ornaments" of the inexhaustible body, speech, and mind of the lama. The essence of the rupakaya is the dharmakaya. The expression of the dharmakaya is the rupakaya. In truth, these two aspects are inseparable, they are the great sameness, the union Vajradhara, Samantabhadra, Vajrasattva the sovereign of all the Buddha families and mandalas, the great primal wisdom pervading all samsara and nirvana, the dharmakaya of the Buddhas. It is because of this crucial point that we say:

> I take refuge in the external universe, the host of glorious lamas;
> I take refuge in the beings of the universe, the host of male and female deities;
> I take refuge in all phenomena, the host of glorious lamas.[277]

Inwardly what is pointed to is the ultimate wisdom, the mind of the teacher, the dharmakaya. And the pointer that points to it is the symbolic teacher who appears in the form of his body, speech, and mind. This is how natural logic is used to prove that the teacher is the Buddha.

(b) Demonstrating This by Scriptural Authority

There are innumerable quotations from the scriptures, such as "The genuinely accomplished Buddha . . . ."*

(B) KNOWING THAT EVERYTHING THE TEACHER DOES IS THE ACTIVITY OF A BUDDHA

There are two kinds of activity: common and supreme.

(1) Common Activities

These refer to the four activities—pacifying, increasing, controlling, and fierce subduing—and these may be on either the spiritual or the worldly plane.

In the first place, if you do not recognize all your teacher's mundane activities as Buddha activities, your thinking of him as a Buddha will be at odds with your considering that his activities are not those of a Buddha. Therefore, if he acts as a great arbitrator and conciliator, settling quarrels and resolving people's differences on a worldly basis, you should think that this is

---

*See page 33.

the activity of pacifying. If he spends his time getting rich, farming the land, building houses, running a successful business, and so on, think that all these activities are the activity of increasing. His charisma may attract men and women alike, but even if he were to seduce a hundred girls daily, see it as the activity of bringing under control. And when he causes trouble, stirring up disputes and so on, even if he slaughters hundreds of animals every day, regard this as the activity of fierce subduing.

Also, imagine him emanating white rays of light and performing the activity of pacifying, removing the eight and sixteen great dangers such as disease, war, and famine; imagine that he emanates yellow rays of light and performs the activity of increasing, spreading the six boons such as longevity, merit, glory, and wealth; imagine that he emanates red rays of light and performs the activity of controlling, using the four types of aspiration such as that of bringing the three worlds under his power; or imagine that he emanates dark green rays of light and performs the activity of fierce subduing, for example, killing, liberating, and destroying all enemies and obstacle makers.

(2) Supreme Activity

This refers to showing beings to be benefited the path of liberation according to the three kinds of enlightenment and bringing them to liberation and omniscience.

(C) KNOWING THAT FOR US, THE TEACHER IS EVEN KINDER THAN THE BUDDHAS

We beings who live in this age of increase in the five degenerations are like paper under a paperweight:[278] none of the Buddhas of the past have been able to benefit us. But gazing at us with great compassion, the Buddha Vajradhara has come in the guise of a human being in order to take us as his disciples. As far as the qualities arising from riddance and realization are concerned, he is the same as all the Buddhas, but as far as we are concerned he is even kinder than they are. Neither your father, nor your mother, nor your lover, nor even the greatest and most beneficent being in the world can help you as much as your teacher.

How, you might ask, does the teacher help us? By teaching us how to give up negative actions, he closes the door of the lower realms. By teaching us how to accomplish positive actions, he sets us on the ladder leading to the higher realms and liberation. By helping us to generate bodhichitta, he sows in us the seed of omniscience. By introducing clear awareness as the dharmakaya, he ultimately bestows on us the legacy of the dharmakaya. So it is important to understand that as far as we are concerned he is even kinder than all the Buddhas.

(D) KNOWING THAT THE TEACHER EMBODIES THE WISDOM OF THE INFINITE REFUGES

Outwardly the teacher embodies the Three Jewels: his body is the Sangha, his speech is the holy Dharma, and his mind is the Buddha.

The mind with nothing to purify or acquire is the Buddha.
Its unchanging, stainless nature is the Dharma.
Its spontaneous qualities are the Sangha.
For this reason, the nature of one's own mind is supreme.

Inwardly, the teacher is the essence of the Three Roots. The root of blessings is the lama: the absolute lama that is pointed to is the great wisdom of his enlightened mind; the symbolic lama who points to it is his body, taking the form of a tantrika or an ordained monk. The yidam is the root of accomplishment: here again, the absolute deity (the absolute nature) is the great primal wisdom of the lama's mind, while the symbolic deities (phenomena),[279] the infinity of peaceful and wrathful yidam deities, are the display of that wisdom. The root of activity is the dakini: this too appears out of the skylike absolute nature of the lama's mind, the great primal wisdom, manifesting as the unobstructed creative power of compassion, liberated as it arises.

Birwapa declares:

Compassion and emptiness in a single body,
Great bliss, the essential nature of the three worlds,
Free from the stains of mental elaborations,
To the Teacher Vajradhara I bow down.

The teacher's mind is the dharmakaya, his speech is the sambhogakaya, his body is the nirmanakaya, his qualities are the wealth deities, and his activities are the Dharma protectors. The one from whom the infinite sources of refuge emanate and in whom they are all incorporated is thus the teacher. Just as the source of all the sun's rays is the sun, and they are essentially incorporated in it, similarly, in one sense the infinite sources of refuge emanate from the great primal wisdom that is the teacher's mind, and in another sense they are incorporated in that same mind. It is in this way that you should know the teacher to be the embodiment that emanates and incorporates all refuges.

(E) KNOWING THAT IF YOU PRAY TO HIM WITH ALL THIS IN MIND, THE WISDOM OF REALIZATION WILL TAKE BIRTH IN YOUR MIND

If you do not convince yourself that the infinite sources of refuge emanate from the teacher's compassionate wisdom like the rays from the sun's orb, and that everything is included and essentialized in the teacher, you will be like the master Marpa: given the choice between his teacher Naropa and the yidam Chakrasamvara, he decided the latter was the more important, and it is said that, as a result, even though his Dharma lineage was longer than a river, his human lineage withered more quickly than a flower.[280] Or like Jomo Cham: because she considered the yidam Vajrakilaya to be more important than her teacher, Guru Padmasambhava, the latter did not take her as a disciple and instead entrusted these teachings to Yeshe Tsogyal.

The compassion of the infinite refuges is like the heat of the sun, our minds are like tinder, and the teacher like a magnifying glass linking the two. If you see your teacher as a Buddha and pray with devotion, neither too tense nor too relaxed, like a well-tensioned bowstring, the wisdom of realization will take birth in your mind, as we mentioned earlier, without your having to rely for a path on other factors such as the generation or perfection phases.

I have given this explanation here even though it concerns the meaning of the sentence in *The Words of My Perfect Teacher*, "[he] has perfect authority, as having the nature of the heruka in every mandala of deities."*

---

*This sentence in WMPT comes later in the chapter on guru yoga; see WMPT page 328.

II. HOW TO PRACTICE GURU YOGA

Bearing these five points in mind, there are a number of ways to accomplish the level of the lama. The outer sadhana is the guru yoga; the inner sadhana is the *Gathering of Vidyadharas*; the secret sadhana is the *Great Compassionate One*; and the most secret sadhana is the *Seal of the Essential Drop*.[281] According to the Great Ominiscient One, outwardly one accomplishes the nirmanakaya, inwardly one accomplishes the sambhogakaya, secretly the dakini, and most secretly the equanimity of the wisdom lama.

Here, however, we are practicing the outer sadhana, the guru yoga. Apu said:

> The way to follow the teacher is with devotion, not with polite speech.
> The way to accomplish the lama's level is through devotion, not by saying prayers.

And the Protector of Beings Gemang Rinpoche declared:

> The activity that boosts the path of the Great Perfection is this yoga, the devotional path of the lama.

So it is most important to develop devotion. Similarly, the Great Master of Oddiyana said:

> If you have no doubts, you can accomplish anything you want;
> Have total confidence, and the blessings will enter you.

and:

> For anyone, man or woman, who has faith in me,
> I, the Lotus Born, have never departed—I sleep on their threshold.

There are two traditions for accomplishing the lama's level with devotion in this way: one in which the teacher's appearance is transformed and another in which it is not. In the tradition of the Omniscient Teacher[282] there is no transformation. Other teachers of the past say that it depends on different individuals or faculties: extraordinary practitioners do not need to transform the teacher's appearance; for the rest, if they do not begin by visualizing the teacher differently they will not be able to see him as a Buddha, and this is why it is important to transform the way the teacher appears.

This practice can be done in one of three ways. If one wants the blessings to enter swiftly, one does the visualization in the manner of "the jewel that includes all";[283] for the refuge practice and when praying, the lamas are visualized one above the other; and for the accumulation of merit they are visualized assembled as a crowd.

As for one's own body, in the refuge practice and purification of obscurations one visualizes oneself in one's ordinary form. For the practice of guru yoga one visualizes oneself as a yidam deity with the teacher above one's head or in ungraspable space. In the present case you should visualize yourself as Vajra Yogini. To think of yourself in your ordinary form is wrong and will prevent the blessings from entering you.

1. Visualizing the Field of Merit

Divide your time into sessions and periods between sessions. After completing the session preliminaries, begin the main practice for the session—the guru yoga—by visualizing the field of merit.

Emaho is an exclamation of contentment and wonder. At what do we wonder? At the perception of the infinite purity of all phenomena. Apu speaks of perceptions as follows:

> Deluded perception due to wrong thoughts is the impure, mistaken perception of the universe and beings as they appear to the deluded consciousnesses of the six classes of beings.
>
> The perception of interdependently arising illusionlike phenomena refers to relative phenomena perceived in the same way as magical illusions, reflections in water, and so on, by Bodhisattvas on the ten levels in the postmeditation period. Of the two kinds of relative phenomena—relative truth and "mere" relative[284]—we are talking here about the second. Such phenomena are perceived like the eight similes of illusion, without being considered to be real.
>
> Authentic perception with primal wisdom corresponds to the actualization of absolute reality, the natural state of all things; it is the object of

knowledge of the authentic primal wisdom; it is the whole of phenomena arising as the kayas and wisdoms.

Deluded perception due to wrong thoughts and the perception of interdependent illusionlike phenomena correspond to the way things appear. Authentic perception with primal wisdom corresponds to the way things are. Ordinary beings cannot see the concord between the way things appear and the way things are. Sublime beings can see it to a small degree. Only Buddhas can genuinely see it.

Here, we take what they see with their omniscience to be true and undeceptive, and we visualize the infinite purity of all phenomena, the mandala of pure phenomena dwelling in the ground, as, in this case (for we are still on the path), arisen from the ground.[285] In the generation phase, the way things appear is visualized as pure, but this is a mentally contrived purity. In the present practice things are visualized the way they are, as the kayas and wisdoms, and this is the uncontrived purity of the natural state of things: visualize everything as this infinitely pure natural state.

Regarding the appearance aspect, the deities, from the principal deity, the Guru Lake-Born Vajra in the center to the lowliest female spirits in the charnel grounds on the outskirts, all appear as main deity and retinue, but in essence their nature is the same, that of the great wisdom mind of the teacher. Their bodies have the major and minor marks, their speech has the melody of Brahma's voice, and their minds are endowed with knowledge, love, and power. They are inseparable from the teacher in the center. Visualize them all complete and perfect, as being in essence the one great wisdom.

Next, in order to counter your ordinary, dualistic thoughts, recite the verse for invoking the field of merit. At that very moment, imagine that the Glorious Copper-Colored Mountain, together with all the deities dwelling there, approaches like a great cloud sailing through the sky, and that all the teachers with whom you have a spiritual connection arrive like vultures descending on carrion.[286] The deities, palace, and all the rest dissolve into those you have visualized.

2. Offering the Seven Branches

On the path of the Sutras we have to accumulate merit for many countless kalpas, but in the Secret Mantrayana this is achieved in as many instants. This important difference is due to pure field and pure intention.

The field is pure because in the Secret Mantrayana it is not the yidams, dakinis, and so forth who are considered the principal objects through which one can accumulate merit, but the lama, who is the supreme, unsurpassable, most sublime field of merit.

The intention is pure in being the wish to attain the union level of Vajradhara in a single lifetime, in a single body, for the sake of others. This is by no means out of self-interest, for when a tantric yogi contemplates beings he sees that though they all have the Buddha nature, they have not realized this, and he feels unbearably intense compassion for them:

> The wise, with little thought of acting for themselves,
> See beings confused, stricken, in misery:
> Overwhelmed by compassion, they weep.
> Turning themselves and others from samsara, they strive to help.

Also the offering is pure, being an offering of pure materials manifested using the deity, mantras, and concentration.

All the various methods for accumulating merit and wisdom are included in the seven branches, and these can be further condensed into three: accumulation, purification, and increase. Prostrations and confession of negative actions are the branches of purification. Rejoicing and dedicating are the branches of increase. And the remaining three are the branches of accumulation.

2.1 Prostration, the Antidote to Pride

Prostration is an antidote to pride. Pride consists in thinking that we are better than others. In ordinary life we consider things such as breeding, from our father's or mother's side, and think, "I'm different from other people, I come from the *x* family, famous for . . . ," and so on. But there are no upper and lower classes, no "thick or thin bones," "big or small flesh."[287] We Tibetans are all descended from an ape, so we are no more than little monkeys.*

In the Dharma world, we become conceited if we have received a little teaching or have done a tiny bit of practice. This is what is referred to in the saying "qualities arise as a demon." When we give things with this sort

---

*See WMPT page 341.

of pride, generosity arises as a demon, "demonic generosity." The same applies to discipline and the other transcendent perfections. This is why it is said:

> Never will the water of good qualities
> Permeate the iron lump of pride.

Neither do we see faults in ourselves, nor can we see good qualities in others. So it is to counteract this attitude that we do prostrations. Instead of vying for a front-row seat,[288] you should treat deferentially even those who have broken the samaya or failed to keep their vows properly; greet them respectfully and speak to them politely.

There are three kinds of prostration. The superior kind is the "recognition of the view." This is to prostrate with the superior view, knowing that there is nothing to conceptualize: no object to which one is prostrating, no person prostrating, and no act of prostration. The middling kind of prostration is "training in meditation": prostrating by mentally emanating countless bodies, each emanating countless heads, with countless tongues singing countless songs of praise. You might think this is a practice of the generation phase, but it is not, for the countless bodies emanated are ordinary, impure bodies. The ordinary kind of prostration is to prostrate with devotion, paying reverence with one's body, reciting praises with one's speech, and exercising devotion with one's mind. Of these three points, the most important is devotion, so ordinary prostration is to perform prostrations keeping in mind the qualities of the infinite sources of refuge.

We should take particular care not to despise or scorn those in the Sangha who have broken samayas or failed to keep their vows. Treat everyone with respect, however good or bad they may be, for as we find in the *Ten Wheels of Kshitigarbha*:

> Whether they keep the precepts or not . . . ,
> My followers, however weak,
> Are worth more than a hundred ordinary people.

For men or women who do not take up the precepts, there is no end to samsara. But of those who do adopt the precepts it is taught that even if they break them, when the Buddha Infinite Aspiration comes to this world they will attain the result of their respective paths as Shravakas, Pratyekabuddhas, and so forth. Just as a hooked fish will sooner or later be drawn out of the water onto dry land, similarly, once they are hooked by virtue, the seed of liberation, they will inevitably, sooner or later, be led to the dry land of liberation. So it is important to cultivate faith and pure perception.

2.2 Offering, the Antidote to Attachment

Offering should serve as an antidote to attachment and miserliness. The term "offering" should include both offering and giving.

Offering can be summed up as three purities: pure field, pure intention, and pure materials. Pure materials are divided into things that belong to an owner and things that are not owned by anyone. The offering of things that have no owner is mentioned in the *Sutra of Skill in the Great Secret*.

It is therefore important to offer the three possessions until you attain enlightenment. At the same time use the deity, mantras, and concentration to bless these offerings, for it will then be as if they had been blessed by Vajradhara. In this way conjure up a mental offering of all things owned and unowned, epitomized by your physical offerings, as described in the life story of Samantabhadra.* Imagine great clouds of offerings, vast as the whole of space, lasting until samsara is emptied and able, as outer, inner, and secret offerings appealing to the Buddhas' six senses, to arouse extraordinary, untainted bliss.

Such mentally emanated offerings are manifestations of the wish-fulfilling jewel that is the mind, so they are especially sublime. If you are able to give mentally, you will never be materially poor. As Geshe Chengawa said, "I began by offering some acrid, poor-quality incense and I ended up offering each time an incense worth five hundred measures of gold."[289]

The teaching

Abandon all other kinds of offering:
Undertake the perfect offering to the teacher

shows that an offering to the teacher, who is the lord of all mandalas, is far superior to any other kind of offering.

*See WMPT page 321.

2.3 Confession of Harmful Actions, the Antidote to Aversion

Confession has to be made completely, employing all the four powers:

1. The outer power of support is to visualize the field of merit. The inner power of support is to take refuge and arouse bodhichitta, but there is no need to recite the refuge and bodhichitta prayers: it is sufficient to keep the relevant attitude in mind.
2. The power of regret is to feel remorse concerning the six doors of negative action that you are purifying.
3. The power of resolution is the vow that, from now on, you will not commit the same negative actions again.
4. The power of action as antidote consists, in this case, of all the remedies to negative actions indicated here in *The Words of My Perfect Teacher*.

2.4 Rejoicing, the Antidote to Jealousy

Whenever you see someone doing positive actions, or hear about or think of them, instead of feeling displeased and letting rivalry and jealousy get the upper hand, you should rejoice at all the sources of good of the Buddhas and Bodhisattvas, the Shravakas and Pratyekabuddhas, and the Vidyadharas, and at those of other, ordinary beings.

By doing so, you yourself will obtain the same merit as others, in no way impaired or diluted:

> The weight of all Mount Merus in a billion worlds could be calculated,
> But not the merit of rejoicing.

What merit, you might wonder, is one to rejoice at? All sources of good, both tainted and untainted. In terms of their essential nature, all sources of good pertaining to the absolute truth are untainted, and all those pertaining to the relative truth are tainted. In terms of the path, all the merit on the path of accumulating and joining is tainted, and the merit on the paths of vision and meditation is untainted. As a source of good, all the accumulation of merit is tainted, and all the accumulation of wisdom is untainted. In terms of meditation and postmeditation, the meditation of sublime beings is untainted, but their sources of good in the postmeditation period are tainted.[290] In terms of accompaniment, all sources of good accompanied by knowledge, whether it be the knowledge of things that can be enumerated or the knowledge of things that cannot be enumerated,[291] are untainted, and all those not accompanied by knowledge are tainted. According to the view of the inseparability of meditation and postmeditation, of samsara and nirvana, the view, meditation, and action of Mahamudra, Mahasandhi,[292] and Madhyamika are untainted in essence, but according to the way things appear, they are tainted merit.[293]

In short, rejoice at all the merit of the past, present, and future Buddhas and Bodhisattvas included in the two truths, from the moment of their first generating bodhichitta, through their accumulation of merit and wisdom, and until their final attainment of perfect enlightenment, or the result of their path,[294] and their subsequent deeds performed for the sake of beings. Next rejoice at all the merit accumulated throughout the three times by their disciples, the Shravakas and Pratyekabuddhas. After that, rejoice at all the merit of the Vidyadharas of the past, present, and future, from the moment of their generating bodhichitta, through their subsequent practice of the yogas of the two phases, until their final realization of their own particular result. Then rejoice at all the sources of good created by all beings in the past, present, and future.

Rejoicing means developing a joyful mind, seeing others' sources of good as something to be happy about, as necessary, as indispensable, without feeling jealous of them. The seven branches can be practiced perfectly well separately, so you should take every opportunity to do so.

2.5 Exhorting the Buddhas to Turn the Wheel of Dharma, the Antidote to Ignorance

In infinite buddhafields reaching to the ends of space, there are Buddhas who have attained perfect buddhahood and yet do not turn the Wheel of Dharma; there are Shravakas, Pratyekabuddhas, Bodhisattvas, and Vidyadharas who, discouraged by the ungrateful behavior of the beings they could help, tarry without teaching the Dharma. In their presence, emanate inconceivable bodies in the form of Brahma and Indra,[295] holding thousand-spoked golden wheels, offering white conches spiraling to the right, and making the following supplication:

> Beat the drum of the supreme Dharma,
> Blow the conch of the supreme Dharma,

Light the lamp of the supreme Dharma,
Hoist the colors of the supreme Dharma,
Raise the victory banner of the supreme Dharma, I entreat you.

You might wonder what Dharma Wheel you should request the Buddhas to turn. Gemang Rinpoche provides the answer: "In accordance with the disposition, faculties, and aspirations of beings to be helped." There are three outer vehicles that liberate from the origin of suffering,[296] three inner vehicles related to ascetic practices in the manner of the Vedic tradition, and three secret vehicles teaching powerful methods of transmutation, each one corresponding to the different dispositions, faculties, and aspirations of different kinds of disciples. It is these three vehicles, further subdivided into nine, that constitute the Wheel of Dharma you are requesting the Buddhas to turn.

2.6 Requesting the Buddhas not to Enter Nirvana, the Antidote to Wrong Views

In infinite buddhafields reaching to the ends of space there are perfect Buddhas who have completed eleven deeds and now wish to perform the twelfth, entering nirvana. There are also their children, the Bodhisattvas, and disciples, the Shravakas and Pratyekabuddhas, as well as Vidyadharas, who wish to depart to other buddhafields. To all of them, pray that they remain until the end of existence without entering nirvana, backing your request by offering all the wealth of gods and humans heaped together. Consider that they accept and agree to remain for a vast number of kalpas.

To pray like this for the long lives of our teacher and vajra brothers and sisters is a very profound practice that clears away obstacles that threaten our own lives.

2.7 Dedication, the Antidote to Uncertainty

Who witnesses your dedication? The Buddhas and Bodhisattvas.

What should you dedicate? All the positive actions you have accumulated, are accumulating, and will in the future accumulate, and as well the untainted sources of good of the Buddhas and Bodhisattvas and the tainted positive deeds of all ordinary beings, all of it imagined together as one whole.

To whom should you dedicate? To all beings, and in particular the sick and those who make them sick,[297] the dead and those who commit murder.

To what end should you dedicate? To both of the two aspects or points,* and especially the second, namely omniscience, the ultimate result.

How should you dedicate? Either with an authentic dedication free from the three concepts, or with a surrogate dedication. Beginners are incapable of performing the authentic dedication free from the three concepts, but they can at least do something approaching it. Sublime beings are free from attachment, and their minds do not cling to the concepts of subject, object, and action: theirs is an authentic dedication that arises out of the emptiness supreme in all aspects, taking the form of dedications and prayers of aspiration.[298] Ordinary beings can approximate this by cultivating the certainty that even though the three concepts of subject, object, and action appear, they are devoid of any inherent nature. Failing this, the teachings say that to try to do as the Buddhas and Bodhisattvas did, reciting the prayer "Emulating the hero Manjushri . . ."† also serves as an effective dedication.

Dedication and prayers of aspiration are not only important in directing one's intentions. The Buddha taught that the result of a source of good is unpredictable, so it is impossible to know where it will take you: it is therefore essential to dedicate with the aim of obtaining what you aspire to, whether it be rebirth in the higher realms or buddhahood or some level in between.

To perform a dedication, you must have a source of good to dedicate. If you have nothing particular to dedicate, you can make a prayer of aspiration, aspiring to a result. When you dedicate and pray in this way, it is important to think that the Buddhas and Bodhisattvas are doing so at the same time.

3. Praying with Resolute Trust

"Resolute" here means praying from the very bottom of one's heart.

With regard to the accomplishments there are five points: the ground of accomplishment, what is to be accomplished, the method for accomplishing it, the manner in which it is accomplished, and the result of accomplishment.

The ground of accomplishment is the sugatagarbha, the absolute, inborn, immovable three doors.[299] Matured through empowerment, realized through the view, attained through the path, what is to be accomplished

---

*Maitreya's two aspects, or points, of bodhichitta. See page 151.
† See the four-line prayer from the *Prayer of Good Actions*, WMPT page 328.

and the result of accomplishment are one and the same. Thus the gross three doors and their nature[300] are the four gross vajras. On the subtle level they are the channels, energies, and essences, along with the nature for which they are the support. On the most subtle level, they refer to the natural state endowed with the three wisdoms.[301] This is the ground of accomplishment.

What is to be accomplished is the level of the four vajras. The pure channels are the vajra body, or nirmanakaya; the pure energies are the vajra speech, or sambhogakaya; the pure mind is the vajra mind, or dharmakaya; and the pure nature is the adamantine inseparability of these three, or svabhavikakaya.

The method for accomplishing this refers to sadhanas such as those of the lama, yidam, and dakini. In the present case it is the sadhana of the lama.

The manner in which it is accomplished is mentally with devotion and verbally through prayer. As Apu said, "The way to follow the teacher is through devotion," but how exactly can one give rise to devotion? You have to cultivate devotion by means of the five ways in which one knows the teacher to be a Buddha. Bear in mind that the teacher's body is the rupakaya, that his mind is the dharmakaya, and that these two are united in him. And when Patrul Rinpoche explains that the teacher "has perfect authority, as having the nature of the *heruka* in every mandala of deities,"* it is because the teacher is the one in whom the absolute space (*he*) and primal wisdom (*ka*) are united (*ru*).

In the same passage he states: "Every individual aspect of each of his qualities is immeasurable." This refers to the wisdom of the inconceivable secrets that are his body, speech, and mind. His dharmakaya is present for as far as space extends. Wherever his dharmakaya is present his sambhogakaya is present, and wherever his sambhogakaya is present his nirmanakaya manifestations are present as well. His all-embracing[302] body, speech, and mind arise as the all-embracing qualities of the major and minor marks, of the melodious voice of Brahma, and of omniscience and love.

Regarding his all-embracing body, he displays the sambhogakaya to Bodhisattvas on the tenth level, while to all others he shows the nirmanakaya and diverse manifestations. His body appears in all possible knowable forms. Take the example of the crown protuberance "whose limit is impos-

---

*See WMPT page 328.

sible to see" on the head of the Tathagata. The Bodhisattva Power Bearer, using his miraculous powers, could look at an inconceivable number of worlds above, but he could not see how far the Buddha's crown protuberance reached. And yet sometimes it seemed that an old beggar woman could take it and hold it on her lap.

His all-embracing speech manifests as all forms of sound, such as the language of the gods, that of the nagas, and so forth.

His all-embracing mind never wavers from the three qualities of knowledge, love, and power, though to us it may appear to be attached, to be angry, and so on.

The passage in *The Words of My Perfect Teacher* that begins, "recite the lines for the practice of receiving the accomplishments, from: 'Precious Lord Guru'"* refers to the mala-recitation[303] of the prayer. When you recite the *Seven Chapters,* recite each chapter at the appropriate time as stated in the text.[304]

The result of accomplishment is the realization temporarily of the four levels of Vidyadharas and ultimately of the level of the four vajras. In the present case, however, through the blessings of practicing and praying in this way, the realization transmitted through the authentic lineage[305] is transferred to one's own mind, and one truly sees the natural state. The sign of the birth of such realization is the growth of love, compassion, bodhichitta, faith, the determination to be free from samsara, and the wisdom that distinguishes all dharmas. But since the signs or qualities of realization can appear either before realization itself or after, it is important to make the distinction between experiences and realization, given that the result of accomplishment is the realization of the dharmata. As Longchenpa said:

> If you are unable to distinguish between experiences and realization,
> You will mistake the experiences that come from habituation for realization.
> When you have realization it is constant, never changing, improving or growing worse.
> As you train in this, good qualities will arise as experiences.[306]

---

*See WMPT pages 328–29.

4. Taking the Four Empowerments

This corresponds to the path empowerment. In general there are three types of empowerment: the ground empowerment, path empowerment, and result empowerment.

1. The ground empowerment is so called because when the nature of mind, sugatagarbha, is realized, this constitutes the "empowerment" of nirvana, and when it is not realized, this constitutes the "empowerment" of the three worlds of samsara. This nature is actually what is to be matured in the ground empowerment of the path empowerment.

2. The path empowerment is divided into three: ground, path, and result. For the *ground empowerment of the path empowerment*, one first receives empowerment from an authentic teacher into the mandala of a deity such as one of the peaceful and wrathful deities from the tantra class or the Eight Herukas from the sadhana class. During the empowerment, a disciple of superior faculties should realize the view related to the empowerment. A disciple of middling faculties should have the experiences of bliss, clarity, and absence of thought. Even disciples of inferior faculties should feel a firm conviction, impervious to distractions, that their body, speech, and mind are the three vajras. An empowerment received in this way will be a proper empowerment that will serve as a basis for following the Vajrayana path. On the other hand, if you just go on receiving empowerment after empowerment without the slightest improvement taking place in your mind, you may end up with a flatter head,[307] but you will still not have received a real empowerment. Regarding the *path empowerment of the path empowerment*, once you have received a proper empowerment, any further empowerment you receive from someone else or self-empowerment that you take yourself is a Mantrayana repair-and-purification[308] or a path empowerment.

The *result empowerment of the path empowerment* refers to the great rays of light empowerment[309] or, according to Mantrayana, the empowerment of indivisible profundity and radiance.

Once these three empowerments have been bestowed, the primal wisdom related to the absolute empowerment destroys all the obscurations of habitual tendencies or the habitual tendencies associated with the changes of the three perceptions.

3. The result empowerment. In the very instant following the result empowerment of the path, one gains mastery of the wisdom of omniscience and has authority over everything in samsara and nirvana.

What we are talking about here is the path empowerment of the path empowerment. This section begins with the passage, "The syllable *Om* between the Guru's eyebrows . . . ."* Rays of light like moonlight purify you of the effects of the three harmful physical actions—taking life and so on—and purify of all obscurations your channels, from which the body develops; the blessings of the vajra body enter you, and you receive the vase empowerment. Through the wisdom related to this empowerment, all your aggregates, elements, and ayatanas are purified as the mandala of the net of magical emanations. The wisdom of appearance and emptiness inseparable takes birth in your mind; appearances, sounds, and thoughts are liberated as the mandala of deities, mantras, and wisdom. Regarding the path, you are empowered to meditate on the generation phase. As for the result, you gain the potential for attaining temporarily the level of the totally matured Vidyadhara and ultimately the level of nirmanakaya.

From the syllable *Ah* emanate rays of light like red lightning. They purify the effects of the four harmful verbal actions—lying and so on—and purify of all obscurations your energies, from which speech develops: "The blessings of the vajra speech" and so on.[310] The wisdom of clarity and emptiness inseparable related to this empowerment takes birth in your mind. The three conditions of the breath—inhaling, exhaling, and remaining—are liberated as mantra.

From the syllable *Hung* rays of light emanate like a long wisp of incense smoke; they purify the effects of the three harmful mental acts—covetousness and so forth—and purify of all obscurations your essence, from which mental processes develop, and so on.[311] The wisdom of bliss and emptiness inseparable corresponding to this empowerment takes birth in your mind, and all your aggregates, elements, and ayatanas are liberated into the state of bliss and emptiness inseparable.

From the syllable *Hung* a second *Hung* streaks down, and so on.[312] It purifies the karma on the ground of all, the obscurations on the consciousness

---

*See WMPT page 329.

of the ground of all, and the conceptual obscurations, the three concepts, and so on.[313] The self-arisen wisdom related to this empowerment takes birth in your mind. Chandrakirti speaks of this wisdom as follows:

> Suchness is unborn and mind itself is also free from birth.[314]

And Apu cites the following quotation:

> If you say that the characteristics of aggregates are separate from space,
> Then how could the aggregates be empty?
> The emptiness found through analysis is not the ultimate meaning . . .[315]

and he comments, "When this wisdom takes birth in your being, all notions of the three doors being separate are liberated into the absolute nature" and so on.

The conclusion is essentially an aspiration transference.[316] Recite this conclusion, "When my life comes to its end . . . ,"[317] and visualize it very clearly. It is a subtle yoga belonging to the common perfection phase.

Between sessions, take everything you do—eating, sleeping, walking, sitting—as the path; in short, turn these activities into the path of pure perception. With devotion to the teacher, take happiness and suffering and their causes as the path. When happiness or its cause befalls you, remind yourself that this is the teacher's kindness and pray to him. Offer him the first part of anything you eat or drink, and see everything as a sign of his kindness. When unhappiness or its cause befalls you, cultivate devotion to the teacher and take it as the path.

If you find yourself unable to feel faith or devotion, pray to the teacher to help you cultivate them. If you feel torpid, pray to your teacher; if you feel agitated, pray to your teacher and apply the physical postures and gazes used to remedy these two problems.

If your view fluctuates and you have doubts, pray to your teacher. If your meditation goes well one moment and badly the next, pray to the teacher. If your action is affected by adoption and rejection,[318] pray to the teacher. If you find yourself having concepts of subject and object,[319] these are impediments to your view, meditation, and action: pray to your teacher. Whatever unwanted things occur—illness, negative forces, obstacles, and so on—use pure vision to see them all as the display of the teacher's wisdom mind and pray to him, meditating on spirits, gyelgongs, and others as being the teacher. In short, remember the following teaching:

> When your health fails, heal yourself with faith;
> Take unfavorable conditions as the path,

and as you experience happy moments or go through difficult times, see your teacher in everything. Cultivate devotion and pray.

Part Three

The Swift Path of Transference

T̲h̲e̲ p̲r̲a̲c̲t̲i̲c̲e̲ o̲f̲ t̲r̲a̲n̲s̲f̲e̲r̲e̲n̲c̲e̲ is a branch of the main practice. As long as your awareness is vulnerable to circumstances, you will need the teaching on transference. But for someone whose awareness is impregnable and perfectly stable, transference is unnecessary. This is why it is said:

> Those without sufficient training can be received through transference.

This refers to the sudden path of transference that is one of the six yogas of Naropa and belongs to the perfection phase. Like a mother with seven children who feels all the more love for the one who is sick, the Buddhas, out of their intense love for beings with exceedingly strong negative emotions and karma, gave these instructions for forcefully transferring the consciousness of great evildoers.

The instructions on transference are referred to as "buddhahood without meditation," but while it is true that they obviate the need to meditate on the generation and perfection phases, one still has to meditate on the visualization in the transference practice itself.

I. THE FIVE KINDS OF TRANSFERENCE

1. Superior Transference to the Dharmakaya through the Seal of the View

The superior transference to the dharmakaya through the seal of the view is practiced by sublime beings who perceive the truth of dharmata on the path of seeing and who have, in this very life, given rise in their minds to the view of the uncontrived natural state and preserved it day and night without interruption. They perform the transference either by following the pith instructions of transferring from the body and transferring into another body in the primordial purity practice of trekchö, or by following those of "entering the interior of clear light" in the spontaneous presence practice of thögal.

Then there are those beings of very pure samaya who, not having achieved the same mastery of awareness, only have control of their perceptions during their waking hours and not when asleep. When they die, once the stages of outer and inner dissolution, as well as the phenomena of clarity, increase, and attainment has taken place, the dharmakaya clear light of the moment of death appears, like the sky in autumn, free from the three obscuring conditions.[320] This is the mother clear light, the moment of the ground. These beings are escorted by the son clear light, the clear light experienced in this life, and when the mother and son clear lights meet, they are liberated in the primordial purity, the original ground.

There are those who have reached the beginning of the increase of experiences and appearances[321] in the practice of thögal. When they die and the dharmakaya clear light of the moment of death appears, they at first fail to recognize it, since they do not at this point have the realization to do so, and they are unable to attain liberation. But when the pure intermediate state of absolute reality arises, they recognize it and remain in oneness with it, and are thus liberated from the spontaneous visions of the intermediate state.[322]

Both these forms of liberation—superior liberation in this life and middling liberation in the intermediate state—count as superior transference to the dharmakaya through the seal of the view.

2. Middling Transference to the Sambhogakaya through the Union of the Generation and Perfection Phases

The middling transference to the sambhogakaya through the union of the generation and perfection stages is practiced by those who have begun to have the wisdom of the perfection phase, have reached one of the four distinctly experienced stages on the path of joining, have given rise to the wisdom of the path of joining, and are able to enter into the concentration of the illusory body and again arise from it. Failing that, they should have been introduced to the pure perceptions that are the display of wisdom, the inseparable union of the generation and perfection aspect of the deity, and have accustomed themselves to this.[323] At the moment of death they dissolve the illusory body into clear light, in the same way as they would practice the dissolution in the generation phase. If in this life they have given rise in their minds to the illustrative clear light, they will recognize the absolute clear light in the intermediate state and subsequently manifest as its postmeditational form, the body of the yidam, the union level of Mahamudra on the path of learning, and thence attain liberation.

3. Lower Transference to the Nirmanakaya through Immeasurable Compassion

This form of transference is practiced by beginners on the path of accumulating who have received empowerment and respected the samayas, have a good understanding of the view, and have practiced the generation phase as the path but have not mastered it.[324] Although they lack the necessary confidence to be liberated in the clear light at the moment of death or in the intermediate state of absolute reality, by taking refuge and praying to their teacher in the intermediate state[325] they can close the way to an unfavorable womb and choose a favorable rebirth. Propelled by compassion and bodhichitta, they depart to a pure buddhafield or, failing that, take birth as a tulku born to parents who practice the Dharma. In that next life they will be liberated.

4. Ordinary Transference Using Three Images[326]

Ordinary transference using three images is for beginners who merely aspire to the supreme Dharma and have no sign of success on the path to presage liberation in this life, at death, in the intermediate state, or in lives to come.

Transference is performed by means of three images—of the central channel as the route, the pure land of Sukhavati as the destination, and the consciousness as a traveler. When signs of approaching death occur, you should check three times whether they are reversible. If there is no turning back and you have time to dispose of all your belongings, do so. But if time is short, give them away mentally so as to be without attachment.

5. Transference Performed for the Dead

Transference to guide the dead must be performed by someone who has supreme realization. The right time to perform it is when the outer breath has stopped but the inner breath is still continuing.[327] Even if the person performing transference at that moment is not a realized being, doing the transference visualization will help the dying person. Though you might not possess the absolute bodhichitta, to have at least the relative bodhichitta can only do good. And if that fails to help, as has been taught, "as long as your mind is positive, you can't go wrong."

With regard to all the above, using the moment of death as the path of dharmakaya is related to the practice of trekchö. Using the pure intermediate state of absolute reality as the path[328] is related to thögal. Using rebirth[329] as the path of nirmanakaya is related to transference and pure vision.

II. THE PRACTICE OF TRANSFERENCE USING THREE IMAGES

In this practice of transference there are two steps: training and actual transference.

1. Training for Transference

Train until you have a sign of success. Afterward, do not leave it at that but recite the practice, or at least do the visualization in its entirety, every day at the end of the evening session, without fail.

2. Actual Transference

Once death is imminent, the actual transference consists in transferring yourself at the moment of death to a pure land. During the gradual process of dissolution, at the clarity stage the consciousnesses of the five senses dissolve into the mind consciousness. During increase the mind consciousness dissolves into the emotional consciousness, and during attainment the emotional consciousness dissolves into the ground of all. At the moment of close attainment[330] the ground of all dissolves into the clear light.

Rid yourself completely of all possessions. Confess and purify the negative actions you have accumulated throughout time without beginning, and then consider that you have but a few. Concentrate especially on confessing any conflicts you may have had with your teacher or your spiritual brothers and sisters. Dedicate all sources of good to the great enlightenment and make prayers of aspiration that in all your series of lives you might encounter the teachings of the Great Vehicle and Mahayana teachers. At the moment of death, instead of being afraid of the painful experiences of the intermediate state, build up your confidence and courage, thinking, "Countless times in the past I have died and been reborn, but this time is different: I have obtained a human existence endowed with the freedoms and advantages; I have met an authentic lama and received profound instructions. Now that I possess the pith instructions on transference, I know how to go to the pure buddhafields. How happy I feel."

When you are training divide your time into sessions and breaks between sessions, and practice transference during the afternoon and evening sessions. Go through the whole preliminary practice as far as "May I swiftly attain the level of Vajradhara," and then begin the training in transference. In the first two-thirds of the session concentrate solely on the visualization. In the last third combine the recitation and meditation.

Hik is a sound that shortens life. As you use it, pull up the energy from below the navel to the upper part of your body and turn your eyes sharply up.

When we speak of energy and mind, the moving aspect is called energy and the knowing one is called mind, but their essence is the same. So when you gather mind and energy, also called the secret empty enclosure of the mind,[331] think that the mind has become a red syllable *Hrih*. Do not think that it can be visualized in some other form.

In between the eight great peacocks bearing Amitabha's throne, visualize the attributes of the five families, wheels, vajras, and suchlike. In the tradition of the *Heart Essence of the Vast Expanse*, the main deity Amitabha is visualized alone. In the *Sky Doctrines* tradition he is visualized with the two Bodhisattvas, and in that of *Inserting the Grass-Stalk*, with the teachers of the lineage.

Practice aspiration transference all the time, when you are eating, sleeping, walking, or sitting: using the three images, keep your awareness constantly focused above your head and recite:

Buddha Amitabha, I pray to you,
Bless me that I may be reborn in the Pure Land of Bliss.

If obstacles occur when you are doing this training, press down the upper air, release the lower air, and fill up the navel region; do the vajra recitation with the three seed syllables,[332] focus your mind on the soles of your feet, and turn your gaze downward. This will dispel the obstacles.

◊ Colophon

When I was eighteen my supreme and peerless teacher, whose name is difficult for me to utter but that I will nevertheless express for the sake of clarity—Lungtok Tenpai Nyima Gyaltsen Pel Zangpo—gave me this teaching up to the section on the bodhichitta of application, but no further.[333] The following year, for two months he gave me detailed explanations, and I received the complete transmission from the Vajrasattva chapter onward, and although he then fell ill and did not manage to go right to the end, I did in fact, taking these two occasions into account, receive the whole teaching. So when Khen Rinpoche Pema Gyaltsen and Tulku Penor persistently urged me to write out my rough notes, and the precious thrice-kind teacher Topden[334] asked me as well, I could not bear the idea of refusing them, and I hastily wrote down what I could. May it be beneficial to all!

Concluding Instructions

HERE IS WHAT THE PRECIOUS omniscient teacher Ngawang Pelzang, also known as Osel Rinchen Nyingpo Pema Lendreltsel,[335] himself wrote on how to practice.

Spend three days on the freedoms,
Four days on the advantages,
One day on the images illustrating the difficulty of obtaining a human rebirth,
One day on the numerical comparisons,
One day each on the eight intrusive circumstances and eight incompatible propensities,
One day on the impermanence of the outer universe,
Three days on the impermanence of beings living in the universe,
One day on the impermanence of holy beings,
One day on the impermanence of those in positions of power,
Three days on other examples of impermanence,
One day on the uncertainty of the circumstances of death,
One day on intense awareness of impermanence,
Three days reflecting on the sufferings of samsara in general,
One day on the hot hells,
One day on the cold hells,
One day on the ephemeral hells and the neighboring hells,
One day on the pretas who live collectively,

One day on the pretas who move through space,
One day on animals living in the depths,
One day on the animals that live scattered in different places,
One day each on the three fundamental types of suffering in the human realm,
One day each on the sufferings of birth, old age, sickness, and death,
One day on each of the four other human sufferings, the fear of meeting hated enemies, and so on,
One day on the asuras,
One day on the gods,
Three days on negative actions,
Three days on positive actions,
Three days on the all-determining quality of actions,
One day on the benefits of liberation,
Three days on how to follow a spiritual friend,
The last third of each of these sessions on taking refuge,
Three days on love,
Three days on compassion,
Three days on sympathetic joy,
Three days on impartiality,
Three days on the essence and classification of bodhichitta,
Three days on considering others as equal to oneself,
Three days on exchanging oneself and others,
Three days on considering others more important than oneself, and
Three days on each of the six transcendent perfections.

Prayers

These prayers are mentioned by Khenpo Ngakchung in the text. The texts of these prayers are included at the end of Chatral Rinpoche's edition. The comments (in italics) are his.

To the Master and Buddhas, guardians of wandering beings,
Who labor for the good of all that lives,
Those mighty ones who scatter every fear,
From this day forth I go for refuge.

In the Dharma that resides within their hearts,
That scatters all the terrors of samsara,
And in the multitude of Bodhisattvas,
Likewise I will perfectly take refuge.

Gripped by dread, beside myself with terror,
To Samantabhadra I will give myself;
And to Manjushri, the melodious and gentle,
I entrust myself entirely.

To him whose loving deeds are steadfast,
O my guardian, Avalokita,
I cry out from depths of misery,
"Protect me now, who am so full of sin."

Now to the noble one, Akashagarbha,
And to Kshitigarbha, from my heart I call.
And all protectors, great, compassionate,
To them I go in search of refuge.

And to Vajrapani, holder of the diamond,
The very sight of whom will rout
All dangers like the deadly host of Yama,
To him indeed I fly for safety.

Formerly your words I have transgressed,
But now I see these terrors all around.
To you indeed I come for help,
And pray you, swiftly save me from this fear.

These are verses from the Way of the Bodhisattva, *with a few words altered to suit the context.*

Courageous One, you who possess the power of compassion—
Linked as we are by the force of karmic connections from the past,
Do not linger uncaring, neither neglect me, nor remain idle.
Look on me now with heartfelt love, compassionate lord of Buddhas.
From "Rudra's Lament and Confession"

Woe is me! Compassionate Three Jewels,
Victorious Ones, whose minds are full of love,
On us who suffer in samsara's six realms
Bestow your blessings now and make us free.
From the Karling Shitro prayer book for practice in four sessions.

These prayers were collated here in one place for the convenience of beginners looking for the texts.

A Brief Recitation for the Four Contemplations That Turn the Mind from Samsara

(Taken from the Sutras)

With these freedoms and advantages so hard to find,
A person can attain enlightenment.
If one does not take advantage of them now,
How will one so well obtain them in the future?

The three worlds are impermanent, like autumn clouds,
The lives and deaths of beings are like a ballet,
A being's life passes like a flash of lightning in the sky,
It rushes on like a mountain torrent.

When the time comes and a king departs,
His wealth, family, and friends do not follow him.
Wherever beings stay, wherever they go,
Their actions follow them like a shadow.

Driven by ignorance, craving, and becoming, all beings—
Humans, celestial beings, and those in the three lower realms—
Circle stupidly in the five realms,
Revolving like a potter's wheel.
The three worlds blaze with the sufferings of old age and sickness,
Here the fire of death rages, and there is no protection.
Beings never have the intelligence to escape from samsara,
They go round and round like bees caught in a jar.

These are the stainless words of the perfect Buddha.

The Seven Branches from the Prayer of Good Actions

To all the Tathagatas, Lions of men,
As many as there are in the three times
And the ten directions of the universe—to all of them
   without exception
I pay homage with clear devotion of body, speech, and
   mind.

Through the power of this prayer of Good Action,
Bowing down to all the Conquerors with bodies
   manifested
By the mind and numerous as the atoms of the universe,
I make full obeisance to all the Buddhas.

Considering all the Conquerors to be gathered
Like the countless atoms on a particle of dust,
Surrounded by Bodhisattvas
And filling the infinity of the absolute space.

And telling the qualities of all the Conquerors
With all sounds of oceanlike branches of melody,
All oceans of inexhaustible praise,
To all the Sugatas I sing praises.

To all the Conquerors I make offerings:
The loveliest flowers and beautiful garlands,
Cymbals, scented water, the precious canopy,
The brightest butter lamps, and the finest incense.

Fine raiment and the most fragrant scents,
And incense powders piled as high as Mount Meru,
Meticulously prepared and arranged as perfectly as
   possible,
I offer to all the Buddhas.

Intending all such offerings, vast and perfect,
For all the Buddhas,
With the strength of confidence in good action
I make offerings with obeisance to all the Conquerors.

Whatever faults I have committed
By body, speech, or mind
Under the influence of craving, hatred, and ignorance,
I confess each one of them.

I rejoice at the merit of all the Buddhas in the ten
    directions,
Of their children the Bodhisattvas,
And of all the Pratyekabuddhas, Arhats,
Practitioners, and all beings.

I exhort all the Protectors, the lights of the universe in the
    ten directions,
Who have attained buddhahood free from attachment
Through the successive stages of awakening,
To turn the incomparable Wheel of Dharma.

To those who would demonstrate the Parinirvana
I fold my hands together and pray:
Remain for the sake of all beings' benefit and happiness
For kalpas as many as the atoms of the universe.

What little merit I have accumulated
By obeisance, offering, confession,
Rejoicing, exhortation, and prayer—
All of it I dedicate to the goal of enlightenment.

Notes

Abbreviations

AZR	Alak Zenkar Rinpoche
PWR	Pema Wangyal Rinpoche
KPS	Khenpo Pema Sherab
Tib.	Tibetan
Skt.	Sanskrit
WMPT	*The Words of My Perfect Teacher*

1. This section on Khenpo Ngakchung's life has been compiled and condensed from the following sources: a summary of Khenpo Ngakchung's autobiography in Tulku Thondup, *Masters of Meditation and Miracles: The Longchen Nyingthig Lineage of Tibetan Buddhism* (Boston: Shambhala Publications, 1996); oral accounts by Nyoshul Khenpo Jamyang Dorje; a recent biography by Sonam Tenpa, the Gyude Khenpo at Kathog; Nyoshul Khenpo Jamyang Dorje's *History of the Dzogchen Lineage*; and E. Gene Smith's introductory essay to Khenpo Ngakchung's autobiography. A complete translation of Khenpo Ngakchung's life story is forthcoming.
2. A butter lamp is more effectively cleaned just after it has finished burning, while it is still warm and the butter still melted; a charging pig can be easily repelled by hitting it on its highly sensitive snout with a pestle (*gtun bu*, the clublike pestle used in Tibet for pounding and milling grain). Similarly, the moment one has a negative thought one should apply the antidote.
3. One will not attain enlightenment merely by growing matted hair and carrying a stick like an Indian sadhu.
4. Ocean Dust (*rgya mtsho'i rdul*), name of a previous incarnation of the Buddha.

5. The Tibetan word for "transmission" (*lung*) literally means a handle.
6. Omniscience (*thams cad mkhyen pa*) is a synonym for buddhahood.
7. Lord of all beings (*skye dgu'i bdag po*). The creator of the universe according to non-Buddhists.
8. A dog that finds itself somewhere high up always looks down and attempts to descend. A bird placed on the ground invariably looks up and attempts to fly up into the air.
9. Khenpo Ngakchung quotes a slightly different version of this verse from that quoted by Patrul Rinpoche in WMPT page 11, ending with *brston par gyis* rather than *shes par gyis*.
10. *bka'*, that part of the Buddhist canon consisting of those teachings given by the Buddha himself or directly inspired by him (for example, the *Heart Sutra*, which is actually a teaching given by the Bodhisattva Avalokiteshvara, in the Buddha's presence).
11. Theoretical treatises by scholars and experiential accounts by realized yogins.
12. These texts constitute Longchenpa's famous Nyingtik Yabshi, the *Four Heart Essences:* the Khandro Yangtik (*Quintessence of the Dakinis*) is Longchenpa's commentary on the Khandro Nyingtik (*Heart Essence of the Dakinis*), the Lama Yangtik (*Quintessence of the Master*) is his commentary on the Vima Nyingtik (Vimalamitra's Sangwa Nyingtik, the *Secret Heart Essence*). In the Zabmo Yangtik (the *Profound Quintessence*) he provided a further commentary on these four.
13. Conch-lettered instructions (*dung yig can*) by Vimalamitra. Part of the Vima Nyingtik. See previous note.
14. The second edition of WMPT contains the following note: The first line of this saying, *mgo ma tshos gong lce snyabs*, can be understood to refer literally to not starting to taste a head that is being cooked until it is ready (the cooking of yaks' or cows' heads being widespread in Tibet, particularly among the nomad pastoralists). However, "sticking your tongue out" can imply expressing agreement or acquiescence, and "the head being cooked" is sometimes used as a metaphor for understanding. An alternate—if less colorful—translation would therefore be "agreeing before you've understood."
15. The Tibetan term (*gzhug shor*) used here literally means to make a mistake, for instance in the preparation of yogurt or wine, where a small error or omission (e.g., in temperature or timing) can ruin the end result.
16. Alternate translation: if the general surrenders, the army is lost.
17. In WMPT the Tibetan word *thun mong* has been translated as "ordinary" and *thun min* as "extraordinary." However it also has the meaning "com-

mon," and it is this sense that is being explained here by Khenpo Ngakchung.
18. These refer to the practices in the generation and perfection phases that purify the processes of birth, death, and the intermediate state
19. Tib. *mdzo*, a cross between a yak and a cow, used as a pack animal.
20. In Tibet, where Buddhist ethics were universally accepted, hunting was generally regarded as a shameful occupation.
21. *dkor ma zhus na*. Lamas or Sangha members who accept offerings from the faithful and subsequently use them for purposes other than the Dharma accumulate very negative karma and have to suffer these and other experiences as hallucinations in the hell realms.
22. Lit. "seal your door with mud," referring to the Tibetan custom of locking meditators doing strict retreat into their hermitages by sealing the entrance door with clay, with only a small hole in the wall through which food was passed.
23. Visualizing the deity in an ordinary way means simply visualizing the deity without the qualities and stages of the generation phase, or visualizing the deity with attachment.
24. This is the second line from *Parting from the Four Attachments*.
25. This is the third line from *Parting from the Four Attachments*.
26. An alternate translation could be: "Nowadays people of all stations say, 'I'm not afraid of death, I'm not deluded. You should meditate.' But it all depends on their attitude, which all too often is entirely self-motivated." (PWR)
27. The two aspects can be understood quite clearly in the Tibetan text, but their order becomes inverted in a "readable" translation. The first aspect, or point, is "for the benefit of others," and the second is "the wish to attain perfect buddhahood."
28. The wish to free all beings from suffering is the compassion aspect. The wish that they may obtain buddhahood, which is ultimate happiness, is the love aspect.
29. This is a quotation from Nagarjuna's *Letter to a Friend*, verse 68. The quotation appears in full on page 141.
30. The criticism and spiteful remarks a mother has to suffer apply to the whole range of remarks and complaints she may receive regarding the nuisance her children cause as she brings them up. They are not directed at the fact that she is pregnant.
31. Shantideva, *The Way of the Bodhisattva*, trans. Padmakara Translation Group (Boston: Shambhala Publications, 1999), I, 28.

32. Someone who has had smallpox can never contract it again. In Khenpo Ngakchung's time smallpox was a common and much feared disease.
33. Merit (Tib. *dge rtsa*). This term has been translated in WMPT as "source of good for the future." For the sake of conciseness in this discussion on how sources of good for the future can be destroyed, we have often translated it simply as "merit." See also Merit in glossary.
34. *Way of the Bodhisattva*, VI, 1.
35. *dung*, a white bead threaded onto the mala to show that one has completed 100 million recitations of the Mani.
36. The city of the gandharvas sometimes appears as a vision, complete with buildings and inhabitants.
37. *Way of the Bodhisattva*, V, 40.
38. Lit. "brahmin like a sal tree, kshatriya like a sal tree, householder like a sal tree." The sal tree is the king of sandalwood trees and therefore used to symbolize excellence.
39. These are the last three lines of the dedication verse: "By these positive actions may all beings / Complete the accumulations of merit and wisdom / And attain the two supreme kayas / Which come from merit and wisdom."
40. The Tibetan speaks of the accumulation of merit as the "apparent" aspect (*snang bcas bsod nams kyi tshogs*) and of the accumulation of wisdom as the "nonapparent" aspect (*snang med ye shes kyi tshogs*). According to Alak Zenkar Rinpoche, these are synonymous with *dmigs bcas* and *dmigs med*, with and without concepts, and have been translated as such for the sake of clarity.
41. This refers to the definition of the Sanskrit word *mantra*, which literally means "mind protect." The Mantrayana is the path in which the mind is protected from emotions easily (without hardship) and quickly (since it is the short path).
42. Union (Tib. *zung 'jug*) refers in this context to the union of the dharmakaya and rupakaya.
43. Lit. "dog accomplishment." Dogs are generally thoroughly despised in the East, and the word is used here to indicate extreme inferiority.
44. The essence of the Vajrayana samaya is pure perception: the five elements (earth, water, fire, wind, and space), for example, are perceived as the five consorts of the Dhyani Buddhas. Perceiving them in an ordinary way constitutes a violation of the samaya.
45. I.e., the dharmakaya.
46. Any one of the five Buddha families. See WMPT glossary, Five Families
47. Although the Buddhas, buddhafields, and so forth are actually present, we are obscured from seeing them as they are, and we therefore have to vi-

sualize or imagine them. We are not imagining something that does not exist.
48. *nges don*. This term has been translated as "real meaning" in WMPT.
49. For example, the injunction in the tantras to "kill the father, kill the mother" refers not to taking life but to destroying hatred and attachment.
50. Four points of reliance (*rton pa bzhi*): "Rely on the teaching, not on the individual. / Rely on the meaning, not on the words. / Rely on the ultimate meaning, not on the expedient meaning. / Rely on wisdom, not on intellectual knowledge."
51. Lit. "you recklessly indulge in the hidden secrets without having realized the covered secrets." "Hidden secrets" refers to practices that are deliberately kept secret until the disciple is ready, such as the practices of union and liberation. "Covered secrets" refers to profound truths, such as the fact that we all have the Buddha nature; they are naturally secret because we have not realized them.
52. Lit. "whether you go up or down."
53. The word "freedom" here refers to liberation (*thar pa*) and not to the freedoms (*dal*) that are the subject of this section.
54. *dge sbyor*. These refer to specifically Dharma-oriented positive actions such as prostrations and circumambulations.
55. Necessary chores, lit. activities outside your retreat room (e.g., going to the toilet) and inside (e.g., cleaning your room or cooking).
56. When doing intensive practice in retreat many practitioners sleep sitting up in a box specifically designed to serve as both meditation seat and bed.
57. Lit. "like a grain of barley." The manner in which one exhales—with ever-increasing force—is illustrated by the shape of the barley grain, which tapers at each end and is widest in the middle, unlike a grain of rice, which is more or less the same width all along its length. (PWR)
58. The technique for expelling the stale breath varies according to the tradition or lineage one is following and in any case can only be properly taught by demonstration.
59. In Tibet, butter is often kept in leather bags, which become hard and stiff when not used.
60. *bsam gtan bzhi pa'i grong*, the fourth heaven of gods in states of concentration. Alak Zenkar Rinpoche says that the place looks like a coal-mining region.
61. Lit. "concentration bodies of void-awareness." These are mental bodies such as we have in dreams. In a dream one is aware of one's body, but it is not a physical body; it is empty. Nevertheless one is still aware of it as a mental body. (PWR)

62. Expedient meaning. The Buddha may have explained this in terms of particular individuals who were reborn to the northeast of where he was teaching his disciples, in India, but as regards the ultimate meaning, there is no actual place where the long-lived gods exist.
63. This is probably a quotation from the Abhidharma. (PWR)
64. Khenpo Ngakchung is explaining here that the long-lived gods do not live in a physical place but rather that those beings who are "reborn" as long-lived gods continue to exist, for immensely long periods of time, in the mentally blank, comatose state in which they died.
65. Khenpo Ngakchung's explanation as to how to deal with the eight intrusive circumstances follows a different order from that of Patrul Rinpoche. In the section that follows, some of the eight incompatible propensities are grouped together. See WMPT pages 30–31.
66. Evil ways of life are not changed or discarded by meditation as a remedy; they have to be given up directly.
67. Lit. "before the sixth of the six periods of a twenty-four-hour day is over."
68. Recitation of the mantra like the flow of a river effectively means doing the practice daily.
69. The tradition of Nagarjuna.
70. The tradition of Asanga.
71. *phyal ba*. The meaning of this word includes "evenness" (*mnyam pa*). (AZR)
72. In other words, nomads and peasants will be born somewhere where they can practice the Dharma.
73. Lit. "to take the essence of the precious human body, the essence of the sacred Dharma." The Tibetan text here is making use of a pun.
74. *Kaya Siddhi Om, Waka Siddhi Ah, Chitta Siddhi Hung*. These are the Sanskrit words recited for blessing the body, speech, and mind respectively in an empowerment or sadhana.
75. Tibetans travel very long distances to get salt; by the time they arrive the dzo may be too weak to carry the salt back.
76. *Way of the Bodhisattva*, VII, 28.
77. *Way of the Bodhisattva*, VII, 30.
78. Infinite Aspiration (*mos pa mtha' yas*), the last of the thousand Buddhas of this kalpa.
79. The vajra hell is said to be located directly below the Vajra Seat (see WMPT glossary).
80. Of the six god realms in the world of desire, the realm of the Four Great Kings is located on the steps of Mount Meru, the Heaven of the Thirty-three on top of Mount Meru, and the four sky abodes in the sky above Mount Meru.

81. In the absence of any living being everything is completely still. There is neither any wind outside nor even the subtle inner wind of beings' breath. And according to interdependence, without wind there can be no rain. (AZR)
82. See, e.g., Kangyur Rinpoche, *Treasury of Precious Qualities,* trans. Padmakara Translation Group (Boston: Shambhala Publications, 2001).
83. These three "paths" refer to three stages during the process of death related to the dissolution of the elements and to the three emotional poisons. An experienced practitioner is able to use these stages as a path toward realization.
84. *blos mi thong,* lit. "that our minds are unable to give away."
85. Alak Zenkar Rinpoche says that these three stages of dusk are seen particularly clearly from an airplane just after sunset.
86. *'khor ba,* Skt. samsara, literally means "circling."
87. *nges 'byung gi 'bras bu,* "determination to be free from samsara as a result," is an irreversible attitude in which one is not swayed by negative emotions or other influences that lead to samsaric existence. It may also refer here to *nges 'byung* as one of the four subdivisions of the third Noble Truth, cessation (*'gog pa'i mtshan nyid bzhi*).
88. Omniscient Father and Son: Kunkhyen Longchenpa and Kunkhyen Jigme Lingpa.
89. The full text is: *Om. Yedharma hetu prabhava hetunte shanta thagato hya vadat. Te shanca yo nirodha evam badi maha shramana. Svaha.* According to the *Maha Vagga* (from the Vinaya Pitaka), this quintessential formulation of the Buddha's teaching, which is often used almost as a mantra, was originally the reply given by the beginner monk Ashvajit when questioned by the young brahmin Shariputra about what the Buddha taught. It so inspired Shariputra and his companion Maudgalyayana that they both began to follow the Buddha and became two of his closest and most accomplished disciples.
90. *dge sbyong che.* A shramana is a homeless renunciant, while the Great Shramana is he who has renounced samsara in its entirety, i.e., the fully enlightened Buddha himself.
91. *rtog ge sde lnga*: (1) *grangs can pa* (Samkhya); (2) *dbang phyug pa* (Aishvara); (3) *rgyal ba pa* (Jaina); (4) *khyab 'jug pa* (Vaishnava); (5) *chad pa'i lta ba* (Nihilists).
92. Gautama: one of Buddha Shakyamuni's names, and the name by which his philosophical opponents, who did not necessarily recognize him as a Buddha, would have known him.
93. *lha chen,* Skt. Mahadeva, "great God"; *dbang phyug chen po,* Skt. Maheshvara, "great almighty one."

94. This is the view of the Samkhya, the eternalist philosophy of atheistic dualism that was systematized in India from about the fourth century onward.
95. *go khug*, lit. "a sack or pouch used for storing grain." Khenpo Ngakchung seems to have adapted this metaphor to his audience. Alak Zenkar Rinpoche explains that the purusha "shakes" this bag and causes particles to "fall out."
96. *ngo tsha*. The Samkhya texts use the simile of a dancer withdrawing, or of a girl concealing herself out of shyness upon being seen.
97. The six non-Buddhist teachers: Maskarí Goshalaputra, Purnakashyapa, Sanjayivairatthiputra, Ajitakeshakambala, Kakudakatyayana, Nirgranthojnatiputra.
98. Bodhisattvas are referred to as the Buddha's children (*rgyal sras*), Shravakas and Pratyekabuddhas as his disciples (*slob ma*).
99. *mi g.yo ba'i las*, "unwavering" actions or karma, so called because their result—rebirth in the form or formless realms—is unwavering or infallible, unlike other actions whose result may depend on circumstances.
100. *bgyi ba dang bcas pa* and *bgyi ba ma mchis pa*, lit. "having something to do" and "not having anything to do."
101. *nyan rang gnyis ka'i sa*, the levels (Skt. bhumis) on the Shravaka or Pratyekabuddha paths, analogous to the Bodhisattva levels. This does not simply mean "the level of a Shravaka or Pratyekabuddha."
102. *nyon mongs pa can ma yin pa'i ma rig pa*, defined by Jamgön Kongtrül as "the conceptual obscuration that obscures omniscience," as opposed to *nyon mongs pa can gyi ma rig pa*, ignorance with negative emotions, defined as "the emotional obscurations that obscure liberation from the causes of samsara."
103. According to Khenpo Yonga's commentary on the *Treasury of Precious Qualities*, these factors of subtle dependent arising operate as follows: on the basis of the subtle kinds of ignorance (*ma rig pa*) mentioned here, the mental body (*yid kyi rang bzhin can gyi lus*) takes support of untainted karma (*zag med kyi las*), actions which are not motivated by the negative emotions and which on this level would be classified as belonging to the truth of the path, and perceives inconceivable (transformations of) death and transmigration (*bsam gyis mi khyab pa'i 'chi 'pho*).
104. According to the Great Vehicle, Arhats after their death will remain for a variable time in a state of suspension of the intellect (the "cessation" they have striven for) and will then be reborn in a buddhafield inside a closed lotus bud until a Buddha's compassion opens the lotus and arouses them

from their concentration to continue on the path of the Great Vehicle until they achieve buddhahood.
105. *rgyud sdom*, lit. "they bind their mindstream."
106. *sems 'byung sems pa*. Mentation (*sems pa, cintana*), sometimes also translated as "thought" or "intention," is one of the "five mental events that accompany everything" (*kun 'gro lnga*) and is described as the (secondary) cognition that moves to and engages with an object, thus bringing the (primary) mind to bear on that object. According to some currents of Abhidharma, however, mentation is assimilated to the primary mind and is not considered a mental event, and so an alternate translation here would be "mental events and mentation."
107. The first of the three kinds of transcendent discipline explained in WMPT page 239.
108. "Mixed" can therefore include a motivation and action that are not continuously consistent. For example, while doing something positive with pure intention, some worldly concept about it might arise and disappear. Unlike the first two kinds of mixed action, where the result depends on the intention, here the cause is mixed and gives a mixed result, rebirth in "happy" realms but with much suffering. There are differences between the four continents of traditional cosmology in terms of the potential for karmic cause and effect (see WMPT, note 60 (note 57, 1st edition)). The scattered god realms are those situated in parts of the universe other than on and above the top of Mount Meru. (JKR)
109. Her story is described in Stanley Frye, trans., *Sutra of the Wise and the Foolish* (Dharamsala, India: Library of Tibetan Works and Archives, 1981). She was born exceedingly ugly. In desperation at her lot, she prayed to the Buddha with great faith and was gradually transformed into a ravishing beauty.
110. The means (*thabs*), the practice of positive actions, has to be completed by wisdom (*shes rab*). For beings of intermediate capacity, wisdom is the realization that the individual has no true existence, as described in the general introduction to this chapter.
111. *kun rdzob*. Often translated as "the relative" or "relative truth."
112. *len pa'i rnam shes*, the basic consciousness that continually identifies with the physical body, as well as with objects of perception. This is equivalent to the consciousness of the ground of all (*kun gzhi'i rnam shes*) in systems that speak of eight consciousnesses or to the mental consciousness (*yid kyi rnam shes*) in systems that speak of six consciousnesses.
113. *de ltar srid zhir 'du byed sogs*. This appears to be a quote from the concluding section of the fourth chapter (on the cause and effect of actions) of

Longchenpa's *sems nyid ngal so*: "All the (actions) that compound (phenomena) as existence and peace / Depend on mind, and the nature of mind is radiant clarity / Like the sky, in which there is no reference to a doer and which is free of conceptual elaborations, / The meaning of the two truths is dependent arising. . . ."

114. *'khrul pa'i ngos nas*, i.e., relatively speaking.
115. Carefulness is realizing that something is awry and then correcting it. When a newlywed bride first comes to live in the bridegroom's house, she desperately needs to create a good impression and therefore does everything extremely carefully for fear of making a mistake. (AZR)
116. *'jig rten pa'i yang dag pa'i lta ba*, the belief in past and future lives and in the law of karma.
117. All three terms here refer to the empowerment.
118. Chatral Rinpoche's edition quotes in full from the *Stages on the Path*: "He is a teacher, holds the treasury of the teachings, has perfected the stream of empowerment, has a sense of responsibility, is versed in the tantras and rituals, possesses the pith instructions, and has attained warmth in the practice: these are the eight qualities he holds."
119. The four empowerments: elaborate, unelaborate, very unelaborate, and extremely unelaborate.
120. This quotation has been translated differently in WMPT (page 188). The present translation accords with Khenpo Ngakchung's explanation and Alak Zenkar Rinpoche's commentary: all schools, whether Buddhist or non-Buddhist, have vows or precepts, but those that lead to liberation cannot be taken without first taking refuge.
121. *Way of the Bodhisattva*, VIII, 4.
122. Of the six kinds of upasaka, the triple-refuge-holder upasaka is the first and most basic, having taken just one vow: the refuge. The others take the refuge vow and in addition the vows respectively to refrain from taking life, stealing, and so forth. Whatever additional vows they may take, they have all taken the refuge vow. The same is of course true for the other forms of Buddhist ordination. The quotation could thus be paraphrased: unless one is a basic upasaka, one cannot take vows.
123. I.e., the first of the three supreme methods.
124. "In the Sugatas of the Three Roots, the true Three Jewels." This is the first line of the refuge prayer in the Longchen Nyingtik preliminary practices; see WMPT page 180. In the light of Khenpo Ngakchung's explanation, this line might be better translated: "In the Sugata, the true Three Jewels, the Three Roots."
125. This means up to the moment when the awareness reaches the wheel of

great bliss in the crown and all the realization and qualities blaze forth like an infinite mass of light rays reaching all beings. (AZR)
126. Because of this inner recognition, the path is without difficulties and thus much easier than the path of the Sutras; it is swift in that it is not necessary to accumulate merit for countless great kalpas. (PWR)
127. The practices related to the three kayas allow one to attain liberation at the moment of death, in the intermediate state, or when taking birth.
128. *ro ma*, lit. "corpselike"; *rkyang ma*, lit. "the solitary one."
129. The gyaling (*rgya gling*) is a Tibetan shawm (reed instrument of the oboe class). Another simile often given for the arrangement of the radial channels is that of the petals of a flower, pointing either up or down according to the particular wheel or chakra.
130. The Tibetan word *rlung* (Skt. *prana*) has generally been translated as "energy," but it should be noted that it can also mean a breeze or wind and, in the body, the breath. In Tibetan medicine this term also covers the circulation, muscular activity, etc. The 120,600 moving energies perhaps refer to the pulse rate, which is generally much faster than the respiratory rate.
131. The Sangha is unchangeable because of its one-pointed concentration and absence of distraction in its practice of discipline.
132. This is not necessarily what the New Traditions actually claim but may be a riposte directed at one of Khenpo Ngakchung's contemporaries.
133. *nges pa lnga*, the five certainties. In WMPT Patrul Rinpoche calls these the five perfections (*phun sum tshogs pa lnga*).
134. Five subfamilies, e.g., in the vajra family: vajra-vajra, vajra-ratna, vajra-padma, etc.
135. Khenpo Ngakchung's comment on "the ever-revolving wheel of eternity" is clearer if the reader understands that "eternity" and "permanent" are both translations of the same Tibetan word, *rtag pa*.
136. *sgren mo bya rog*. Animal names in Tibetan vary from one region to another. Probably a bat (lit. "a naked—i.e., featherless—bird"). But this could possibly be two words, meaning a porcupine and a crow.
137. Vishvakarma (*bzo rgyal karma bi shva*) was the greatest artist of the Buddha's time. Three statues that he made representing the Buddha were blessed by the Buddha himself.
138. *dkar po rnam par 'phel ba'i tshong zongs*. Books, statues, and paintings increase merit for both the artisan and buyer when created and purchased (or commissioned) for the purposes for which they are intended.
139. This is a quotation from the *Sutra Remembering the Three Jewels*.
140. The eight forms of pratimoksha are: fully ordained monks and nuns (bhikshus and bhikshunis), probationer nuns, male and female shramaneras,

male and female upasakas, and those who take the one-day vow of purificatory fasting.
141. "Seeing the truth" (Tib. *bden pa mthong*) refers to gaining realization of emptiness.
142. The two traditions (*srol gnyis*): Nagarjuna's tradition of the Profound View and Asanga's tradition of the Vast Activity.
143. The other four hundred are: to know perfectly the blessings of one hundred Buddhas, to remain alive for one hundred kalpas, to know one hundred past and present kalpas, and to open one hundred doors to the Dharma.
144. Bodhisattvas on the second level have twelve hundred thousand qualities, those on the third level twelve hundred million, and so on.
145. *lta gon*. The preparatory section of the empowerment that is held the day before the actual empowerment.
146. Making beer can be as tricky as making mayonnaise; if the wrong person is around it curdles. When we are in strict retreat and people from outside visit us, they can bring in their wake all sorts of forces detrimental to our practice. (PWR)
147. Lit. "that with the Mantrayana vows they can, as it were, recklessly ford rivers without taking off their shoes," referring to the necessary custom in Tibet of removing one's shoes and tucking up one's *chuba* before wading across a river. The Khampas of eastern Tibet, who have a reputation for recklessness, are reputed to charge through rivers fully clothed. (PWR)
148. These three objects refer to three stages of expertise in the generation phase. As a result of long periods of practice visualizing the deity, the visualization progresses from an incredibly clear and "real" mental image to a point where the practitioner feels he or she can actually touch the deity, and finally to a stage in which the power of concentration influences the sense organs and the practitioner can actually see the deity with his or her own eyes and even influence other people's perception of him or her. (AZR)
149. *phyi lus kyi stong ra*, lit. "the outer fence of emptiness," referring to the outer form of the deity, which is hollow and encloses the system of channels.
150. Four features of the vase exercise: inhaling, holding, turning, and exhaling.
151. Repeated group practice: repeated if the result is not obtained.
152. During the liberation practice the yogis liberate otherwise irretrievably negative beings. The three satisfactions are: the negative being's mind is liberated in the dharmadhatu, the dharmapalas receive the flesh and blood of the deceased being transformed into wisdom nectar, and the yogi's life force increases.

153. In the practice of the channels and energies (*rtsa lung*), one first trains on one's own. Once one has achieved proficiency in this, one can make further progress "relying on another's body," that is, training with a consort. It should be emphasized that this sort of practice requires stable realization of emptiness by both practitioners.
154. This is the oral lineage that comes down from Zurpoche Shakya Jungne.
155. The nine objects to which we go for refuge are the Three Jewels, the Three Roots, and the Three Kayas.
156. The three special features are the special motivation, special duration, and special object.
157. "As for that wisdom . . ." This would appear to be the wisdom referred to by the Third Turning of the Wheel, but Khenpo Ngakchung's text is not clear here, and Alak Zenkar Rinpoche thinks it possible that there are words missing from the text.
158. The "inspirational deity" *(mos lha)* is the deity to whom we feel spontaneous devotion; the "destined deity" *(phog lha)* is the deity on whom one's flower falls during the empowerment (PWR).
159. I.e., in the form of a deity or as you normally perceive him.
160. Umdze (Tib. *dbu mdzad*), the monk who leads the music and chanting in a monastery.
161. Although in many traditions the practitioner accumulates the required one hundred thousand prostrations while reciting the refuge prayer one hundred thousand times, in the Longchen Nyingtik tradition it is more usual to accumulate the one hundred thousand prostrations while reciting the offering of the seven branches in the guru yoga. There is nothing however to stop practitioners, if they feel so inspired, from performing prostrations while reciting the refuge prayer.
162. Lit. "make pure dedication and wishing prayers," i.e., prayers that are devoid of selfish motivation and free of the three concepts.
163. The Tibetan metaphor used here seems to be that of rubbing or working leather to make it softer and more pliable.
164. *Way of the Bodhisattva*, I, 5.
165. This refers to the fact that the Three Jewels are embodied in the teacher: his body is the Sangha, his speech the Dharma, and his mind the Buddha. The merit we gain by making offerings to the teacher, who is alive, rather than to statues and books, is more powerful.
166. As a result of taking refuge in the Sangha one will become a teacher who has controlled his negative emotions gathering around him a Sangha of Shravakas and Bodhisattvas who control their negative emotions (*'dul ba*); a teacher who has pacified his emotions gathering around him a Sangha of

disciples who pacify their emotions (*zhi ba*); or a teacher who has completely eradicated the negative emotions and attained perfect peace gathering around him a Sangha of disciples who completely eradicate the negative emotions (*nye bar zhi ba*). These three aspects of being disciplined, peaceful, and perfectly peaceful are related to the Three Trainings, respectively discipline, concentration, and wisdom.

167. The nine levels of the three realms of samsara (*khams gsum sa dgu*) are: the desire realm, the four concentrations of the form realm, and the four formless absorptions.
168. The hell beings, pretas, animals, humans, and gods.
169. The first four of the thirty-seven elements of enlightenment are more usually described as the four close mindfulnesses.
170. These constitute the second of the twenty-one sets of immaculate qualities of the Buddha's wisdom dharmakaya.
171. This sentence also implies that in the preliminary practice for the session one also develops the four boundless qualities, though in less detail than in the main practice that now follows. (AZR)
172. He might be considered a hero for defeating us. (AZR)
173. Going to the temple, reciting mantras with a mala, reading Dharma texts, and so on, before actually taking ordination. (AZR)
174. The notion of karmic debts is illustrated in the story of Katyayana. See WMPT pages 50–51.
175. Nagarjuna's *Letter to a Friend*, verse 68, last two lines. See also WMPT page 62.
176. Lit. "the shins become (as sturdy as) pillars and the down (on the body) becomes (like) stalks."
177. Here Khenpo Ngakchung has changed the usual order of these first two links.
178. Lit. "actually in front of you, with all her aggregates, dhatus, and ayatanas, just as they were when she was alive."
179. A Tibetan expression for ingratitude.
180. *Way of the Bodhisattva* I, 28, last two lines. The first two lines make up the next quote below.
181. The world of form and the formless world.
182. See note 27.
183. One's body, wealth, and merits. See *Way of the Bodhisattva*, III, 11: "My body, thus, and all my goods besides, / And all my merits gained and to be gained / I give them all away withholding nothing / To bring about the benefit of beings."

184. *sems dvangs ba*, a pure, clear state of mind free from negative emotions and discursive thoughts.
185. The special motivation, special duration, and special object.
186. *Way of the Bodhisattva*, II, 26.
187. *Way of the Bodhisattva*, III, 23, 24.
188. *Way of the Bodhisattva*, III, 26.
189. *Way of the Bodhisattva*, III, 27.
190. *Way of the Bodhisattva*, III, 28.
191. *Way of the Bodhisattva*, III, 34.
192. When one takes the Bodhisattva vow, one's teacher gives one a Bodhisattva name.
193. The five pure abodes.
194. Lit. "apart from going down and bouncing straight up again like a silk ball, they will not have to go to the lower realms." This refers to a silk ball on an elastic string used as a toy.
195. *Way of the Bodhisattva*, VIII, 130.
196. Chandrakirti, *Introduction to the Middle Way*, trans. Padmakara Translation Group (Boston: Shambhala Publications, 2002), I, 1.
197. Tib. *'bri*, a female yak.
198. In Tibet juniper is often burned as an incense offering and makes a thick white smoke. (AZR)
199. As taught by Langri Thangpa in his *Eight Verses*.
200. The Tibetan text does not state explicitly which is the fourth.
201. This line is quoted from Atisha's *Seven-Point Mind Training*. See Dilgo Khyentse Rinpoche, *Enlightened Courage*, trans. Padmakara Translation Group (Ithaca, N.Y.: Snow Lion Publications, 1992), 37.
202. "Giving" (*gtong ba*) has the sense of letting go, relinquishing. "Handing over" (*byin pa*) is giving physically. "Dedicating" (*bsngo ba*) includes investing on behalf of others; mentally transferring.
203. The seed here refers mainly to habitual tendencies.
204. Lit. "pure conduct" (*tshang par spyod pa*), which within the context of the pratimoksha vows has come to mean celibacy.
205. Ceremonies conducted by visiting lamas for the benefit of the sick, the dead, etc.
206. Sponsor's accumulations: the merit the sponsor accumulates from making the offerings for the ceremony.
207. One such confession and fulfillment that includes the four sections and four essential elements is the Confession and Fulfilment That Churns the Depths of Hell (*na rag skong bshags*).

208. That is, the promise and the iron resolve not to break that promise.
209. *Way of the Bodhisattva*, VI, 1.
210. *Way of the Bodhisattva*, VI, 2.
211. *Introduction to the Middle Way*, III, 6.
212. *Way of the Bodhisattva*, VII, 2.
213. There are three kinds of laziness: (1) indolence, idleness, and procrastination; (2) being attracted to unwholesome actions and involved in trivial activity; and (3) discouragement or feeling inadequate.
214. The *Prayer of Good Actions* includes the following lines: "I shall purify infinite realms, / Liberate infinite beings, / Understand infinite dharmas, / Realize infinite wisdoms, / Perfect infinite actions, / Fulfill infinite aspirations, / And serve infinite buddhas, / And do this, without ever growing weary, through infinite kalpas!" Note that the Tibetan term for "infinite" here is "oceanlike" (*rgya mtsho*), indicating vastness and depth.
215. *Way of the Bodhisattva*, VII, 28. This verse in the Tibetan has been slightly adapted by Khenpo Ngakchung, and in translation we have done the same.
216. Although *sbyor ba'i brtson 'grus* has been translated in WMPT as "diligence in action," we have opted for "diligence in application," as this seems more consistent with what follows in Khenpo Ngakchung's commentary.
217. The paragraphs that follow were originally aimed at a male monastic audience and include teachings based on ancient Indian attitudes. They have been slightly edited to apply to modern Western readers.
218. *Way of the Bodhisattva*, VIII, 4.
219. *Way of the Bodhisattva*, V, 40.
220. *khru do*, lit. "two cubits," or twice the distance from the elbow to the tip of the middle finger.
221. Lit. "the concentration practiced by the childish."
222. *Treatise of the Middle Way Called Wisdom*, XXIV, 8.
223. *Introduction to the Middle Way*, XI, 13.
224. The Chinese monk defeated by Kamalashila in the great debate at Samye.
225. Khenpo Ngakchung is referring here more to the Vaibhashika school than to Shravakas in general.
226. *rang stong* and *gzhan stong*, lit. "emptiness of self" and "emptiness of other."
227. These three were the successive holders of Shri Gupta's lineage.
228. These are the four extremes. For the eight extremes see Eight conceptual extremes in glossary.
229. Chandrakirti's original verse reads: "The nature of phenomena, enshrouded

by our ignorance, is 'all-concealed.' / But what this ignorance contrives appears as true. / Therefore the Buddha spoke of 'all-concealing truth.'"
230. *Refutation of Objections*, verse 29.
231. *dgag bya'i snang tshul*. What we need to refute is the nature as it appears (*snang tshul*), as opposed to the nature as it is (*gnas tshul*).
232. In this section, the same Tibetan term, *sems*, has been translated as "mind" or "thoughts" to suit the context.
233. The body is the organ of touch.
234. In the Vajrayana, the aggregates, elements, and ayatanas are seen with pure perception as the mandala of the forty-two peaceful deities.
235. *nyes byas*, the 112 wrong actions or minor faults that constitute the fifth of the five classes of precepts to be observed by a fully ordained monk.
236. This is the second of the fourteen root downfalls included in the Vajrayana samayas and refers to transgressing the three levels of vows.
237. Any thought with negative emotions.
238. The "causal downfall" is the negative action that subsequently ripens as the "resultant downfall." E.g., taking life leads to one falling into hell. In this case the cause is called a downfall after its result.
239. I.e., someone who is practicing the same path.
240. While WMPT speaks of the power of resolution (*sdom pa'i stobs*), Khenpo Ngakchung uses the term "power of restoration" (*sor chud pa'i stobs*). The heading "power of resolution" has been added in the Chengdu edition, following WMPT.
241. "The manner of a fish leaping from water," a common phrase in visualization instructions to denote that the deity appears instantaneously, in its complete form, not gradually.
242. The point here is that a vow not to commit a particular negative act creates much greater merit than the simple avoidance of that act.
243. I.e., to assume a higher rank than one has.
244. For details of all these different vows, see *Treasury of Precious Qualities* and Dudjom Rinpoche, *Perfect Conduct: Ascertaining the Three Vows*, trans. Khenpo Gyurme Samdrub and Sangye Khandro (Boston: Shambhala Publications, 1996).
245. Common to the traditions of both the Ancient and New Translations.
246. The vehicle of the six transcendent perfections (*phar phyin theg pa*) is another name for the Vehicle of Characteristics.
247. Lit. "the support and the supported" (*rten dang brten*), the palace and the deity visualized in the palace.
248. Khenpo Pema Dorje, also known as Khenchen Pema Damchö Ozer, was

a khenpo at Dzogchen Monastery. He was a contemporary of Patrul Rinpoche and an important holder of the Nyingtik lineage.
249. *ye she rin po che*, lit. "precious primal wisdom."
250. I.e., one imagines each of the Buddhas, palaces, and goddesses in their different "versions," one for each of the five families: Buddha/Body, Vajra/Mind, Jewel/Quality, Lotus/Speech, and Karma/Activity.
251. This is a round-shaped stupa, different from the eight standard designs. It resembles the Kalachakra stupa. The reason for the name is not clear; it is not apparently connected with the Kadampa school. (AZR)
252. *zhing khams sbyang ba*, lit. "purifying the universe," i.e., one's perception of it, by visualizing one's surroundings as a buddhafield or pure realm. This is related to the third of the Bodhisattva's activities of completion, maturation, and training.
253. *tshams pa tshang* refers to Patrul Rinpoche's teacher Jigme Gyalwai Nyugu, the disciple of Rigdzin Jigme Lingpa.
254. This is one of the names of Jamyang Khyentse Wangpo.
255. *Way of the Bodhisattva*, II, 1.
256. The text refers to what the Tibetans call "dark and pale gold," the former being more highly valued.
257. This is the twelve-line prayer in the text of the Longchen Nyingtik Ngondro.
258. *lus sbyin*, translated in WMPT as "offering the body." The Tibetan word for "giving" here is the same as "generosity."
259. He does not dwell with the main gods in the city of Tushita.
260. Haunted places (*mnyan sa*), lit. "sensitive places," so called because of the sensitivity and aggressive reactions of the many spirits who inhabit such places and who tend to thwart all attempts to do anything there.
261. Bodhisattvas who are already on the fourth, fifth, or even eighth level and who enter the Mantrayana in order to complete the path, so that at this point they are already on one of the four Vidyadhara levels. (AZR)
262. *rgyal-po*, a class of spirit antithetical to the Dharma, and *'gong-po*, a class of spirit antithetical to the state.
263. *sdig pa'i bshes gnyen*, the opposite of the Tibetan *dge ba'i bshes gnyen*, or "spiritual friend"; literally "a friend in evil," as opposed to a friend in virtue.
264. This condensed sentence refers to the analysis of the object (material things) into particles and the subject (the consciousness) into instants of time.
265. Approach, a stage in sadhana practice and recitation. See WMPT glossary, Approach and accomplishment.

266. Springs are the abodes of powerful, dangerous *naga*s, so to have visited one hundred springs is something of a qualification for a Chö master. (AZR).
267. Superior (*lhag*) means here that the teacher should have greater knowledge than the disciple. (KPS)
268. The verse quoted mentions only nine qualities explicitly, the quality of endeavor being understood.
269. *Way of the Bodhisattva*, I, 34.
270. *Way of the Bodhisattva*, I, 35 (first two lines).
271. Much of what follows is described in slightly more detail in part 1, chapter 1.
272. *thun mong rig pa'i dbang lnga*, five preliminary empowerments in the three outer tantras: water, crown, vajra, bell, and name.
273. At the end of a sadhana one usually receives the accomplishments or result of the practice symbolically, using both visualizations and ritual objects.
274. Sogpo Lhapel was one of the twenty-five disciples of Padmasambhava. A blacksmith by trade, he received teachings from both Nyak Jnanakumara and Guru Rinpoche. He could seize savage beasts of prey with his bare hands.
275. The duration of the Buddha's teaching in this world is said to be ten periods of "five hundred." Some traditions claim that this means not five hundred years but five hundred cycles of prosperity and decline linked to the advent of holy beings on the one hand and evil beings on the other.
276. Profundity refers to emptiness, and clarity to wisdom.
277. When we understand the nature of the lama, all our perceptions become pure. The external world is a palace, appearing through the creative power of the lama's compassion. The beings it contains are deities, self-manifestations of the lama himself. (KPS)
278. Like pieces of paper under a paperweight that cannot be blown away by the wind, we are trapped in samsara by our negative emotions, beyond the help of the Buddhas of the past. (KPS)
279. *chos can*, the phenomena that have that absolute nature (*chos nyid*).
280. The lineage of the Kagyu teachings has continued to this day, but Marpa's family line ended with his son Tarma Dode.
281. These are the four lama sadhanas in the Longchen Nyingtik cycle, the *Heart Essence of the Vast Expanse*, respectively the guru yoga described here, the sadhana of Guru Rinpoche and the Eight Vidyadharas, that of Avalokiteshvara, and that of Longchenpa.

282. *kun mkhyen bla ma* probably refers in this case to Kunkhyen Jigme Lingpa rather than Longchenpa.
283. In this manner the lama himself, or the main deity, embodies all the others.
284. Relative truth is the illusory phenomena that deluded beings perceive as true. "Merely relative phenomena" are the phenomena perceived by supreme beings who recognize them as untrue. (KPS)
285. "Dwelling on the ground" (*gzhir gzhugs*) refers to the spontaneous arising from the absolute nature, or Buddha nature. "Arisen from the ground" (*gzhir gzhengs*) refers to visualizing oneself as deity. (KPS)
286. This simile is intended to illustrate the fact that the recitation of the Prayer in Seven Lines causes the deities thus invoked to be drawn irresistibly to the practitioner.
287. This is a Tibetan play on words; "bones" refers to the father lineage, and "flesh" to the mother lineage.
288. *gral mgo*, lit. "the head of the row," i.e., a position of rank in the rows of monks in a monastery.
289. This quote could also be understood to mean that Geshe Chengawa began by offering different kinds of incense, such as Mongolian incense made from four ingredients, burning so much that he created a tremendous fog in his room, and then he gradually progressed to offering very costly incense. (PWR)
290. In meditation those on the Bodhisattva levels dwell in emptiness, so their meditation cannot be tainted by the dualistic perception of an observing mind and an observed object (*gnyis snang*). In the postmeditation, however, this dualistic perception is still present to a greater or lesser extent, and it is for this reason that Bodhisattvas' actions are said to be tainted.
291. Things that can be enumerated are concepts (true, false, etc.), and those that cannot be are beyond concepts (e.g., emptiness). (AZR)
292. Mahasandhi (Skt.), the Great Perfection.
293. Seen from the point of view of the way things appear, all actions of body, speech, and mind are tainted. From the point of view of the way they are in reality (i.e., emptiness), they are not tainted. (KPS)
294. I.e., the ultimate attainment of the particular one of the five paths the Bodhisattva is on: clear understanding as the attainment of the path of accumulating, experience on the path of joining, realization on the path of seeing, and freedom on the path of meditation.
295. Brahma and Indra were the first to request Buddha Shakyamuni to turn the Wheel of Dharma after his enlightenment at Bodh Gaya.
296. Alternate translation: "three outer vehicles that guide beings, taking the origin of suffering as the starting point."

297. For example, evil spirits. (AZR)
298. They dedicate and pray without separating from the emptiness supreme in all aspects. (AZR)
299. The absolute three doors are the three vajras (see glossary).
300. Their nature (*chos nyid*) is emptiness. (AZR)
301. The three wisdoms (*ye shes gsum*) are the wisdoms of the void essential nature, of the natural expression that is clarity, and of the all-pervading compassion. (KPS)
302. Their essence is one; therefore they are together, inseparable. (KPS)
303. *dzab*, repeated recitation while counting the repetitions on a mala.
304. The times of day recommended for reciting each chapter are stated at the end of the seventh chapter, *The Prayer for the Spontaneous Fulfillment of Wishes* (*bsam pa lhun 'grub ma*): *The Prayer to the Guru's Three Kayas* should be recited whenever one remembers one's refuge, the teacher; the prayer given to King Trisong Detsen should be recited in the evening; the prayer given to Yeshe Tsogyal should be recited in the morning; the one given to Namkhai Nyingpo at dawn; that given to Nanam Dorje Dudjom in the afternoon; that given to Prince Mutri Tsenpo at midnight; and the prayer given to the King of Gungthang (that is, the seventh chapter) at noon. In general these prayers can be recited whenever one is threatened with suffering. A complete translation of the *Seven Chapters* appears in Ngawang Zangpo, *Guru Rinpoché: His Life and Times* (Ithaca, N.Y.: Snow Lion Publications, 2002), 217 et seq.
305. *don brgyud*, the authentic lineage or transmission of the realization, not just of the words or even the empowerments. (PWR)
306. One should distinguish between experiences coming from mere perceptions (*snang nyams*) and experiences coming from realization (*rtogs nyams*). (AZR)
307. Flattened by all the ritual objects symbolically placed on it during the empowerment.
308. *sngags kyi gso sbyong*. This is the Mantrayana equivalent of the pratimoksha repair-and-purification ritual involving the confession of downfalls.
309. The empowerment of great lights rays (*'od zer chen po'i dbang*). According to the Sutrayana, when a Bodhisattva is about to become a Buddha, light rays emanate from between the eyes of the myriad Tathagatas of the ten directions and vanish into the Bodhisattva's crown, and buddhahood is attained. See Dudjom Rinpoche, *The Nyingma School of Tibetan Buddhism* (Boston: Wisdom Publications, 1991), 142, 912.
310. Here Khenpo Ngakchung is referring to the preliminary practice text recited at this moment: "The blessings of the vajra speech enter me, / I

316   NOTES

receive the secret empowerment / I become a suitable vessel for mantra recitation. / The seed is sown for attaining the level of Vidyadhara with mastery of the duration of life. / The potential for attaining the sambhogakaya level is established in me."

311. The text continues: "The blessings of the vajra mind enter me, / I receive the primordial wisdom empowerment, / I become a suitable vessel for the *tummo* (mystic heat) practice of bliss and emptiness, / The seed is sown for attaining the level of Mahamudra Vidyadhara, / The potential for attaining the dharmakaya level is established in me."

312. The text continues: "Again from the *hung* in the heart / A second *hung*, like a shooting star, / Streaks down and mixes completely with my mind. . . ."

313. The text continues: "The blessings of the vajra primal wisdom enter me, / I receive the absolute word empowerment, / I become a suitable vessel for the Great Perfection practice of primordial purity, / The seed is sown for attaining the level of spontaneously accomplished Vidyadhara, / The potential for attaining the ultimate result, the svabhavikakaya, is established in me."

314. *Introduction to the Middle Way*, XI, 13.

315. The meaning of this quote is that aggregates and space (meaning emptiness) are not two separate things; they are inseparable. (KPS)

316. It is the aspiration to transfer one's mind into the lama's mind, at the end of the guru yoga. See WMPT page 330.

317. "When my life comes to its end, / May I perceive the Glorious Mountain of Ngayab, / The union nirmanakaya buddhafield. / There, my body transformed into Vajra Yogini, / A mass of brilliant, shining light, / May I attain buddhahood, / Inseparable from the Lotus-Born Lord. / From the display of the great primal wisdom, / Manifesting as bliss and emptiness, / May I be inspired by the Lotus Lord / As a sublime leader, a guide / For all beings in the three worlds. / With this prayer from the depth of my heart, / Words that I have not simply mouthed, / May you bless me from the expanse of your mind / And grant my wishes, I pray."

318. Adoption and rejection: notions of having to undertake positive actions and give up negative ones.

319. In the Great Perfection the view, meditation, and action are respectively the understanding of the absolute nature, the habituation to that understanding, and the action based on it; any concepts of subject and object necessarily run counter to such understanding.

320. *slong byed kyi rkyen gsum*, cloud, mist, and fog. The simile here refers to the

three subtle states of attachment, aversion, and bewilderment that no longer obscure the clear light of the dharmakaya once they have dissolved.
321. I.e., the second of the four visions of thögal.
322. They do not have to experience the manifestation of the five Dhyani Buddhas and the other visions of the intermediate state.
323. I.e., those who have attained firmness in the practice of the generation phase. (KPS)
324. *mos pa tsam*, lit. "with mere interest or aspiration," i.e., without actual realization.
325. I.e., the intermediate state of becoming.
326. *'du shes*, lit. "idea, thought, mental image." This term has been translated in WMPT as "metaphor."
327. The moment when the breath has ceased but the heart has not yet stopped beating.
328. This means taking as the path the pure phenomena arising during the intermediate state of absolute reality. (KPS)
329. "Rebirth" here implies the intermediate state of becoming (*srid pa'i bar do*).
330. This is the moment when one recovers consciousness after the complete blackout of the moment of attainment.
331. Visualize your mind and energy gathered in the form of the essential drop (*tig le*) (KPS). The outer empty enclosure is the body; the inner empty enclosure is the central channel.
332. The three seed syllables are *Om, Ah,* and *Hung,* connected with inhaling, holding the breath, and exhaling.
333. According to the ancient tradition in India, to refer to one's teacher directly by his name was considered disrespectful, and it was the custom to refer to him simply by a title, such as "the Vajradhara," or "Refuge Lord." This can make it difficult to identify the teachers mentioned in the colophon of some texts, so rather than risk confusion Khenpo Ngakchung prefers here to do away with convention and to spell his teacher's name out in full.
334. *bka' drin sum ldan.* Various explanations of the threefold kindness have been given. According to the Sutra tradition, the teacher possesses the kindness of giving vows, transmission, and explanation. According to the Mantrayana it is the kindness of bestowing empowerment, explaining or transmitting the tantras, and giving the pith instructions. The thrice-kind teacher is also the one who through kindness is one's root teacher, the teacher who guides one, and a teacher in the lineage.
335. These are two names of Khenpo Ngakchung.

Glossary

Absolute nature – *chos nyid*, Skt. *dharmata*, the nature that is emptiness.

Aggregates – *phung po*, Skt. *skandha*. See Five aggregates.

Apu – *a bu*, the name by which Patrul Rinpoche was familiarly known in the Dzogchen area of Kham, eastern Tibet.

Arhat with residue – *lhag bcas pa'i dgra bcom pa*, one who is completely rid of the negative emotions but whose aggregates remain.

Arhat without residue – *lhag med pa'i dgra bcom pa*, one who is not only completely rid of the negative emotions but has also left behind the aggregates.

Ayatanas – *skye mched*, the six sense organs and their corresponding sense objects.

Basic Vehicle – *theg dman*, Skt. *Hinayana* (lit. "lesser vehicle," in relation to the Mahayana or Great Vehicle), the vehicle of the Shravakas and Pratyekabuddhas.

Bhikshu – *dge slong*, a fully ordained monk.

Birwapa – *bir wa pa*, the Indian Mahasiddha Virupa, whose Path and Result (*lam 'bras*) teachings have been continued mainly in the Sakya and Kagyu traditions.

Causal Vehicle of Characteristics – *rgyu mtshan nyid theg pa*, the vehicle that teaches the path as the cause for attaining enlightenment. It includes the vehicles of the Shravakas, Pratyekabuddhas and Bodhisattvas (that is, those Bodhisattvas practicing the sutra path and not that of the mantras). It is distinct from the Resultant Vehicle of the Mantras, which takes the result (enlightenment) as the path.

Chöpa – *gcod pa*, someone who practices the Chö, the kusali's offering of the body.

Completion, maturation, and training – *rdzogs smin sbyang*, completing the two accumulations: maturing or ripening beings and training in perception.

Conceptual parts or particles – *phyogs cha*, lit. "directional parts." Parts or particles that, because they have a top, a bottom, and sides, can logically be further divided, however small they are, ad infinitum.

Damaru – *da ma ru,* Skt. *idem,* a hand drum consisting of two bowl-shaped drums fixed back to back, with a double thong acting as the beater when the drum is twisted rapidly back and forth. Damarus are sometimes constructed from the tops of two skulls and therefore described as skull drums.

Deity, mantras, and concentration – *lha sngags ting nge 'dzin,* visualizing oneself as the deity, reciting mantras, and using the power of concentration to bless offerings, etc.

Dhatu – *khams,* lit. "space" or "sphere." The eighteen dhatus comprise the six senses, their six objects, and the six corresponding consciousnesses.

Disillusionment – *skyo shas,* disillusionment, sadness, or weariness, the sadness that comes with seeing the suffering inherent in samsara.

Driza – *dri za,* Skt. *gandharva,* lit. "smell eater," a spirit that feeds on smells. Also a being in the intermediate state: since it inhabits a mental body, it feeds not on solid food but on odors.

Eight concentrations and formless absorptions – *bsam gzugs brgyad,* an abbreviation of *bsam gtan bzhi dang gzugs med pa'i snyoms 'jug bzhi,* the four concentrations and four formless absorptions. These concentration practices, if practiced as an end in themselves, aim merely at higher states of existence and are then not considered to be part of any of the Buddhist vehicles because their goal is still within samsara. They are sometimes practiced in a Buddhist context as part of a more far-sighted training in meditation.

Eight conceptual extremes – *spros mtha' brgyad,* the eight extreme views: arising and ceasing, eternalism and nihilism, going and coming, and single and multiple.

Eight consciousnesses – *tshogs brgyad,* the consciousnesses of the five senses, the mind consciousness, the emotional consciousness, and the consciousness of the ground of all.

Eight great dangers (or fears) – *'jigs pa chen po brgyad,* those of lions, elephants, fire, snakes, water, chains, robbers, and flesh eaters (harmful spirits).

Eight similes of illusion – *sgyu ma'i dpe brgyad,* a dream, a magic show, a visual aberration, a mirage, an echo, a city of gandharvas, a reflection, a city created by magic. See WMPT page 252.

Eighteen distinctive qualities – *ma 'dres pa bco brgyad,* eighteen special attributes that only a fully enlightened Buddha can have. Six concern a Buddha's conduct and six his realization, three describe his wisdom in terms of the three times and three in terms of the deeds of his Body, Speech, and Mind. A detailed description is to be found in *Treasury of Precious Qualities* (see bibliography).

Five aggregates – *phung po lnga*, the five psychophysical components into which a person can be analyzed and which together produce the illusion of a self. They are form, feeling, perception, conditioning factors, and consciousness.

Five elements – *'byung ba lnga*, the five elements that constitute all matter, namely earth, water, fire, wind (air), and space.

Five powers – *rnam byang dbang po lnga*, five of the thirty-seven elements leading to enlightenment: confidence (or faith), diligence, mindfulness, concentration, and wisdom.

Five sense organs – *dbang po lnga*, the eyes, ears, nose, tongue, and body (or skin, the organ of touch).

Four black dharmas – *nag po'i chos bzhi*, or four unwholesome deeds. These are: (1) intentionally deceiving or lying to someone who is worthy of veneration, such as the teacher or abbot; (2) with a negative attitude, regretting or causing someone to regret an action that is actually positive in nature; (3) blatantly disrespecting, by verbal criticism or negative thoughts, a Bodhisattva or a spiritual practitioner who possesses the bodhichitta; and (4) deceiving sentient beings through negative behavior.

Four causes that exhaust one's store of merit – *dge rtsa zad pa'i rgyu bzhi*, failing to dedicate, getting angry, regretting one's virtuous deeds, and showing off.

Four causes that lead to downfalls – *ltung ba 'byung ba'i rgyu bzhi,* (1) not knowing the precepts; (2) carelessness; (3) a great many negative emotions; and (4) lack of devotion or respect.

Four ends of impermanence – *mi rtag mtha' bzhi,* these are defined in a famous quotation from the *Collection of Deliberate Sayings*, I, 22:

> The end of all gathering is dispersing,
> The end of all living is dying.
> The end of all meeting is parting,
> The end of all rising is falling.

Four families – *rigs bzhi*, the three Buddha families plus one family combining the Action (karma) and Jewel (ratna) families.

Four guests – *mgron bzhi*, (1) the Buddhas and Bodhisattvas; (2) the Dharma protectors; (3) the beings of the six realms; and (4) those with whom we have karmic debts. *See also* Offering and giving.

Four Noble Truths – *bden pa bzhi*, Skt. *caturaryasatya*, suffering, the origin of suffering, cessation, and the path. These were the subject of Buddha Shakyamuni's first discourse.

Four root vows of the pratimoksha – *so thar gyi rtsa ba bzhi po*, to refrain from killing, taking that which is not given, sexual misconduct, and lying.

Four vajras – *rdo rje bzhi*, vajra body, vajra speech, vajra mind, and vajra wisdom.

Gemang Rinpoche – *dge mang rin po che*, refers to Gyelse Shenphen Thaye (1800– ?), a holder of the Longchen Nyingtik lineage and contemporary of Patrul Rinpoche.

Ghandhapa – *dril bu pa,* one of the eighty-four Mahasiddhas of India.

Hevajra – *kye rdo rje*, one of the main yidam deities in the Sakyapa tradition.

King Indrabhuti – *rgyal po indra bhu ti*, the king of Oddiyana at the time Padmasambhava appeared in this world.

Kumaraja – *ku ma ra dza* (1266–1343) a great master and root teacher of Longchen Rabjam, who studied with him for six years.

Kyurura – *skyu ru ra*, a medicinal fruit, emblic myrobalan or *Emblica officinalis*. The young fruit is so transparent that all the finest details of its internal structure can be clearly seen. The seeds are like transparent jellylike pearls.

Lesser Vehicle – *theg dman*, the Hinayana or Basic Vehicle.

Mala – *phreng ba*, the 108 prayer beads used for counting recitations of prayers and mantras.

Merit – *bsod nams,* Skt. *punya,* the first of the two accumulations. "Merit" is also sometimes used loosely to translate the Tibetan terms *dge ba* (virtue, positive action) and *dge rtsa* (sources of good for the future).

Mudra – *phyag rgya*, Skt. *mudra,* a term with various meanings dependent on context. They include: a seal, a hand gesture, a spiritual consort.

Nagabodhi – *klu'i byang chub*, one of the eighty-four Mahasiddhas of India. Nagarjuna's disciple and successor, he was renowned for his miraculous powers.

Nirvana with residue – *lhag bcas myang 'das*, the state of nirvana of an Arhat with residue.

Nirvana without residue – *lhag med myang 'das*, the state of nirvana of an Arhat without residue.

No-self – *bdag med. See* WMPT glossary, Egolessness.

Offering and giving – *mchod sbyin*. The distinction is usually made, particularly in such practices as the incense (*gsang*) offering and burned (*gsur*) offerings, between *offering* to sublime beings "above" such as the Buddhas and Bodhisattvas and *giving* (as part of the practice of generosity) to ordinary beings "below," including animals and spirits. *See also* Four guests.

Omniscience – *thams cad mkhyen pa*, a synonym for buddhahood.

Path of earnest aspiration – *mos spyod kyi lam*, comprises the paths of accumulating and joining. The level of earnest aspiration is a sort of prelevel before one reaches the first of the ten Bodhisattva levels. Practitioners on the paths of accumulating and joining have not yet realized emptiness and cannot therefore practice the six transcendent perfections in a truly transcendental way. Their practice is more a question of willingness than of the genuine practice of a mature Bodhisattva. (AZR)

Renunciation – *nges 'byung*, usually translated here as "determination to be free."

Root downfall – *rtsa ltung*, a vow the observance of which is fundamental to successfully accomplishing the path. Defined as follows: if the vow is kept, it is the root that gives rise to all the excellent qualities of the path and result; if it is not kept, it becomes the cause of lower realms and the root of suffering, and as a result one falls further and further down in subsequent lives.

Rudra – *ru dra*, Skt. *rudra*, a kind of demon.

Sadhana – *sgrub thabs*, the method for accomplishing the level of a particular deity, for example, the lama, yidam, or dakini.

Saha world – *mi mjed 'jig rten*, the world of no fear, our universe, which is the buddhafield of Buddha Shakyamuni.

Sakya Pandita – an important Sakyapa master (1182–1251), also known as Kunga Gyaltsen.

Samaya deity – *dam tshig sems dpa'*, Skt. *samayasattva*, the deity one "creates" by visualization.

Shakya – the name of the family clan into which the Buddha Shakyamuni was born.

Shastra – *bstan bcos*, a commentary on the Buddha's teachings. The term *shastra* does not necessarily apply to a commentary on one particular teaching (a named sutra, for example) but includes works by both Indian and Tibetan masters that provide condensed or more accessible expositions of particular subjects.

Shramanera – *dge tshul*, the first stage in monastic ordination. Shramaneras do not observe all the precepts of fully ordained bhikshus, but it is incorrect to refer to them as novices in that many of them remain shramaneras throughout their lives without necessarily progressing to bhikshu ordination.

Six elements of a person – *skyes bu khams drug*, the six elements of a person: earth, water, fire, air, space, consciousness.

Six yogas – *chos drug*: the yogas of psychic heat (*gtum mo*), the illusory body (*sgyu lus*), dream (*rmi lam*), luminosity (*'od gsal*), consciousness transference (*'pho ba*), and the intermediate state (*bar do*).

Sixteen great dangers (or fears) – *'jigs pa chen po bcu drug*, those related to (1) earth (earthquakes, landslides); (2) water (oceans, drowning); (3) fire; (4)

wind (cyclones); (5) lightning; (6) weapons; (7) imprisonment and the law; (8) robbers; (9) ghosts; (10) wild elephants; (11) lion; (12) poisonous snakes and food poisoning; (13) epidemics and disease; (14) untimely death; (15) poverty; and (16) not accomplishing one's wishes. (TPW) Another source lists these as dangers and fears related to (1) obstacles created by gyalpo spirits; (2) celestial beings; (3) sicknesses caught from *sadag* spirits; (4) diseases such as leprosy; (5) famine; (6) war; (7) harm caused by *sadhu*s; (8) harm caused by elemental spirits; (9) lightning; (10) frost and hail; (11) earthquakes; (12) fire; (13) water; (14) falling stars; (15) outer space; and (16) nightmares.

Sixteen subdivisions of the Four Noble Truths – suffering, impermanence, emptiness, and selflessness are the four aspects of the truth of suffering; cause, arising, appearance, and condition are those of the truth of origination; cessation, quiescence, excellence, and renunciation those of the truth of cessation; and path, method, attainment, and liberation are the four aspects of the truth of the path.

Sugatagarbha – *bde gshegs snying po*, lit. "essence of those gone to bliss," a synonym of the Buddha nature. Sugatagarbha is often thought to be the same as *tathagatagarbha* (*de bzhin zhegs pa'i snying po*); they differ in that the former is related to the ground (*bzhi*) whereas the latter is related to the result (*'bras bu*).

Ten transcendent perfections – *pha rol tu phyin pa bcu po*, the six transcendent perfections to which are added the transcendent perfections of skillful means (*thabs*), prayer or aspiration (*smon lam*), strength (*stobs*), and primal wisdom (*ye shes*).

Three appearances – *snang ba gsum*, also *snang gsum 'pho ba'i bag chags*, changes of the three perceptions. These are the three perceptions related to the dissolution of the three poisons experienced by a dying person.

Three doors of perfect liberation – *rnam thar sgo gsum*: (1) the nature is empty; (2) the cause is without characteristics; (3) the result is not to be wished for.

Three families – *rigs gsum*, the Buddhas Manjushri, Avalokiteshvara, and Vajrapani; the Tathagata, Lotus, and Vajra families.

Three great systems (views of the) – *chen po gsum gyi lta ba*, the views of the Great Seal (Mahamudra), the Great Perfection (Dzogchen or Mahasandhi), and the Great Middle Way (Maha-madhyamaka) (*phyags rdzogs dbu gsum*).

Three kinds of enlightenment – *byang chub gsum*, the enlightenment of the Shravakas, Pratyekabuddhas, and Bodhisattvas.

Three possessions – *yongs su 'dzin pa'i gzhi gsum,* lit. "three grounds of grasping or bases for clinging." One's body, wealth, and merits.

Three Trainings – *bslab pa gsum,* the threefold training in discipline, concentration, and wisdom.

Three types of merit – *gsod nams bya ba'i dngos po gsum,* merit that comes from generosity, from discipline, and from meditation.

Three vajras – *rdo rje gsum,* the vajra body, vajra speech, and vajra mind of the deity.

Three ways of pleasing the teacher – *mnyes pa gsum,* by (1) making material offerings; (2) helping him through physical, verbal, or mental tasks; and (3) practicing what he teaches. See WMPT page 145.

Twelve branches of excellent speech – *sde snod bcu gnyis.* See WMPT glossary, Twelve categories of teaching in the pitakas.

Twelve deeds of a Buddha – *mdzad pa bcu gnyis,* (1) descending from the Tushita heaven; (2) entering the womb of his mother; (3) being born; (4) enjoying youthful sports; (5) taking pleasure in his entourage of queens; (6) renouncing the world; (7) practicing asceticism; (8) going to the Vajra Seat under the Bodhi tree; (9) vanquishing Mara; (10) attaining perfect buddhahood; (11) turning the Wheel of Dharma; and (12) passing into nirvana.

Twelve links of interdependent arising – *rten 'brel bcu nyi,* (1) ignorance; (2) conditioning factors; (3) consciousness; (4) name and form; (5) the sense powers; (6) contact; (7) feeling; (8) craving; (9) grasping; (10) becoming; (11) birth; and (12) old age-death. See *Treasury of Precious Qualities.*

Twenty-one sets of immaculate dharmas – *zag med kyi chos sde tshan nyi shu rtsa gcig,* twenty-one groups of qualities of the Buddha's dharmakaya wisdom: (1) the thirty-seven elements leading to enlightenment; (2) the four boundless qualities; (3) the eight perfect freedoms; (4) the nine successive absorptions; (5) the ten limitless ayatanas; (6) the eight dominant ayatanas; (7) the nonarising of negative emotions; (8) the knowledge of wishes and aspirations; (9) the five kinds of clairvoyance; (10) the four perfect knowledges; (11) the four complete purities; (12) the ten powers; (13) the ten strengths; (14) the four fearlessnesses; (15) the threefold absence of secretiveness; (16) the threefold limpidity; (17) the absence of forgetfulness; (18) the complete destruction of habitual tendencies; (19) great compassion for all that lives; (20) the eighteen distinctive qualities; and (21) omniscience.

Two extremes – *mtha' gnyis,* the extreme of samsara and the extreme of nirvana.

Ultimate meaning – *nges don.* See WMPT glossary, Real meaning.

Untainted – *zag med*, lit. "unstained," uncontaminated by negative emotions, including concepts due to the negative emotion of ignorance. *See also* WMPT glossary, Tainted (action).

Upasaka – *dge bsnyen*, the most basic form of Buddhist ordination, the so-called lay person's vow. Anyone who has taken the refuge vow is an upasaka, though the term is often understood to imply someone who has taken the five basic vows of refraining from taking life, taking what is not given, sexual misconduct, lying, and the consumption of intoxicants.

Vehicle of Characteristics – *mtshan nyid theg pa*. *See* Causal Vehicle of Characteristics.

Wisdom deity – *ye shes sems dpa'*, Skt. *jnanasattva*, the "true" deity one invites to come and bless the samaya deity one has visualized.

World of desire – *'dod khams*, Skt. *kamaloka* or *kamadhatu*, the first of the three worlds.

World of form – *gzugs khams*, Skt. *rupadhatu*, the second of the three worlds.

World of formlessness – *gzugs med khams*, Skt. *arupyadhatu*, the third of the three worlds.

Worldly Vehicle – *'jig rten pa'i theg pa*, the vehicle of those who strive to achieve happiness but without attempting to attain liberation from samsara. Those who follow the "unmistaken" worldly vehicle seek liberation from the lower realms by winning rebirth in the higher realms; they believe in the law of cause and effect and practice the avoidance of negative actions and adoption of positive actions. Those who follow the "mistaken" worldly vehicle do not believe in the law of cause and effect or in past and future lives. In both cases, liberation from samsara is impossible.

The Three Worlds

The Three Worlds	The Six Realms		The individual realms	
World of form-lessness	Gods	Gods of the world of formlessness	The four formless realms at the peak of existence	Sphere of neither existence nor non-existence Sphere of Utter Nothingness Sphere of Infinite Consciousness Sphere of Infinite Space
World of form	Gods	The seventeen classes of gods of the world of form	The five pure abodes	Unexcelled (Akanishtha) Good Vision Manifest Richness Without Distress Not Greater
			The twelve ordinary realms of the four concentrations	
			Fourth concentration	Great Result Merit-Born Cloudless
			Third concentration	Flourishing Virtue Limitless Virtue Lesser Virtue
			Second concentration	Clear Light Measureless Radiance Dim Light
			First concentration	Great Pure Ones Priests of Brahma The Pure

The Three Worlds

The Three Worlds	The Six Realms		The individual realms	
World of desire	Gods	The six classes of gods of the world of desire	Gods of the four sky abodes	Mastery of Others' Creations Enjoying Magical Creations The Joyous Realm (Tushita) Heaven Free of Conflict (Yama)
			Gods on top of Mount Meru	Heaven of the Thirty-three
			Gods on the steps of Mount Meru	Four Great Kings
	Asuras			Asuras
	Humans			Humans of the four continents
	Animals			Animals living in the depths Animals that live scattered in different places
	Pretas			Pretas who live collectively Pretas who move through space
	Hells			The eight hot hells The neighboring hells The eight cold hells The ephemeral hells

The Five Bodhisattva Paths and the Thirty-seven Elements Leading to Enlightenment

	The Five Paths			*The Thirty-seven Elements of Enlightenment*
PATH OF LEARNING	*Path of accumulating*	lesser	Four close mindfulnesses	1. mindfulness of the body 2. mindfulness of feeling 3. mindfulness of consciousness 4. mindfulness of mental objects
		middle	Four genuine restraints	5. halting of negative thoughts not yet arisen 6. rejection of negative thoughts already arisen 7. solicitation of positive thoughts not yet arisen 8. protection from decline of positive thoughts already arisen
		greater	Four bases of miraculous powers	9. concentration based on the power of the will 10. concentration based on endeavor 11. concentration based on one-pointed mindfulness 12. concentration based on analysis

330   THE FIVE BODHISATTVA PATHS

The Five Paths		*The Thirty-seven Elements of Enlightenment*	
Path of joining	the four distinctly experienced stages		
	warmth	Five powers	13. confidence
			14. diligence
	peak		15. mindfulness
			16. concentration
			17. wisdom
	acceptance	Five irresistible forces	18. confidence
			19. diligence
			20. mindfulness
	supreme mundane level		21. concentration
			22. wisdom
Path of seeing	First Bodhisattva level	Seven elements leading to enlightenment	23. mindfulness
			24. perfect discernment
			25. diligence
			26. joy
			27. flexibility
			28. concentration
			29. evenness
Path of meditation	Second–Tenth Bodhisattva levels	Eightfold Noble Path	30. right view
			31. right thought
			32. right speech
			33. right conduct
			34. right livelihood
			35. right effort
			36. right mindfulness
			37. right concentration
PATH OF NO MORE LEARNING	*Path of no more learning*		

A Comparative Glossary: Alternative Translations with Tibetan and Sanskrit Equivalents

WESTERN TRANSLATORS HAVE YET to standardize the translation of Tibetan terms. This table, compiled at the request of Alak Zenkar Rinpoche, will, we hope, contribute toward a fuller appreciation of Tibetan terms and help to remove the confusion that arises from reading texts translated by different individuals, each with his or her own preferences and reasons for using a particular English word or for using the Sanskrit equivalent. The first column contains the English terms generally adopted in the translation of the present text and *The Words of My Perfect Teacher*. This list cannot pretend to be exhaustive but may overcome some of the terminological difficulties readers might encounter and enrich their understanding of these terms.

English Term Used in This Translation	Tibetan (Wylie)	Sanskrit	Alternative English Translations
absolute nature	chos nyid	dharmata	intrinsic nature of reality, intrinsic reality
absolute truth	don dam	paramarthasatya	ultimate truth
acceptance (on the path of joining)	bzod	kshanti	patience, forbearance, patient acceptance, receptiveness
action (view, meditation and)	spyod pa	carya	activity, conduct
actions	las	karma	karma, action
activity	phrin las	karma	enlightened activity

Comparative Glossary

English Term Used in This Translation	Tibetan (Wylie)	Sanskrit	Alternative English Translations
adventitious	glo bur	agantuka	incidental
analytic meditation	dpyad sgom	vicarabhavana	investigative meditation
antidote	gnyen po	pratihara, pratipaksha	remedy
apparent	snang bcas		perceptible, with concepts
asura	lha ma yin	asura	demigod, jealous god, titan, antigod
attachment	'dod chags	raga	desire
aversion	zhe sdang	dvesha	hatred, anger
basic vehicle	theg dman	hinayana	lesser vehicle, fundamental vehicle
beings	sems can/'gro ba	sattva, jagat	sentient beings
beings of great capactiy	skye bu che	mahapurusha	superior beings, beings of highest capacity
beings of lesser capacity	skye bu chung		inferior beings, beings of limited capacity
beings of middling capacity	skye bu 'bring		mediocre, middling beings, beings of intermediate capacity
beings to be benefited	gdul bya		beings to be tamed, to be converted, disciples, beings
bewilderment	gti mug	moha	ignorance, confusion, stupidity
bhikshu	dge slong	bhikshu	monk
bodhichitta	byang chub sems	bodhicitta	mind turned toward enlightenment, thought of enlightenment, enlightened mind, altruistic mind
Capable One	thub pa	muni	Mighty One
channel	rtsa	nadi	vein, subtle vein
Chittamatra	sems tsam pa	cittamatra	Mind Only school

Comparative Glossary

English Term Used in This Translation	Tibetan (Wylie)	Sanskrit	Alternative English Translations
clear light	'od gsal	prabhasvara	luminosity, luminous
concentration	bsam gtan	dhyana	meditative concentration, absorption, contemplation
concentration	ting nge 'dzin	samadhi	contemplation
conceptual obscurations	shes bya'i sgrib pa	jneyavarana	cognitive obscurations, obscurations veiling knowledge, obstructions to knowledge
Conqueror	rgyal ba	jina	Victorious One
crucial point	gnad	marma	key point, important point, vital point
dependent arising	rten 'byung	pratityasamutpada	dependent origination, interdependence
determination to be free	nges 'byung	nihsarana	renunciation
dharmakaya	chos sku	dharmakaya	absolute body, Dharma body, body of truth
diligence	brtson 'grus	virya	endeavor, strenuousness, effort, exertion
discipline	tshul khrims	shila	ethics, morality, ethical discipline
discipline, keep/observe	rgyud sdom/bsdam		bind one's mind/being
dualistic grasping	gnyis 'dzin	dvayastha	dualistic clinging/notions/thoughts/concepts, conceptualization
eight consciousnesses	tshogs brgyad	ashtavijnana	eight gatherings of consciousness
eighteen distinctive qualities	ma 'dres pa bco brgyad	avenikadharma	eighteen distinct attributes
elaborations	spros	prapanca	mental constructs, concepts
emptiness	stong pa nyid	shunyata	voidness

334 Comparative Glossary

English Term Used in This Translation	Tibetan (Wylie)	Sanskrit	Alternative English Translations
energy	rlung	prana	vital energy, wind, breath
equanimity (rest in)	mnyam bzhag	samapatti	meditation, formal meditation, meditative equipoise
essence	thig le	bindu	essential drop, subtle essence
essence	ngo bo	vastu	essential nature, nature
essential nature	ngo bo	vastuta	essence
expedient meaning	drang don	neyartha	provisional meaning
extraordinary	thun min	asadharana	uncommon
five irresistible forces	stobs lnga	pancabala	five powers, five unshakable forces
five masteries	mngon byang lnga	abhisambodhi	five awakenings, five familiarizations
five powers	dbang po lnga	pancendriya	five faculties, five controlling powers, five perfect capacities
four bases of miraculous powers	rdzu 'phrul gyi rkang pa bzhi	riddhipada	four types of absorption, supports for miraculous ability
four close mindfulnesses	dran pa nyer bzhag bzhi	smrityupasthana	four objects of inspection, essential recollections, foundations of mindfulness
four distinctly experienced stages of the path of joining	byor lam nges 'byed cha bzhi	prayogamarga	
four genuine restraints	yang dag par spong ba bzhi	samyakprahana/ samyakpradhana	four attempts at rejection and acquisition, correct trainings
four points of reliance	ston pa bzhi	catuhpratisharana	four reliances, four kinds of reliance, four supports
four powers	stobs bzhi	caturbala	four strengths, four forces

Comparative Glossary

English Term Used in This Translation	Tibetan (Wylie)	Sanskrit	Alternative English Translations
freedoms and advantages	dal 'byor	kshanasampada	unique occasion and right juncture, unfavorable and favorable circumstances, leisures and wealths/endowments
friend	gnyen	mitra	relative, dear one, close one
generation phase	bskyed rim	utpattikrama	development phase, creation stage
generosity	sbyin pa	dana	giving, giving generously
ground	gzhi		basis, basic nature, foundation
habitual tendencies	bag chags	vasana	inclinations, habitual patterns, latencies, impregnations
illustrative (clear light/wisdom)	dpe'i 'od gsal/ ye shes		symbolic, example
infinite	rgya mtsho	samudra	oceanlike
innate	lhan skyes	sahaja	coemergent
interdependence	rten 'byung	pratityasamutpada	interdependent arising, dependent origination
intermediate state	bar do	antarabhava	bardo
kalpa	bskal pa	kalpa	eon, age
knowing as it really is	ji lta ba mkhyen pa	yathabhuta-parijnana	knowing the nature of phenomena
knowing each and every thing	ji snyed mkhyen pa	yathavad vyavasthana parijnana	knowing the multiplicity of phenomena
level	sa	bhumi	ground
listen (reflect and meditate)	thos (bsam sgom)	shruta	hear, study, receive (teachings)
love	byams pa	maitri	loving-kindness

Comparative Glossary

English Term Used in This Translation	Tibetan (Wylie)	Sanskrit	Alternative English Translations
Madhyamika	dbu ma pa	madhyamika	Middle Way school
master	bla ma	guru	guru, teacher
measureless (kalpa)	grangs med	asamkhya	countless, uncountable
mental event	sems 'byung	caitta	mental factor, mental function
mentation	sems pa	cintana	thought, intention
mind consciousness	yid kyi shes pa	manovijnana	mental consciousness
natural expression	rang bzhin	prakriti	nature, intrinsic existence
natural state	gnas tshul		way it is, way things are
natural state	gnas lugs		natural condition
nature	rang bzhin	prakriti	intrinsic existence
nature	ngo bo		essence, essential nature
negative action	sdig pa	papa	defilement, sin, bad karma
negative actions	mi dge ba	akushala	nonvirtue, nonmeritorious deeds
negative emotions	nyon mongs pa	kleshas	afflictive emotions, obscuring emotions, passions, afflictions, disturbing conceptions, delusions
nirmanakaya	sprul sku	nirmanakaya	emanated body, body of manifesation, tulku
nonapparent	snang med		imperceptible, without concepts
nonexistence, omnipresence, unity and spontaneous presence (four samayas of Atiyoga)	med pa phyal ba gcig pu lhun grub		nothingness, plainness, uniqueness, spontaneous presence
nonthought	mi rtog pa	acinta	absence of conceptualization, absence of thoughts, absence of thoughts, nonconceptuality

Comparative Glossary

English Term Used in This Translation	Tibetan (Wylie)	Sanskrit	Alternative English Translations
no-self	bdag med	nairatmya	egolessness, selflessness, absence/lack of true existence, insubstantiality
obscuration	sgrib	avarana	defilement, veil
ordinary	thun mong	samanya, sadharana	common
ordinary concerns (eight)	'jig rten gyi chos	ashtalokadharma	worldly concerns, ordinary preoccupations
path of accumulating	tshogs lam	sambharamarga	path of provisions, of preparation
path of joining	sbyor lam	prayogamarga	path of connection, of application
path of meditation	sgom lam	bhavanamarga	path of practice
path of no more learning	mi slob pa'i lam	ashaikshamarga	
path of seeing	mthong lam	darshanamarga	path of insight, of vision
peak (on the path of joining)	rtse		climax, summit
peak of existence	srid rtse	bhutakoti	summit of existence, pinnacle of existence
perfection phase	rdzogs rim	sampannakrama	completion stage
permanent	rtag pa	nitya	eternal, everlasting
pitakas (three)	sde snod	(tri)pitaka	baskets
positive actions	dge ba	kushala	positive acts, virtue, good deeds, meritorious actions, good karma, wholesome deeds
practitioner of sudden realization	cig car ba		person who progresses in instantaneous leaps
practitioner whose realization develops gradually	rim gyis pa		person who progresses in gradual stages
Prasangika	thal 'gyur pa	prasangika	Consequentialist

English Term Used in This Translation	Tibetan (Wylie)	Sanskrit	Alternative English Translations
pratimoksha	so sor thar pa	pratimoksha	individual liberation
pratyekabuddha	rang sangs rgyas	pratyekabuddha	buddha for himself, solitary realizer
preta	yi dvags	preta	hungry ghost, famished spirit
primal substance	gtso bo	pradhana	primal matter
primal wisdom	ye shes	jnana	primordial wisdom, gnosis, wisdom, pristine cognition
primordial purity	ka dag		
profound insight	lhag mthong	vipashyana	insight
realize/realization (1) (riddance and realization)	rtogs pa	abhisamaya	
realization (2)	dgongs pa		wisdom mind, intention, intent, wisdom
relative (truth)	kun rdzob	samvrittisatya	the relative, all-concealing, deceptive appearance, conventional truth, the conventional
remedy	gnyen po	pratipaksha	antidote
resting meditation	'jog sgom	sthapyabhavana	settling meditation, contemplative meditation
result	'bras bu	phala	fruit, fruition
riddance	spangs		elimination, abandonment
Saha (world of)	mi mjed	saha (lokadhatu)	world of no fear, world of patient endurance
samaya	dam tshig	samaya	promise, oath, sacred commitment, sacred precept, sacred bond
sambhogakaya	longs spyod rdzogs pa'i sku	sambhogakaya	body of perfect enjoyment, body of bliss
Sautrantika	mdo sde pa	sautrantika	Sutra school

English Term Used in This Translation	Tibetan (Wylie)	Sanskrit	Alternative English Translations
self (individual)	gang zag gi bdag	pudgalatma	personal self
self (phenomena)	chos kyi bdag	dharmatma	intrinsic/true existence (in phenomena)
sentient being	sems can	sattva	being
serious fault	lci ba		heavy, weighty, consequential fault
shramanera	dge tshul	shramanera	novice
shravaka	nyan thos	shravaka	listener, auditor, hearer
skillful means	thabs	upaya	means, method
spontaneous presence	lhun grub		natural presence, spontaneous accomplishment
supreme mundane level (on the path of joining)	chos mchog		supreme recognition of reality, highest worldly realization
surrogate	rjes mthun pa		substitute, akin to, similar to, concordant with, referential
sustained calm	zhi gnas	shamatha	calm abiding, quiescence, tranquillity
Svatantrika	rang rgyud pa	svatantrika	Autonomist
tainted	zag bcas	sasrava	contaminated
tantrika	sngags pa	tantrika	mantra practitioner
teacher	bla ma	guru	lama, guru, master
Teacher	ston pa	shasta	Buddha Shakyamuni
thögal	thod rgal		direct crossing, leap over, all-surpassing realization, overstepping, surpassing
thoughts	rnam rtog	vitarka	discursive thought/thinking
three doors of perfect liberation	rnam thar sgo gsum	vimokshadvaratraya	three liberating factors

English Term Used in This Translation	Tibetan (Wylie)	Sanskrit	Alternative English Translations
three possessions	yongs su 'dzin pa'i gzhi gsum		three grounds of grasping, bases for clinging, foundations of ownership
three worlds	khams gsum	triloka, trailokya	three realms
trekchö	khregs chod		cutting through resistance
ultimate meaning	nges don	nitartha	real meaning, definite meaning, definitive meaning
uncontrived	ma bcos pa		unfabricated
unfabricated	ma bcos pa		uncontrived
universe of one thousand million worlds	stong gsum 'jig rten gyi khams	trisahasra mahasahasra lokadhatu	three-thousand-fold universe, trichiliocosm
untainted	zag med	anasrava	uncontaminated
upasaka	dge bsnyen	upasaka	lay Buddhist, householder
Vaibhashika	bye brag smra ba	vaibhashika	Great Exposition school
Vajrayana	rdo rje'i theg pa	vajrayana	Diamond Vehicle, Adamantine Vehicle
vidyadhara	rig 'dzin	vidyadhara	knowledge holder, awareness holder
warmth (on the path of joining)	drod	ushman	meditative heat
wheel	'khor lo	chakra	center, chakra
wisdom	shes rab	prajna	supreme knowledge, awareness, supreme intelligence, transcendent knowledge
worldly vehicle	'jig rten pa'i theg pa		mundane vehicle
yidam	yi dam	ishtadevata	deity, tutelary deity, divinity

Bibliography

Works Quoted in the Text

Collection of Deliberate Sayings – *Udanavarga, ched du brjod pa'i tshoms*. A collection of verses from the Buddhist canon compiled by Dharmatrata. It is similar in content and style to the famed Dhammapada found in the Pali canon.

Conch-Lettered Instructions – *dung yig can*. Part of the Vima Nyingtik by Vimalamitra.

Condensed Transcendent Wisdom – *Prajnaparamita-samcayagatha, phar phyin bsdus pa*. A shastra by Aryashura.

Confession of Downfalls – *ltung gshags*. Another name for the *Sutra in Three Parts*.

Detailed Commentary on the Condensed Meaning – *dgongs 'dus rnam bshad*. A commentary written by Jigme Lingpa on the cycle of practices called *bla ma dgongs 'dus* by Sangye Lingpa.

Diamond Cutter Sutra – *Vajracchedika-prajnaparamita, 'phags pa shes rab kyi pha rol du phyin pa rdo rje gcod pa*.

Eight Verses of Langri Thangpa – *glang thang pa'i tshig brgyad ma*. Eight stanzas on the bodhicitta practice of mind training by the Kadampa Geshe Langri Thangpa.

Essay on the Mind of Enlightenment – *Bodhicitta-vivarana, byang chub sems 'grel*, by Nagarjuna.

Five Stages – *rim lnga*.

Five Treatises on the Middle Way – *dbu ma rig pa'i tshogs*. Five treatises on Madhyamika philosophy by Nagarjuna: *Prajna-mula-madhyamaka-karika* (*dbus ma rtsa ba shes rab*), *Yukti-sastika-karika* (*rigs pa drug cu pa*), *Vaidalya-sutra* (*zhib mo rnam 'thag*), *shunyata-saptati-karika* (*stong nyid bdun cu pa*), *Vigraha-vyavartani-karika* (*rtsod pa bzlog pa*).

Four Hundred Verses on Madhyamaka – *Madhyamaka catuhshataka, dbu ma bzhi brgya pa*. A shastra by Aryadeva.

Great Array of Ati – *a ti bkod pa chen po*. A tantra on Atiyoga.

Hagiography of Purna – *gang po'i rtogs rjod*. Purna was a merchant from western India who became a disciple of the Buddha.

Heart Essence of the Vast Expanse – *klong chen snying gi thig le*. A treasure rediscovered by Jigme Lingpa, one of the most famous heart essence teachings. Published by Lama Ngödrup for H.H. Dilgo Khyentse Rinpoche, Paro, Bhutan, 1972, 4 volumes.
Heruka Galpo – a tantra.
Hevajra Tantra – *Hevajra-tantra-raja, rgyud brtags gnyis*.
Inserting the Grass-Stalk – *'pho ba 'jag 'dzugs ma*. A prayer by Nyi Da Sangye recited in the practice of transference.
Introduction to the Middle Way – *Madhyamakavatara, dbu ma 'jug pa*, by the seventh-century Indian master Chandrakirti.
Jewel Garland of the Middle Way – *Ratnavali, dbu ma rin chen phreng ba*, by Nagarjuna.
Letter to a Friend – *Suhrllekha, bshes pa'i spring yig*, by Nagarjuna.
Madhyamaka Collections on Reasoning – *dbu ma rigs pa'i tshogs* by Nagarjuna.
Magical Net of Manjushri – *'jam dpal sgyu 'phrul dra ba*. Another name for the *Manjushri-nama-samgiti, 'phags pa 'jam dpal gyi mtshan yang dag par brjod pa*, the Litany of the Names of Manjushri.
Nirvana Sutra – *Mahaparinirvana-sutra, mya ngan las 'das pa'i mdo*.
Ocean of Liberation – *dam tshig rnam grol rgya mtsho*. A text on samaya by Longchenpa which forms part of the Lama Yangtik.
Ornament of Clear Realization – *Abhisamayalankara, mngon rtogs rgyan*, by Maitreya-Asanga.
Ornament of the Mahayana Sutras – *Mahayana-sutralankara-karika, mdo sde rgyan*, by Maitreya-Asanga.
Ornament of the Middle Way – *Madhyamakalankara, dbu ma rgyan*, by Shantarakshita.
Parting from the Four Attachments – *zhen pa bzhi bral*. An important Sakyapa text written by Sachen Kunga Nyingpo (1092–1158).
Prayer of Good Actions – *Bhadracaryapranidhana, bzang spyod smon lam*. A prayer from the *Avatamsaka Sutra, phal po che*, often recited at the end of rituals.
Prayer of Maitreya – a prayer requested by Maitreya from the Buddha Shakyamuni, taken from the forty-first chapter of the *Ratnakuta, The Jewel Mound Sutra, dkon mchog brtsegs pa*.
Refutation of Objections – *Vigrahavyavartani, rtsod pa bzlog pa*, by Nagarjuna.
Seven Chapters – *le'u bdun ma*. Seven prayers to Padmasambhava that he gave at the request of five of his principal disciples before his final departure from Tibet. They were then concealed and later revealed by the fourteenth-century terton Zangpo Tragpa.
Seven-Point Mind Training – *slob sbyong don bdun ma*, by Atisha.

Seven Treasures – *mdzod bdun*, a famous set of works by Longchenpa, covering all aspects of the Buddhist teachings and in particular the subtleties of the Great Perfection. The seven are listed in the bibliography of *The Words of My Perfect Teacher.*

Seventy Stanzas on Refuge – *skyabs 'gro bdun bcu pa.*

Stages on the Path – *lam rim.* (The Tibetan literature includes numerous works of this genre. It has not been possible to ascertain with certitude which particular work is referred to here.)

Sublime Continuum – *Uttaratantra-shastra, rgyud bla ma,* by Maitreya-Asanga.

Sutra Designed Like a Jewel Chest – *Arya-ratna-karandavyuha-sutra, mdo sde za ma tog bkod pa,* in the *Mani Kahbum* of Songtsen Gampo.

Sutra in Three Parts – *Triskandha-sutra, phung po gsum.*

Sutra of a Hundred Actions – *Karmashataka-sutra, mdo sde las brgya pa.*

Sutra of Great Liberation – *Mahamoksha-sutra, thar pa chen po'i mdo.*

Sutra of Skill in the Great Secret – *Mahaguhya-upaya-kaushalya-sutra, gsang chen thabs la mkhas pa'i mdo.*

Sutra of Sublime Dharma of Clear Recollection – *Saddharmanu-smrityu-pasthana-sutra, dam pa'i chos dran pa nye bar bzhag pa'i mdo.*

Sutra of the Descent to Lanka – *Lankavatara sutra, lang kar gshegs pa'i mdo.*

Sutra Remembering the Three Jewels – *Triratna-anusmrti-sutra, dkon mchog rjes dran.*

Sutra Requested by Sagaramati – *Sagaramati-paripriccha-sutra, blo gros rgya mtshos zhus pa'i mdo.*

Sutra Requested by Shrimaladevi Simhanada – *Shrimaladevi-simhanada-sutra, dpal phreng senge sgra zhus pa'i mdo.* Shrimaladevi-simhanada was the daughter of King Prasenajit.

Ten Wheels of Ksitigarbha – *Dasacakra-ksitigarbha-sutra, sa snying 'khor lo bcu pa.*

Torch of the Three Methods – *Nayatraya-pradipa, tshul gsum sgron me.* A shastra by Tripitakamala.

Treasury of the Abhidharma – *Abhidharmakosha, chos mngon pa dzod,* by Vasubandhu.

Treatise of the Middle Way Called Wisdom – *Madhyamikakarika, dbu ma rtsa ba'i shes rab,* by Nagarjuna.

Two Truths – *Satyadvayavibhanga, bden gnyis,* by Jnanagarbha.

Vajra Pinnacle tantra – *Vajrasekhara-mahaguhya-yogatantra, rdo rje rtse mo'i rgyud.* One of the four major sections of yoga tantra.

Vajrapani's True Empowerment – *phyag na rdo rje mngon par dbang bskur ba'i rgyud.*

Way of the Bodhisattva – *Bodhicharyavatara, byang chub sems dpa'i spyod pa la 'jug pa,* by Shantideva.

Bibliographical Sources Used by the Translators

Works in Tibetan

mkhas 'jug – Mipham Rinpoche's *Introduction to Scholarship*.

sdom gsum 'bru 'grel – Dudjom Rinpoche's commentary on Ngari Panchen's *sdom gsum rnam nges, Ascertaining the Three Vows*.

bod rgya tshig mdzod chen mo – *The Great Tibetan Chinese Dictionary* published by Alak Zenkar Thubten Nyima Rinpoche (Chengdu, China: Minorities Publishing House).

byang chub sems dpa'i spyod pa la 'jug pa – Shantideva's *The Way of the Bodhisattva*.

rdzogs pa chen po klong chen snying thig gi ngon 'gro'i khrid yig kun bzang bla ma'i zhal lung – Patrul Rinpoche's *The Words of My Perfect Teacher*.

yon tan rin po che'i mdzod kyi 'grel pa bden gnyis gsal byed zla ba'i sgron me – Khenpo Yonten Gyamtso's commentary on the sutra section of Jigme Lingpa's *Treasury of Precious Qualities*.

bshes spring mchan 'grel – Kangyur Rinpoche's commentary on Nagarjuna's *Letter to a Friend* (a translation is in preparation).

sems nyid ngal so – Longchenpa's *The Mind at Rest*.

Works in English

Chandrakirti. *Introduction to the Middle Way*. With commentary by Jamgön Mipham. Translated by the Padmakara Translation Group. Boston: Shambhala Publications, 2002.

Dudjom Rinpoche. *The Nyingma School of Tibetan Buddhism: Its Fundamentals and History*. Translated by Gyurme Dorje and Matthew Kapstein. Boston: Wisdom Publications, 1991.

———. *Perfect Conduct: Ascertaining the Three Vows*. Translated by Khenpo Gyurme Samdrub and Sangye Khandro. Boston: Shambhala Publications, 1996.

Eckel, Malcolm D. *Jnanagarbha's Commentary on the Distinction between the Two Truths*. Albany: State University of New York Press, 1987.

Frye, Stanley, trans. *Sutra of the Wise and the Foolish*. Dharamsala, India: Library of Tibetan Works and Archives, 1981.

Gampopa. *The Jewel Ornament of Liberation*. Translated by Khenpo Konchog Gyaltsen Rinpoche. Ithaca, N.Y.: Snow Lion Publications, 1998.

———. *The Jewel Ornament of Liberation*. Translated by Herbert V. Guenther. London: Rider, 1970.

Hopkins, Jeffrey. *Meditation on Emptiness*. London: Wisdom Publications, 1984.

Kangyur Rinpoche. *Treasury of Precious Qualities.* Translated by the Padmakara Translation Group. Boston: Shambhala Publications, 2001.

Khyentse, Dilgo. *Enlightened Courage: An Explanation of Atisha's Seven Point Mind Training.* Translated by the Padmakara Translation Group. Ithaca, N.Y.: Snow Lion Publications, 1993.

Klein, Anne. *Knowing, Naming, and Negation.* Ithaca, N.Y.: Snow Lion Publications, 1991.

Lingpa, Jigme. *The Dzogchen Innermost Essence Preliminary Practice.* Translated with commentary by Ven. Tulku Thondup. Edited by Brian Beresford. Dharamsala: Library of Tibetan Works and Archives, 1982.

Loden, Geshe Acharya Thubten. *The Fundamental Potential for Enlightenment.* Melbourne: Tushita, 1996.

Nagarjuna and Lama Mipham. *Golden Zephyr: A Letter to a Friend.* Translated by Leslie Kawamura. Emeryville, Calif.: Dharma Publishing, 1975.

Padmasambhava and Jamgon Kongtrul. *Light of Wisdom.* Boston: Shambhala Publications, 1995.

Patrul Rinpoche. *The Words of My Perfect Teacher.* Translated by the Padmakara Translation Group. San Francisco: HarperCollins, 1994; Second edition, Boston: Shambhala Publications, 1999.

Rigzin, Tsepak. *Tibetan-English Dictionary of Buddhist Terminology,* Second edition. Dharamsala, India: Library of Tibetan Works and Archives, 1993.

Shantideva. *The Way of the Bodhisattva.* Translated by the Padmakara Translation Group. Boston: Shambhala Publications, 1997.

Zangpo, Ngawang. *Guru Rinpoche: His Life and Times.* Ithaca, N.Y.: Snow Lion Publications, 2002.

Index

Absolute Mother, 249, 250
abysses, three, 63, 301n85
accomplishment(s), 113, 117, 255, 256, 257, 260, 313n273
    five points of the, 274–76
accumulation of merit and wisdom, 30–31, 53–54, 130, 234–36, 268, 271–72, 298n40
    See also mandala; merit; wisdom
actions
    as antidote, 227
    cause and effect, 74–78, 303n110
    choice and, 81–82
    chronology of result of, 78
    mixed, 76, 303n108
    negative, 74, 161, 187–92, 271
    positive, 29, 75, 91
    unwavering, 71, 302n99
    See also karma
acts, eight perverse, 230–31
aggregates, the, 184, 210–11, 213, 225, 248–49, 274 *passim*, 312n264
Akshobya, 112
Amitabha, 112, 285–86
Amitayus, 59
Amoghasiddhi, 113
Ananda, 35, 104, 260
Ancient Tradition, 102, 123, 134
anger, 27–28, 63, 162, 192–93
animal realm, 45–46
Anuttarayoga, 114
    outer tantra, 112–14, 255
Aparantaka, 76
appearances, deceptive, 81, 303n111
Apu (Patrul Rinpoche), 19, 52, 129, 148, 169, 204, 205, 228, 236, 240, 251, 275
    on bodhichitta, 168, 169
    on perception, 266–67
    on self-arisen wisdom, 279
    on the two truths, 205
Arhat, 72, 84, 95, 96, 110, 254, 302n104
Aryadeva, 33, 208
Asanga, 69
Atisha, 148
attachment, 197–98
attitude(s)
    according to the capacity of beings, 20–22
    correcting the, 43
    negative, neutral, and positive, 18–20
    right, 17, 18, 52
Avalokiteshvara, 255
Avatamsaka Sutra, 161

Basic Vehicle, 9, 10, 14, 96, 253–54 *passim*
    See also Shravakas and Pratyekabuddhas
beings
    five classes of, 133, 308n168
    forsaking, 162–63
Bhaviveka, 208
Birwapa, 263
Black Ishvara, 68
Black Spearman, 76
bodhichitta
    absolute, 155–56
    application, 181–84
    arousing, 24, 96, 134–35, 155–60
    aspiration, 52, 162–81
    benefits of, 164, 194
    Chö and, 247

classification, 152–55
  intention and, 27, 37, 96, 133–34, 181, 299n49
  and the Mahayana, 134
  relative, 22, 134, 155, 156
  structured, 100–101
  two aspects of, 22–27, 151–52, 172, 190, 274, 297nn27–28, 308n199
Bodhisattva, 24, 50, 97, 101, 160, 247, 271, 272 *passim,* 309n192, 314n294
  accomplishments, 256
  connection with a, 176
  levels, 101–2, 152–53
  qualities, 111, 112, 306nn143–44
  skillful means of a, 174–75, 179
  vehicle, 254–55
  vow(s), 51, 156–60, 191
  See also sangha
boundless qualities, four, 134–36, 160, 167, 308nn169–70
  compassion, 136, 148–51, 250, 259, 268, 283
  impartiality, 136–45, 165
  love, 136, 145–47
  sympathetic joy, 136, 150–51, 172
Brahma, 7, 69, 87, 272, 275 *passim,* 314n295
  four states of, 135–36
Branches of Excellent Speech, Twelve, 6, 9, 107
breath
  expulsion of stale, 42–43, 124, 299nn57–58
  outer and inner, 284, 316n327
buddhafield(s)
  Akanishtha, 34, 114
  cosmography, 236–39
  Dense Array, 23
  Potala (Glorious Copper Colored) Mountain, 255, 267
  Sukhavati, 184
buddhahood, 9, 26, 100, 122, 152, 160, 164, 182, 223–24 *passim*

Buddhalochana, 115
Buddhapalita, 208
Buddhas, the, 3, 77, 86, 157, 164, 178, 272 *passim*
  of the five families. *See* Hemasagara Buddhas
Buddha, the, 3–4, 5, 7, 29, 37, 97–98, 136, 164, 224, 260 *passim*
  activities, 105
  definition, 102
  edicts of, 221–23
  essence, divisions and qualities of, 101–7
  nature, 224–25
  omniscience of, 70, 163
  qualities, 136, 308n170
  teachings, 9, 296n10
  See also Buddha Shakyamuni; Gautama; Great Glorious One; Great Shramana; kayas; Sugata; Tathagata; Teacher; Three Jewels

Captain Compassionate Heart, 76
carefulness, 82, 304n115
Causal Vehicle of Characteristics, 31–32, 121, 233, 245, 246
cause and effect. *See* actions
certainties, five, 103, 305n133
  See also perfections, five
Chakrasamvara, 123, 264
Chandrakirti, 134, 164, 205, 209, 279
channels, the, 100–101, 305n129
Chatral Rinpoche, 289
Chengawa, Geshe, 270, 314n289
Chittamatrins, 77, 156, 206–7, 309n184
Chö, 156, 244–51
  Ninefold Black, 248n263
Chöpas
  recumbent cow, 247
  yapping dog, 248, 312n263
circumstances intrusive to Dharma practice, eight, 48–49, 300n65

Collection of Deliberate Sayings, 3
conceit. *See* self-centeredness
concerns, eight ordinary, 19, 173–74, 175, 180, 250
Conch-Lettered Instructions, 13, 296n13
Condensed Transcendent Wisdom, The, 29, 30
conduct
  evil, 49, 300n66
  right, 17, 18
  to be adopted, 38–39
  to be avoided, 35–38
confession, 50, 225–29, 271
  the four sections and essential elements of, 189, 309n207
Confession of Downfalls, 229–30
consciousness(es)
  dissolution of, 284–85
  impermanence of, 57–58
  six sense, 210, 217
  that seizes, 81, 303n112
continents, four, 76, 303n108
courage, three degrees of, 26, 152

Dagpo, 19
daka, 119, 120, 128
dakini. *See* Three Roots
death, 57–58, 142, 245, 301n83
  preparing for, 58–62
  See also intermediate state; transference
defects of the pot, 35
delusion, 47, 81–82, 127, 128, 209–10, 219, 225, 304n114
demon(s), 7, 38, 164, 169, 172
  four, 244–51
  See also Lord of Death; self-centeredness
dependent arising, 68, 71, 78–82, 214, 302n103
  See also interdependence
desire, 63, 74, 75
  sexual, 198–200, 310n217

Detailed Commentary on the Condensed Meaning, 239
determination to be free, 3, 40, 49, 65–66, 215 *passim,* 301n87
Devadatta, 8–9, 70
devotion, 258–59, 265–66, 275–76
Dharma, 4–9, 60 *passim*
  circumstantial and individual advantages and, 47–48
  essence, 107
  qualities, 108
  of realization, 84, 96, 108, 123
  of transmission, 6, 84, 96, 107–8, 123
  See also Three Jewels
dharmas, four black, 160
dharmata, 81, 120, 153, 168, 183, 207, 224–25, 260, 276, 282
difficulties, 175–76
discouragement, 36–37
disillusionment, 49
distraction(s), 36, 196–201, 245–46
doors of negative action, six, 228–29
doors, three, 114, 189, 207, 274–75, 279, 315nn299–300
  See also vajras
downfalls. *See* vows
driza, 23, 141
Drom Tönpa, 21
dung, 28, 298n35

effort, 36
Ekajati, 11
emptiness, 6, 70, 79–82, 134, 213–14, 218
  four approaches to, 80
  four experiences of, 116–17
enemies, 138
energies, 100, 101, 116, 119, 305n130
environment, purifying the, 240, 312n252
equalities, four, 178
equality of self and others, 165–68
Essay on the Mind of Enlightenment, 81
essences, 100–101, 116, 118, 119

eternalism, 68–69, 80, 302n94
exchange of self and others, 169–75, 309n199
extremes, four conceptual, 209, 310n228
extremes, two, 26, 80–81, 94

factors, three supreme, 155–56
faith, 4–5, 36, 49, 226, 254–55
   four kinds of, 9
faults, four serious, 230
fear(s), 5, 18
Five Stages, 122
Five Treatises on the Middle Way, 207, 208
forces, four, 196
Four Hundred Verses on Madhyamaka, 208
Four Noble Truths, 63–64, 70, 71–73, 81, 302n100
   See also truth
freedoms, eight, 44–47
freedoms and advantages, causes of, 50–54
friends, 139
Fundamental Treatise on the Middle Way, 208

gandharvas, 28, 298n36
Gathering of Vidyadharas, 265
Gautama, 8–9, 68, 301n92
   See also Buddha, the
Gemang Rinpoche, 265, 273
Ghandhapa, 259
giving and taking, practice of (tonglen), 169–77, 179
God, 6, 301n96
god realms, 56, 76, 300n80
gods, 7, 46, 56, 80 *passim*, 299n61, 300n62, 300n64
good, sources of, 84, 85, 255, 271–72, 314n29
   See also merit
Great Array of Ati, 10–11

Great Compassionate One, 265
Great Glorious One, 116
   See also Buddha, the
Great Master of Oddiyana, 82
Great Middle Way, 108
Great Omniscient One, 81, 265, 303n113
   See also Longchenpa
Great Perfection, 6, 10, 51, 54, 86, 88, 108, 304n119
   See also Mahasandhi
Great Shramana, 67, 301n90
   See also Buddha, the
Great Vehicle, 9, 10, 85, 96, 103, 133, 224, 225
Ground of All, 77
Guhyagarbha Tantra, 239
Guhyasamaja Tantra, 123
Guru Lake-Born Vajra, 267
Guru of Oddiyana, 125
guru yoga, the practice of, 265–80
   four empowerments, 277–79, 315nn306–7

Hagiography of Purna, 65
happiness, 24–25, 53, 129–30, 165–66, 171
Hashang, 205, 310n224
hatred, 65, 193
Heart Essence of the Great Expanse from the Great Perfection, 12, 285
Heart Sutra, 212
hell beings, 44, 56
hell(s), 41, 56–57, 64–66
   hot and cold, 44
   of Ultimate Torment, 57, 180
Hemasagara Buddhas, 103, 237, 238, 305n134
heruka, 275
Herukas, Eight, 114, 277
Heruka Galpo, 224
Hevajra practice, 21
Hevajra Tantra, 34, 123, 224–25
higher worlds, two, 149, 308n181

human body, the, 62
    four essential elements of, 189
    giving away, 176
    impermanence and, 57–58, 213–14
    misuse of, 19, 297n21
    offering(s), 249–51
    proper use of, 41, 52–53
human existence
    causes of, 50–53
    potential, 53–55

ignorance, 25, 63, 71, 272–73, 302n102
illusion, magical, 137, 208, 219
impermanence, 39, 49, 61, 198, 245
    See also consciousness; human body
Indra, 25, 272, 314n295
Indrabodhi, 117
Infinite Aspiration, Buddha, 56, 269, 300n78
infirmity, 38
Inserting the Grass Stalk, 285
instructions. *See* teacher and disciple
interdependence, 110–12
    See also dependent arising
intermediate state, 62–63, 282, 316n322
    See also death; transference
Introduction to the Middle Way, 134, 209

Jambudvipa, 37
jealousy, 151, 271
Jetsun Mila, 58
Jewel Garland of the Middle Way, 74
Jigme Lingpa, 32, 40–41, 148, 259
    See also Omniscient Teacher
Jnanagarbha, 208
Jomo Cham, 264

Kadam Stupa, 239, 312n251
kalpa(s), 55–58, 85
    Complete Array, 5
    Strewn Flowers, 5
Kamalashila, 208

karma, 48–49, 56, 63, 72, 179
    See also actions
kayas
    four, 102–4
    dharmakaya, 5, 31, 33–34, 73, 102, 122; recitation, 232
    nirmanakaya, 5, 102, 305n138; four kinds of, 103–4
    rupakaya, 31, 34, 99, 106; recitation, 232
    sambhogakaya, 5, 102, 103, 122
    svabhavikakaya, 102
    three, 99, 224, 304n127
    See also Buddha, the
Khandro Nyingtik, 11
Khandro Yangtik, 11
kindness
    four sorts of, 141–42
    repaying, 143–45
    of the teacher. *See* teacher
King Ajatashatru, 69
King Bimbisara, 69
King Indrabhuti, 8
King Prasenajit, 76
King of the Shakyas, 5, 73
knowledge, 69–70
Kumaraja, 13
kyangma, 100, 304n128

Lady of Beauty, 238
lama, 60, 87, 88, 89, 97, 260, 261, 263, 266, 268, 313n277, 314n283
    eight qualities of a, 88, 304n118
    See also teacher; vajra master
lama sadhanas, 265, 313n281
Lama Yangtik, 12
laziness, 49, 195, 310n213
Lesser Vehicle, 133
liberation, attaining, 8–9, 17, 27, 40, 83–86, 262
liberation practice, 118, 306n152
lineage
    authentic, 276, 315n305

352   INDEX

Kagyu, 13
  Marpa's, 264, 313n280
  of Zur, 118, 307n154
links
  four, 144, 165–66
  three, 25, 65
Longbeard of Khyungpo, 219
Longchenpa, 11, 13, 17, 27, 276
  See also Great Omniscient One
Lord of Death, 59, 245
Lord of Supreme Joy, 246, 312n259
Lord of the Paranirmitavasavartin realm, 69
Lord of the Universe, 7, 296n7
louse, 222, 311n234
Lungtok Tenpai Nyima Gyaltsen Pel Zangpo, 286, 317n333

Machik Labdrön, 248
Madhyamika(s), 77, 156, 272
  Prasangika, 207–8, 209–10
  Svatantrika, 207–10
Magical Net of Manjushri, 5
Mahamudra, 118, 214, 272
Mahasandhi, 272, 314n292
  See also Great Perfection
Maitreya, 22, 69, 151, 207
Maitriyogi, 178
mandala, the
  accomplishment, 239
  dharmakaya, 239
  nirmanakaya, 237
  offering, 236, 240–43
  sambhogakaya, 238
  See also accumulation of merit and wisdom
Manjushri, 5, 7, 69, 76, 184, 255
  mantra, 99
Mantrayana, the, 51, 77, 99, 107, 115, 191, 277, 304n126
  distinguishing features of, 31–32, 298n42
  vows, 115, 306n147 (*see also* samaya(s))

  See also Vajrayana
Mara, 50, 180
Mayadevi, 96
Medicine Buddha, 59
meditation
  sessions, 41–47, 124
  sustained calm, 202
mentation, 76, 303n106
merit, 230, 271–72 *passim*, 298n33, 311n242
  dedication of, 29–31, 46, 127, 273–74, 307n162
  field of, 266–67
  four causes of exhausting the store of, 27–29, 77
  giving away one's, 177–81
  sponsor's accumulation of, 189, 309n206
  See also accumulation of merit and wisdom; good, sources of
metaphors, four, 38
methods, three supreme, 27–31, 304n123
Milarepa. *See* Jetsun Mila
mind, the
  analyzing, 215–19
  nature of, 263
  visualization of, in transference practice, 285, 317n285
  uncreated, 205, 278
  See also thoughts
mindfulness, 82
Mindroling Prayer Book, 240
Mipham, 204, 205
miserliness, 154, 186, 187
mother, 23–24, 148–49
mother sentient beings, 23, 24–26, 140–47
motivation, 18–20, 78, 83, 84, 85
Mount Meru, 55, 57
mudra practice, 118, 307n153
Munis, Six, 103

Nagabodhi, 259

Index

Nagarjuna, 30, 79, 134, 204, 207, 208, 210n230
Naropa, 259, 281
New Tradition(s), 10, 102, 123, 201, 204, 257, 305n132
Ngari Panchen, 242–43
Ngawang Pelzang, (Osel Rinchen Nyingpo Pema Lendretsel), 287, 317n335
nihilism, 68, 80
nirvana 9, 26, 78, 81, 94 *passim*
    causes of, 69–70
    cessation and, 70–73
Nirvana Sutra, 103–4
non-Buddhist
    teachers, 69, 302n97
    traditions, 6, 68–69
Nonreturners, 96, 110
no-self, 53, 72, 173, 184, 203, 254
    of persons and phenomena, 210–15
Nyingmas, 10

obscurations, 73, 154–55, 223–24, 225 *passim*
obscuring conditions, 282, 316n320
Ocean Dust, 5, 295n4
Ocean of Liberation, 13
offering, 130, 185, 186–87, 270 *passim*
    perfect, 270
    the Seven Branches, 267–68
    See also mandala offering
omniscience, abandoning, 163
Omniscient Father and Son, 66, 301n88
Omniscient Teacher, 265, 314n282
Once Come King, Buddha, 5
Once Returners, 96, 109
ordinary concerns, eight, 19, 173–74
Ornament of Clear Realization, 207
Ornament of the Mahayana Sutras, 155
Ornament of the Middle Way, 209
others
    benefiting, 191–92
    importance of, 177–81

Padmasambhava, 11, 264
    See also Great Master of Oddiyana; Guru Lake-Born Vajra; Guru of Oddiyana
path
    conditions and, 279–80
    of superior training, 6
path of accumulating, 119, 120, 153, 187, 203 *passim*
path of joining, 120, 153, 187, 203 *passim*
path of meditation, 72, 120, 184 *passim*
path of no more learning, 72, 120
path of seeing, 72, 111–12, 118, 119, 120, 153, 163, 184, 187, 204 *passim*
Parting from the Four Attachments, 19, 39
Patrul Rinpoche. *See* Apu
Peak of Existence, 180
Pema Dorje, Khenpo, 236, 311n248
Pema Gyaltsen, 286
Penor, Tulku, 286
perception, 266–67
perfections, five, 32–34, 298n47
    See also certainties, five
perfections, six transcendent, 49, 163, 182–85 *passim*
    as they apply to the teacher, 38–39
    concentration, 108, 196–204
    diligence, 193–96
    discipline, 51, 53, 75, 93, 138, 187–92, 201, 303n105, 303n107, 309n203
    generosity, 51–52, 53, 138, 163, 184–87
    patience, 138, 192–93
    wisdom, 49, 204–19
    See also wisdom(s)
perfections, ten, 183
Perfect Joy, 153–54
phenomena, 32, 67–69, 79, 204, 212–19, 263, 266, 313n279, 314n284
poisons, three, 38, 74–75, 223, 245
possessions, three, 156, 247, 308n183
posture. *See* Vairochana
Power Bearer, 276
powers, four, 48, 226–27, 228–32

Prajnaparamita, 248
Prajnaparamita sutras, 108, 207, 239, 280
prakriti, 68–69, 302nn95–96
pratimoksha, 115, 191, 222, 311n235
    eight forms of, 109, 305n140
Pratyekabuddhas. *See* Shravakas and Pratyekabuddhas
prayer, essential points of, 124
Prayer of Good Actions, 85, 195, 240, 243, 310n214
Prayer of Maitreya, 161
preliminaries, ordinary and extraordinary, 14, 296n17
pretas, 45, 186
pride, 36, 268–69 *passim*
Profound View tradition, 51, 156, 190, 231, 300n69
promises. *See* vows
propensities incompatible with Dharma practice, eight, 49–50
prostrations, 125, 189, 268–70, 307n161
purification. *See* confession; environment; Vajrasattva practice
purusha, 68–69

Rabga the Gandharva, 106
Rabga the Wanderer, 106
Rangtong, 207, 310n226
Rare and Supreme Ones, three. *See* Three Jewels
Ratnasambhava, 112, 238, 280
realization, 102, 109, 153, 156, 276
    obstacles to, 221
rebirth, 52, 62, 63, 65, 75–76, 85, 284
refuge
    approaches according to the capacity of beings, 95–97
    benefits of, 130–31, 307n166
    causal, 98–99, 121–22
    definition of, 93–94
    generation phase, 116, 306n148
    nine objects of, 121, 307n155
    perfection phase, 116–20
    practice, 124–28
    prayer, 97
    precepts, 128–30
    resultant, 12, 99
    three special features of, 121, 157, 307n156, 309n185
    vows, 93–94, 304n120
    See also Three Jewels; Three Roots; vows
regret, 28, 49, 227, 228, 271
rejoicing, 48, 58–60, 271–72
reliance, four points of, 37, 299n50
remembering, wrong ways of, 37–38
renunciation. *See* determination to be free
resolution, 45, 155, 187, 188, 190, 227, 311n240
rigs chad, 49
ris chad, 49
roma, 100, 304n128
Rudra, 20, 38

Saha world, 5
Sakya Pandita, 20–21, 133–34
Samantabhadra, 5, 30, 33, 34, 46, 261, 270
samaya(s), 33, 50, 51, 88, 115, 117, 190–91 *passim,* 298n44, 306nn146–47
    See also vows
samsara, 26, 78, 81, 94 *passim,* 301n86
    causes of, 69–70
    cessation and, 70–73
    four contemplations that turn the mind from, 17, 39–42
    meditation on the defects of, 64–66
    three realms of, 67, 133, 308n167
    See also suffering
Sangha, the, 7, 101 *passim,* 305n131
    Bodhisattva, 111–12
    divisions, 108–10
    essence, 109
    Pratyekabuddha, 110–11

qualities, 121
Shravaka, 109–10
Vidhyadhara, 112–20
See also Three Jewels; Three Roots
Sangwa Nyingtik, 11
Saraha, 9
Sautrantikas, 206
Seal of the Essential Drop, 265
sea monster, 106
seclusion, 196–97, 198, 200–201
Secret Mantra Vajrayana. *See* Mantrayana; Vajrayana
secret practices, 38, 299n51
seed syllables, three, 286, 317n332
self-centeredness, 162–64, 173–74, 178–79
  See also demon(s)
sense objects, six, 216
sense organs, six, 216–17, 311n233
serious faults, four, 230
Seven Chapters, 276, 315n304
Seven Treasures, 11
Seventy Stanzas on Refuge, 94
Shabdrung, Tulku, 240, 242, 312n254
Shakyamuni Buddha, 5, 37
  See also Buddha, the
Shantarakshita, 208
Shantideva, 28, 135, 156, 163–64, 195, 226
Sharava, 69
shastras, 9
Shentong, 207, 310n226
showing off, 28
Shravakas and Pratyekabuddhas, 9, 10, 26, 69, 71, 95, 133–34, 135, 206, 247, 302n98, 302n101
  See also Basic Vehicle; Sangha, the
Shri Gupta, 208
Shuddhodana, 96
Single Verse, 240
six month group practice, 117–18
skandhas. *See* aggregates
Sky Doctrines, 285
Sogpo Lhapel, 259, 313n274

spiritual friend. *See* teacher
stains, six, 36
Stages on the Path, 118
Stream Enterers, 96, 109, 111
stupidity, 48
Sublime Continuum, 154
suchness, 184, 205, 223, 279
suffering, 25, 149, 273 *passim*, 314n296
  causes of, 129
  dispelling, 166–69
  experienced as a result, 129
  See also Four Noble Truths; samsara
Sugata, 97, 304n124
  See also Buddha, the
sugatagarbha, 98, 121–22, 277
Sutra Designed Like a Jewel Chest, 194
Sutra in Three Parts, 225
Sutra of a Hundred Actions, 65
Sutra of Great Liberation, 225, 226
Sutra of Skill in the Great Secret, 270
Sutra of Sublime Dharma of Clear Recollection, 64, 65
Sutra of the Descent to Lanka, 81
Sutra of the Prayer of Good Actions, 85, 195, 240, 243, 310n214
Sutra Remembering the Three Jewels, 240
Sutra Requested by Sagaramati, 29
Sutra Requested by Shrimaladevi Sinhanada, Daughter of King Prasenajit, 71
Sutrayana, 6, 31, 84, 98

tantras
  secret cycle of, 11, 296n11
  three outer, 10, 255–56, 313n272; Kriya, 86, 112–13, 123; Upa, 86, 113, 123; Yoga, 86, 113–14, 123
tarka schools, 68, 301n91
Tathagata, 35, 63, 140, 204 *passim*
  See also Buddha, the
Teacher, the, 5, 6, 73 *passim*
  See also Buddha, the
teacher, the
  activities, 261–62

as Buddha 32–34, 122–24, 258–62, 265, 298n45
as the Fourth Jewel, 130, 307n165
disciple and, 10, 13–14, 17, 24, 31, 33, 40, 48
examination of, 87–89
field of merit and, 266–67
kindness of, 262–63, 286, 317n334
qualities, 254, 313n268
as source of refuge, 128, 263–64
visualization of, 43–44, 124, 125, 307n156
wisdom mind of, 260–61
See also kayas; lama; vajra master
Ten Wheels of Kshitigarbha, 269
thögal, 11, 12, 63–64, 85, 236, 282, 284 *passim*, 317n321
thought(s)
discursive, 198–201
four. See samsara, four contemplations that turn the mind from
three types of, 3, 175
wrong, 223, 311n237
See also mind
Three Appearances, 10
Three Jewels, 8, 65–66, 94, 95, 96
compassion of, 129–30
essence, divisions and qualities, 101–7
See also Buddha; Dharma; refuge; Sangha
Three Pitakas. See Tripitaka
Three Roots, 97, 101, 122–23, 263
time, 103, 305n135
tonglen. See giving and taking, practice of
Topden, 286
Torch of the Three Methods, 31
traditions, two, 111, 306n142
training, threefold, 6, 54, 84, 108, 184
Trakpa Gyaltsen, 50
transcendent vehicle, 9
transference, 14–15, 279, 281, 297n18, 316n316, 317n329

attainment and, 284, 311n330
five kinds of, 282–84
practice of, 284–86
See also death; intermediate state; *Treasury of the Abhidharma*, 199
trekchö, 11, 63–64, 86, 235–36, 258
Tripitaka, 6–7, 9, 84, 96, 108
truth(s)
absolute, 31–32, 70, 195, 205
all-concealing, 209–10, 310n229
four. See Four Noble Truths
relative, 195, 204
secret, 38, 299n51
two, 81, 204–10
Tshampa Tshang, 240, 312n253
turtle, blind, 54
Tushita, 246
Twelve Deeds of the Buddha, 240
Two Truths, 208
Two Verses, 240

uma, 100
universe, formation and destruction of, 55–57
upasaka, 94, 189, 304n122
Vairochana, 113, 237, 238
posture of, 42, 124, 202
Vajra, 76, 303n109
Vajra Bhairava, 116
vajra body, 100–101, 238, 278
Vajra Cutter Sutra, 49
Vajradhara, 5, 33, 34, 85, 113, 114, 258, 261–63, 268, 270, 285
Vajra Essence, 97, 100
Vajrakilaya, 264
Vajra King, 113
vajra master, 123, 255, 256–57, 280
See also lama; teacher
Vajrapani, 59
Vajrapani's True Empowerment, 115
Vajra Pinnacle, 3
Vajrasattva, 3, 222, 238, 261
purification and, 225–26, 232

practice, 227–32
Vajra Seat, 56, 300n79
vajras
 four, 275, 276
 three, 34, 114, 191, 192, 277
 See also doors, three
Vajrayana, 5, 6, 10, 51, 77 *passim*
 See also Mantrayana
Vajra Yogini, 250, 266
vase exercise, 11, 306n150
Vast Activity Tradition, 51, 156, 190, 231, 300n70
Vidyadhara(s). *See* Sangha, the
views
 correct worldly, 84, 304n116
 four extreme, 209
 high and low, 254
 wrong, 68, 79, 80, 273
view
 arrived at through mental analysis, 214
 derived through inference, 153
 of ground, path and result, 28
 meditation and action, 271, 279, 314n293, 316n319
 of primordial purity, 73
 of primal wisdom, 214
vigilance, 82
Vimalamitra, 11, 13, 296n12
Vishvakarma, 104, 305n137
visions, four, 120
vows, 49–52, 93, 179–80, 188–90, 191, 201, 229–32 *passim*
 and downfalls, 221–23, 225, 311n238
 See also Bodhisattva vows; refuge vows; samayas

Way of the Bodhisattva, 53, 129, 148, 161, 192

Wheel of Dharma, the, 272–73
 Second Turning, 121
 Third Turning, 121
wheel(s), the
 of the celestial gods, 98, 304n125
 five, 100
wealth, 177
Wicked Black Demon, 246
wisdom(s)
 five, 104–5
 of omniscience, 95, 102, 105, 154, 223, 278
 primal, 32, 34, 98, 101, 115, 154, 214, 239, 261, 277, 312n249
 self-arisen, 279
 self-cognizing, 205, 207, 209, 214
 that realizes no-self. *See* no-self
 three, 275, 315n301
 See also perfection(s), six transcendent
wish-fulfilling gem, 8, 39
worldly vehicle, 9, 10, 14
Words of My Perfect Teacher, 12, 27, 36, 74, 99, 239, 264, 272, 276 *passim*

Yama's henchmen, 63
Yedharma, 67, 69, 70, 301n89
Yeshe Tsogyal, 264
yidam. *See* Three Roots
yoga(s), the three inner
 Anuyoga, 73, 86, 119–20, 235, 236, 257–58
 Atiyoga, 73, 120, 235, 258–59
 Mahayoga, 86, 114–19, 235, 236, 256–57
yogi(s), 117, 249, 268
Yogatantra, 123

Zabmo Yangtik, 12, 296n12
Zur. *See* lineage

Gönpo Lekden

Gönpo Maning Nagpo

Ekajati

Khyabjuk Rahula

Damchen Dorje Lekpa

Tseringma

It is traditional in Tibetan books to have pictures of the Dharma protectors at the end.